Excel® 2007 Workbook
For Dummies®

Cheat Sheet

Access Keys for Common File Commands

Access Keys	Excel Ribbon Command	Function
Alt+FN	Microsoft Office Button | New	Displays the New Workbook dialog box, where you can open a blank workbook or one from a template.
Alt+FO	Microsoft Office Button | Open	Displays the Open dialog box, where you can select a new Excel workbook to open for editing or printing.
Alt+FS	Microsoft Office Button | Save	Saves changes to a workbook. When you first select this command for a new workbook, Excel displays the Save As dialog box.
Alt+FA	Microsoft Office Button | Save As	Display the Save As dialog box where you can modify the filename, location where the file is saved, and format that the file is saved in.
Alt+FP	Microsoft Office Button | Print	Displays the Print dialog box to send the current worksheet, workbook, or cell selection to the printer.
Alt+FD	Microsoft Office Button | Send	Sends the current workbook as an e-mail attachment or faxes it using Internet Fax.
Alt+FC	Microsoft Office Button | Close	Closes the current workbook without exiting Excel.
Alt+FI	Microsoft Office Button | Excel Options	Displays the Excel Options dialog box, where you can change default program settings and modify the buttons on the Quick Access toolbar.
Alt+FX	Microsoft Office Button | Exit Excel	Quits the Excel program and closes all open workbooks after prompting you to save them.

Access Keys for Common Formula Commands

Access Keys	Excel Ribbon Command	Function
Alt+MF	Formulas | Insert Function	Opens the Insert Function dialog box (same as clicking the Insert Function button on the Formula bar).
Alt+MUS	Formulas | AutoSum | Sum	Selects the occupied range above and to the left of the cell cursor and inserts the SUM formula to total the range.
Alt+MUA	Formulas | AutoSum | Average	Selects the occupied range above and to the left of the cell cursor and inserts the AVERAGE formula to calculate the average in the range.
Alt+MUC	Formulas | AutoSum | Count Numbers	Selects the occupied range above the cell cursor and inserts the COUNT formula to count the number of values in the range.
Alt+MI	Formulas | Financial	Opens a drop-down menu listing all Financial functions — click name to insert function into current cell.
Alt+ME	Formulas | Date & Time	Opens a drop-down menu listing all Date and Time functions — click name to insert function into current cell.
Alt+MN	Formulas | Name Manager	Opens Name Manager dialog box showing all range names in workbook where you can add, edit, and delete names.
Alt+MMD	Formulas | Define Name	Opens New Name dialog box where you can assign a name to the cell selection or define a new constant.
Alt+MS	Formulas | Use in Formula	Displays drop-down menu with range names in workbook that you can insert into current formula by clicking.
Alt+MC	Formulas | Create from Selection	Opens Create Names from Selection dialog box, where you indicate which rows and columns to use in naming cell selection.
Alt+MH	Formulas | Show Formulas (Ctrl+`)	Displays and then hides all formulas in cells of the worksheet.

For Dummies: Bestselling Book Series for Beginners

Excel® 2007 Workbook For Dummies®

Cheat Sheet

Access Keys for Common Editing Commands

Access Keys	Excel Ribbon Command	Function
Alt+HVP	Home | Paste | Paste	Pastes the currently cut or copied cell selection or graphic objects in the worksheet.
Alt+HX	Home | Cut	Cuts the cell selection or selected graphic objects out of the workbook and places them on the Windows Clipboard.
Alt+HC	Home | Copy	Copies the cell selection or selected graphic objects to the Windows Clipboard.
Alt+HFP	Home | Format Painter	Activates the Format Painter.
Alt+HFO	Home | Clipboard Dialog Box Launcher	Displays and hides the Clipboard task pane.
Alt+HII	Home | Insert | Insert Cells	Opens Insert dialog box so you can indicate the direction in which to shift existing cells to make room for the ones being inserted.
Alt+HIR	Home | Insert | Insert Sheet Rows	Inserts blank rows equal to the number of rows in the cell selection.
Alt+HIC	Home | Insert | Insert Sheet Columns	Inserts blank columns equal to the number of columns in the cell selection.
Alt+HIS	Home | Insert | Insert Sheet	Inserts a new worksheet in the workbook.
Alt+HDD	Home | Delete | Delete Cells	Opens Delete dialog box so you can indicate the direction in which to shift existing cells to replace the ones being deleted.
Alt+HDR	Home | Delete | Delete Sheet Rows	Deletes rows equal to the number of rows in the cell selection.
Alt+HDC	Home | Delete | Delete Sheet Columns	Deletes columns equal to the number of columns in the cell selection.
Alt+HDS	Home | Delete | Delete Sheet	Deletes the current worksheet after warning you of data loss if the sheet contains cell entries.
Alt+HEA	Home | Clear | Clear All	Clears the contents, formatting, and comments from the cell selection.
Alt+HEF	Home | Clear | Clear Formats	Clears the formatting of the cell selection without removing the contents and comments.
Alt+HEC	Home | Clear | Clear Contents	Clears the contents of the cell selection without removing the formatting and comments.
Alt+HEM	Home | Clear | Clear Comments	Clears all comments in the cell selection without removing the formatting and contents.

Copyright © 2007 Wiley Publishing, Inc. All rights reserved. Item 6937-7. For more information about Wiley Publishing, call 1-800-762-2974.

For Dummies: Bestselling Book Series for Beginners

Excel® 2007 Workbook

FOR
DUMMIES®

by Greg Harvey, PhD

Wiley Publishing, Inc.

Excel® 2007 Workbook For Dummies®

Published by
Wiley Publishing, Inc.
111 River Street
Hoboken, NJ 07030-5774
www.wiley.com

For general information on our other products and services, please contact our Customer Care Department within the U.S. at 877-762-2974, outside the U.S. at 317-572-3993, or fax 317-572-4002.

For technical support, please visit www.wiley.com/techsupport.

Wiley also publishes its books in a variety of electronic formats. Some content that appears in print may not be available in electronic books.

Library of Congress Control Number: 2007932459

ISBN: 978-0-470-16937-7

Manufactured in the United States of America

10 9 8 7 6 5 4 3 2

WILEY

Dedication

To Chris, my partner and helpmate in all aspects of my life, and Shandy and Tara, my constant companions.

About the Author

Greg Harvey has authored tons of computer books, the most recent being *Grieving For Dummies* and *Excel Workbook For Dummies*, and the ever-popular *Excel 2007 For Dummies* and *Excel 2007 All-In-One Desk Reference For Dummies*. He started out training business users on how to use IBM personal computers and their attendant computer software in the rough-and-tumble days of DOS, WordStar, and Lotus 1-2-3 in the mid-'80s of the last century. After working for a number of independent training firms, he went on to teach semester-long courses in spreadsheet and database management software at Golden Gate University in San Francisco.

His love of teaching has translated into an equal love of writing. *For Dummies* books are, of course, his all-time favorites to write because they enable him to write to his favorite audience, the beginner. They also enable him to use humor (a key element to success in the training room) and, most delightful of all, to express an opinion or two about the subject matter at hand.

Greg received his doctorate degree in Humanities in Philosophy and Religion with a concentration in Asian Studies and Comparative Religion last May. Everyone is glad that Greg was finally able to get out of school before he retired.

Author's Acknowledgments

I'm always very grateful to the many people who work so hard to bring my book projects into being, and this one is no exception. This time, preliminary thanks are in order to Andy Cummings and Katie Feltman for giving me this opportunity to write in this wonderful workbook format.

Next, I want to express great thanks to my project editor, Linda Morris (a more knowledgeable person about the *For Dummies* series and better editor you'll never find), and to my partner in crime, Christopher Aiken (I really appreciate all your editing, additions, and comments on this one). Thanks also go to Joyce Nielsen for the great technical edit, Jennifer Theriot for coordinating its production, and everybody in the Wiley Publishing Composition Services department for their proofreading, indexing, and layout work.

Publisher's Acknowledgments

We're proud of this book; please send us your comments through our online registration form located at www.dummies.com/register/.

Some of the people who helped bring this book to market include the following:

Acquisitions, Editorial, and Media Development

Project Editor: Linda Morris

Acquisitions Editor: Katie Feltman

Copy Editor: Linda Morris

Technical Editor: Joyce Nielsen

Editorial Manager: Jodi Jensen

Media Development Manager: Laura VanWinkle

Editorial Assistant: Amanda Foxworth

Sr. Editorial Assistant: Cherie Case

Cartoons: Rich Tennant (www.the5thwave.com)

Composition Services

Project Coordinator: Jennifer Theriot

Layout and Graphics: Carrie Foster, Denny Hager, Stephanie D. Jumper

Proofreaders: Broccoli Information Management, Christy Pingleton

Indexer: Broccoli Information Management

Anniversary Logo Design: Richard J. Pacifico

Publishing and Editorial for Technology Dummies

   Richard Swadley, Vice President and Executive Group Publisher

   Andy Cummings, Vice President and Publisher

   Mary Bednarek, Executive Acquisitions Director

   Mary C. Corder, Editorial Director

Publishing for Consumer Dummies

   Diane Graves Steele, Vice President and Publisher

   Joyce Pepple, Acquisitions Director

Composition Services

   Gerry Fahey, Vice President of Production Services

   Debbie Stailey, Director of Composition Services

Contents at a Glance

Table of Contents

Table of Exercises

Introduction

*E*xcel is the most sophisticated spreadsheet program available in the world of personal computing. As such, this program is much more than just an electronic version of an accountant's familiar green sheet for crunching numbers. For millions of users the world over, Excel is also their number-one forms designer, their interface to the corporate database, as well as their premier charting program.

Given Excel's indisputable versatility, it should come as no surprise that mastering the basics of the program, not to mention its finer points, is no small undertaking. My experience, however, in teaching adults to use all manner of Excel's capabilities has convinced me that this mastery is greatly accelerated with just a modicum of hands-on experience judiciously applied to rather simple *but* realistic data-related problems.

About This Book

As its name suggests, *Excel 2007 Workbook For Dummies* is designed to give you the kind of hands-on experience with all the major aspects of the program you need to start using the program for business or home with a certain degree of confidence and efficiency. As you'd expect from this type of book, the workbook is primarily composed of questions and exercises that give you plenty of opportunities to experience the purpose and benefits of Excel's many features.

It's my hope that as a result of doing the exercises in this workbook, you'll not only be in firm command of the basic skills necessary to work with confidence in the Excel spreadsheet, but also have a good idea of the overall power of the program through experience with its features beyond the spreadsheet.

Conventions Used in This Book

By convention, all the text entries that you type yourself appear in **bold**. In addition, all filenames appear in *italic* type even though they are not italicized when you see their names in the Windows Explorer or the Excel Open dialog box.

When it comes to instructions in the exercises throughout the workbook, you'll notice two conventions:

✔ Ribbon commands often follow the sequence of the tab, command button, and drop-down menu option. For example, the command Home | Format | Column Width means that you should select the Home tab, followed by the Format command button, and then finally the Column Width option on the menu that appears.

✔ Ribbon hot keys are often given following the Ribbon command sequence. For example, Alt+HOW selects the Home tab, followed by the Format command button, and then the Column Width, entirely from the keyboard.

One other convention that you'll notice used throughout the text is the display of the names for Excel Ribbon commands, Quick Access toolbar buttons, and dialog box options in the title case, wherein all major words are capitalized except for prepositions. The title case is used to make these names stand out from the rest of the text. Often, however, especially in the case of dialog box options, Microsoft does not always follow this convention, often preferring to capitalize only the first letter of the option name.

Foolish Assumptions

I assume that you're a new user of Microsoft Office Excel 2007 motivated to master its essentials either for work or at home. Further, I assume that you're someone who learns by doing at least as well as, if not better than, by reading alone.

To complete most of the exercises in this workbook, you only need to have Microsoft Excel 2007 installed on a computer running a version of Microsoft Windows XP or Vista. For some of the printing exercises, you will benefit from having a printer installed on your system (although you can complete most of their steps and get the gist of the lessons without actually printing the sample worksheets).

This workbook is designed exclusively for users of Microsoft Office Excel version 2007. As such, all the practice material utilizes features (such as the Ribbon command structure, Live Preview, and style galleries) that are newly introduced and limited to Excel 2007, and the sample Workbook files are all saved in the new Microsoft Office 2007 XML file format. If you're a user of an earlier version of the application program (including Excel 97 through 2003), don't buy this workbook! Instead, get your hands on a copy of the original *Excel Workbook For Dummies* (Wiley). That edition covers the same material, exercises, and Excel features as this workbook following the classic command structure. Moreover, its sample files are saved in the classic workbook file format that your version of Excel can open.

How This Book Is Organized

This workbook is organized into six Parts, the first five of which contain the chapters with exercises you perform to become proficient in the use of particular Excel commands and features. Each of these chapters follows a similar pattern of introductory text followed by exercises. In some of the chapters, you'll also encounter question and answer sections that are designed to stimulate your thinking regarding the features you're about to practice in the subsequent exercises. Note that although the exercises within any given chapter do build on one another, you're certainly not expected to complete them in strict chapter order. Feel free to work on the exercises in any order that feels comfortable and fits your learning needs.

Part 1: Creating Spreadsheets

This part contains the most exercises of any in the workbook. It is made up of five chapters designed to give you practice in all the spreadsheet basics, all the way from starting Excel to editing a completed spreadsheet:

- Chapter 1 introduces you to the new user interface in Excel 2007 in the form of the Office menu, the Ribbon, and the Quick Access toolbar.

- Chapter 2 enables you to practice entering spreadsheet data.

- Chapter 3 runs you through formatting spreadsheet data.

- Chapter 4 gives you training in all aspects of printing the completed spreadsheet.

- Chapter 5 gives you plenty of experience with making modifications to the completed spreadsheet.

Part 11: Using Formulas and Functions

This part gives you all the practice you need with creating and using formulas in the spreadsheet. Chapter 6 introduces you to formula-making just as Chapter 7 introduces you to the all-important topic of formula copying.

Because of the importance of Excel's built-in functions in formula building, the remaining seven chapters in this part concentrate on building formulas using a particular category of functions:

- Chapter 8 gets you up and running on date and time formulas.

- Chapter 9 trains you in the use of financial formulas.

- Chapter 10 gives you practice creating formulas using Excel's Math functions.

- Chapter 11 concentrates on exercises in creating formulas using statistical functions.

- Chapter 12 introduces you to the creation of formulas using Lookup functions.

- Chapter 13 runs you through the creation of formulas using the Logical functions, the performance of which depends upon prevailing conditions in the spreadsheet.

- Chapter 14 introduces you to the creation of text formulas that manipulate and change text entries in the spreadsheet.

Part 111: Working with Graphics

This part takes you into the graphical aspects of Excel, the most important of which is its rich and versatile charting capabilities covered in Chapter 15. In addition to charts, in Chapter 16, you get practice in working with other type of graphics in the spreadsheet, both those that you generate with the program's own drawing tools and those that you import from other sources such as clip art and digital photos.

Part IV: Managing and Securing Data

This part is concerned with the management and security of the vast amounts of data that you accumulate in your worksheets. Chapter 17 gives you practice in creating, maintaining, sorting, and querying database tables and data lists in the worksheet. Chapter 18, on the other hand, gives you practice using Excel's various methods for protecting your data and worksheets from illicit viewing and unwanted changes.

Part V: Doing Data Analysis

This part takes you the next step of using the Excel spreadsheet by introducing you to two different kinds of data analysis. Chapter 19 gives you practice in doing various types of what-if analysis that enable you to look at different potential outcomes in the spreadsheet. Chapter 20 concentrates on training you in the use of pivot tables, a dynamic type of data table that you can use to summarize vast amounts of data.

Part VI: Macros and Visual Basic for Applications

This part introduces you to the topic of creating and using macros to both streamline and customize your work in Excel. Chapter 21 introduces you to recording your actions as Excel macros and then playing them back in the worksheet. Chapter 22 gives you practice using Excel's Visual Basic Editor to edit macros and extend macros you've recorded as well as to create your own user-defined functions.

Part VII: The Part of Tens

This part gives you tips for using Excel on your own after you complete the exercises in this workbook. Chapter 23 gives you the lowdown on what I consider to be the top ten features in Excel 2007. Chapter 24 is full of tips on using some of the many features you've practiced in the workbook like a professional.

Using the Practice Material on the CD-ROM

The CD-ROM that comes with this workbook is an integral part of the workbook experience. It contains not only the practice material that you need to complete most of its exercises, but also freestanding and self-running demos that introduce you to essential techniques utilized in many of the exercises throughout the workbook, as well as those that introduce new features specifically covered in the exercises in a chapter.

Running the Essential Technique Demos before you begin doing any of the exercises in the workbook and the Feature Demos before you attempt the exercises in a particular chapter should help you understand the technique you're about to undertake as well as visualize the end result, thereby aiding you later in completing the exercise steps in the workbook in Excel on your own.

For details on the CD-ROM and how to use its files, see the About the CD appendix.

Icons Used in This Book

Icons are sprinkled throughout the text of this workbook in high hopes that they draw your attention to particular features. Some of the icons are of the heads-up type, whereas others are more informational in nature:

This icon indicates the start of a question and answer section in the workbook.

This icon indicates a hint that can help you perform a particular step in the exercise.

This icon indicates that a step in your workbook exercise utilizes an essential technique (such as saving a workbook in a different folder with a new filename or comparing your completed worksheet against one in a Solved workbook) that is covered in one of the self-running Essential Technique Demos included on this book's CD-ROM.

This icon indicates that the Excel features or techniques utilized in the exercises you're about to undertake in a particular chapter are demonstrated in a particular self-running demonstration video included on this book's CD-ROM.

This icon indicates a tidbit that, if retained, can make your work somewhat easier in Excel.

This icon indicates a tidbit that is essential to the topic being discussed and is, therefore, worth putting under your hat.

This icon indicates a bit of trickery in the topic that, if ignored, can lead to some real trouble in your spreadsheet.

Where to Go from Here

This workbook is constructed such that you don't have to start working through the exercises in Chapter 1 and end with those in Chapter 22. That being said, it is still to your benefit to complete all the exercises within a particular chapter, if not in a single work session, at least in a short time period.

If you're a real newbie to Excel and have no experience with any of the earlier versions of the program, I urge you to complete the exercises in Part I, Chapters 1 through 5, before you take off in your own direction. The exercises in this part are truly fundamental and are meant to give you a strong foundation in the basic features that all Excel users need to know.

Please keep in mind that I designed the exercises in this workbook to work with my Excel companion books, *Excel 2007 For Dummies* and *Excel 2007 All-In-One Desk Reference For Dummies* (Wiley). They can therefore provide you with additional information about the Excel features you're using either at the time you go through the workbook exercises or afterwards. To facilitate this crossover usage, I have, wherever possible, used the same example files in the exercises of this workbook as you see illustrated and explained at length in these references.

Whatever you do next and wherever you go in this workbook, just be sure that you enjoy yourself!

Part I
Creating Spreadsheets

The 5th Wave   By Rich Tennant

"Unless there's a corrupt cell in our spreadsheet analysis concerning the importance of trunk space, this should be a big seller next year."

In this part . . .

The chapters and exercises in Part I form the core skills on which all spreadsheet users rely. These skills run the gamut from using the Ribbon user interface, customizing the Quick Access toolbar, and basic data entry, to more complex data editing with cell formatting and worksheet printing in between. When you have these skills under your belt, you are well on your way to mastering Excel.

Chapter 1

Getting Familiar with the Excel 2007 Interface

*T*he Excel 2007 interface has been completely revamped and redesigned compared to the older versions of Excel we're all used to. In place of the old pull-down menus, so prominent in all earlier versions of the program, Excel 2007 now relies primarily on the Ribbon, a block of commands displayed at the top of the screen and divided into distinct blocks called tabs. All that's left of the old pull-down menus is the pull-down menu opened with the Office Button, which replicates most of the File commands. Also, in place of the many toolbars of previous Excel versions, Excel 2007 offers a single toolbar called the Quick Access toolbar.

The exercises in this first chapter are designed to get you familiar with the new Excel 2007 interface. As a result of doing these exercises, you should be comfortable with all aspects of the display screen and the command structure and ready to do all the rest of the exercises in this book.

Identifying the Parts of the Excel Display Screen

Before you can start using Excel 2007, you have to be familiar with its display screen. Figure 1-1 shows you the Excel 2007 display screen as it first appears when you launch the program. Note the names of the different parts of the display screen before you perform Exercise 1-1.

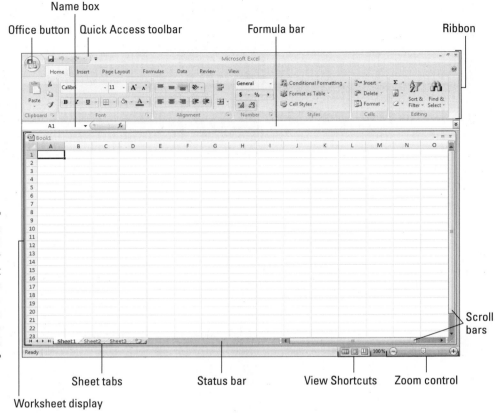

Name box

Office button | Quick Access toolbar | Formula bar | Ribbon

Figure 1-1:
The Excel 2007 display screen as it appears when you first launch the program.

Scroll bars

Sheet tabs | Status bar | View Shortcuts | Zoom control

Worksheet display

Q. What are the primary functions of the commands on the Office menu?

A. To open, close, save, and print your Excel spreadsheet files and change the Excel program options.

Q. What is the primary function of the Quick Access toolbar?

A. To enable you to quickly select Excel commands that you use all the time without having to open the Office menu or use the Ribbon commands.

Q. What's the primary function of the Ribbon in Excel 2007?

A. To group related Excel commands together and give you quick access to these commands.

Selecting Commands on the Office Menu

Clicking the Office Button opens the only pull-down menu in Excel 2007. Almost all the commands on this pull-down menu are related to actions that affect the entire file, such as saving and printing. If you prefer, you can open this menu by pressing Alt+F (F for File) instead of clicking the Office Button.

Solve It

Exercise 1-1: Opening the Office Menu and Selecting Its Commands

In this exercise, you get familiar with the commands on the Office menu as you practice opening the Office menu and selecting some of its commands. Make sure that Excel 2007 is running and an empty Sheet1 worksheet is active on your computer monitor (see Chapter 2 if you need information on launching Excel).

1. Highlight the Office Button (by hovering the mouse pointer over it without clicking the mouse button) and wait until its ScreenTip appears.

The ScreenTip shows you an image of the menu and gives you a brief description of its function.

2. Click the Office Button to open its pull-down menu.

Note the commands New through Close in the left menu pane. Also note the Excel Options and Exit Excel command buttons at the very bottom of the menu.

3. Highlight the Save As command on the Office menu (but don't click it).

Note all the Save a Copy sub-options that now appear in the right menu pane.

4. Now, click the Save As command on the Office menu to select it.

Excel opens the Save As dialog box where you can modify the name, location, and type of Excel workbook file before saving a copy of it.

5. Press the Esc (Escape) key on your keyboard to close the Save As dialog box.

6. Press Alt+F to open the Office menu again, this time from the keyboard.

This time, small letters appear on each command as well as on the sub-option buttons attached to the Save As and Print commands. These are the access keys that you can type to select an option rather than clicking its name or button.

7. Type **W** to display the Print command sub-options, and then type **V** to select the Print Preview sub-option.

Excel displays an alert dialog box indicating that there's no data in the Sheet1 worksheet to preview. Note the appearance of the dashes in the Excel worksheet display showing where the pages would be divided.

8. Click OK in the alert box and then press Alt+FI to open the Excel Options dialog box.

The Excel Options dialog box contains all the options for changing the Excel program and worksheet options. These options are divided into categories Popular through Resources.

9. Click the Advanced button in the left pane to display all the Advanced options in the right pane. Next, scroll down to the Display Options for This Worksheet section and click the Show Page Breaks check box to remove its check mark before you click the OK command button to close the dialog box.

Note that deselecting the Show Page Breaks option in the Excel Options dialog box removes all the dashed page break lines from the Sheet1 worksheet.

Selecting Commands from the Ribbon

The Excel Ribbon contains the bulk of all the commands that you use in creating, editing, formatting, and sharing your spreadsheets, charts, and data lists. As shown in Figure 1-2, normally the Ribbon is divided into seven tabs: Home, Insert, Page Layout, Formulas, Data, Review, and View. The commands that appear on each tab are then further divided into Groups, containing related command buttons. Also, many of these groups contain a Dialog Box Launcher button that appears in the lower-right corner of the Group. Clicking this button opens a dialog box of further options related to the particular Group.

Tab

Figure 1-2:
The normal
Excel 2007
Ribbon.

Group   Dialog Box launcher

 Exercise 1-2: Selecting Commands from the Ribbon

In Exercise 1-2, you get practice selecting commands from the Ribbon. Make sure that Excel 2007 is running and an empty Sheet1 worksheet is active on your computer monitor.

1. Click the Formulas tab to displays its commands.

Note that the commands on the Formulas tab are divided into four Groups: Function Library, Defined Names, Formula Auditing, and Calculation.

2. Press the Alt key.

Note the access-key letters that now appear on the Office button, Quick Access toolbar options and the Ribbon Tabs.

If you prefer selecting Excel commands from the keyboard, you'll probably want to memorize the following access keys for selecting the seven tabs:

Home tab: Alt+H

Insert tab: Alt+N

Page Layout tab: Alt+P

Formulas tab: Alt+M

Data tab: Alt+A

Review tab: Alt+R

View tab: Alt+W

3. Type **W** to display the contents of the View tab and then type **VG** to remove the check mark from the Gridlines check box in the Show/Hide Group.

4. Click the Gridlines check box to select it again and redisplay the gridlines in the worksheet.

   As you may have noticed, the Ribbon takes up quite of bit of screen space that is otherwise used to display worksheet data. You can take care of this by setting Excel to minimize the Ribbon each time you select one of its commands to display only the tab names.

5. Click the Customize Quick Access Toolbar button (the button with the line and downward-pointing triangle at the end of the Quick Access toolbar) and then click the Minimize the Ribbon option at the very end of this menu.

   Excel immediately minimizes the toolbar to display only the seven tab names. As long as this option is selected on the Customize Quick Access toolbar menu (indicated by a check mark in front of its menu option), Excel continues to reduce the Ribbon to its tab names any time after you select one its commands.

   Keep in mind that you can expand the Ribbon to display all the command buttons on the currently selected tab any time that the Ribbon is minimized simply by double-clicking the tab or pressing Ctrl+F1.

6. Click Data on the minimized Ribbon.

   Excel expands the Ribbon to display all of the Data tab command buttons.

7. Click anywhere in the worksheet area to minimize the Ribbon once again.

   The only problem with this minimized Ribbon arrangement is that the temporarily expanded Ribbon covers the first three rows of the worksheet. This makes it very difficult to work with data at the top of the worksheet. For that reason, as well as to help you get comfortable with unfamiliar Ribbon commands, you will work with the Ribbon expanded at all times in all remaining exercises in this workbook.

8. Click the Customize Quick Access Toolbar button and then click the Minimize the Ribbon option to deselect this option by removing its check mark. Then, click the Home tab to displays its command buttons.

   The Ribbon now remains fully displayed at all times as you select any of its tabs and command buttons without ever obscuring any part of the worksheet display.

Selecting Commands on the Quick Access Toolbar

When you first start working with Excel 2007, the Quick Access toolbar contains only the following three simple command buttons:

✔ **Save** to save changes to your current workbook file

✔ **Undo** to reverse the effect of the last change you made to a worksheet

✔ **Redo** to restore the last change you reversed with the Undo button

Customizing the Quick Access toolbar

In addition to the three default command buttons, the Quick Access toolbar contains a Customize Quick Access Toolbar button (the one with the line above a downward pointing triangle) that when clicked opens a pull-down menu. The options on this pull-down menu enable you to quickly customize the command buttons on this toolbar. In addition, you can change the placement of the toolbar by moving it down so that it appears immediately below the Ribbon and above the Formula bar.

Solve It | ### Exercise 1-3: Quickly Customizing the Quick Access Toolbar

In Exercise 1-3, you get practice customizing the contents and position of the Quick Access toolbar using options that appear on the Customize Quick Access Toolbar menu. Make sure that Excel 2007 is running and an empty Sheet1 worksheet is active on your computer monitor (see Chapter 2 for information on launching Excel).

1. Click the Customize Quick Access Toolbar button and then click the Show Below the Ribbon option on its menu.

The Quick Access toolbar with its three command buttons and the Customize Quick Access Toolbar button now appears immediately above the Formula bar.

2. Click the Customize Quick Access Toolbar button and then click the Quick Print option.

Excel adds the Quick Print button to the Quick Access toolbar that you can click to send the current worksheet to the printer.

3. Use the same technique to add the New, Open, and Print Preview command buttons to the Quick Access toolbar on your own.

Use the ScreenTips attached to each button to verify that you've correctly added the Quick Print, New, Open, and Print Preview buttons to the Quick Access toolbar, noting the shortcut keys listed.

Adding more commands to the Quick Access toolbar

When customizing the command buttons on the Quick Access toolbar, you aren't limited to the selection of commands that appear on the Customize Quick Access Toolbar pull-down menu. Using command options that appear in the Excel Options dialog box, you can add buttons for any of the commands that appear on the various tabs of the Ribbon as well as some Excel commands that remain completely unavailable until you add them to the Quick Access toolbar.

Solve It

Exercise 1-4: Adding Commands from the Excel Options Dialog Box to the Quick Access Toolbar

In Exercise 1-4, you get practice customizing the contents of the Quick Access toolbar using commands that appear in the Excel Options dialog box. Make sure that Excel 2007 is running and an empty Sheet1 worksheet is active on your computer monitor (see Chapter 2 for information on launching Excel).

1. Click the Customize Quick Access Toolbar button and then click the More Commands option on its menu.

Excel opens the Excel Options dialog box with the Customize tab selected (see Figure 1-3). This dialog box contains two list boxes:

- **Choose Commands From** list box on the left where you select the commands to add to the toolbar

- **Customize Quick Access Toolbar** list box on the right, showing the buttons on the toolbar and their order

To add a new command to the toolbar, you select it in the Choose Commands From list box and then click the Add button. To reorder the buttons on the toolbar, you click its command button in the Customize Quick Access Toolbar list box and then click the Move Up or Move Down buttons (with the black triangles pointing up and down, respectively) until the selected button is in the desired position.

2. Click the drop-down button on the Choose Commands From drop-down list box and then click the Commands Not in the Ribbon option on its drop-down menu.

The Choose Command From list box now contains only command buttons that are not found on the various tabs of the Excel Ribbon.

3. Click the AutoFormat command option in the Choose Commands From list box (the one with the lightning bolt on top of a small table) and then click the Add button.

The AutoFormat command option is now listed at the very bottom of your Customize Quick Access Toolbar list box, indicating that it is now the last button on the Quick Access toolbar.

Figure 1-3:
Customizing the Quick Access toolbar using the Excel Options dialog box.

4. On your own, add the Calculator, Draw Borders, Form, Speak Cells, Speak Cells – Stop Speaking Cells, Speak Cells by Columns, Speak Cells by Rows, and Speak Cells on Enter command options to the Quick Access toolbar.

You may have to scroll down the list of command options in the Choose Commands From list box in order to select and add the Draw Borders, Form, and the different Speak Cells command options to the Quick Access toolbar.

Next, you want to modify the order in which the command buttons appear on your customized Quick Access toolbar so that they appear in this order arranged in four groups:

- New, Open, Save, Quick Print, and then Print Preview
- Undo and then Redo
- AutoFormat, Calculator, Draw Borders, and Form
- Speak Cells, Speak Cells – Stop Speaking Cells, Speak Cells by Columns, Speak Cells by Rows, and Speak Cells on Enter

5. Click the New command option in the Customize Quick Access Toolbar list box to select it and then click the Move Up button (the one with the black triangle pointing upward) until New is the first command in this list (four times).

6. Use the same technique to move the Open command button up until it appears between the New and the Save button.

7. Use the Move Down button to move the Undo and Redo buttons so that they now appear in the same order below the Quick Print and Print Preview buttons.

   The command buttons for your customized version of the Quick Access toolbar now appear in the correct order in the Customize Quick Access Toolbar list box in the Excel Options dialog box. The only other thing you need to do is to divide them into groups by adding a vertical bar called a separator.

8. Click the Print Preview command option in the Customize Quick Access Toolbar list box to select it and then click the Separator option at the very top of the Choose Commands From list box to select this option. Click the Add button.

   Excel inserts a separator between the Print Preview and Undo command options in the Customize Quick Access Toolbar list box.

9. Use this same technique to add a Separator between the Redo and AutoFormat command options and the Form and Speak Cells command options in the Customize Quick Access Toolbar list box.

   Your customized Quick Access toolbar now contains four groups of command buttons created by the three Separator options that appear after the Print Preview command option, Redo command option, and the Form command option.

10. Click OK to close the Excel Options dialog box. On the Quick Access toolbar, click the Customize Quick Access Toolbar button followed by the Show Above the Ribbon option on its menu.

    The final version of your customized Quick Access toolbar now appears once again above the Ribbon to the immediate right of the Office button. Check the buttons on your customized toolbar against those shown in the toolbar in Figure 1-4.

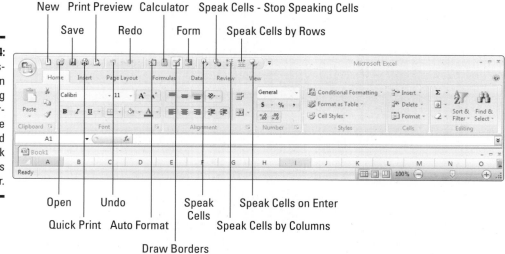

Figure 1-4: Excel display screen showing the final version of the customized Quick Access toolbar.

Chapter 2

Entering the Spreadsheet Data

. . . .

In This Chapter

▶ Launching Excel and opening a new workbook

▶ Moving around the workbook

▶ Selecting cell ranges in a worksheet

▶ Doing simple data entry in a worksheet

▶ Using AutoFill to create data series and copy formulas

▶ Saving the spreadsheet as an Excel workbook file

. . . .

Data entry is the bread and butter of any spreadsheet you create or edit. As a result of doing the exercises in this chapter, you will have practice in launching Excel, moving around a new spreadsheet, the many aspects of doing data entry, and, most importantly, saving your work.

Launching Excel

Excel 2007 is only one of the primary application programs included as part of Microsoft Office 2007. In order to be proficient in its use, you need to be familiar with all the various ways of launching the program.

Q. How many ways are there to start Excel 2007?

A. You should be familiar with all these methods:

✔ Click Start on the Windows XP taskbar and then highlight All Programs and Microsoft Office before clicking Microsoft Office Excel 2007. If you're using Windows Vista, you click the Start button, type **ex** in the Start Search text box and then press Enter while the Microsoft Excel 2007 Office 2007 option is selected at the top of the Programs menu.

✔ Double-click the Microsoft Excel 2007 program shortcut icon on your Windows desktop.

✔ Click the Excel 2007 shortcut button on the Windows Quick Launch toolbar.

✔ Double-click an Excel workbook file in any folder on any drive to which your computer has access.

Q. Can I have Excel launch automatically each time I start my computer?

A. Copy the Microsoft Office Excel 2007 option to the Startup submenu on the All Programs menu by holding down the Ctrl key as you drag this option from the Microsoft Office menu to the Startup menu.

Solve It

Exercise 2-1: Adding Excel 2007 Shortcuts to the Windows Desktop and Quick Launch Toolbar

In Exercise 2-1, you add the Microsoft Excel 2007 program icon to your Windows desktop and the Quick Launch toolbar and then launch Excel 2007 using each of these two methods:

1. Launch Excel 2007 from the Windows XP or Vista Start menu (as described in the Q & A on the different ways to start Excel immediately preceding this exercise). Then, click Office Button | Exit Excel or press Alt+FX to close the program.

   Excel closes and the Microsoft Office Excel 2007 program name is added to the Windows Start menu as a recently opened application.

2. Click Start on the Windows taskbar and then right-click Microsoft Office Excel 2007 on the Start menu, before you click Send To and Desktop (Create Shortcut) on the submenus.

   Excel adds a program shortcut icon called Microsoft Office Excel 2007, although only a part of this shortcut name (something like Microsoft Office Ex . . .) appears on the desktop. You can then launch Excel 2007 by double-clicking this program shortcut on the Windows desktop.

3. Drag the Microsoft Office Excel 2007 program shortcut icon to the Quick Launch toolbar and then drop this icon onto the bar some place in between its displayed buttons.

   As soon as you drop the icon on the Quick Launch toolbar, Windows pastes a copy of the Excel program shortcut on the toolbar. You can then launch Excel 2007 by clicking this Excel 2007 button on the Quick Launch toolbar.

4. Practice launching Excel by double-clicking the Excel 2007 program shortcut on the Windows desktop and then exiting the program. Then launch Excel again, this time by clicking the Excel 2007 button on the Windows Quick Launch toolbar.

   You can leave Excel 2007 running for Exercise 2-2.

Opening a New Workbook

Each time you launch Excel (using any method other than double-clicking an Excel workbook file icon), a new workbook containing three blank worksheets opens. You can build your new spreadsheet in this workbook, using any of its sheet pages.

The blank workbook that opens with Excel is given a temporary filename such as Book1, Book2, and so on, that appears after the application's name on the program window's title bar. If you want to start work on a spreadsheet in another workbook, click the New command button on your customized version of the Quick Access toolbar (assuming that you performed Exercise 1-4 in Chapter 1).

When Excel opens a blank workbook, the new workbook follows the Blank Workbook template (which controls the formatting applied to all its blank cells). You can also open new workbooks from other, specialized templates or from a workbook that you've already created. To do this, click Office Button | New or press Alt+FN. Excel opens the New Workbook dialog box where you can click the template or file to use (see Figure 2-1).

Figure 2-1: The New Workbook dialog box enables you to create a new workbook file from an installed template file.

Q. What's so special about an Excel template file?

A. A template is a particular type of Excel file designed to automatically generate new workbooks that use both its data and formatting. Each time you open a template, Excel opens a copy of the template file rather than the original (by appending a number to the template's original filename). Excel template files use the filename extension .xltx to differentiate them from regular Excel workbook files that carry an .xlsx filename extension.

Q. What's the difference between opening a new workbook file from an Excel template file rather than an existing Excel workbook file?

A. None, provided that you open the new file in the New From Existing Workbook dialog box — opened by clicking the New From Existing option in New Workbook dialog box (Alt+FN) — rather than in the regular Open dialog box (doing this opens not a copy of the template or workbook file, but the original file for editing).

Q. How do you create templates out of your own Excel workbook files?

A. Build a spreadsheet in a new or existing workbook file. To this spreadsheet add all the stock text and data, calculating formulas, and formatting required in all the files you will generate from its ensuing template and then save this file with the Office Button | Save As command. In the Save As dialog box, select Excel Template (*.xltx) in the Save As Type drop-down list box and edit the dummy filename (without removing the .xltx filename extension) before you click the Save button.

Solve It

Exercise 2-2: Opening a New Workbook from the Blank Workbook Template

In Exercise 2-2, you launch Excel 2007 (if it's not already running) and then open a new workbook (Book2). Switch back to Book1 (notice the change in the Excel program title bar) and then close the workbook. Notice what happens to Book2 when you close Book1. Leave Book2 open for the next exercise.

To switch from Sheet1 of Book2 and make Sheet1 of Book1 active, click the Book1 icon on the Windows taskbar or press Ctrl+Tab (to switch back to Book2, click the Book2 icon on the taskbar or press Ctrl+Tab again so that Sheet1 of Book2 is selected). To close a workbook file, choose Office Button | Close or press Alt+FC.

1. If necessary, launch Excel 2007 and, in the program title bar, note that Book1 is the current workbook file.

2. Click Office Button | New or press Alt+FN.

Excel opens the New Workbook dialog box. Note that the Blank Workbook template icon is automatically selected.

3. Click the Create button or press Enter.

Excel closes the New Workbook dialog box and creates a new workbook file, indicated by Book2 in the program title bar. Note the appearance of Book1 and Book2 program icons on the Windows taskbar.

4. Press Ctrl+Tab to make Book1 active and then click the Book2 program icon on the Windows taskbar to make Book2 active.

You can use either method to switch between open Excel workbook files.

5. With Book2 still active (indicated by Book2 in the program title bar), click Office Button | Close or press Alt+FC.

Excel closes Book2 and returns you to Book1. Note that the program would have prompted you to save changes to Book2 before closing it if you had made any data entries in the first worksheet of this workbook. Leave the Book1 workbook open for the next exercise.

Solve It

Exercise 2-3: Open a New Workbook File from an Installed Template File

In Exercise 2-3, you open a new workbook from the Personal Monthly Budget template installed with Excel 2007.

1. Click Office Button | New or press Alt+FN.

   Excel opens the New Workbook dialog box. This time, you will select a home budgeting template to use in creating your new workbook file.

2. Click Installed Templates in the left pane and then click the Personal Monthly Budget icon.

   Excel displays a preview of this template and its name in the preview pane on the right.

3. Click the Create button or press Enter.

   Excel closes the New Workbook dialog box and inserts a copy of the budget template as a new workbook automatically named PersonalMonthlyBudget1 in the Excel program title bar. This template is all set for you to start editing its values.

4. Close the PersonalMonthlyBudget1 workbook file. Click No in the alert dialog box that appears asking you if you want to save changes to this file.

   Excel returns you to your Book1 workbook file that you leave open for the next exercise.

You can also create the new workbook and close the New Workbook dialog box by double-clicking the desired template icon.

Moving Around the Workbook

The key to doing both data entry and data editing in any spreadsheet is selecting the cell or cells you want to fill or modify. Doing this cell selection almost always entails moving the cell cursor (or pointer) to another part of the current worksheet. Sometimes, it also involves activating a different worksheet in the workbook file.

Excel gives you plenty of choices in techniques for moving the cell cursor, some of which use the mouse and others of which are keyboard-driven.

Moving within the displayed area

Here's a recap of the most important ways to move the cell cursor to a new cell within the area of the worksheet that is currently displayed onscreen:

- ✔ Click the target cell with the white-cross mouse pointer.
- ✔ Press the arrow keys until the cell pointer is in the target cell.
- ✔ Click the Name Box at the beginning of the Formula Bar, enter the reference of the target (by column letter and row number as in D12), and press Enter.

Exercise 2-4: Moving the Cell Cursor in a Displayed Area of the Worksheet

For Exercise 2-4, make sure Sheet1 of the blank workbook, Book1, is active before you start practicing moving the cell cursor to different cells in the displayed area using the mouse, arrow keys, and Name Box:

1. Move the cell pointer to cell F9 with the mouse.

2. Move the cell pointer to cell C13 using just the down and left arrow keys.

3. Move the cell pointer to cell A1 using only the Name Box.

Keep in mind that you can always move the cursor to cell A1 (also known as the Home cell) of any active worksheet simply by pressing Ctrl+Home.

Moving to a new area of the worksheet

Many times you have to make cell entries in areas that aren't currently displayed in the active worksheet. One of quickest ways to do this is by entering the reference of the cell you want to go to in the Name Box. You can also use any of the following techniques to scroll to new parts of the current worksheet:

✔ To scroll up and down rows of the worksheet by windows, press the Page Up or Page Down or click the blank area above or below the scroll box in the vertical scroll bar.

✔ To scroll left and right columns of the worksheet by windows, click the blank area to the left or right of the scroll box in the horizontal scroll bar.

✔ To quickly scroll through rows or columns of the worksheet, hold down the Shift key as you drag the scroll box up or down in the vertical scroll bar, or left and right in the horizontal scroll bar.

✔ If you use a mouse with a wheel button, scroll up and down the rows of the worksheet by rotating the wheel button forward (to scroll up) and backward (to scroll down).

✔ If you use a mouse with a wheel button, pan through the rows and columns of the worksheet by clicking the wheel button and then dragging the triangular mouse pointer in the direction you want to scroll.

Don't forget that scrolling is not the same as selecting! After scrolling to a new part of the worksheet in view, you still have to select a cell by clicking in it to set the cursor in it.

Exercise 2-5: Moving the Cell Cursor to Unseen Parts of a Worksheet

In Exercise 2-5, you get practice moving the cell cursor to cells in the same worksheet that are not currently displayed on your screen.

1. Move the cell cursor to cell C125 with the Name Box on the Formula Bar.

Type **c125** into the Name Box and then press the Enter key.

2. Move the cell cursor to cell CA125 using the horizontal scroll bar.

   Hold down the Shift key as you drag the scroll box in the horizontal scroll bar to the right until column CA appears and then click cell CA125 to put the cell cursor in it.

3. Move the cell cursor to cell CA63560 using the vertical scroll bar.

   Hold down the Shift key and drag the scroll box in the vertical scroll down until row 63560 appears and then click cell CA63560 to put the cursor in it.

4. Move the cell cursor directly to cell A1 (the Home cell) in a single operation.

   Simply press Ctrl+Home.

Hold down the Shift key to scroll quickly through columns and rows by dragging the scroll box in the horizontal or vertical scroll bar. After scrolling into view the region with the cell you want to select, you still need to click in the cell to select it.

Q. What's the most efficient way to move between ranges of data that are spread out across a worksheet?

A. Use the Ctrl key in combination with any of the four arrow keys to jump from occupied cell to occupied cell in a particular direction.

Solve It **Exercise 2-6: Moving the Cell Cursor Using the Ctrl and Arrow Keys**

In Exercise 2-6, you get practice moving the cell pointer around a blank worksheet and between data entries with the Ctrl key and the arrow keys in Sheet1 of Book1.

1. Press Ctrl+→, Ctrl+↓, Ctrl+←, and Ctrl+↑ in succession to jump the cell cursor from one corner to the next of the entire Sheet1 worksheet.

   The first time you press Ctrl+→, the cell cursor jumps from cell A1 all the way to cell XFD1. When you next press Ctrl+↓, the cursor jumps from cell XFD1 all the way down to cell XFD1048576. When you then press Ctrl+←, the cursor jumps all the way left to cell A1048576, and from there all the way back up to cell A1 when you press Ctrl+↑. All this corner-to-corner jumping happens because there are no occupied cells in a particular direction, so the cursor jumps right to the cell on each border of the worksheet.

2. Move the cell cursor to cell A18, type **Stop,** and press Ctrl+Home. Next, press Ctrl+↓.

   The cell cursor stops in cell A18 rather than A1048576 because A18 is now occupied with the label *Stop.*

3. Move the cell cursor to cell AB18, type **Stop** again, and then press Home. Now, press Ctrl+→.

   This time, the cell cursor stops in cell AB18 rather than XFD18 because AB18 is now occupied.

4. Press the Delete key and then press Ctrl+← to move to cell AB1. Then, press the Delete key again, this time followed by Ctrl+Home.

Both entries in cells A18 and AB18 are deleted and the cell cursor is back in the home cell, A1.

Moving to a different sheet in the workbook

Each new workbook you start uses the general Excel Worksheet template that automatically includes three blank worksheets that you can fill with data. If you need more space for a particular spreadsheet, you can add additional worksheets by clicking the Insert Worksheet button that appears immediately following the last sheet tab in the workbook or by pressing Shift+F11. If you want all new workbooks you open to have more worksheets, open the Excel Options dialog box (Alt+FI) and then enter a new value in the Include This Many Sheets text box in the section called When Creating New Workbooks.

Each sheet in a workbook is automatically given the next available numeric name, such as Sheet1, Sheet2, and the like, but you can easily replace these generic names with something descriptive: Double-click the tab you want to rename, type the new sheet name, and press Enter. You can also color-code a sheet tab by right-clicking it, clicking Tab Color on the shortcut menu, and then selecting the color square on the pop-up palette.

Of course, you must know how to move between the sheets in order to be able to add and edit data in them. The most direct way to select a new worksheet is to click its sheet tab, although you can also use the shortcut keys Ctrl+Page Down to select the next sheet and Ctrl+Page Up to select the previous sheet.

If you add so many worksheets to your workbook that their sheet tabs can't all be displayed at one time, you can use the Tab scroll buttons to the immediate left of the sheet tab to bring into view the tabs you want to select. You can also display more tabs by reducing the width of the horizontal scroll bar (by dragging to the right the split bar that appears when you position the mouse pointer on the vertical bar at the beginning of the scroll bar).

Solve It

Exercise 2-7: Practice Moving the Cell Cursor to Different Sheets of the Same Workbook

In Exercise 2-7, you get practice moving the cell cursor to specific cells in different worksheets of the workbook named Book1, which should be open in Excel.

1. Move the cell cursor to cell J10 on Sheet2.

If used in a formula on another worksheet, this cell reference is indicated as Sheet2!J10.

2. Select cell M21 on Sheet3.

When you move the cell cursor to a cell, you, in essence, select that cell. If you were to refer to this cell in a formula on another worksheet, this cell would be designated as Sheet3!M21.

3. Select cell J10 on Sheet3 and then click the Sheet2 sheet tab to activate it.

   Note that when the cell cursor is located in the same cell on different worksheets and you then move between them, you don't notice any difference on the screen. The only way to tell that you're on a different sheet is by looking at which sheet tab is selected (indicated by the sheet name in boldface type).

4. Rename Sheet1 to Spring Sale.

   The easiest way to rename a tab is to double-click it, type the new name, and then press Enter. Leave the Book1 workbook with the renamed tab open for the next exercise.

Selecting Cell Ranges

When entering, editing, or formatting a single cell, all you have to do is move the cell cursor to it as you practiced in the earlier exercises. You can also enter the same data as well as do the same type of editing and formatting in a bunch of cells at one time, but to do so, you must first select the cells where all this is going to happen.

Most of the time when selecting multiple cells in a worksheet, you select a discrete block of cells of so many rows high and so many columns wide. Such a block is known as a *cell range* in parlance of spreadsheet software.

A cell range is most often described by the reference of its first and last cell (that is, the cell in the upper-left corner and the lower-right corner of its block, respectively). When written, it's separated by a colon as in B15:F20, for a six-row and five-column cell range whose first cell is B15 and last cell is F20. To select this cell range, you move the cursor to cell B15 and then drag over and down (or down or over) to cell F20; or hold down the Shift key as you click cell F20; or use the ↓ and → keys to move the cursor to cell F20.

Excel, however, does not limit you to selecting a single cell range for data entry, editing, or formatting. You can select as many cell ranges (even those as small as a single cell) by holding down the Ctrl key as you add a new range to the cell selection.

Always think of the Shift key when you want to select a single range of cells and the Ctrl key when you want to select more than one cell range at one time.

Q. How do you select cell ranges that include complete rows and columns of the active worksheet?

A. Click the letter of the column or the number of the row whose cells are to be selected in the column and row header, respectively. To select multiple columns or rows, hold down the Shift key and drag through them if they are consecutive, or click them as you hold down the Ctrl key if they are non-contiguous. Press Ctrl+A or click the box at the junction of the column and row header with the folded corner icon to select all the columns and rows in the active worksheet (in other words, the entire worksheet).

Q. How do I select the same cell ranges that span different worksheets of the active workbook?

A. Click the tab of the first worksheet and then hold down Shift as you click the last sheet before you select the cell range or ranges on the active sheet.

Solve It

Exercise 2-8: Practice Assigning Fill Colors to Selected Cell Ranges

In Exercise 2-8, you get to practice assigning different fill colors to cell ranges you select in the Spring Sale worksheet of Book1. You can assign these fill colors directly from the Ribbon, using the Fill Color drop-down button in the Font Group.

1. Drag the Zoom slider on the right side of the Status bar to the right until you've increased the magnification of the worksheet to 200%.

Increasing the magnification of the worksheet display makes it easy to work on a particular section.

2. Drag through the cell range A2:E2 to select this cell range; click the Fill Color drop-down button on the Home tab and click the White, Background 1, Darker 15% square in the drop-down color palette.

This square is the one located in the first column of the palette, the third row down.

3. Select the cell ranges A3:A9 and B3:E3 as a single cell selection (I'm sure you can ConTRoL it) and then assign Light Blue as the fill color by selecting its square on the Fill Color palette.

The Light Blue fill color is located in the row of Standard Colors in the Fill Color drop-down palette. It's the turquoise square that's fourth from the right.

4. Select the cell range B4:E9 and then assign Yellow as the fill color for this range before you position the cell cursor in cell A1 (Ctrl+Home).

The Yellow fill color is located in the row of Standard Colors in the Fill Color drop-down palette (fourth from the left).

Making Cell Entries

As you may already be aware, Excel recognizes only two types of cell entries: text (label) and number (or value). Numeric cell entries are those that consist solely of numbers or calculable formulas. Text entries are those that consist of all letters or a combination of letters, numbers, and punctuation on which Excel can perform no sort of calculation.

Anything you enter into a cell or cell selection is immediately analyzed as either being a number or text entry. Because the general Excel Worksheet template automatically left-aligns all text entries and right-aligns all numeric ones, you can often tell immediately how your entry has been classified by noting how it's aligned in its cell.

When you make a numeric entry in a worksheet, Excel not only right aligns the value in its cell, but also assigns the General number format to it. In this format, only significant digits are displayed. This means that all trailing zeros after the decimal point are dropped. Also, if the number you enter contains more than can fit within the current column width, Excel automatically converts the value to scientific notation (as in 5.00E+11 for 500,000,000,000).

Sometimes you have to override Excel's number/text assignment in order to obtain the desired cell entry. The most famous example of this is a ZIP code or numeric part or item number that begins with a zero, as in 00105. If you try to enter this ZIP code into a cell simply by typing its five digits, Excel interprets it as a numeric entry and in assigning the General format to it, retains only the value 105 in the cell. In order to retain the preceding zeros, you need to force the entry to be recognized as text by typing an initial apostrophe, as in '**00105** (this apostrophe does not appear in the cell, although you can see it on the Formula bar).

Entering data in a single cell

Most cell entries are made by typing from the keyboard (although later versions of Excel do support voice and ink text entry). After typing the characters, which appear both in the cell and on the Formula bar, you must still complete the entry.

Any time prior to completing the cell entry, you can press the Esc key to clear the cell of all characters you typed there.

Q. How many ways are there to complete an entry in the current cell?

A. You should be familiar with all these methods:

- Click the Enter box on the Formula bar (the one with the check mark).
- Press the Enter key.
- Press one of the arrow keys.
- Press Tab, Shift+Tab, Home, Ctrl+Home, Page Up, Page Down, Ctrl+Page Up, Ctrl+Page Down or, any of the other cursor-movement key combinations.

Click the Enter box on the Formula bar when you want the cell cursor to remain in the cell where you just made the entry (so that you can format it in some fashion). Press Enter when you want to move the cell cursor to the next row in order to make another entry.

Solve It

Exercise 2-9: Practice Entering Data in a Simple Table

In Exercise 2-9, you get practice doing data entry for the simple Spring Sale table shown in Figure 2-2. You make these data entries in the cells that you colored in Exercise 2-8.

1. Enter the table title Spring Sale Markdowns in cell A2.

2. Enter the column headings in row 3 as follows:

- **Code** in cell A3

- **Description** in cell B3

- **Retail Price** in cell C3

- **% Discount** in cell D3

- **Markdown** in cell E3

3. Enter the code numbers in column A as follows (don't forget how to override Excel and enter these codes as text entries by prefacing each of them with an apostrophe):

- **02-305** in cell A4

- **02-240** in cell A5

- **04-356** in cell A6

- **01-234** in cell A7

- **03-003** in cell A8

- **01-240** in cell A9

4. Enter the furniture descriptions in column B as follows:

- **36-inch round table** in cell B4

- **72-inch rectangle table** in cell B5

- **76-inch hutch** in cell B6

- **Side chair** in cell B7

- **Arm chair** in cell B8

- **Armoire** in cell B9

5. Enter the retail prices of the furniture in column C as follows:

- **1250** in cell C4

- **1400** in cell C5

- **2500** in cell C6

- **350** in cell C7

- **500** in cell C8

- **1750** in cell C9

6. Enter the discount percentages in column D as follows:

  - **25%** in cells D4, D5, and D6

  - **15%** in cells D7 and D8

  - **25%** in cell D9

Use the View Side by Side feature to check your completed spreadsheet table against the one in *Solved2-9.xlsx*. (Open this workbook in the Chap2 folder inside the Excel Workbook folder that you've copied into your My Documents folder on your hard disk or on the CD-ROM that came with this book.)

Entering data in a cell range

Sometimes you want to make the same entry in several different cells in the same worksheet. To do this, select all the cells and cell ranges and then press Ctrl+Enter to both complete the entry you make in the active cell and simultaneously insert it into all the other selected cells.

Figure 2-2: The new Spring Sale table after completing the initial data entry.

	A	B	C	D	E
1					
2	Spring Sale Markdowns				
3	Code	Description	Retail Price	% Discount	Markdown
4	02-305	36-inch ro	1250	25%	
5	02-240	72-inch re	1400	25%	
6	04-356	76-inch hu	2500	25%	
7	01-234	Side chair	350	15%	
8	03-003	Arm chair	500	15%	
9	01-240	Armoire	1750	25%	
10					
11					

Filling in a data series with the Fill handle

The tiny black square in the lower-right corner of the cell cursor is known as the Fill handle. The Fill handle is your key to the AutoFill feature that makes it super-easy either to fill in a continuous range with the same entry or with data series (such as Monday, Tuesday, Wednesday, and so on, or 101, 102, 103, and the like).

To create a sequential series that increments by one unit (day, hour, month, widget number), you enter the first entry in the series in a blank cell and then drag the Fill handle in the direction you want the series to appear (down or to the right are the most common directions). To create series that increment by other units (every other day, every third month, every fourth hour, every tenth widget), you enter the first two entries in the series (that serves as an example of the increment to be used) in two adjacent blank cells and then, after selecting them both, drag the Fill handle in the appropriate direction.

Instead of filling in a data series with AutoFill, you can force Excel to copy the entry you've made in the current cell by holding down the Ctrl key as you drag the Fill handle. Excel indicates that it copies rather than fills a range by displaying a tiny plus sign to the side of the Fill handle mouse pointer.

Before you attempt Exercise 2-10, you may want to play the AutoFill.exe demo located in the Excel Feature Demos folder on your workbook CD-ROM. This feature demonstration shows you how to use the Fill handle in an Excel worksheet to create different types of data series.

Exercise 2-10: Creating a Series of Entries with the Fill Handle

In Exercise 2-10, you practice making the same data entry in multiple ranges and using the Fill handle to create various data series in its Sheet1.

1. Make Sheet2 of Book1 active.

2. Enter today's date, following the date format *25-Oct-07*, in the cell selection A1, D3:F3, and B4:B6.

   Don't forget to hold down the Ctrl key when you're selecting the three ranges in the cell selection.

   Be sure to complete the current date entry into all the cells of the selection by pressing Ctrl+Enter.

3. Use AutoFill to create a data series with all twelve months in the cell range A8:A19 starting with January.

4. Use AutoFill to create a data series with the names of all the days of the week in cell range D8:J8 starting with Monday.

5. Use AutoFill to create a data series with hours from 8:00AM to 8:00PM in cell range C10:C22.

6. Use AutoFill to create a data series in cell range E10:H10 containing the headings Qtr1, Qtr2, Qtr3, and Qtr4.

7. Use AutoFill to create a series in cell range E12:E21 containing 1st Team, 2nd Team, 3rd Team, and so on all the way up to 10th Team.

8. Use AutoFill to create a data series in cell range G12:L12 that contains the name of every other month starting with November and ending with September.

Don't forget that you need to indicate the every-other-month increment to Excel (by entering January in cell H12 and then selecting the range G12:H12) before using the Fill handle to create the data series.

9. Use AutoFill to copy the data entry New Budget in the cell range G14:G19 (don't let this one get out of ConTRoL).

Copying a formula with the Fill handle

AutoFill is not only useful for filling in a data series or copying a static data entry to a continuous cell range, but also for copying a formula across a row or down a column of a data table. When you copy a formula, Excel automatically adjusts the column and row references in the copies so that they refer to the right data.

Don't forget that Excel automatically uses the so-called relative column and row cell references in all formulas you create. If you ever need to override this so that all or part of a cell reference is not adjusted in the copied formulas, you enter a $ (dollar sign) before the cell's column letter or row number (you can have Excel do it for you by pressing F4 while building the formula on the Formula bar).

Exercise 2-11: Copying Formulas with the Fill Handle

In Exercise 2-11, you complete the Spring Sale table by entering the formula that calculates the amount of the markdown in cell E4 and then using AutoFill to copy that formula down the cell range E5:E9.

1. Switch to the Spring Sale sheet of Book1 and then move the cell cursor to cell E4.

2. Type = (equal) to start the formula for calculating the sale price of the 36-inch round table.

Remember that all Excel formulas start with the equal sign.

3. Click cell C4 and then type * (asterisk) before you click cell D4.

Remember that Excel uses the asterisk (*) as the sign of multiplication. Your formula should now read =C4*D4 on the Formula bar.

4. Click the Enter box on the Formula bar and then drag the Fill handle of the cell cursor in cell E4 down to E9.

As soon as you click the Enter button, Excel inserts the formula in the cell. The formula =C4*D4 appears in the Formula bar and the calculated markdown amount of 312.5 appears in cell E4. As soon as you release the mouse button after dragging the Fill handle, Excel makes copies of the original formula in the cell range E5:E9.

5. Use the Side by Side feature to check your results against those in the Spring Sale table shown in *Solved2-11.xlsx* in the Chap2 folder. (The Chap2 folder is in the Excel Workbook folder on your hard disk or the CD-ROM that comes with this book.)

Saving the Spreadsheet Data in a Workbook File

Now all that remains to do is to save the spreadsheets you created while performing the exercises in this chapter before exiting Excel. As you know, all work that you do in between the times you save the worksheet is at risk because you immediately lose it if your computer experiences even the briefest power interruption.

The first time you save your spreadsheet in a workbook file, the Save As dialog box appears giving you have the opportunity to rename the file (replacing the Book1, Book2 monikers with something more descriptive) in the File Name text box, and indicate the folder in which it should be saved in the Save In drop-down list box. After that, you can use the Save command to save all additional changes to the same file without opening any dialog box.

Excel 2007 uses a new XML (eXtensible Markup Language File) default file format (indicated by the .xlsx extension to the filename). If you need to create a workbook file that users of older versions of Excel (97-2003) can open and use, you need to save your workbook in the older Excel file format (indicated by the .xls filename extension). To do this, you select Office Button | Save As | Excel 97-2003 Workbook or press Alt+FF9 to open the Save As dialog box with the old .xls file format selected.

Excel saves the current position of the cell cursor in the worksheet when you save its workbook. Therefore, always position the cursor in the cell you want to be current when you next open the workbook for editing before doing the final save of your work session.

Q. How many ways do you know for saving changes to your workbook file?

A. You should be familiar with all these methods:

- ✔ Click the Save button on the Quick Access toolbar (the one with the disk icon).

- ✔ Choose Office Button | Save or press Alt+FS (Office Button | Save As or Alt+FA if you want to open the Save As dialog box again so that you can rename or save a copy in a new folder).

- ✔ Press F12 (Shift+F12 to open the Save As dialog box).

Exercise 2-12: Saving a Workbook File

In Exercise 2-12, save the Spring Sales table in a new Excel 2007 Practice folder inside the My Documents (Windows XP) or Documents (Vista) folder on your hard disk:

1. With the Spring Sales table displayed onscreen, select cell A2 before you click the Save button on the Quick Access toolbar.

    Excel opens the Save As dialog box.

2. Click My Documents or Documents (Vista) in the left pane and then click the Create New Folder button or New Folder (Vista) on the toolbar of the Save As dialog box; Type **Excel 2007 Practice** in the Name text box of the New Folder dialog box and click OK.

    The new folder name, *Excel 2007 Practice*, now appears at the top of the Save As dialog box.

3. Replace Book1.xls in the File Name text box by typing **Spring Furniture Sale** and then clicking the Save button.

4. Close the Spring Furniture Sale workbook by exiting Excel (Office Button | Exit Excel or Alt+F4).

Chapter 3

Formatting the Spreadsheet

· ·

In This Chapter

▶ Resizing columns and rows in a worksheet

▶ Formatting cells with the Home tab of the Ribbon

▶ Formatting cells with the Format Cells dialog box

▶ Using Cell Styles

▶ Using Conditional Formatting

▶ Hiding columns and rows in a worksheet

· ·

*I*n Excel, formatting means formatting cells of the worksheet. Therefore, the formatting you assign a cell not only affects the cell's current contents but any contents you enter into it. The exercises in this chapter give you a chance to practice widening and narrowing the columns and rows of a worksheet to suit the formatting and contents of its cells. In addition, you discover a full array of techniques for assigning formatting to cells in worksheets, including the Format Cells dialog box and the AutoFormat and Conditional Formatting features.

Resizing Columns and Rows

In all new workbooks generated from the general Excel Worksheet template, the columns of its worksheets are a standard 8.43 characters or 64 pixels wide and all the rows are 15 points or 20 pixels high. You can, if you need, change this default column width for an entire worksheet by clicking its sheet tab to select it before choosing Format | Default Width on the Ribbon's Home tab (Alt+HOD). Then, you enter the new default width in the Standard Column Width text box (in characters) before you select OK.

Note that Excel does not provide any way for setting a new row height default in a worksheet. The 15-point default value is universal for all worksheets you deal with unless you manually override this height. This is probably because Excel always automatically increases the height of all rows to suit the formatting of its cell entries. Column widths, on the other hand, are automatically widened only under certain circumstances (when applying certain AutoFormat styles and building data tables with later versions of Excel).

Making column widths suit the data

Resizing particular columns to suit the data they contain is one of the most common formatting tasks you perform in creating and editing a spreadsheet.

You need to widen a column in a worksheet whenever it contains cells with numerical data having too many digits to be displayed in the current column width (indicated by a string of #### signs in the cells) or text data with characters cut off (because they spilled over into cells in columns to the immediate right that were then truncated by entries made in the adjacent column).

Q. How many ways exist for resizing particular columns in a worksheet?

A. You should be familiar with all the following methods:

   ✔ Drag the column's right border in the column header to the left (to narrow) or right (to widen) — to resize several columns at once, drag through their column letters in the header or Ctrl+click them before dragging the right border of one of them.

   ✔ Double-click the column's right border in the column header to resize it with AutoFit — to resize several columns at once, drag though their column letters in the header or Ctrl+click them before double-clicking the right border of one of them.

   ✔ Select the column or columns to resize and then choose Format | Column Width on the Home tab or press Alt+HOW. Enter the new width (in characters) in the Column Width dialog box and then select OK.

   ✔ Select the cell range or selection whose columns need resizing and then choose Format | AutoFit Column Width on the Home tab or press Alt+HOI. (Excel widens or narrows the columns in the cell selection to display all the digits and text in the cells in the selection.)

   ✔ Select the column or columns to resize to standard column width (of 8.43 characters) and then choose Format | Column Width on the Home tab or press Alt+HOW. Type **8.43** in the Column Width text box and select OK in the Column Width dialog box.

Solve It **Exercise 3-1: Changing Column Widths in a Worksheet Table**

In Exercise 3-1, you practice changing the column widths in your Spring Sale Markdowns table.

   1. Launch Excel and then open the *Spring Furniture Sale.xlsx* workbook you created in the exercises in Chapter 2 and saved in the Excel 2007 Practice folder. If you didn't do these exercises, open the *Exercise3-1.xlsx* file in the Chapter 3 folder inside the Excel 2007 Workbook folder.

If *Spring Furniture Sale.xlsx* is not listed as one of the Recent Documents in the right-hand pane of the Office menu (opened by clicking the Office Button or pressing Alt+F), click the Open button on the Office menu, open the *Exercise3-1.xlsx* file in the Chap3 subfolder inside the Excel 2007 Workbook folder. Play the File Open on Windows XP or the File Open on Windows Vista essential technique demo if you need help in performing this step.

2. Use the AutoFit feature to widen Column B containing the furniture descriptions and Column D containing the discount percentages sufficiently so that none of these descriptions are cut off.

3. Drag the right border of Column C to the left until the column is 34 pixels wide and then release the mouse button (note the appearance of ### indicators in all but two cells in the Sale table). Next, use AutoFit to widen Columns C and D so that all the entries in these columns are displayed.

4. Use the Column Width dialog box to set column E to a width of 10 characters or 75 pixels.

5. Narrow column A to 7.14 characters or 55 pixels wide (use any method that works).

6. If you've been modifying your *Spring Furniture Sale.xlsx* file, click the Save button on the Quick Access toolbar or press Ctrl+S to save your changes. If you've been modifying the *Exercise3-1.xlsx* file, choose the Office Button | Save As or press F12 to open the Save As dialog box and then rename *Exercise 3-1.xlsx* as **Spring Furniture Sale.xlsx** in the File Name text box. Select Excel 2007 Practice folder inside My Documents as the location in the Save In drop-down list before you select Save.

Manipulating the height of certain rows

You don't find yourself having to resize the rows of a worksheet all that much. Most of the time, Excel does all the work for you by automatically resizing them just right to accommodate any and all formatting change you make to their cells.

About the only time you might want to increase the height of a row on your own is when you want to increase the space between the contents of one row and the contents of the row immediately above without going through the trouble of inserting a blank row as a spacer between them.

Q. What are the two ways you can manually modify the height of selected rows in a worksheet?

A. You should be familiar with both these methods for changing row height:

↳ Drag the lower border of the number of the row to modify in the row header either up (to shorten the row) or down (to heighten the row) — to modify multiple rows at one time, select the rows (by dragging through or Ctrl+clicking their row numbers in the row header) and then drag just the lower border of just one of the selected rows.

↳ Position the cell cursor in any one of the cells in the row to be modified, and then choose Format | Row Height on the Home tab or press Alt+HOH. Enter the number of points in the Row Height text box before you select OK — to modify multiple rows at one time, select the rows before opening the Row Height dialog box.

Exercise 3-2: Changing Row Heights in a Worksheet

In Exercise 3-2, practice modifying row height in the Spring Furniture Sale workbook.

1. Increase the height of Row 2, containing the table title, to 26.25 or 35 pixels by dragging the row's border.

Note how the spreadsheet title sinks down when the row height is increased.

2. Restore the height of Row 2 to it original height with AutoFit Row Height.

HINT

Double-click the lower border of a row in the row header and modify its height using AutoFit. Alternatively, place the cell cursor somewhere in the row and choose Format | AutoFit Row Height on the Home tab or press Alt+HOA.

Cell Formatting Techniques

Cell formatting can run the gamut from changing the font, color, attribute, or alignment of a cell entry to the color, borders, and protection status of the cell itself. You can accomplish most of the formatting in a typical spreadsheet with the command buttons on the Home tab of the Ribbon. The rest you can accomplish with the options available on the various tabs of the Format Cells dialog box.

REMEMBER

The first rule of formatting is to remember to select all the cells that need formatting before you select the desired button on the Formatting toolbar or option on one of the tabs in the Format Cells dialog box.

Formatting cells with the Ribbon's Home tab

The Home tab of the Ribbon contains five groups with lots of command buttons for formatting your spreadsheets:

- ✔ **Font** group with command buttons changing the font, font size, font attribute, font color, and fill color.

- ✔ **Alignment** group with command buttons for changing the alignment and orientation of entries in a cell range as well as wrapping entries on different rows and merging cells.

- ✔ **Number** group with command buttons for assigning the most popular number formats to cell ranges.

- ✔ **Styles** group with command buttons for assigning conditional formatting, formatting a cell range as a table, and applying styles to a cell range.

- ✔ **Cells** group with command buttons for inserting and deleting cells as well as formatting the widths of worksheet columns and the heights of rows.

Before you attempt Exercise 3-3, you may want to play the Formatting Cell Range as Table.exe demo located in the Excel Feature Demos folder on your workbook CD-ROM. This feature demonstration shows you the basic process of formatting a cell range as a table.

Exercise 3-3: Applying the Format As Table Option to Your Markdown Data Table

In Exercise 3-3, you get practice formatting the sale furniture markdown data table in the Spring Sale worksheet of the Spring Furniture Sale workbook using the Merge & Center and Format As Table command buttons on the Home tab of the Ribbon.

1. Center the title of the markdown table in cell A2 over the range A2:E2 and make it bold.

Click the Merge & Center button in the Alignment group after selecting the range of cells over which you want to center the text that's entered in the first cell of the range (the range A2:E2 in this case). Click the Bold button in Font group to make the centered title bold.

Next, you want to remove all of the fill colors you earlier assigned to the markdown table so that you can then format the range as a table.

2. Select the table's cell range A3:E9 and then click the Fill Color drop-down button in the Font group and click No Fill on the drop-down menu.

Excel removes all the fill colors from this cell range. You will now format this cell range as a table. Doing this makes it possible for you to instantly change its formatting using Excel's new Table Styles gallery. This gallery uses the new Live Preview feature that lets you preview any table style in the gallery in the table in your worksheet before you actually select the style and apply it to the table's cell range.

3. Click the Format as Table command button in the Styles group and then click Table Style Light 1 (the first one in the first row) of the drop-down palette.

You must select an initial table format from the Table Styles gallery and specify the cell range of the table before you can use Live Preview to see how any of the other table formats in the gallery suit your particular table. Note that the Format As Table dialog box not only displays the range address of the cell range that it selects in the worksheet (indicated by the marquee or marching ants) but also automatically selects the My Table Has Headers check box.

When the My Table Has Headers check box is selected, Excel automatically considers the data entries in the first row of the cell range as the column headings of the table (to which it adds drop-down buttons called AutoFilter buttons). If you remove the check mark from the My Table Has Headers check box, Excel inserts an additional row in your table with generic column headings such as Column1, Column2, and so forth.

4. Click OK in the Format As Table dialog box without making any changes to its settings.

Excel adds AutoFilter buttons to the column headings in row 3 of the table — Code, Description, Retail Price, and so on — you'll find out how to use these buttons to sort and filter your data in Chapter 17. It also applies the Table Style Light 1 style (with the alternating lightly banded rows) to your markdown table.

Now, you can have some fun using Excel's Live Preview feature to see how your table would look if you were to apply one of the many other styles in the Table Styles gallery to its data. Note that the end of the Ribbon now contains an additional Design tab (under the label *Table Tools*). You can use the command buttons on the Table Tools Design tab to select a new table style as well as to customize the one currently selected.

This Table Tools Design tab and the others like it that you'll encounter as you work with different object in Excel 2007 worksheets are referred to as Contextual tabs. A Contextual tab and all its command buttons appears at the end of the Ribbon only as long as you select the object (a formatted table, in this case) to which its options can be applied.

5. Click cell A2 containing the table title in the Spring Sale worksheet to select it.

The moment you select a cell outside of your formatted data table, the Contextual Table Tools Design tab and its command buttons immediately disappear from the Ribbon. To bring this Contextual tab and all its options back, all you have to do is select a cell in the data table.

6. Click cell A3 with the column heading Code to select this cell.

The Design tab immediately reappears at the end of the Ribbon. You will now use Live Preview to preview your markdown table in some of the other styles in its Table Styles gallery.

7. Click the Design tab at the end of the Ribbon to make this tab active and display its command buttons and Table Styles gallery. Position your mouse pointer (but don't click) on the thumbnail of each of the other four or so styles (Table Style Light 2, Light 3, and so on) that are normally displayed in the Table Styles group to the right of the Table Style Light 1 thumbnail.

As you mouse over each thumbnail in the gallery, Excel's Live Preview displays the data in your markdown table in that style. These few light styles whose thumbnails are currently displayed in the Tables Styles gallery on the Ribbon are not, however, your only choices.

8. Click the More button (the button with the line and the downward pointing triangle) located in the lower-right corner of the Table Styles group to expand the gallery and then experiment by mousing over the different Medium and Dark styles. (You have to use the scroll bar to display the thumbnails of the Dark table styles.)

Previewing a style in the gallery is not the same as selecting it. To apply a new style, you must click the thumbnail after previewing it.

9. Format your markdown table with Table Style Medium 23 in the Table Styles gallery.

Note that the thumbnails displayed in the single row of the Table Styles gallery on the Ribbon changes to display currently selected Medium 23 style as well as other Medium styles in its row. You can use the Up and Down buttons that appear above the More button at the end of the gallery to display rows above and below the current one without expanding the gallery so that it obscures cells in the worksheet.

10. Use the Save As command on the Office menu or press Alt+FA to save your changes to the workbook under the new filename, **Spring Furniture Sale Table Fmt.xlsx**.

Be sure that you don't change the folder (you want to save this version in the Excel 2007 Practice folder on your hard drive) or the type of file when you rename it in the Save As dialog box. Simply append **Table Fmt** to the main filename before you click Save.

Solve It

Exercise 3-4: Customizing the Table Formatting for Markdowns Data Table

In Exercise 3-4, you get practice customizing the table formatting applied to the Spring Sale Markdowns data table of your Spring Sale worksheet in the Spring Furniture Sale Table Fmt workbook. Check the program title bar to be sure that the Spring Furniture Sale Table Fmt workbook is the one open and active in Excel. If you didn't complete Exercise 3-3, open the *Exercise3-4.xlsx* file in the Chap3 subfolder of your Excel 2007 Workbook folder.

1. Click the Contextual Design tab under Table Tools at the end of the Ribbon to display its command buttons.

If your Ribbon doesn't have Table Tools displayed at the end with a Design tab underneath it, this means that none of the cells of your formatted Spring Sale Markdowns table is currently selected. Remember that Excel only adds Contextual tabs for an object on the Ribbon when that object is selected in the worksheet. Click one of the cells in your markdowns table to display the Table Tools Design Contextual tab.

2. Click the Last Column check box in the Table Style Options group in the Table Tools Design tab.

Excel displays the calculated markdowns for each item in Column E in boldface type.

3. Click the Total Row check box in the Table Style Options group of the Table Tools Design tab.

Excel now adds a total row in row 10 of your data table with a formula in cell E10 that totals the markdown amounts in column E. This feature is very useful when you need totals to appear at the bottom of your data table. However, it makes no sense here because the markdown amounts are not cumulative.

4. Deselect the Total Row check box in the Table Style Options group to remove the Total row from your data table and then rename the data table by clicking Table1 under Table Name in the Properties group and replacing it with the name Markdowns.

Now you're ready to further customize the Markdowns table by formatting some of its contents using command buttons on the Home tab.

5. Select the values in the cell ranges C4:C9 and E4:E9. Next, click the Home tab and there click the Accounting Number Format button in the Number group.

Excel immediately adds a dollar sign and two decimal places to all the values in these two cell ranges. Now experiment with the Decrease Decimal and Increase Decimal buttons in the Number group.

6. Click the Decrease Decimal button in the Number group twice to remove all the decimal places from the values in the selected cell ranges and then click the Increase Decimal button twice to bring the decimal places back.

Now try changing the number formatting for the selected cells ranges.

7. Click the Comma Style button in the Number group to change the number formatting from Accounting to Comma Style.

The Table Styles gallery is not the only feature to use Live Preview. This feature also works when you want to assign a new font or font size to a cell selection.

8. Select the entire data table as a cell selection (A3:E9) and then click the Font Size drop-down button in the Font group. Highlight larger and smaller font sizes in this list with the mouse before you click 10 to make 10 point the new font size.

Note that each time you highlight a new size on the Font Size drop-down list, Excel displays all the table data not obscured by the list itself in the new font size.

9. Click the Font drop-down button and highlight different fonts in the drop-down list before you click Arial to make it the new font.

Each time you highlight a new font on the Font drop-down list, Excel displays all the table data not obscured by this list in the new font.

10. Use the Borders button in the Font group to add a border around all the cells in the cell selection (A3:E9).

To draw a border around a block of cells, select its cell range (A3:E9 in this case), and then click the Borders drop-down button in the Font group of the Home tab. Click the All Border option on the Borders drop-down list (the one divided into four quadrants).

Next, you're going to remove the AutoFilter buttons that Excel automatically adds to the row containing the column headings of a table when you select a table style with the Format As Table button on the Home tab. (You only need these AutoFilter buttons when you intend to sort or filter the table's data, which you don't need to do here, and, besides, you can always bring these buttons back should need them later.)

11. Click A3 to select it and then click the Sort & Filter button in the Editing group of the Home tab and, finally, click Filter on its drop-down menu.

Excel removes all the AutoFilter buttons from all the cells in row 3 of your markdowns table.

Use the View Side by Side feature to check your fully formatted table against the one entered on the Spring Sale sheet in the workbook file *Solved3-4.xlsx*, located in the Chap3 Folder in your Excel 2007 Workbook folder.

12. When your work checks outs, click cell A1 and then use the Save As command on the Office menu or press Alt+FA to save your changes to the workbook under the new filename, **Spring Furniture Sale Cust Fmt.xlsx**.

Be sure that you don't change the folder (you want to save this version in the Excel 2007 Practice folder on your hard drive) or the type of file when you rename it in the Save As dialog box. Simply replace Table with **Cust** in the main filename before you click Save. Leave the *Spring Furniture Sale Cust Fmt.xlsx* workbook open in Excel for the next exercise.

Solve It

Exercise 3-5: Using the Format Painter and AutoFormat Features

In Exercise 3-5, you get practice using the Format Painter and AutoFormat buttons to format a cell range. The Format Painter button in the Clipboard group of the Ribbon's Home tab enables you to pick up all the formatting you've already assigned a cell in the worksheet and apply this formatting to a range you select. The AutoFormat button, which you added as part of customizing the Quick Access toolbar in Exercise 1-4, is not normally a part of Excel 2007. This button enables you to use an earlier table formatting feature (available in Excel 97-2003) to apply complex formatting to data tables in a single operation.

1. Click cell A3 containing the first column heading, Code, in the markdowns data table and then click the AutoFormat button on the Quick Access toolbar.

Excel opens an AutoFormat dialog box that contains a list box with samples of various table formats you can apply to your table arranged in two columns. Scroll down the list to see all the table formats available.

2. Click the Classic 3 sample in the AutoFormat dialog box and then click OK.

Excel immediately applies the Classic 3 table format with its vivid blue coloring to all the data in your table (cell range, A3:E9).

3. With cell A3 still selected, click the Format Painter button (the one with the paintbrush icon) in the Clipboard group of the Ribbon's Home tab.

A marquee (of marching ants) now appears around the border of cell A3, indicating that the formatting applied to this cell will be copied to whatever cell or cell range you select next.

4. Use the Paintbrush mouse pointer to click cell A2 containing the table title to select this cell and simultaneously copy the formatting from cell A3 to it.

Excel immediately applies the dark blue fill and bold white font color to the title in cell A2. Unfortunately, the program also applies the Align Text Left formatting while at the same time removing the merge you applied to cells A2:E2.

5. Click the Merge & Center button in the Alignment group of the Home tab and then increase the size of the title font to 14 points using the Font Size button in the Font group.

Excel converts the range A2:E2 into a super-cell in which it now horizontally centers the table title.

6. Save your formatting changes to this table in a new workbook file named **Spring Furniture Sale Classic 3.xlsx** in your Excel 2007 Practice folder and then close the workbook file.

Formatting cells with the Format Cells dialog box

You rely on the Format Cells dialog box for applying more complex formatting than assigned by the command buttons in the Font, Alignment, and Number groups on the Ribbon's Home tab. This includes applying any number formats other than the standard Accounting, Percent, and Comma number formats from the Number tab as well as applying custom alignment angles not available from the Orientation button's drop-down list from the Alignment tab. You can also use its options on the Font tab for selecting more font attributes and its Fill tab for applying patterns along with fill-in colors for cell backgrounds, and the Protection tab to change locked or hidden status of cells that goes into effect as soon as you protect the worksheet (see Chapter 17 for details).

When you click the dialog box launcher buttons in the lower-right corner of the Font, Alignment, and Number groups in the Ribbon's Home tab, Excel opens the Format Cells dialog box with the respective Font, Alignment, and Number tabs of the Format Cells dialog box selected. You can also open the Format Cells dialog box with the tab selected by pressing Ctrl+1 (that's the Ctrl key and the number 1 on the top row of the QWERTY keyboard).

The options on the Number tab for applying the various and sundry number formats that Excel has to offer as well as for creating your own custom number formats is possibly the most important one in the Format Cells dialog box (see Figure 3-1). This tab organizes the ready-made number formats by category from General, the default for all cells in a new worksheet which retains only significant digits, to Custom, where you can create your own number formats. Here's a quick rundown on the other ten categories of number formats that you will probably use more often:

- ✔ **Number** to apply a number format to numeric entries in which you determine the number of decimal places to display, whether to use the comma as a thousands separator, and the appearance of negative numbers (either with a negative sign or enclosed in parentheses in black or red).

- ✔ **Currency** to apply a number format to numeric entries in which you determine the currency symbol (the dollar sign is the default), the number of decimal places to display, and the appearance of negative numbers (either with a negative sign or enclosed in parentheses in black or red).

- ✔ **Accounting** to apply a number format to numeric entries in which you determine the currency symbol (the dollar sign is the default) and the number of decimal places to display (the difference between Accounting and Currency is that Accounting always uses two decimal places and aligns the currency symbol and decimal points in their cells).

- ✔ **Date** to select a new date format for numeric entries that Excel recognizes as representing dates of the year (because it was entered following one of these date formats).

- ✔ **Time** to select a new time format using either a 12- or 24-hour clock for numeric entries that Excel recognizes as representing times of the day (because it was entered following one of the time formats).

- ✔ **Percentage** to multiply the numeric entries by 100 with a percent sign and the number of decimal places you designate.

- ✔ **Fraction** to select a fractional number format for the decimal places in your numeric entries.

- ✔ **Scientific** to apply scientific notation to numeric entries by applying an exponent and the number of decimal places you designate.

✔ **Text** to have numeric entries formatted as though they were text entries.

✔ **Special** to format numeric entries following the styles for ZIP Code, ZIP Code + 4 (with leading zeros retained), Phone Number (with parentheses added to the first three digits as the area code and dashes between the third and fourth digits of the next seven indicating the prefix and main number), or Social Security Number (with dashes between the third and fourth, and fifth and sixth digits of the nine-digit number).

Figure 3-1:
The Number tab of the Format Cells dialog box gives you access to a wide variety of number formats.

Before you attempt Exercise 3-6, you may want to play the Formatting Numbers.exe demo located in the Excel Feature Demos folder on your workbook CD-ROM. This feature demonstration shows you the basic process of assigning appropriate number formatting to different types of values in a spreadsheet using the command buttons in the Number group on the Home tab and options on the Number tab of the Format Cells dialog box.

Solve It

Exercise 3-6: Practice Formatting Various Values with the Format Cells Dialog Box

In Exercise 3-6, you get practice formatting different types of values using some of the number formats found in the Format.

1. Open a new workbook (Book2) by clicking the New button you added to the Quick Access toolbar or by pressing Ctrl+N, and then rename Sheet1 **Number Formats** and use it to practice applying following number formats using the Number tab on the Format Cells dialog box.

Next, you increase the magnification to make it easier to see your work.

2. Increase the worksheet magnification for the blank Sheet1 worksheet to 150% using the Zoom slider on the Status bar.

3. Format the cell range B2:B5 in the blank Sheet1 using the Currency number format with two decimal places, the dollar sign, and negative values set in red parentheses in the Format Cells dialog box.

When you assign a number format to a blank cell range, any values later entered in those cells pick up that number format rather than the General format.

4. Enter the following values the cell range:

   • **1234.75** in cell B2

   • **23500** in cell B3

   • **-1450.5** in cell B4

   • **100.345** in cell B5

Note how Excel automatically adds the Currency format using the parameters you selected in the Format Cells dialog box, including enclosing the negative value -1450.5 in parentheses without a minus sign and displaying the value in red.

5. Apply the Text format to cell B7 from the Format Cells dialog box and then enter **200.25** in this cell and select cell B7, if necessary.

Note how Excel left-aligns the value and the appearance of the Number Options drop-down button in later versions of Excel (the diamond with the exclamation point in the upper-left corner of cell B7).

6. Create a formula in cell B7 that currently contains the value 200.25 formatted with the Text format that adds the values in cells B4 and B5 together (=B4+B5).

Uh, oh. Instead of adding the cells together, Excel inserts the text of the formula =B4+B5 into cell B7. You have to assign a number format to cell B7 and recreate the formula to get Excel to calculate the sum of the values in cells B4 and B5.

7. With the cell cursor in cell B7, select the Accounting format on the Number tab of the Format Cells dialog box and then replace the text by recreating the formula to add the values in cells B4 and B5.

This time when you click the Enter button, Excel enters the formula into cell B7, displaying the calculated answer (1350.16) in the cell and =B4+B5 on the Formula bar.

8. Enter the date **02-15-08** in cell B9.

Note how Excel automatically converts this entry to 02/15/2008.

9. Format cell B9 with Date format on the Number tab of the Format Cells dialog box that follows the pattern March 14, 2001.

Excel displays the date entered into cell B9 as February 15, 2008.

10. Format cell B9 with General number format, this time by clicking the Number Format drop-down button in the Number group on the Home tab and then clicking General at the top of its drop-down list.

Note the appearance of the date serial number 39493 indicating that this date represents the 39,493rd day since the dawn of the twentieth century.

11. Click the Undo button on the Quick Access toolbar or press Ctrl+Z to restore the previous date formatting.

Excel restores the previous date format and February 15, 2008 reappears in cell B9.

12. Enter the number 00401 in cell B11 and then format it with Special ZIP Code format on the Number tab of the Format Cells dialog box.

Note that Excel immediately drops the preceding two zeros when you complete the cell entry in B11 (so that only 401 appears) and then redisplays them the moment you apply the ZIP Code format to the value.

13. Enter the number **4155551122** in cell B13 and then format it with the Special Phone Number format.

Note how Excel parses the number into area code, prefix, and main number by formatting it as (415) 555-1122.

14. Enter the number **20012551** in cell B15 and then format it with the Special Social Security Number format.

Note how Excel formats the value as the Social Security Number 020-01-2551.

15. Open the *Solved3-6.xlsx* workbook file in the Chap3 folder of your Excel 2007 Workbook folder and use the Side by Side feature to check your formatted values against those in its Number Formats sheet.

16. When everything checks out, click cell A1 and then save your practice workbook in your Excel 2007 Practice folder under the filename **Number Formatting Practice.xlsx** and then close the workbook file.

Exercise 3-7: Modifying the Alignment of Labels in a Spreadsheet

Between the command options in the Alignment group of the Ribbon's Home tab and those on the Alignment tab of the Format Cells dialog box, Excel gives you almost total control not only over the horizontal alignment of cell entries (that is, between the left and right borders of their columns) but over vertical alignment (between the top and bottom borders of their rows) and the orientation (direction of the text with regard to a horizontal baseline at 0 degrees). In addition, its Text Control options (Wrap Text, Shrink to Fit, and Merge Cells) enable you to accommodate longer cell entries to restricted column widths.

In Exercise 3-7, you get practice modifying the alignment of various labels in the markdowns data table using both the command buttons in the Alignment group of the Home tab and the options on the Alignment tab of the Format Cells dialog box (Ctrl+1). To do this exercise, you need to open your *Spring Furniture Sale Cust Fmt.xlsx* saved in your Excel 2007 Practice folder.

1. Click the Office Button and then click *Spring Furniture Sale Cust Fmt.xlsx* in the Recent Documents list on the right side of the pull-down menu to open the file in Excel.

If this filename is not listed in your Recent Documents list, click Open on the Office menu and then click open your Excel 2007 Practice folder and click the *Spring Furniture Sale Cust Fmt.xlsx* file icon before you click the Open button.

2. Select cell A2 in the Spring Sale worksheet and then increase the height of row 2 from the default 15 points (20 pixels) to 30 points (40 pixels).

   It's not until you increase the row height that you really notice the bottom vertical alignment of text in its cell.

3. Click the Middle Align button in the Alignment group of the Ribbon's Home tab to change the vertical alignment of the table title in cell A2 from bottom to center.

   Excel moves the title of the table up in its super-cell so that the text is now vertically centered between the cell's top and bottom borders.

4. Italicize the table title using the Italic command button in the Font group of the Home tab of the Ribbon and then increase the size of the table title from 11 points to 16 points using the Font Size button's drop-down list.

   The title of the table is now nicely emphasized in the super-cell created out of the cell range A2:E2.

5. Select the cell range B4:B9 containing the furniture descriptions and then click the Wrap Text command button on the Home tab. Next, narrow Column B to 15 (110 pixels) and use AutoFit to increase the height of rows 4:9 to accommodate the wrapping of the text in cells B4 and B5.

   To select the rows 4:9 in the worksheet, click 4 in the row headings column and then drag down to row 9. To apply AutoFit to the selected rows, double-click the lower-right border of row 9's heading.

   When you use the Wrap Text button, Excel automatically wraps the text to other lines in the selected cells whenever you narrow their columns sufficiently that their text can no longer be displayed all on a single line.

6. Select the cell ranges A4:A5 and C4:E5 and then click the Top Align command button on the Home tab to change the vertical alignment of their data entries from bottom to top.

   Excel aligns the data entries in the cell ranges A4:A5 and C4:E5 with the top line of the wrapped furniture description text entries in cells B4 and B5.

7. Select the cell range A3:E3 and then change the orientation of their column headings from 0 degrees to 60 degrees counterclockwise, and then increase the height of row 3, if necessary, so that all the text in the now diagonal column headings are displayed.

   The Orientation button in the Alignment group of the Home tab only supports rotating the text clockwise or counterclockwise 45 degrees. To rotate the text up or down any other number of degrees, you need to open the Alignment tab of the Format Cells dialog box. Entering positive numbers in the Degrees text box on the Alignment tab of the Format cells dialog box moves the orientation of the text up, counterclockwise to the baseline; whereas entering negative numbers in the Degrees text box moves the text orientation down, clockwise from the baseline.

8. Remove the fill color from the merged, super-cell A2 by selecting the merged cell A2 and then clicking the No Fill option on the Fill Color button's drop-down list.

   Next, you need to remove the border around cell A2.

9. Remove the borders from the merged, super-cell A2 by clicking the No Border option on the Border button's drop-down list.

Next, you need to convert the A2 super-cell back into separate cells and return the title text back to its default bottom vertical alignment.

10. Unmerge cell A2 and return it to the bottom vertical alignment before you use AutoFit to return the height of the row to its default.

- To unmerge a super-cell and convert it back into the original block of individual cells, select it and then click the Merge & Center button on the Ribbon's Home tab.

- To restore bottom vertical alignment, click the Bottom Align button in the Alignment group of the Ribbon's Home tab.

Finally, you are going to move the table title from cell A2 to the home cell, A1.

11. Click cell A2 and then click the Cut button in the Clipboard group of the Home tab. Click cell A1 and press the Enter key.

When you press Enter, Excel pastes the table title in cell A1.

12. Use the Zoom slider on the Status bar to reduce the worksheet magnification down to 100% or full size.

Use the Side by Side feature to check the changes you've made to the formatting of your markdowns table in the Spring Sale worksheet against those shown in that worksheet in the *Solved3-7.xlsx* workbook file located in the Chapter 3 folder of the Excel 2007 Workbook folder.

13. When everything checks out, close the *Solved3-7.xlsx* workbook file and save your alignment changes in the Spring Furniture Sale file in a new workbook called **Spring Furniture Sale Aligned.xlsx** located in your Excel 2007 Practice folder. Then, close the new workbook.

Using cell styles

Excel 2007 makes it really easy to assign complex formatting to selected cells of a spreadsheet. The program's Cell Styles gallery gives you access to a whole range of varied predefined cell styles that you can try on for size with Live Preview before assigning to the current cell selection.

Exercise 3-8: Practice Applying Cell Styles

In Exercise 3-8, you get practice applying the predefined cells styles to cell ranges from the Cell Styles gallery. For this exercise, open a completely unformatted version of the markdown data table you've been using.

1. Click the Open button on your customized Quick Access toolbar or press Ctrl+O. Then, in the Open dialog box, click My Documents in the left-hand pane before you double-click the Excel 2007 Workbook folder icon followed by the Chap3 folder icon in the main area. Finally, double-click the *Exercise3-8.xlsx* file icon.

Excel opens the *Exercise3-8.xlsx* workbook file that contains an unformatted version of the now very familiar markdowns table.

2. Click cell A2 and then click the Cell Styles command button in the Styles group on the Ribbon's Home tab.

   Excel displays the Cell Styles gallery divided into various sections: Good, Bad, and Neutral; Data and Model; Titles and Headings; Themed Cell Styles; and Number Format.

3. Position the mouse pointer on the Heading 1 style sample, the first one in the Titles and Headings section of the Cell Styles gallery. Highlight the samples of the other title styles in this row and then click the Heading 4 sample to assign it to cell A2.

   Note how Live Preview shows how the title, Spring Sale Markdowns, that's entered in cell A2 looks in each of the heading styles as you highlight their samples in the Cell Styles gallery.

4. Select the cell range A3:E3 containing the table's column headings and then preview how these headings look with the samples in the Data and Model section of the Cell Styles gallery before applying the Note style to this range.

   Excel applies the Note cell style to the range A3:E3 so that these cells now use this Data and Model style's borders and light shading.

5. Select the cell range A4:E9 with the table's data and then apply the Input cell style to this cell selection.

   Excel applies the Input cell style to the range A4:E9 so that these cells now use this Data and Model style's font color, borders, and shading.

6. Select the cell ranges C4:C9 and E4:E9 containing the table's values and then apply the Currency cell style to this cell selection.

   Excel applies the Currency cell style to these two ranges so that the values in these cells now use this Number Format style's dollar signs, commas, and two decimal places.

7. Click cell A1 and then save your cell style formatting changes to this version of the workbook under the filename **Spring Furniture Sale Cell Styles.xlsx** in the Excel 2007 Practice folder on your computer's hard disk. Then, close the workbook file.

Using conditional formatting

Conditional formatting enables you to set up a particular type of formatting that goes into effect only when a condition or a series of conditions that you define actually go into effect in the spreadsheet. This type of formatting is useful when you want to apply a special type of formatting (such as a red fill color or underlining) to a cell to alert you when its calculated data entry reaches a particular (high or low) value. In Excel 2007, you can even use conditional formatting to apply different colored data bars, color scales, and icons sets to a range of values to instantly depict their relative values in a highly visual manner.

Solve It

Exercise 3-9: Practice Applying Conditional Formatting to a Target Cell

Exercise 3-9 gives you practice applying conditionally formatting to a particular cell in a spreadsheet so that its formatting changes depending upon the value that the cell currently contains.

1. Open the *Exercise3-9.xlsx* workbook located in the Chap3 subfolder inside your Excel 2007 Workbook folder.

   You will use its Income Statement to get practice in applying and using Conditional Formatting to a particular target cell in an Income Statement spreadsheet so that Excel changes the cell formatting when the value in this target cell is greater than, less than, or exactly equal to an anticipated value.

2. Select cell B10 containing the formula for calculating the total operating income or loss, and then click the Conditional Formatting command button in the Styles group of the Ribbon's Home tab.

   Excel opens the Conditional Formatting drop-down menu.

3. Click Highlight Cells Rules on the Conditional Formatting drop-down menu and then click the Greater Than option on the continuation menu.

   Excel opens a Greater Than dialog box that contains two boxes: a text box on the left that currently contains the value 99,440 currently in cell B10; and a drop-down list box on the right that contains the style, Light Red Fill with Dark Red Text.

4. Type 100000 (1 and five zeros) in the text box on the left and then select Green Fill with Dark Green Text as the formatting to use in the drop-down list box on the right before you click OK.

   Excel will now automatically format any value in cell B10 that is greater than 100,000 with a green fill color and dark green font color.

5. Use the same technique to assign a conditional format to cell B10 that formats this cell with Yellow Fill with Dark Yellow Text when its value is less than 100,000.

   Select Highlight Cells Rules > Less Than and then enter 100000 in the text box. Select Yellow Fill with Dark Yellow Text in the drop-down list box in the Less Than dialog box before you click OK.

   Note that Excel applies this dark yellow text on yellow fill to cell B10 because the Operating Income (Loss) cell, B10, currently contains a calculated value below 100,000.

6. Assign a third conditional format to cell B10 that formats the cell with a custom format that uses a dark blue font color against a light blue fill color with a dark cell border when its value is equal to 100,000.

   After entering **100000** in the text box, select Custom Format at the bottom of the drop-down list box in the Equal To dialog box (opened by selecting Highlight Cells Rules > Equal To on the Conditional Formatting button menus). In the Format Cells dialog box, click the Dark Blue square on the Color palette on the Font tab, the Outline sample on the Border tab, and a light blue square on the Fill tab before you click OK twice.

7. Reduce the Product Costs in cell B6 from the current -12,175 to **-2175**.

   Note that as soon as you change this value, Excel applies your dark green text on a green fill color to cell B10 because the Operating Income (loss) in this cell has risen to 109,440 so that the calculated value now meets the greater than 100,000 condition.

   To replace an existing entry with a new entry, simply select the cell and enter the new entry as though the cell were still blank.

8. Replace the Revenues value in cell B3 from the current 150,250 with 140,810.

Excel now applies the custom conditional formatting to the calculated value in cell B10 because it now contains the anticipated value of 100,000 exactly.

Use the Side by Side feature to check your Income Statement with conditional formatting against the one shown in *Solved3-9.xlsx* located in the Chap3 subfolder of your Excel 2007 Workbook folder.

9. When everything checks out, click cell A1 and then save your work as a new workbook called **Income Statement 08 Cond Fmt.xlsx** in your Excel 2007 Practice folder inside My Documents on your hard disk, and then close the workbook.

Before you attempt Exercise 3-10, you may want to play the Formatting Conditionally.exe demo located in the Excel Feature Demos folder on your workbook CD-ROM. This feature demonstration shows you how to use conditional formatting to apply different data bars, scales, and icon sets to a cell range containing a series of sequential values.

Exercise 3-10: Practice Applying Conditional Formatting to a Range of Values

In Exercise 3-10, you get practice using Excel's conditional formatting to apply different data bars, scales, and icon sets to a cell range containing a series of sequential values. These colored data bars and scales and icon sets that you apply then call attention to the relationship between the values in this sequence.

1. Open a new blank workbook and then position the cell pointer in cell C1. Then enter the value **1** in cell C1 — be sure to complete the cell entry by clicking the Enter button on the Formula bar so that the cell cursor remains in cell C1.

Now you use the Fill handle to create a sequential series of numbers in column C.

2. Hold down the Ctrl key as you drag the Fill Handle down column C until you reach cell C12 and the ScreenTip says 12.

Now, use the Fill handle to create a descending series of values in this column that ends with 0 in cell C24.

3. Enter **11** in cell C13 and then select cells C12 and C13. Next, drag the Fill handle in cell C13 down column C until you reach cell C24 and the ScreenTip says 0.

Note that you don't have to hold down the Ctrl key to create this descending sequential series because cells C12 and C13 are selected as a range and these cells show Excel how to model the series by decreasing each cell by 1.

4. Select the cell range C1:C24. Then click the Conditional Formatting button in the Styles group of the Ribbon's Home tab and highlight Data Bars on the Conditional Formatting drop-down menu.

Excel displays a Data Bars continuation menu with thumbnails of the various colored data bars that you can assign to your cell selection. You can use Live Preview to see how these colors look in your worksheet before you select them.

5. Highlight each of the different colored data bar thumbnails in the Data Bars continuation menu before you click the Purple Data Bar thumbnail to assign it to the cell range C1:C24.

Next, you'll use the Fill handle to create a range of temperatures from 0 to 120 degrees that increases sequentially in 10-degree increments. Then you'll use Excel's Conditional Formatting to assign the Red – Yellow – Blue Color Scale to this cell range.

6. Use the Fill handle to create a range that begins with 0 in cell F15 and 120 in cell R15 incremented by 10 in each succeeding cell to the right.

Enter **0** in cell F15 and **10** in cell G15. Then, select the cell range F15:G15 and drag the Fill handle to the right until you reach cell R15 and the ScreenTip says 120.

7. Use the Conditional Formatting button on the Home tab to assign the Red – Yellow – Blue Color Scale to the cell range F15:R15 after using Live Preview to see how the range would look in all the other color scale combinations.

Finally, you'll use the Fill Handle to create a cell range containing a series of percentages ranging from 0% to 100% that increases sequentially by 10% in each succeeding cell. Then, you assign the Three Traffic Lights (Unrimmed) Icon Set to this cell range.

8. Use the Fill handle to create a range that begins with 0% in cell F20 and 100% in cell R20 incremented by 10 percent in each succeeding cell to the right.

Now, play with the different Icon Sets before selecting the Three Traffic Lights (Unrimmed) set for cell range F20:P20.

9. Use the Conditional Formatting button on the Home tab to assign the Three Traffic Lights (Unrimmed) Icon Set to the cell range F20:P20 after using Live Preview to see how the range would look in all the other icon set combinations.

Use the Side by Side feature to check your conditionally formatted ranges against those in Sheet1 of the *Solved3-10.xlsx* workbook file located in the Chap3 folder inside your Excel 2007 Workbook folder.

10. When your work checks out, select cell A1 and the save your workbook in your Excel 2007 Practice folder under the filename **Conditional Fmt Practice.xlsx** and then close the workbook file.

Hiding Columns and Rows

Excel makes it easy to hide entire columns and rows in your worksheet. You can use this facility to conceal sensitive data (such as salaries and the like) in spreadsheets that are used in formula calculations but that are not for everyone's eyes.

Hiding columns and rows is a lot like modifying their width and height (in fact, if the truth be known, a hidden column is just one whose width is reduced to zero and a hidden row one whose height is shrunk down to zero): Select the column or columns to hide and then in the Cells group of the Home tab, choose Format | Hide & Unhide | Hide Columns (Alt+HOUC) or the row or rows to hide and Format | Hide & Unhide | Hide Rows (Alt+HOUR).

To redisplay concealed columns, select the remaining columns on either side (left and right) of the hidden columns and then choose Format | Hide & Unhide | Unhide Columns (Alt+HOUL). To redisplay concealed rows, select the rows on either side (above and below) the hidden rows and then choose Format | Hide & Unhide | Unhide Rows (Alt+HOUO). Excel then redisplays all the formerly hidden columns or rows, which are automatically selected, and all you have do is click a single cell anywhere in the worksheet to deselect them.

Q. Is there any way to hide individual cell entries in the worksheet rather than entire columns and rows?

A. Although Excel does not provide a command for hiding individual cells or cell ranges, you can accomplish this by creating a Custom number format on the Number tab of the Format Cells dialog box and then applying this custom number format to selected cells from this dialog box. To create this Custom number format, click Custom in the Category list box and then click any of the formatting codes in the Sample list box on the right. Replace its codes with three semicolons in a row with no spaces in between (;;;) before you click. Be aware, however, that applying this ;;; Custom number format hides only the entries as they appear in the worksheet itself but does nothing to cloak their appearance on the Formula bar when the cell cursor is in them. This limits the usefulness of this method to the distribution of printed copies of the spreadsheet because all the entries in electronic copies are vulnerable via the Formula bar.

Solve It

Exercise 3-11: Practice Hiding Columns and Rows

1. Open the *Exercise 3-11.xlsx* workbook file located in the Chap3 folder of your Excel 2007 Workbook folder. Use its twelve-month Regional Income table to practice hiding columns and rows.

2. Hide the column ranges B:D, F:H, J:L, and N:P and then put the cell cursor in cell A1 so that only columns A, E, I, M, Q, and R are displayed at the far left of the Income Analysis worksheet.

3. Select the column range A:Q and then choose Format | Hide & Unhide | Unhide Columns on the Ribbon or press Alt+HOUL. Click cell A1 and then verify that all the erstwhile hidden columns of spreadsheet are redisplayed.

4. Hide the row ranges 4:8, 12:16, and 20:24 and then scroll up to verify that only rows 1, 2, 3; 9, 10, 11; 17, 18, 19; and 25 are displayed at the top of the Income Analysis worksheet.

5. Select the row range 3:25 and then redisplay all the hidden rows by choosing Format | Hide & Unhide | Unhide Rows or pressing Alt+HOUO. Click cell A3 and then verify that all the missing rows are now redisplayed in the worksheet.

6. Close the *Exercise 3-11.xlsx* workbook file without saving your changes and exit Excel.

Chapter 4

Printing Spreadsheet Reports

· ·

In This Chapter

▶ Previewing pages in the Page Layout view

▶ Using Page Break Preview to adjust the paging

▶ Adding readymade and custom headers and footers to a report

▶ Adjusting various Page and Print Settings

▶ Printing all or portions of a workbook

· ·

*P*rinting easy-to-read and well organized reports from your spreadsheets is one of the most important tasks you do in Excel. The exercises in this chapter give you a chance to practice printing many types of spreadsheet reports using Excel's Page Layout view, Page Break Preview, headers and footers, and print titles features. Don't worry if you don't have access to a printer while completing these exercises: In almost all cases, you can use Excel's Print Preview feature to get an idea of how the report would appear on the printed page.

Previewing Pages in the Worksheet Area

Page Layout view is your first line of defense against wasting paper on useless reports that contain bad page breaks, one which separates columns and rows of the spreadsheet from data that needs to appear together on a page. In Page Layout view, Excel turns on the display of the horizontal and vertical rulers in the border area as well as shows representations of the pages in the worksheet area. The depictions of each page include the pages' margins, any headers or footers you've assigned (as well as an area to click if you haven't assigned a header or footer and decide you want to), along with the worksheet data. You can then use the Zoom slider on the status bar to zoom in and out on the pages by increasing and decreasing the screen magnification to ensure that none of the data is being printed on the wrong pages.

Always switch to Page Layout view to check the pages of your report before sending the worksheet to the printer unless it's a worksheet to which you've made no editing changes and one that you've already successfully printed in the past.

Solve It | ### Exercise 4-1: Previewing the Pages in Page Layout View

In Exercise 4-1, you get practice using Page Layout view to check out the paging of an Income Analysis spreadsheet. You then use this sample Income Analysis spreadsheet in later printing exercises in this chapter.

1. Open the *Exercise4-1.xlsx* workbook file in your Excel 2007 Workbook folder.

The Income Analysis worksheet that charts regional sales data for all four quarters of 2008 opens in Excel.

2. Click the Page Layout button on the program's Status bar (that's the middle button of the three that appear immediately to the left of the Zoom slider below the worksheet area).

Excel switches to Page Layout view indicated by the appearance of the rulers in the worksheet headings area above and to the left of the worksheet; the page representation in the worksheet area; and the current page and total page indicator on the Status bar.

You can also switch into Page Layout mode by clicking View | Page Layout on the Ribbon or pressing Alt+WP.

3. Drag the Zoom slider on the Status bar to the left and click the Zoom out button (the one with the minus sign) until the screen magnification is reduced to 40%.

At this magnification, depending upon your screen resolution, you may be able to see the page depictions for two or possibly three and a half pages including the top rows of the worksheet. Note that the first three pages (1, 3, and 5) are complete depictions that show you all four page margins (left, right, top, and bottom).

4. Use the vertical scroll bar to scroll down the Income Analysis worksheet until you can see the bottom of margins of the pages for the lower rows of the Income Analysis worksheet (pages 2, 4, and 6).

Remember that, by default, Excel numbers pages down the rows of data in your worksheet and then to the columns to the right. Thus the pages in this 10-page report are 1, 3, 5, 7, 9 in the top row of pages proceeding left to right and 2, 4, 6, 8, and 10 in the row of pages below.

Note the top part of the blank pages that are not part of the printed report below pages 2, 4, 6, 8, and 10 (indicated by the Click to Add Data indicators).

5. Use the Zoom slider to return the screen magnification to 100%.

The quickest way to do this is by clicking the center marker of the slider.

6. Press Ctrl+Home to select cell A1 in the Income Analysis worksheet and then click the Normal view button on the Status bar.

You can also select the normal worksheet view by selecting View | Normal on the Ribbon or by pressing Alt+WL.

7. Close the *Exercise4-1.xlsx* workbook file without saving changes.

Adjusting Page Breaks

Whereas Print Layout alerts you to all sorts of potential problems in the printed report by showing you everything on the page as it will print, Page Break Preview only shows you where the page breaks occur. Page Break Preview does this by drawing lines between columns and rows in the worksheet that indicate the limits of each page in the report. You can then manipulate the page breaks by dragging these page break indicators to new columns and rows.

Before you attempt Exercise 4-2, you may want to play the Report Page Layout & Breaks.exe demo located in the Excel Feature Demos folder on your workbook CD-ROM. This feature demonstration shows you the basic process of using Page Layout view to spot bad page breaks and Page Break Preview to fix them.

Solve It | **Exercise 4-2: Using Page Break Preview to Fix Bad Page Breaks**

In Exercise 4-2, you get practice using Excel's Page Break Preview view to first identify and then fix page break problems in a report created from another version of the Income Analysis worksheet you first worked with in Exercise 4-1.

1. Open the *Exercise4-2.xlsx* workbook file in the Chap4 folder located in Excel 2007 Workbook folder.

Excel opens another, slightly different version of the Income Analysis worksheet you used in Exercise 4-1.

2. Click the Page Break Preview button on the Status bar (the one on the right of the three buttons grouped together to the left of the Zoom slider).

The first time you select Page Break Preview view, Excel displays the Welcome to Page Preview dialog box that briefly describes the function of this mode.

3. Click OK in the Welcome to Page Break Preview dialog box.

Excel closes the dialog box and displays page breaks as dark blue dotted lines between worksheet columns and rows. The program also displays the page numbers in the center of each page and automatically reduces the magnification of the screen to 60% of normal. Note that there are now 12 pages in this report.

4. Scroll down the first row of pages and then remove the first bad page break that occurs between rows 38 and 39.

Here, the page break automatically placed between rows 38 and 39 separates the Regional Ratio Analysis heading in row 36, the month headings in row 37, and the Gross Profit on Sales heading in row 38 on pages 1, 3, 5, 7, 9, and 11 from the actual regional analysis data on pages 2, 4, 6, 8, 10 and 12 below.

To fix this bad page break, you need to drag the page break line between rows 38 and 39 up three rows so that the break now occurs between rows 35 and 36. The Regional Analysis Heading and all the other headings associated with the percentage data will be printed together on pages 2, 4, 6, 8, 10, and 12 of the report.

5. Scroll to up until you can see the headings in row 2 of the worksheet. Adjust the page break between pages 1 and 3, and 2 and 4 so that all the Qtr 1 income figures are printed on pages 1 and 2 of the report.

To fix this bad break, drag the page break line between columns D and E to the right one column so that the break now occurs between column E and F, putting all the Qtr 1 figures together on pages 1 and 2.

6. Adjust the page break between pages 3 and 5, and 4 and 6 so that all the Qtr 2 income figures are printed on pages 3 and 4 of the report.

To fix this bad break, drag the page break line between columns J and K to the left one column so that the break now occurs between column I and J, putting all the Qtr 2 figures together on pages 3 and 4.

7. Adjust the page break between pages 5 and 7, and 6 and 8 so that only the Qtr 3 income figures are printed on pages 5 and 6 of the report.

Note that after taking care of all the bad page breaks in the original report the total number of pages is reduced from 12 to 8 pages.

8. Put the worksheet into Page Layout view and then use Zoom slider and the scroll bars to check the layout and content of all eight pages of the report.

Make sure that all the quarterly data are now printed together on their respective pages.

9. Click the Page Layout tab on the Ribbon and then click the Page Setup Dialog Box Launcher button to open the Page Setup dialog box.

The Page Setup dialog box opens with the Page tab selected.

10. Click the Margins tab in the Page Setup dialog box and then click the Horizontally and Vertically check boxes to select them in the Center on the Page section before you click OK.

Excel centers the headings and data on each page of the report between the left and right, and top and bottom margins.

11. Remove the column and row gridlines from the report by removing the check mark from the Print check box in the Gridlines section of the Sheet Options group on the Ribbon's Page Layout tab.

You can also deselect and select this particular Print check box by pressing Alt+PPG.

Note that you continue to see the worksheet gridlines in the Page Layout view even after you remove the check mark from the Print check box. To make sure that the worksheet gridlines will not appear in your printed report, you need to switch to Print Preview mode. Print Preview enables you to examine each page of the report.

12. Click the Print Preview button you added to your custom Quick Access toolbar in Exercise 1-3 or press Ctrl+F2 to open the Print Preview window.

Note that the gridlines no longer appear on the first page of the report in Print Preview mode. Also note that you can zoom in on each previewed page by clicking the page with the Magnifying glass mouse pointer or by clicking the Zoom button on the Print Preview tab.

13. Preview all eight pages of the final report using the Page Down key to advance to the next page and the Page Up key to return to the previous page (make sure that you've zoomed out on the previewed page before pressing these keys or you only end up scrolling around the same page).

When you've zoomed in on the report pages in Print Preview, you need to click the Next Page and Previous Page buttons on the Print Preview tab to display the next and previous pages.

14. When you've checked all the pages in the Print Preview window, click the Print button on the Print Preview tab to print the report if you have access to a printer; otherwise, click the Close Print Preview button to close the Print Preview window.

Now all that's left to do is to return the worksheet to Normal view.

15. Click the Normal button on the Status bar and then save your changes in a new file named **Income Analysis Report.xlsx** in your Excel 2007 Practice folder on your hard disk.

Adding Headers and Footers

Excel 2007 makes it really easy to add a heading in the top margin (called a header) and the bottom margin (called a footer) of each page (or every other page) of your printed reports. The program supports two types of headers and footers: prefabricated headers and footers that print only stock information such as the current page number, date, and name of the worksheet, and custom headers and footers that enable you to mix this type of stock information with information of your own.

To add a custom header or footer to a report, you insert codes that retrieve information about the report or workbook file that you can mix with your own text (such as the company or department name) in one of three sections:

- **Left-hand Section** for information to be left-aligned against the page's left margin
- **Center Section** for information to be centered between the left and right margins
- **Right-hand Section** for information to be right-aligned against the page's right margin

Q. What is the easiest way to add a new prefabricated header and footer to my report?

A. Put the worksheet into Page Layout view (by clicking the Page Layout button on the Status bar) and then click the left, center, or right section of the header or footer area at the top or bottom of the first page (indicated by Click to Add Header and Click to Add Footer message). Finally, click the Header or Footer button on the Design tab of the Header & Footer Tools contextual tab and select the type of header or footer text to insert on its respective pull-down menu.

Q. Can I customize a prefabricated header or footer?

A. Yes, you can: Simply click the section containing the prefab header or footer you want to customize in Page Layout view. Then, to insert custom text or codes, type the text or click the appropriate command button in the Header & Footer Elements group of the Header & Footer Tools Design tab.

Before you attempt Exercise 4-3, you may want to play the Report Headers & Footers.exe demo located in the Excel Feature Demos folder on your workbook CD-ROM. This feature demonstration shows you the basic process of adding a header and footer to your printed report.

Solve It

Exercise 4-3: Adding a Header and a Footer to a Worksheet Report

In Exercise 4-3, you get practice adding both a header and footer to a report generated from a version of the Income Analysis worksheet that you've been working on throughout this chapter. This report will have an alternating header that changes the placement of the current page number depending on whether the page is odd or even and a standard footer that is printed on every page.

1. Open the *Exercise4-3.xlsx* workbook file in the Chap4 folder located in Excel 2007 Workbook folder.

Excel opens a version of the Income Analysis worksheet you used in Exercise 4-2 without any headers or footers defined.

2. Put the Income Analysis worksheet into Page Layout view by clicking the Page Layout button on the Status bar and then clicking the right-hand section of the header area immediately above row 1 to select this section.

When you position the mouse pointer in this area to the right of the text Click to Add Header, the section turns blue. When you click the pointer in this section, Excel sets the insertion pointer or cursor at the right edge of this section (all text in this is right-aligned so that any characters you type proceed from right to left).

3. Type **Page** and press the space bar one time. Then, click the Page Number button in the Header & Footer Elements group of the Header & Footer Tools Design tab.

When inserting codes in a custom header or footer, you need to insert spaces between the codes and any custom stock text you type if you don't want the code and custom text to all run together. To change the font or assign an attribute to the codes or stock text you add to a section of a custom header or footer, drag through them to select them, and then click the appropriate Font command button on the Ribbon's Home tab.

The right section of the header now contains the text you typed, Page, followed by the code, &[Page], that calculates and returns the current page number.

4. Press the space bar, and then type **of** and press the spacebar again. Click the Number of Pages button in the Header & Footer Elements group.

The right-hand section of the header now contains the following combination of custom stock text and codes: Page &[Page] of &[Pages].

5. Click cell A1 to select it.

   As soon as you click out of the right-hand section, Excel replaces the codes so that your custom header on the first page of the report now reads Page 1 of 6.

6. Click the right-hand section of the header area once again and then click the Different Odd & Even Pages check box in the Options group of the Header & Footer Tools Design tab.

   The Odd Page Header indicator appears right above the left-hand section of the header area, indicating that the custom header you've defined will appear only on odd-numbered pages of the report.

7. Scroll down the worksheet until you can see the top margin area of page 2 of the report (indicated by the heading, Regional Ratio Analysis, in cell A36 right below the empty top margin).

   You will now create the same custom header for a second page except that this even-page header will appear in the left-hand rather than the right-hand header section.

8. Click the left-hand section of the header area right above cell A36 and then use the Page Number and Number of Pages buttons in the Header & Footer Elements group to create the same Page &[Page] of &[Pages]. Then, click cell A36 to de-select the left-hand section of the header area.

   The even-page header for the second page of the report now reads Page 2 of 6.

9. Scroll up, if necessary, until you see the text Click to Add Footer. Click this text before you click the selection near the bottom of the Footer button's menu that displays Prepared by followed by your name, the current date, and then the page number (as in Prepared by Greg Harvey 4/25/08 Page 1).

   Excel places the Prepared by followed by your name and the current date in the center section and the page number in the right-hand section of the footer.

10. Click the right-hand section and delete the Page &[Page] information by pressing the Delete key.

    Note that the footer with your name and the date is an odd-page footer that prints only on the odd pages of the report. You need to copy this footer to the second page so that it is also printed on the even pages.

11. While stock footer text and &[Date] code are selected in the odd-page footer, press Ctrl+C to copy this information to the clipboard. Then, click the center section of the footer area on the second page below row 81 and then press Ctrl+V to paste this same information in as the even-page footer.

    The same footer information now appears in the center section of the even-page footer at the bottom of the second page of the report.

12. Click cell A81 and then put Excel into Print Preview mode (Ctrl+F2) and check its pages to make sure that the page number appears aligned with the right margin on all odd-numbered pages and aligned with the left margin on all even-numbered pages and that the footer appears centered on all pages.

13. If the header and footer check out, close the Print Preview window, select cell A1, return the worksheet to Normal view, and then save the changes to *Exercise4-3.xlsx* workbook file with the name **Income Analysis-HdrFtr.xlsx** in your Excel 2007 Practice folder. Then, close the workbook (Ctrl+W).

Adding Print Titles to a Report

In Excel reports, you use Print Titles to print the column and row headings from the worksheet on every page. If you don't bother to add Print Titles to multi-page reports, only the first pages of the report contain the headings that identify the related data, and your readers have no way of identifying the data on the later pages of the report.

Before you attempt Exercise 4-4, you may want to play the Report Print Titles.exe demo located in the Excel Feature Demos folder on your workbook CD-ROM. This feature demonstration shows you the basic process of designating a column of a worksheet as the titles of a report to be printed on each of its pages.

Exercise 4-4: Adding the First Worksheet Column as the Print Title for a Report

In Exercise 4-4, you get practice adding the column A of the Income Analysis worksheet as the print title for a printed report. You do this so that the row headings in column A appear on all the pages of the report.

1. Open the *Exercise4-4.xlsx* workbook file located in the Chap4 folder in the Excel 2007 Workbook folder on your hard disk.

In this version of the Income Analysis worksheet, all the bad page breaks have been removed. However, because the report lacks any print titles, the row headings entered in column A of the worksheet appear only on its first two pages.

2. Open the Print Preview window (Ctrl+F2) and then preview each of its eight pages to verify that the row headings in column A appear only on pages 1 and 2.

When pages 3 through 8 are printed, the reader will have no references with which to identify the financial data.

3. Click the Close Print Preview button on the Print Preview tab of the Ribbon.

Excel returns you to the regular Income Analysis worksheet.

4. Click Page Layout | Print Titles on the Ribbon or press Alt+PI.

Excel opens the Page Setup dialog box with the Sheet tab selected. This tab contains a Print Titles section where you can define rows of worksheet data to repeat at the top of each printed page as column headings, and columns of worksheet data to repeat on the left side of each printed page as row headings.

5. Click the Columns to Repeat at Left text box in the Page Setup dialog box and then click column A in the worksheet to select it (indicated by marching ants around the column).

Click the Collapse Dialog Box button to the immediate right of the Columns to Repeat at Left text box if the Page Setup dialog box obscures column A of the worksheet, making it difficult to click the column and select it. Then, after clicking column A, click the Expand Dialog Box on the right side of the collapsed dialog box to expand and restore its display.

Excel inserts the absolute column range reference $A:$A in the Columns to Repeat at Left text box.

6. Click OK to close the Page Setup dialog box. Then open the Print Preview window and preview each of its now 10 pages to verify that the row headings in column A appear on every page of the report.

Repeating the row headings in column A of the worksheet on each printed page has increased the total number of pages from 8 to 10.

7. Go to page 3 of the report in the Print Preview window and zoom in on this page either by clicking on the page with the magnifying glass mouse pointer or by clicking the Zoom button on the Print Preview tab.

Note that the worksheet title, 2008 Regional Income, is truncated at the top of this page (it looks more like 2008 Regional Inco). You need to widen the column to display all of the letters in this title.

8. Click the Show Margins check box in the Preview group of the Print Preview tab to put a check mark in it.

Excel now displays margin and column markers at the top of the page 3 preview (see Figure 4-1). You can drag these markers to manipulate and change the margin settings and/or column widths.

9. Use the vertical scrollbar to display the top margin and column markers. Then position the mouse pointer on the first column marker. When the mouse pointer becomes a double-headed arrow (Figure 4-1), drag the marker slightly to the right and then release the mouse button.

When you release the mouse button, Excel shows as many letters as the new width accommodates. Continue to adjust the column marker in this manner until all the letters in Income are displayed in the first column of page 3.

10. Reduce the preview to full page (by clicking page 3 or clicking the Zoom button again) and then check its pages to make sure that the complete worksheet title will be printed on all pages.

Next, you need to remove the margin markers from the Print Preview window and the gridlines from the printed report.

11. Click the Show Margins check box to removes its check mark. Click the Page Setup button and then click the Gridlines check box on the Sheet tab of the Page Setup dialog box to remove its check mark before you click OK.

Note that the gridlines are now removed from the page shown in Print Preview.

12. Close the Print Preview window, and then with cell A1 selected, save the changes to *Exercise4-4.xlsx* workbook file with the name **Income Analysis-PrntTitle.xlsx** in your Excel 2007 Practice folder. Then, close the workbook (Ctrl+W).

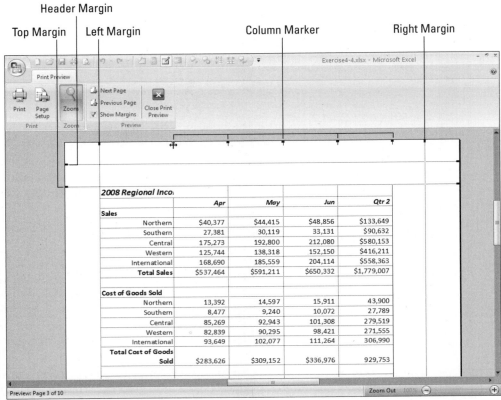

Figure 4-1:
Displaying
the margin
and column
markers in
the Print
Preview
window.

Modifying the Print Setting for a Report

Regardless of what type of printer you use, Excel has a number of default print settings that it automatically puts into effect when you first print a spreadsheet. These print settings include

- Portrait rather than landscape orientation for the printing (so that the printing runs with the shorter width of the page rather than with the longer length)

- Printing at 100% of normal size

- Print quality medium (on printers that support different print quality modes)

- Letter (8.5 x 11 inch) paper size

- Top and bottom margins of 0.75 inch

- Left and right margins of 0.7 inch

- Header and footer margin of 0.3 inch (with no header or footer defined)

- No printing of the column and row gridlines that define the cells in the worksheet

✔ No printing of the column letters and row numbers associated with the cells within the Print Area in the worksheet

✔ No printing of the comments attached to cells included in the Print Area (see Chapter 5 for more on comments)

✔ Printing of error values returned by formulas as they appear in the worksheet (see Chapter 6 for more on error values)

✔ Paging order down the rows of the Print Area and then across the columns

✔ Printing a single copy of all the pages generated from a Print Area that includes all the data in the active worksheet(s)

Many times you may find that you can solve minor paging problems in a report simply by modifying the orientation of the printing, the percentage of normal size on the Page tab of the Page Settings dialog box, or the margin settings on the Margins tab.

If your intention is simply to produce a facsimile of the worksheet for reviewing its data, you should include the worksheet gridlines and column and row headings in the print-out. To do this, you select the Page Layout tab on the Ribbon and then make sure that Print check box under Gridlines and Print check box under Headings are both selected (indicated by a check mark) in the Sheet Options group. If you also want to print the comments, click the Page Setup group's Dialog Box Launcher button and then click the Sheet tab and select the At End of the Sheet or As Displayed on Sheet option on the Comments drop-down list box on this tab before you click OK.

Exercise 4-5: Modifying Various Print Settings for a Report

In Exercise 4-5, you get practice changing different print settings for a report including changing the orientation of the printing from portrait to landscape and using the Scale to Fit option.

1. Open the *Exercise4-5.xlsx* workbook file in the Chap4 folder in the Excel 2007 Workbook folder.

This CG Media sales workbook opens with the Total Sales worksheet displayed. The spreadsheet on this worksheet is quite wide as it tracks the monthly sales with quarterly totals for different types of media for the entire year 2008.

2. Switch to Page Layout view (Alt+WP) and use the worksheet scroll bars to check out the pages for a report that prints all the data in the Total Sales worksheet in the default portrait mode.

Because this spreadsheet uses more columns than rows, the printed report might be easier to read if you switched the orientation of the printing to landscape.

3. Click Page Layout | Orientation on the Ribbon or press Alt+PO and then click the Landscape option on the drop-down menu.

Excel immediately switches the printing orientation and redraws the page depictions in Page Layout view. Note how many more columns of data fit on the first page of the report in this print orientation.

4. Use the horizontal scroll bar to check out the page breaks for printing the report in landscape mode.

   Note that the third page now contains an "orphaned" column with the annual total sales. You will fix this bad page break using the Width option located in the Scale to Fit group on the Ribbon's Page Layout tab.

5. Click the Width drop-down button in the Scale to Fit group and then click 2 Pages on its drop-down menu.

   Note that when you select 2 Pages for the Width setting, Excel immediately scales the printing size down to 97% now shown in the Scale combo box. Note also that the Scale combo box remains grayed out (unavailable) whenever you set either the Width or Height options in the Scale to Fit group to any other setting besides Automatic.

   Using the Scale to Fit Width and Height options on the Ribbon's Page Layout tab to constrain the printing to a particular number of pages rather than using the Scale option to set a specific scaling percentage is often a much more effective way to eliminate pages with orphaned columns or rows of data.

6. Switch back to Normal view (Alt+WL). Then, click Qtr1 sheet tab to make this worksheet active and then switch the view back into Page Layout for this sheet (Alt+WP).

   Note that the bad page break for this worksheet report orphans the first quarter totals by printing them on the second page separated from all the supporting monthly sales data printed on the first page.

7. Fix the bad page break by changing the orientation of the printing so that the quarterly totals are no longer orphaned and all the first quarter sales data print together on the first and only page of the report.

   Next, you need to add a header to the one-page report.

8. Add a header to the report that prints the name of the worksheet (Qtr1) in its left-hand section, the word Confidential in its center section, and the current page number (Page 1) in its right-hand section.

   Finally, you need to add to gridlines and the column and row headings to the printout of the first quarter sales data on the first page.

9. Turn on the printing of the column and row gridlines, and the row and column headings in the printed report.

   To display the gridlines, you need to select the Print check box under the Gridlines heading in the Sheet Options group of the Ribbon's Page Layout tab (Alt+PPG). To display the row and column headings, you select the Print check box under Headings in this same group (Alt+PPH).

10. If you have access to a printer, print the Qtr1 worksheet; otherwise, switch back to the Total Sales worksheet and then save the workbook as **CGMedia-PrntSettings.xlsx** in your Excel 2007 Practice folder before you close the workbook.

Printing All or Part of the Workbook

As noted in the previous section on default print settings, the Print Area that defines which cell ranges are included in the printout consists of whatever worksheet or worksheets that you've selected at the time of printing. Many times you need to reduce the Print Area to just a range of cells within the active worksheet or to increase it to include the data on all the worksheets in the entire workbook. The exercises in this section give you practice in printing not only Print Areas of different sizes but also printouts that include the contents of formulas in the spreadsheet (as opposed to their calculated values) and charts that you've created (see Chapter 15 for practice on charting spreadsheet data).

If you want to print all the data on the active worksheet using the print settings currently in effect for that sheet, simply click the Quick Print button you added to the Quick Access toolbar in Exercise 1-3: Excel then sends the print job directly to the default printer without ever opening the Print dialog box.

Printing a range of cells

Many times you only need to print a particular table or list of data on the active worksheet (as opposed to all the data on the sheet). To do this, select the cell range or ranges that encompass this data in the active worksheet and then click the Selection option button in the Print What section in the Print dialog box (Office button | Print or Ctrl+P). Then send the print job to the printer by selecting OK.

If you have a table or list in a worksheet whose updated data you need to print regularly, name the range and use the Go To feature (as covered in Chapter 5) to quickly select it for printing.

Solve It

Exercise 4-6: Printing a Range of Cells in a Worksheet

In Exercise 4-6, you get practice printing just the range of cells in a worksheet containing the quarterly and annual sales totals without the embedded clustered bar chat that accompanies the data.

1. Open the *Exercise4-6.xlsx* workbook file in the Chap4 folder in the Excel 2007 Workbook folder.

The 2008 Sales worksheet in the *Exercise4-6.xlsx* workbook file opens. In this sales worksheet, all the columns with supporting monthly sales figures are hidden so that only the quarterly totals and yearly total are now displayed. They appear above the clustered bar chart that is created from these quarterly sales figures.

2. Select the cell range A1:R15 in the 2008 Sales worksheet and then open the Print dialog box by clicking Office button | Print or pressing Ctrl+P.

The Print dialog box opens with the Active Sheet(s) option button selected.

3. Click the Selection option button and then click the Preview button at the bottom of the Print dialog box to verify that only the CG Media – 2008 Quarterly Totals sales table, and not the embedded clustered bar chart immediately beneath it in the 2008 Sales worksheet, will be printed.

   Next, you will change the orientation of the printing from the default portrait to landscape in the Page Setup dialog box opened in the Print Preview window.

4. Click the Page Setup button on the Print Preview tab of the Ribbon.

   Excel opens the Page Setup dialog box.

5. Click the Landscape option button on the Page tab of the Page Setup dialog box.

   Next, center the printing horizontally between the left and right margins.

6. Click the Margins tab of the Page Setup dialog box and then click the Horizontally check box.

   Finally, you will add a prefabricated header that prints the name of the worksheet (2008 Sales) in the left-hand section, Confidential in the center, and the current page number (Page 1) in the right-hand section.

7. Click the Header/Footer tab of the Page Setup dialog box and then click the Header drop-down button before you click 2008 Sales, Confidential, Page 1 on its drop-down menu. Then, click the OK button to close the Page Setup dialog box.

   When the Page Setup dialog box closes, the preview of the printed page shows the new landscape page orientation along with the prefabricated three-part header and the table data centered to be printed between the left and right margins.

8. If you have access to a printer, print this worksheet by clicking the Print button; otherwise, just close the Print Preview window, select cell A1 and then save the workbook as **CGMedia-PrntSelection.xlsx** in your Excel 2007 Practice folder before you close the workbook.

Printing the entire workbook

Printing all the data in the entire workbook is a snap: Simply open the Print dialog box (Office button | Print or Ctrl+P) and then select the Entire Workbook option button in the Print What section before sending the print job to the Printer by selecting the OK button.

Q. How can I print data on multiple worksheets without printing the entire workbook?

A. Select the tabs for all the worksheets in the workbook that contain data you want printed (remember to Ctrl+click to select multiple sheet tabs) before sending the job to the printer.

7. Following the technique outlined in Step 6, assign the same type of custom header and prefab footer to Sheet 07, Sheet 06, and Sheet 05 worksheets in the *Exercise4-7.xlsx* workbook.

   Next, you need to take care of the orphaned data on the third page of each of the four worksheets in the workbook. You do this by changing the orientation of the printing, if need be, and then using the Scale to Fit Width option.

8. Click the Sales 08 sheet tab and then click the Landscape option on the Orientation button's drop-down menu on the Ribbon's Page Layout tab. Then, click the 2 Pages option on the Width button's drop-down menu in the Scale to Fit group.

   Immediately following the Ready indicator, the Status bar should now read Page 1 of 2.

9. Following the technique outlined in Step 8, reduce the number of printed pages from three to two for Sheet 07, Sheet 06, and Sheet 05 worksheets in the *Exercise4-7.xlsx* workbook by changing the orientation of the printing from portrait to landscape.

   Immediately following the Ready indicator, the Status bar should now read Page 1 of 2 for when you selected each of the three Sheet tabs, Sales 07, Sales 06, and Sales 05.

10. Once again Open the Print dialog box (Ctrl+P) and then select the Entire Workbook option button in the Print What section before selecting Preview to open the Print Preview window.

    Excel displays the first page of what is now an eight-page report in the Print Preview window.

11. If you have access to a printer, print this eight-page report; otherwise, just close the Print Preview window, select cell A1 on Sheet 08 and then save the workbook as **CG Media 08-05 PrntWrkbk.xlsx** in the Excel 2007 Practice folder before you close the workbook.

Printing charts in the spreadsheet

Charts that you create from the data in your spreadsheets are either embedded in the same worksheet that contains the data or on a separate Chart sheet (see Chapter 15). Embedded charts are printed as part of the worksheet unless you select just the data ranges they're created from as the print selection. Note, however, that charts placed on their own Chart sheets are not printed unless you select their sheets as part of the print selection.

When you print a chart placed on its own Chart sheet, Excel adds a Chart tab to the Page Setup dialog box. The Chart tab contains options for scaling the chart instead of printing it full page and for printing the chart in black and white instead of color. You get experience using these options in Exercise 4-8 that follows.

Solve It | ## Exercise 4-8: Printing a Chart in a Report

In Exercise 4-8, you get practice printing a clustered bar chart that has been added to a workbook on its own chart sheet.

1. Open *Exercise4-8.xlsx* workbook file in the Chap4 folder of the Excel 2007 Workbook folder.

   This workbook contains two worksheets: Qtrly 08 Sales and Clustered Bar Chart.

2. Click the Clustered Bar Chart sheet tab to display the bar chart and activate its sheet. Then, click the Print Preview button you added to the Quick Access toolbar in Exercise 1-3 or press Ctrl+F2.

   You can also open the Print Preview window by clicking Office button | Print | Print Preview or pressing Alt+FWV.

   Note that Excel automatically selects landscape as the printing orientation for the chart and scales the chart so that it prints full-size on the page.

3. Click the Page Setup button on the Print Preview tab.

   Note that Page Setup dialog box now contains a fourth tab Chart, in addition to the other standard Page, Margins, and Header/Footer tabs.

4. Click the Chart tab in the Page Setup dialog box and then click the Print in Black and White check box.

   Use the Print in Black and White option to print an initial printout of a chart for proofing in black and white even when you're printing it with a color printer. That way, you can check the chart before you print it in color so that you don't waste any colored ink.

5. Click the Header/Footer tab in the Page Setup dialog box and then click the Custom Footer button.

   Excel opens the Footer dialog box which divides the custom footer into three sections: Left, Center, and Right. Note that the cursor is automatically positioned in the Left section.

6. Click the Insert Date button to insert the &[Date] code into the Left section. Then, click the Center section and click the Insert File Name button to insert the &[File] code in the center section. Finally, click the Right section and then click Insert Sheet Name button to insert the &[Tab] code in the Right section before you click OK.

   The custom footer in the Footer drop-down list box now contains the current date, the filename, and sheet name as in 03/30/2008, Exercise4-8.xlsx, Clustered Bar Chart.

7. Click OK to close the Page Setup dialog box.

   The previewed page with the chart now contains your three-part custom footer.

8. If you have access to a printer, print the chart from the Print Preview window; otherwise, close the Print Preview window and then make the Qtrly 08 Sales sheet active. Save the workbook as **CG Media 08 Qtrly Totals - ChartSht.xlsx** in the Excel 2007 Practice folder and then close the workbook.

Printing the spreadsheet formulas

When you print a worksheet, Excel prints the entries exactly as they appear in their cells of the worksheet. As a result, when you print a section of worksheet that contains formulas, the printout shows only the results of the calculations performed by the formulas, not the contents of the formulas themselves. In addition to a printout showing the results, you may also want to print a copy of the worksheet showing the formulas by which these results were derived. You can then use this printout of the formulas when double-checking the formulas in a worksheet to make sure that they are designed correctly.

To help you identify the cell reference of each formula in your printout, be sure to include the gridlines and column and row headings as part of the printout.

Exercise 4-9: Printing Spreadsheet Formulas in a Report

In Exercise 4-9, you get practice getting a worksheet ready to print with its formulas, gridlines, and column and row headings displayed.

1. Open the *Exercise4-9.xlsx* workbook in the Chap4 folder of the Excel 2007 Workbook folder.

The 08 Schedule sheet of this workbook contains a target production schedule for various part numbers with monthly quotas for the entire year of 2008.

2. Click the Show Formulas command button on the Formulas tab of the Ribbon or press Alt+MH.

Excel displays all the formulas in the cells of the 08 Schedule worksheet. Note that the table title in cell A1, Target Production Schedule for 2008, is now truncated to Target Production (the remainder of the heading no longer spills over into the adjacent cells in row 1 even though these cells are empty).

3. Press Ctrl+~ (tilde) to turn off the formula display and return to the normal worksheet display.

The tilde key is located on the ` key (accent grave) that is usually located to the immediate left of the 1 key on the top row of the QWERTY keyboard.

Ctrl+~ (tilde) is a toggle key combination: The first time you press it, it turns on the formula display and the second time turns it off.

4. Press Ctrl+~ (tilde) again, this time to turn the formula display back on and then switch to Page Layout view before you change the following settings with the command buttons on the Page Layout tab of the Ribbon:

  • Change the orientation of the printing from portrait to landscape.

  • Add a centered header that contains the text **Formula Check** and a centered prefab footer that displays the current page number and total pages in the report.

  • Add the gridlines and the row and column headings to the printout.

  • Make the rows $1:$2 the Rows to Repeat at Top and column $A:$A the Columns to Repeat at Left.

Now you need to check the pages in Print Preview.

5. Open the Print Preview window and check the three pages of the report.

Note that each of the three pages contains the row and column print titles you assigned.

6. Close the Print Preview window. Then switch to Page Break Preview view and dispense with the Welcome dialog box.

In Page Break Preview view, you will page the report so that there are four pages, each with the months of a quarter: Jan through Mar on Page 1, Apr through Jun on Page 2, Jul through Sep on Page 3, and Oct through Dec (along with the annual totals) on Page 4.

7. Move the page markers so that Page 1 contains only Part No. column along with the Jan, Feb, and Mar production quota columns; Page 2 only the Apr, May, and Jun columns; Page 3 only the Jul, Aug, and Sep columns; and Page 4, only the Oct, Nov, and Dec quota columns along with Total column with the grand total formulas.

The page breaks of the report now divide the production quota figures into four quarters.

8. Return the worksheet to Normal view and then open the Print Preview window again and check the pages of the report.

Each page should have the row and column print titles along with the row and column headings to help you identify which cell contains what formula.

9. If you have access to a printer, print the worksheet report showing the formulas; otherwise, close Print Preview and hide the display of the formulas in the cells before you save the workbook as **Target Schedule 08 -frmls.xlsx** in your Excel 2007 Practice folder.

Chapter 5

Modifying the Spreadsheet

- -

In This Chapter

▶ Selecting the cell ranges that require editing

▶ Finding data entry errors with Text to Speech

▶ Inserting and deleting cell ranges

▶ Moving and copying cell ranges

▶ Using comments in the spreadsheet

▶ Finding and replacing cell entries and spell checking the spreadsheet

▶ Editing worksheets as a group

- -

Some of the spreadsheets you work with require constant updating, whereas others need only the occasion revision. Whichever is the case, being able to revise an existing spreadsheet without disturbing either its underlying structure or its current contents is essential. The exercises in this chapter give you a chance to practice all aspects of basic editing, including locating the workbook file to open, finding the area in the worksheet that needs editing, and making all the necessary editing changes.

Finding and Identifying the Region That Needs Editing

As you're already well aware, an Excel worksheet represents an extremely large space in which to work. Often the biggest challenge in editing a spreadsheet is just finding and identifying the data ranges in the worksheet that are in need of revision. To help in this endeavor, you can often use the following three features to good advantage:

- ✔ **Zoom** to gain an overview of the worksheet and its data ranges by zooming out on the worksheet and then using it to gain a close-up view of the particular range in the sheet you need to edit

- ✔ **Freeze Panes** to prevent the rows and columns containing the column and row headings from scrolling so that these headings remain visible at all times while you are scrolling through their data entries

- ✔ **Custom Views** to name and save a combination of different worksheet display settings (including frozen panes and various magnification settings) so that you can put them into effect by simply selecting them

Q. What is the range of zoom settings I can select for my worksheet display?

A. You can set the worksheet display magnification setting anywhere in the range of 10% to 400% of normal by doing any of the following:

✔ Drag the Zoom button in the Zoom slider on the Status bar to the left to decrease the magnification percentage or to the right to increase it.

✔ Click the Zoom In or Zoom Out buttons at either end of the Zoom slider to increase or decrease magnification respectively in 10% increments.

✔ Click the Zoom Level located to the immediate left of the Zoom slider that displays the current percentage to open the Zoom dialog box. In the Zoom dialog box, you can select the 200%, 100%, 75%, 50%, 25%, or Fit Selection options or enter the value of the new magnification percentage directly into the Custom option's text box in single-degree increments.

Solve It

Exercise 5-1: Creating Custom Views in a Worksheet

In Exercise 5-1, you get practice creating custom views of a worksheet that use different zoom magnification settings and panes that freeze specific rows and columns on the screen. By saving custom views you create as a part of a workbook file, you can restore their screen settings in a jiffy simply by selecting the custom view.

1. Open the *Exercise5-1.xlsx* workbook file in the Chap5 folder in your Excel 2007 Workbook folder.

This workbook contains a version of the Income Analysis worksheet that you can use to practice creating and selecting custom views.

2. Use the Zoom slider to reduce the screen magnification of the Income Analysis worksheet to 50%.

Note that even at one-half of normal, not all of the data ranges are visible on screen.

3. Click the Zoom Level to open the Zoom dialog box and then click the Custom option button and type **45** in the Custom option's text box before you press Enter.

At a magnification setting of 45% of normal, you can now see all the data entered in the Income Analysis worksheet.

4. Change the screen magnification percentage back to 50% and then select the cell range J20:M25 by carefully dragging through this range in the worksheet. Click the Zoom Level to open the Zoom dialog box and then click the Fit Selection option button before you press Enter.

Excel responds by setting the magnification to something over 200% so that all of the cells in the selected range J20:M25 are visible in the display. Note, however, that without the row and column headings, it is impossible to identify these entries in this range.

5. Put the cell cursor in cell A1 (Ctrl+Home) and move it to the empty cell B3. Then, click View | Freeze Panes | Freeze Panes or press Alt+WFF.

Because the cell cursor is in the row immediately beneath the one with the table's column headings and the column immediately to the right of the one containing the row headings, Excel draws a horizontal line between rows 2 and 3 and a vertical line between columns A and B indicating the limits of the frozen panes — any entries above the horizontal line and to the left of the vertical line remain on-screen as you scroll through their columns and rows.

6. Use the Tab key to scroll new columns on the right into view.

Note how the column headings in row 2 as well as the table title in row 1 remain displayed as you move other columns of the table into view.

7. Use the Page Down key to scroll new rows lower in the worksheet into view.

Note how the row headings in column A remain displayed on the screen as you move new rows of the table into view.

8. Repeat Step 4 in this exercise, select the cell range J20:M25, and set the magnification to fit the display of this selection.

Note that this time with the addition of the frozen panes that retain the associated row and column headings, you can tell right away that you're looking at the 3rd Qtr operating expenses for all the divisions.

9. Return the Zoom setting to 100% and then position the cell cursor in cell B3 which you used to freeze the row and column headings.

Now you're going to save this screen magnification and frozen pane display as a custom view that you can reuse.

10. Click Custom Views button on the Ribbon's View tab or press Alt+WC to open the Custom Views dialog box.

The Custom Views dialog box enables you to create new custom views as well as to select the views that you've already created.

11. Click the Add button in the Custom Views dialog box to open the Add View dialog box. Then, type **100% w/Row & Col Headings** in the Name text box, leaving the Print Settings and Hidden Rows, Columns and Filter Settings check boxes selected. Click OK.

Excel adds your 100% custom view and closes the Custom Views dialog box. Next, you create another custom view that hides columns so that only the four quarterly subtotals and yearly grand totals are displayed.

12. Hide the column ranges B:D, F:H, J:L, and N:P. Next, select cell E3 and then, following Steps 10 and 11, name this view **100% w/4 Qtrs Display**.

To hide columns, you select their column headings (by dragging through them — use the Ctrl key to select nonadjacent column ranges) and then select Home | Format | Hide & Unhide | Hide Columns on the Ribbon (Alt+HOUC).

13. Open the Custom Views dialog box and click the 100% w/Row & Col Headings view before you select the Show button.

Excel immediately unhides all the columns you hide in Step 12, while at the same time repositioning the cell cursor in cell B3.

14. Open the Custom Views dialog box again and this time double-click the 100% w/4 Qtrs Display view to apply it to the worksheet. Hide the following row ranges: 4:8, 12:16, 20:24, 28:32 and then select cell E3; save this view under the name **100% w/4 Qtrs Total Display**.

To hide rows, you select their row headings (by dragging through them — use the Ctrl key to select nonadjacent row ranges) and then select Home | Format | Hide & Unhide | Hide Rows on the Ribbon (Alt+HOUR).

15. Return the worksheet to the 100% w/Row & Col Headings view, and then choose Freeze Panes | Unfreeze Panes on the Ribbon or press Alt+WFF to remove the panes.

Excel immediately removes the lines indicating the frozen panes.

16. Position the cell cursor in cell A1. Save this version of the Income Analysis worksheet with the custom views under the filename **Income Analysis - CustViews.xlsx** in the Excel 2007 Practice folder and close the workbook.

Selecting the Ranges to Edit

Selecting occupied cells in the worksheet for editing is very much the same process as selecting blank cells for pre-formatting or data entry with one important exception. Because the cells already contain data, in addition to dragging through the ranges and clicking the first and last cell while holding down the Shift key, you can use a technique known as AutoSelect to quickly select an entire block of occupied cells in a couple of mouse clicks.

Moreover, you can use Excel's Go To and range name features to combine locating a cell range that needs editing and selecting its cells all at the same time!

Before you attempt Exercise 5-2, you may want to play the Cell Ranges Selecting.exe demo located in the Excel Feature Demos folder on your workbook CD-ROM. This feature demonstration shows you how to select a range of cell entries in a worksheet using both AutoSelect and the Go To dialog box.

Solve It | ### Exercise 5-2: Selecting Cell Ranges for Editing

In Exercise 5-2, you get practice using various techniques for selecting the cell ranges in a worksheet that require editing. These techniques include using AutoSelect, the Go To dialog box, and naming a cell range and then selecting its cells by selecting its range name in the Name box on the Formula bar.

1. Open the *Exercise5-2.xlsx* workbook file in the Chap5 folder inside the Excel 2007 Workbook folder.

You can use the 08 Schedule worksheet in this workbook to practice selecting cell ranges for editing.

2. Position the mouse pointer on the bottom edge of the cell cursor in cell A2, and then when the Arrowhead mouse pointer appears, click the bottom edge.

AutoSelect extends the selection down to row 7, the last row in this range formatted as a table.

3. Continue to hold down the Shift key as you double-click anywhere on the right edge of the extended cell cursor.

AutoSelect extends the cell selection to column N, the last occupied column in the data table, effectively selecting all of its cells in the range A2:N7.

4. Click cell A10 in the worksheet to position the cell cursor in this cell while at the same time deselecting the cell range A2:N7.

Now you will practice selecting the cells in the data table using Excel's Go To feature, which is normally used to position the cell cursor in a new cell in the worksheet.

5. Press F5 or Ctrl+G to open the Go To dialog box and then type **A2** (it's all right to enter the reference as **a2**) and press Enter.

The Go To dialog box disappears and the cell cursor jumps to cell A2, making it current.

6. Press F5 or Ctrl+G to open the Go To dialog box again and then type **N7** (or **n7**). This time, however, hold down the Shift key as you press Enter.

Excel jumps the cell pointer to cell N7 and, because you held down the Shift key, the program also selected all the cells in between (if you don't hold down the Shift key, the program just moves the cursor from A2 to N7).

7. Position the cell cursor in cell A1 and use AutoSelect on your own to select the cell range A1:N7.

Note that this time you need to position the mouse pointer on the cell border between cell A1 and A2 and then, when the black downward-pointing arrow mouse pointer appears, hold down the Shift key before you click the mouse. This extends the cell selection down to row 7 so that you can then double-click the right edge of this selection to extend it to column N. Next, you're going to name this cell selection.

8. Click the Name Box on the Formula bar that currently displays A1 and type **Target_sched** (with an underscore and no space) and press Enter.

Excel assigns the range name Target_sched to the cell selection, A1:N7.

9. Use the Go To feature to move the cell cursor to cell IV4000 in the worksheet.

Next, select the target production schedule cell range by selecting its range name on the Formula bar.

10. Click the drop-down button attached to the Name Box on the Formula bar and then click Target_sched on its drop-down list.

When you click Target_sched, Excel responds by selecting the range A1:N7 and repositioning the worksheet so that this range is in view and displaying this range name in the Name box on the Formula bar.

Note that this worksheet already contains two other range names: Print_Titles given to column A when it was defined as the print title for this worksheet (see Chapter 4) and Table1 that was defined as the range with the table data when the cell range A2: N7 was formatted as a table (see Chapter 3).

11. Select the cell range A3:N7 by selecting the Table1 range name on the Name Box drop-down menu.

Save your 08 Schedule worksheet with your Target_sched range name.

12. Click cell A1 to deselect the range A3:N7, and then save this workbook with the filename **Target Schedule 08 - named.xlsx** in your Excel 2007 Practice folder and close the workbook file.

Editing Data Entries

In the previous exercises in this chapter, the sole technique you've used to modify the entry in a cell is to replace it completely by entering the new value into that cell as though it were still blank. This method is fine as long as the replacement entry is short and easy to type. It is not, however, the preferred method when you only need to make slight corrections to a long text entry or a complex formula. Rather than replace the original entry, you need to put Excel into Edit mode so that you can edit its contents as you would a word or phrase in a word-processing program, such as Microsoft Word 2007.

Excel gives you a choice of techniques for putting the program into Edit mode:

- Click the I-beam cursor at the place in the current cell entry that needs editing on the Formula bar and then edit its contents on the Formula bar.

- Double-click the white-cross mouse pointer at the place in the cell entry in the worksheet that needs editing and then edit its contents in the cell.

- Press F2 to place the insertion point at the end of the current cell entry in the worksheet and edit its contents in its cell.

After you've placed Excel in Edit mode and positioned the insertion point somewhere in the entry, you can then use ← and → to move the flashing pointer in front of or immediately after the characters to modify. Press the Delete key to remove characters to the right of the insertion point or the Backspace key to remove characters to its left. To insert new characters at the insertion point and move existing characters out the way and to the right, just type them.

After you finish modifying the contents of the entry, you still need to complete the edit as you do a new entry. Only, in this case, you need to rely on the Enter box, Enter key, Tab, or clicking another cell as you can't use any of the arrow keys (↑, ↓, ←, or →). In Edit mode, these cursor keys only move the insertion point within the characters of the entry.

If you need to abandon an edit without entering the changes you've made in the cell or on the Formula bar, press the Esc key. If you complete a mistaken editing change, click the Undo button on the Quick Access toolbar or press Ctrl+Z to undo the change (and keep in mind that Excel supports multiple levels of undo).

Solve It

Exercise 5-3: Making Simple Edits to Cell Entries

In Exercise 5-3, you get practice manually editing the contents of existing cell entries without replacing them.

1. Open the *Exercise5-3.xlsx* workbook file in the Chap5 folder in your Excel 2007 Workbook folder.

   You can use the 08 Sales sheet in this workbook file to practice making simple editing changes to the contents of particular cells in the spreadsheet.

2. Increase the screen magnification to 150% using the Zoom slider and its Zoom In and Zoom Out buttons.

   Now, insert new text in the title of the worksheet table.

3. Click the I-beam pointer in front of the C in Category on the Formula bar, and then type **Media and** followed by a space to insert this text into the title. Click the Enter box to complete this edit in cell A1.

   The edited title in cell A1 now reads, CG Media – 2008 Sales by Media and Category.

4. Position the white-cross mouse pointer after the *s* in Discs in the row heading in cell A3 and then double-click to set the insertion point in this cell. Then, remove this extraneous *s* and the extra space between Compact and Disc.

   Use ← and → to position the insertion point immediately after the extra *s* in Discs and, later, immediately in front of the D and, then in each instance, press the Backspace key to first remove the extra letter and then the extra space.

   The edited row heading in cell A3 now reads, Compact Disc Sales.

5. Position the cell cursor in cell A14, press F2, and then replace Cassette in the row heading with **Tape** and press Tab to complete the edit.

   Use ← to position the insertion point immediately after the final *e* in Cassette and then press the Backspace key until you have deleted its letters. Then, type **Tape** before you press Tab.

   The row heading in cell A14 now reads, Total Tape Sales.

6. Select cell A1 again and save your editing changes in a new file named **CG Media 08 - edits.xlsx** in your Excel 2007 Practice folder and then close the workbook file.

Catching Errors with Text to Speech

In Excel 2007 you can use the Text to Speech feature to catch data entry errors by listening to them, provided that you first add the Speak Cells buttons to the Quick Access toolbar (the command buttons for the Text to Speech feature are not found on the Excel 2007 Ribbon). Text to Speech reads the entries in a data table or list out loud, enabling you to check their accuracy by keeping your eyes focused on the printed source from which they were originally entered.

If you're running Excel 2007 on Windows XP, the Text to Speech feature uses a male mechanical voice named Microsoft Sam. If, however, you're running Excel 2007 on Windows Vista, the Text to Speech feature uses a female voice named Microsoft Anna.

Solve It

Exercise 5-4: Using Speak Cell Buttons to Hear Cell Entries Spoken

In Exercise 5-4, you use the Speak Cells buttons that you added to the Quick Access toolbar way back in Exercise 1-4 so that you can verify cell entries and locate any that need editing. (If you didn't complete Exercise 1-4 or reset the buttons on the Quick Access toolbar, you need to do so before you can do this exercise.)

1. Open the *Exercise5-4.xlsx* workbook in the Chap5 folder in your Excel 2007 Workbook folder.

This workbook file contains a Markdown Table worksheet with a version of the Spring Sale Markdowns table that you can use to practice hearing cell entries read aloud to check their accuracy and eliminate errors.

2. Click the Speak Cells by Rows button on the Quick Access toolbar and then click the Speak Cells button. Listen to the entries in cell A1 and then across the column headings in row.

As soon as you click the Speak Cells button, Excel selects the cell range of the entire table. As Microsoft Sam or Anna reads the entries across each column in succeeding rows, note how Excel highlights the cell currently being spoken in the selected table.

3. When you hear "zero two to three hundred five" spoken for the code entry 02-305 in cell A3, immediately click the Speak Cells - Stop Speaking Cells button.

Notice how Microsoft Sam (on Windows XP) or Microsoft Anna (on Vista), pronounces the code number entered in cell A3 as "zero two to three hundred five" rather than "zero two dash three hundred five" (Text to Speech interprets the dash as indicating a range).

4. Click the Speak Cells by Columns button on the Quick Access toolbar and then click the Speak Cells button again and listen to the rest of the entries in the Markdowns Table.

When you select the Speak Cells by Columns button, Text to Speech reads the entries down each row in succeeding columns. Note how Text to Speech automatically stops when the program reaches the last cell in the table selection.

In addition to listening to entries already made in a spreadsheet, you can have Text to Speech read back as you make each entry. Try this in Sheet2 of the *Exercise5-4.xlsx* workbook.

5. Click the Sheet2 tab to activate this blank worksheet and then click the Speak Cells on Enter button on the Quick Access toolbar.

When you click the Speak Cells on Enter button, Microsoft Sam or Anna tells you that "cells will now be spoken on Enter."

6. Make the following entries down column A of Sheet2:

   • **Northeast Consortium** in cell A1

   • **Alfred E. Neuman** in cell A2

- **-89.45** in cell A3

- **CD-ROM** in cell A4

- **395-11-0034** in cell A5

- **415-555-0023** in cell A6

- **3678.6** in cell A7

- **Feb 12, 2008** in cell A8

Now, each time you complete one of these cell entries, Sam or Anna reads back that entry out loud. Note that Microsoft Sam has some difficulty pronouncing Neuman as "Newman;" he says something closer to "Noyman." Also, notice that both Sam and Anna correctly interpret your entry in cell A6 as a telephone number by saying, "area code four, one, five; five, five, five; zero, zero, two, three" but fail to recognize the Social Security Number in cell A5, saying "three hundred ninety-five; eleven; zero, zero, three, four."

7. Click the Speak Cells on Enter button on the Quick Access toolbar a second time to deselect the button and turn off Text to Speech.

    When you click the Speak Cells on Enter button a second time, Microsoft Sam or Anna tells you that "turned off Speak on Enter."

8. Rename Sheet2 to Speech Practice, and then switch back to the Markdown Table worksheet, select cell A1 and then save the workbook as **Spring Furniture Sale - speakcells.xlsx** in your Excel 2007 Practice folder before you close the workbook file.

Deleting and Inserting Data and Cells

Deletions in a worksheet are a little more complicated than in other software programs. This is because Excel gives you a choice between deleting only the cell entry, leaving intact the cell structure and all assigned formatting attributes; clearing the cell of all its contents without disturbing its structure; and removing the cell structure along with everything its contains, causing remaining cell entries in neighboring cells to adjust to fill in the gap:

↙ Press the Delete key to remove only the entry in the current cell.

↙ Click the Delete button in the Cells group of Ribbon's Home tab to remove the entry in the current cell plus all formatting attributes and comments (Excel automatically shifts up any cell entries in rows below).

↙ Choose Delete | Delete Cells in the Cells group of the Home tab (Alt+HDD) to open the Delete dialog box. Choose between the Shift Cells Up or the Shift Cells Left options to remove the cell along with all its contents, formatting, and comments, and to adjust remaining cells in rows below or in columns on the right.

Choosing Insert | Insert Cells (Alt+HII) in the Cells group of the Home tab is the opposite of Delete | Delete Cells. You use it to open the Insert dialog box, where you can Shift Cells Right or Shift Cells Down to insert blank cells in regions where you need to squeeze in data entries that were somehow left out. In the process of squeezing in these blank cells, you also shift existing entries down to rows below or to columns to the right. Note that if you click the Insert button in the Cells group of the Home tab, Excel automatically shifts existing cell entries in the same column down to rows below.

You can delete entire rows and columns containing the cell cursor from the worksheet by choosing Delete | Delete Sheet Rows (Alt+HDR) or Delete | Delete Sheet Columns (Alt+HDC) in the Cells group of the Home tab. Likewise, you can insert an entire row or column by choosing Insert | Insert Sheet Rows (Alt+HIR) or Insert | Insert Sheet Columns (Alt+HIC). To delete or insert multiple rows or columns in the worksheet, select their row or column headings before you choose these commands.

Be very cautious about deleting *or* inserting entire rows or columns in any worksheet, especially one that you didn't create or are not that familiar with. You can easily take out vital data from tables and lists located in unseen regions of the worksheet when doing a deletion. Inserting new columns and rows can be almost as dangerous, however, as your insertions can just as well corrupt the accuracy or even disrupt the functionality of the formulas in these unseen tables and lists. To stay on the safe side, constrain your cell deletions and insertions to just the cell ranges in the region you're working in.

Solve It

Exercise 5-5: Deleting and Inserting Cells in the Worksheet

In Exercise 5-5, you get practice inserting and deleting cells in an existing worksheet without disturbing existing entries and by adjusting them as needed to accommodate the editing changes.

1. Open the *Exercise5-5.xls* workbook file in the Chap5 folder of the Excel 2007 Workbook folder.

The Home Sales 2008 worksheet in this workbook file contains a copy of a House Sales table that you can use to practice deleting and inserting cells and cell entries.

2. Select cell C4 with the selling price of the first house on Elm Street and delete just this entry by pressing the Delete key.

Excel deletes the contents of this cell.

3. Enter **1250000** in now-blank cell C4.

Because you only deleted the contents in cell C4, Excel applies the remaining Currency style number format with no decimal places to the new entry you made, so it immediately appears as $1,250,000 in the cell.

4. Delete everything in cell C4 by clicking Clear | Clear All in the Editing group of the Ribbon's Home tab or press Alt+HEA.

This time, Excel deletes the contents of the cell as well as its number formatting.

5. Enter **735000** in the now-blank cell C4.

This time, Excel does no number formatting to the 735000 value because you cleared the cell of formatting plus contents.

6. Use the Format Painter to restore the Currency style number format with no decimal places to cell C4.

Position the cell cursor in cell C5 that still contains this Currency number formatting. Click the Format Painter button in the Clipboard group of the Home tab and then click cell C4 to copy just the formatting from cell C5.

7. Select the cell range A5:C5 listing a house sale on Apple Drive. Then click the Delete button in the Cells group of the Ribbon's Home tab (be sure you don't the click the drop-down button that appears either to the side or beneath the Delete button's icon).

Excel removes the cells in the selected cell range A5:C5 while at the same time pulling up the data in the rows below so that there are no gaps in the table.

8. Click the Undo button on the Quick Access toolbar or press Ctrl+Z to restore the deleted cell range.

Now you'll insert blank cells in the table for a new home sale listing.

9. Leave the cell range A5:C5 selected and then click the Insert button in the Cells group of the Home tab.

Excel inserts three blank cells above the Apple Drive sales information, shifting the remaining entries in this table down. Note the appearance of the Insert Options button at the Fill handle in the lower-right corner of the extended cell cursor: You display its drop-down button by positioning the mouse pointer over the button and then use its options to copy cell formatting from the cells in the row below (it automatically uses the formatting in the cells in the row above) or to clear all formatting from the newly inserted cells.

10. Make the following entries in the new, empty cell selection, A5:C5:

- The address, **500 King Street**, in cell A5
- The selling date, **4/1/2008**, in cell B5
- The selling price, **820000**, in cell C5

11. Select cell A1 and then save your editing changes to the Home Sales 2008 worksheet in a new workbook named **Home Sales 08 - rev.xlsx** in your Chap5 folder inside the Excel 2007 Practice folder.

Moving and Copying Data and Cells

Excel provides two methods for moving and copying a cell selection (along with its contents and formatting) to a new place in the same worksheet. You can either use

- ✔ Drag-and-drop to manually take the selection or a copy of it with the mouse pointer and drop it into its new place in the sheet
- ✔ Cut and paste to cut or copy the selection to the Windows clipboard and then paste it into its new position after moving the cell cursor to the first cell of that range

Keep in mind that you must use the cut-and-paste method to move or copy cell ranges from one worksheet to another in the same workbook or from one workbook to another.

When using the cut-and-paste method, you can select what part of the cut or copied data is transferred when pasting it into their new position in the worksheet or workbook. You do this by selecting one of the options on the Paste button's drop-down menu (Formulas, Paste Values, No Borders, Transpose, or Paste Link) on the Home tab or by selecting Paste Special option on this button's drop-down menu and then selecting the appropriate Paste option in the Paste Special dialog box (see Table 5-1).

Table 5-1	The Paste Options in the Paste Special Dialog Box
Paste Option	**What It Does**
All	Pastes all types of entries (numbers, formulas, and text), their formats, and comments from the selection in the paste area
Formulas	Pastes only the entries (numbers, formulas, and text) from the selection in the paste area
Values	Pastes only numbers and text from the selection in the paste area, converting all formulas to their current calculated values so they're pasted into the worksheet as numbers
Formats	Pastes only the formats from the selection into the paste area
Comments	Pastes only the comments from the selection into the paste area
Validation	Pastes only the entries in cells that use data validation into the paste area
All Using Source Theme	Pastes all types of entries with their formats using whatever theme is assigned to the cut or copied cells (from the pop-up gallery attached to the Themes button on the Ribbon's Page Layout tab)
All Except Borders	Pastes everything but the borders assigned to the cell selection into the paste area
Column Widths	Pastes everything into the paste area and adjusts the column widths in this area to match those of the original cell selection
Formulas and Number Formats	Pastes only the formulas and number formatting (omitting all text and numeric entries) from the cell selection into the paste area
Values and Number Formats	Pastes only the numbers and number formatting (omitting all text and converting all formulas to their calculated values) from the cell selection into the paste area

Use the Transpose option on the Paste button's drop-down menu or the Transpose check box in the Paste Special dialog box to transpose the data in the table so that data that used to run across the columns now run down the rows and vice versa.

Before you attempt Exercise 5-6, you may want to play the Cell Ranges Moving and Copying.exe demo located in the Excel Feature Demos folder on your workbook CD-ROM. This feature demonstration shows you how to move a cell range using the drag-and-drop method and copy the range to a new place on the same worksheet and to a new worksheet in the same workbook using cut and paste.

Exercise 5-6: Moving and Copying Cells in a Workbook

In Exercise 5-6, you get practice moving and copying cells in a workbook using both the drag-and-drop method as well as copy-and-paste.

1. Open the *Exercise5-6.xlsx* workbook file in the Chap5 folder inside your Excel 2007 Workbook folder.

You use the Target Production Schedule table in its 08 Schedule sheet to practice moving and copying cells and their data entries. Note that this worksheet contains the range name Target_sched assigned to the cell range A1:N7 that you can use to select its cells.

2. Select the table's cells (A1:N7) and then use drag-and-drop to move it so that it now occupies the range B5:O11.

Position the white-cross mouse pointer somewhere on the bottom edge of the extended cell cursor and when the pointer changes to an arrowhead, drag the selected range of cells to its new position. When the ScreenTip at the bottom of the outline representing the cell selection you're moving reads B5:O11, release the mouse button to drop it in place.

3. Use drag-and-drop to copy the table you've just moved to the cell range B5:O11 to the cell range B13:O19.

Hold down the Ctrl key as you drag the outline of the copy of the selected cell range to its new position in the worksheet.

4. Cut the copy of the original Target Production Schedule table you moved to the cell range B5:O11 to the Clipboard by selecting this range and then clicking the Cut button in the Clipboard group of the Ribbon's Home tab or by pressing Ctrl+X.

Excel puts a marquee (marching ants) around the cell selection B5:O11 and displays the message "Select Destination and Press ENTER or choose Paste" on the Status bar.

5. Click the Sheet2 tab to make this worksheet active, move the cell cursor to cell B2, and then press Enter.

The moment you press the Enter key, Excel moves the table to the cell range B2:O8 on Sheet2 of the workbook.

6. Switch back to the 08 Schedule sheet and select cell A1.

Excel deselects the cell range B5:O11 on the 08 Schedule worksheet that used to contain the table you just moved to the cell range B2:O8 on Sheet2.

7. Click the drop-down button on the Name Box on the Formula bar and then click Target_sched on its drop-down menu.

   Excel selects the cell range B2:O8 on Sheet2 of the *Exercise5-6.xlsx* workbook file. When you move a cell range that you've named to a new sheet in the same workbook, Excel can still identify and select the range using that name.

8. While the cell range B2:O8 is still selected on Sheet2, click the Copy button in the Clipboard group of the Home tab or press Ctrl+C to copy the cell selection to the Windows Clipboard.

   Again, Excel places a marquee around the cell selection and displays the message, "Select Destination and Press ENTER or choose Paste" on the Status bar.

9. Select cell B2 in the 08 Schedule worksheet, and then click the Paste command button in the Clipboard group of the Home tab followed by Paste Values on its drop-down menu or press Alt+HVV.

   Excel makes a copy of the table without the formulas. Note also that this copy of the table contains none of the formatting assigned to the original; thus the decimal numbers in the cells in this table that were calculated by formula.

10. Click cell D4 in the 08 Schedule sheet to verify that the formulas are missing from this copy of the table.

    In place of the formula =C4+(C4*0.055) on the Formula bar, the value 527.5 appears showing that the formula has been replaced by its calculated result.

11. Select the range B2:O8 and use drag-and-drop to move this table down until the ScreenTip reads B8:O14. Then, release the mouse button.

    Excel displays an alert dialog box asking you if you want to replace the contents of the destination cells.

12. Click the Cancel button to close this alert dialog box.

    As soon as you click Cancel, Excel undoes the move after closing the alert dialog box.

13. Use drag-and-drop to move this cell range selection with the copy of the table containing only values so that this table is temporarily located in the cell range B21:O27 beneath your original copy of the table that still contains formulas.

    Next, you'll move the original copy of the table up near the top of the worksheet and then the copy with values only up so that it's right underneath.

14. Select the cell range B13:O19 and then move this original copy of the table up to the cell range B2:O8. Then, select the cell range B21:O27 with the values-only table and move it up to the cell range B10:O16 so that it is now directly beneath the original copy of the table in the worksheet.

    Next, you use the Transpose option with the original table you moved to Sheet2 to see how you can use this Paste command to change the orientation of your data.

15. Switch to Sheet2 by clicking its sheet tab. Select the cell range B3:N7 that contains the headings and data in the original table and then click the Copy button on the Home tab or press Ctrl+C.

Excel places a marquee around the selected cell range B3:N7, indicating that it's copied to the Clipboard and ready to Paste.

16. Select cell B10 in Sheet2 and then click the Paste button followed by the Transpose option on its drop-down menu or press Alt+HVT.

Excel copies the selected table data to the cell range B10:F22 so that part numbers are now the column headings and the months of the year form the row headings (see Figure 5-1).

17. Rename Sheet2 to **Trans Schedule**. Press the Esc key and then click cell A1 in the Trans Schedule worksheet.

Pressing the Escape key always removes a marquee from a cell selection. It does not, however, remove the cut or copied data from the Clipboard.

18. Select cell A1 in the 08 Schedule worksheet and then save your work in a new workbook file named **Target Schedule 08 - cutncopy.xlsx** in your Excel 2007 Practice folder. Then, close this workbook.

Figure 5-1:
Sheet2 after
transposing
the pasted
table into
the cell
range
B10:F22.

Using Notes in the Spreadsheet

Excel makes it easy to attach notes to the cells of a spreadsheet. You can use these notes (officially called comments in the program) to remind yourself or your coworkers of changes that need to be made in the spreadsheet or data that needs to be reviewed and verified.

The key to adding and managing notes in a worksheet is the Comments group in the Review tab on the Ribbon. This group contains all the command buttons you need to add, edit, delete, display and hide, and move from comment to comment in the worksheet.

Solve It

Exercise 5-7: Adding and Using Comments in a Worksheet

In Exercise 5-7, you get practice annotating a worksheet by adding comments to it. In addition, you also get experience with hiding comments until you select them and finding all the comments you've added to a worksheet.

1. Open the *Exercise5-7.xlsx* workbook file in the Chap5 folder inside your Excel 2007 Workbook folder.

   This file contains an Employee List worksheet with table of employees that you can use in practicing how to use comments in a spreadsheet.

2. Select cell J2 and then click the Review | New Comment button on the Ribbon or press Alt+RC.

   Excel inserts a new text box with an arrow pointing to cell J2 containing your name.

3. Type **Verify this employee's status** as the text of this comment and then resize the text box, making it wide enough for all the comment text to appear on a single line of the box and short enough that there's no longer lines of empty space below the text.

   To resize a text box, position the mouse pointer over one of the eight sizing handles that appear as circles at the four corners and midpoints around the perimeter of the box. When the mouse pointer changes into a double-header arrow, drag the sides of the box until it is the size and shape you want (note that Excel automatically reflows the text in the box to accommodate these changes).

4. Select cell E6 and then add a comment to this cell reminding you to change Cindy's department from Accounting to Human Resources as of 01-01-08.

   Notice that the text box for this comment is in the way of salary and location information in the employee list for several individuals.

5. Move the text box for this comment you added to cell E6 so that the box no longer obscures cell entries in the employee list by locating it to the right somewhere in the blank columns of K, L, and M in the worksheet.

   To move a text box, position the mouse pointer anywhere on the outline of the box outside of the eight sizing handles and then drag the outline of the box until it is positioned in the desired place in the worksheet.

6. Select cell F20 and then add a note to this cell reminding you to verify Miriam's salary and then resize to remove its unused space and reposition the comment's text box outside of the list in the empty columns K, L, and M.

7. Position the cell cursor in cell A1, and then position the mouse pointer over each of the three cells, J2, E6, and F20, that now contain comments.

   Note that positioning the mouse pointer over a cell with a comment causes that comment's text box to be displayed. Also note that each of these three cells now contains a tiny red triangle in the upper-right corner, indicating that the cell has a comment attached to it.

8. Click the Show All Comments command button on the Ribbon's Review tab or press Alt+RA.

   Note this command button is a toggle switch that shows or hides all the comments in a worksheet.

9. Hide all three comments and then click the Next button on the Review tab or press Alt+RN to display each of the three comments in succession.

   Note that the Edit Comment and Delete command buttons become active on the Review tab as you use Next to move to each of the three comments in succession. You use the Edit Comment button to position the insertion point at the end of the comment text in its box. You use the Delete button to remove a comment.

10. When you reach the last comment attached to cell F20, select the text of the comment and then right-click the border of the text box and click Format Comment on the shortcut menu to open the Format Comment dialog box.

    The Format Comment dialog box enables you to modify all sorts of format settings for the selected text box, including the font and fill color it uses.

11. Change the comment text to 10-point Calibri bold italic and the fill color of the text box to Gray-25%. Then, change the formatting of the other two comments-in cells J2 and E6 to match.

    To change the fill color for a comment's text box, click the Colors and Lines tab in the Format Comment dialog box. Then, click Color option to display its drop-down color palette and click the color square you want to use.

12. Click cell A1 and then save this version of the Employee List worksheet with your notes with the filename **Employee List - notes.xlsx** in your Excel 2007 Practice folder and then close the workbook.

Using Find and Replace and Spell Checking

Just like Microsoft Word 2007, Excel is equipped with a Find, Find and Replace, and Spelling checking feature that you can use in editing your spreadsheets:

- **Find** (Find & Select | Find on the Home tab or Ctrl+F) enables you to search for and locate text or values in the spreadsheet that potentially need changing.

- **Find and Replace** (Find & Select | Replace on the Home tab or Ctrl+H) enables you to select whether Excel replaces one set of text or values it locates in the spreadsheet with another set that you specify.

- **Spelling** (Spelling command button on the Review tab or F7) enables you to catch and correct spelling errors using either the built-in dictionary or a custom dictionary you build.

Keep in mind when using Find and Find and Replace to locate entries in the spreadsheet that you can change any of the following search options to refine the search. You can use the

- ✔ **Within** drop-down list box to choose between Sheet (the default) to look for the search text only in the cells of the current worksheet or Workbook to search the cells on all the sheets in the workbook.

- ✔ **Search** drop-down list box to choose between By Rows (the default) to conduct the search across the rows and then down the columns of the worksheet or By Columns to conduct the search down each column and then across each row.

- ✔ **Look In** drop-down list box to choose among Formulas (the default) to look for matches to the search text in the entries as they appear on the Formula bar, Values to look for matches in the entries as they appear in the cells of the worksheet, or Comments to look for matches in the comments added to the cells of the worksheet.

- ✔ **Match Case** check box to match the upper- and lowercase spelling in the cell entries with the search text.

- ✔ **Match Entire Cell Contents** check box to match the entire contents of a cell with the search text.

- ✔ **Format** button to specify formatting that the cell or cell entries must match.

Solve It

Exercise 5-8: Editing with Find and Replace

In Exercise 5-8, you get practice using Find and Replace and some of its many options to locate and modify cell entries that need updating.

1. Open the *Exercise5-8.xlsx* workbook file in the Chap5 folder inside your Excel 2007 Workbook folder.

This workbook file contains a number of numeric (variations of 2500 and a variety of dates in 2007) and text (different Italian pastas, yum!) cell entries that you can use to practice using the Find, Find and Replace, and Spell checking features in Excel.

2. Click Find & Select | Find on the Ribbon's Home tab or Ctrl+F to open the Find and Replace dialog box with the Find tab selected. Then, enter **25?** in Find What text box and click the Find Next button or press Enter.

You can use the wildcard characters, ? (question mark) or * (asterisk), to stand for missing characters in the search text. The first time you select Find Next, Excel moves the cell cursor to cell A2 in the worksheet.

3. Continue to click the Find Next button to locate all the matches in the Find, Replace & Spell worksheet, and Excel returns the cell cursor to the cell with the first match.

Note that Excel considers the 2500 entered in cells A2, D2, and D5 as matches, but not the 2500 that's displayed in cell A7. This is because the 2500 in cell A7 is the calculated result of the formula =A5+A6 and not a static value entered on the Formula bar. The program also considers the date, May 25, 2007, entered in cell A17 as a match because of the 25 in the date.

4. Click the Options button in the Find and Replace dialog box to display the search options and select Values on the Look In drop-down list, and then select the Find All button to display the locations of all the cells with matching entries.

   This time, Excel considers the 2500 calculated in A7 as well as those entered into cells A2 and D5 as matches along with the May 25, 2007 date in cell A17. However, when Values is set as the Look In search option, the program no longer considers the $2,500.00 in D2 with its Currency Style number formatting as a match.

5. Select Comments in the Look In drop-down list in the Find and Replace dialog box and then select the Find Next button.

   Excel jumps the cell cursor to cell C12 in the spreadsheet.

6. Position the mouse pointer over cell C12 and verify that the comment attached to this cell contains the value 25.

   Excel considers this a match because the message, "We need 25 lbs." in the comment contains the value 25.

7. Modify the search text in the Find What box slightly by adding a comma between the 2 and the 5 so that **2,5?** now appears in this text box. Then, select Values again in the Look In drop-down list before you select the Find All button.

   Now, Excel considers $2,500.00 in D2 as the only match because none of the other 25s or 2500s have a comma between the 2 and 5 as these entries appear in the cells of the Find, Replace & Spell worksheet.

8. Modify the search text in the Find What box again by prefacing 500 with a question mark wildcard character so that **?500** appears in this text box. Then, select the Find All button.

   This time, Excel includes all the cells containing 2500 (including the $2,500.00 in cell D2) as matches as well as the 1500 entered into cell A6.

9. Select the Match Entire Cell Contents check box in the Find and Replace dialog box before you select the Find All button.

   When the Match Entire Cell Contents check box is selected, the $2,500.00 in cell D2 is no longer considered to be a match because of the decimal point and two zeros that trail the 500 (the question mark wildcard only pertains to characters that precede 500).

10. Click the Replace tab in the Find and Replace dialog box and then set up the following conditions:

    • Position the cell cursor in cell A1 of the Find, Replace & Spell worksheet.

    • Enter **25** in the Find What text box on the Replace tab.

    • Enter **27** in the Replace With text box on the Replace tab.

    • Deselect the Match Cell Entire Contents check box on the Replace tab.

11. Click the Find Next button in the Find and Replace dialog box to locate the first instance to be replaced.

    Excel positions the cell pointer in cell A2, the first cell containing an occurrence of the search text (25 in 2500).

12. Click the Replace button in the Find and Replace dialog box.

As soon as you click Replace, Excel changes 2500 in cell A2 to 2700 and immediately moves the cell cursor to the next instance of the search text in the worksheet (cell D2).

13. Continue to search out the remaining cells containing values of 2500 and replace them with 2700. Do not, however, replace the date, May 25, 2007 with May 27, 2007 in cell A17.

After Excel finds the final occurrence of your search text in the worksheet, the program no longer moves the cell pointer from the cell containing the last occurrence (cell A17 with May 25, 2007 in this case).

14. Select the 2007 Prod Sch worksheet by clicking its sheet tab and then use the Find and Replace feature to globally update the years in all the dates in the spreadsheet from 2007 to 2008.

Enter **2007** in the Find What text box and **2008** in the Replace With text box and then select the Replace All button — Excel then displays an alert dialog box indicating the number of replacements made (10 in this case).

Be extra careful with performing global replacements in your own worksheets as you can all too easily wreak havoc in the spreadsheet at the click of the Replace All button — should you make a major boo-boo with this feature, remember to hit the Undo button with all due haste.

15. Close the replacement alert dialog box and the Find and Replace dialog box and then rename the 2007 Prod Sch worksheet to **2008 Prod Sch** by editing its sheet tab. Click the Find, Replace & Spell sheet tab to select this worksheet and leave the *Exercise5-8.xlsx* workbook open for the following exercise.

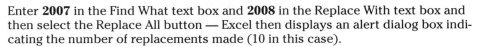

Exercise 5-9: Spell Checking the Worksheet

In Exercise 5-9, you get practice spell checking your worksheet to eliminate typos in your cell entries. You also find out how to add new words to the spelling dictionary.

1. Click cell A1 in the Find, Replace & Spell worksheet of the *Exercise5-8.xlsx* workbook and then click the Spelling command button on the Ribbon's Review tab or press F7 to spell check the entries in this worksheet.

Excel displays the Spelling: English dialog box and positions the cell cursor in E10 containing the unknown word Fetticine. This is a misspelling, so you must change it.

2. Accept the Spelling Checker's suggestion of Fettuccine by clicking the Change button.

Excel moves the cell cursor to the cell with the second unknown spelling, Maccaroni, in cell E12. This is also a misspelling, so you must change it.

3. Accept the Spelling Checker's suggestion of Macaroni by selecting the Change button.

The third unknown spelling occurs with Capellini in cell C14. This is a correct spelling so you can either ignore it once, ignore all occurrences, or add it to the dictionary.

4. Add the word to the dictionary by selecting the Add to Dictionary button.

When you click the Add to Dictionary button, Excel adds the unknown word to the main dictionary. If you wish to add the word to a custom dictionary, click the Options button in the Spelling dialog box to open the Excel Options dialog box with the Proofing tab selected. There, click the Custom Dictionaries button to open the Custom Dictionaries dialog box, where you can add a new custom dictionary or select one for spell checking your worksheet.

5. Close the alert dialog box indicating that the spelling check is complete by selecting OK, and then select cell A1. Save this edited version of the workbook under the filename **FindReplaceSpell.xlsx** in your Excel 2007 Practice folder. Then, close the workbook.

Group Editing

Group editing enables you to save time by making the same editing changes to multiple sheets in the workbook at the same time. To put Excel in Group Edit mode, all you have to do is select all the sheets in the current workbook that you want to edit together — Excel indicates that a workbook is in Group Edit mode by appending [Group] to its filename on the Excel program window's title bar.

Q. How do I select individual, non-adjacent worksheets to be included for group editing?

A. Ctrl+click the sheet tab of each worksheet you want to include in the group.

Q. How can I quickly select all the sheets in a workbook for group editing?

A. Right-click one of the sheet tabs and then select the Select All Sheets item on the shortcut menu.

Q. How can I easily take the workbook out of group editing mode?

A. Click any single visible sheet tab on the status bar other than the one for the active worksheet (indicated by the sheet tab name in bold lettering).

Solve It

Exercise 5-10: Editing Multiple Worksheets Selected as a Group

In Exercise 5-10, you get practice making simultaneous editing changes to three worksheets in a practice workbook that you select as a group. As long as these sheets are grouped together, any changes that you make to the active worksheet is reflected in all the others as well.

1. Open the *Exercise5-10.xl*s workbook file in the Chap5 folder inside your Excel 2007 Workbook folder.

   This version of the CG Media Sales workbook file contains three worksheets, 2005 Sales, 2006 Sales, and 2007 Sales, that you can use to practice group editing.

2. Examine each of the three worksheets by clicking their sheet tabs in succession and then return to the first sheet, 2005 Sales.

   As you can see, all three of these sales tables are laid out in a similar manner and all contain the same level of detail.

3. Select all three worksheets for group editing.

   To select a group of adjacent worksheets, hold down the Shift key as you click the tab of the last sheet in the group (2007 Sales in this case) — note the appearance of [Group] after the workbook's filename on the Excel program window's title bar as in Exercise5-10.xlsx [Group].

4. Click the Cell Styles button on the Ribbon's Home tab or press Alt+HJ to open the Cell Styles palette. Then, click the Title sample in the Titles and Headings section of this palette to apply this cell style to the spreadsheet title in cell A1.

   As soon as you click Title in the Cell Styles palette, Excel applies all of this style's formatting to the spreadsheet title in cell A1 of the 2005 Sales worksheet.

5. Verify that this Title style has been applied to cell A1 in the 2006 Sales sheet and then the 2007 Sales sheet by clicking their sheet tabs in succession.

   Note that the moment you click the sheet tab of the 2006 Sales worksheet, Excel automatically takes the workbook out of Group mode.

6. Click the 2005 Sales sheet tab again and then regroup the three worksheets, 2005 Sales, 2006 Sales, and 2007 Sales. Select the cell ranges A3:A15 and B2:R2 and then select the Heading 4 sample in the Cell Styles palette.

   Excel formats all the row and column headings in these two ranges in the Heading 4 style.

7. Select the cell ranges B4:R8 and B10:R15 and then click the Comma [0] cell style in the Number Format section of the Cell Styles palette.

   Excel formats all the values in these two selected ranges in Comma style number format with no decimal places.

8. Select the cell range A15:R15 and then click the Total sample in the Titles and Headings section of the Cell Styles palette.

   Excel formats all the cells in this range with the formatting included in the Total cell style (bold text and a double-underline in the cells).

9. Edit the heading in cell A14 so that instead of Total Cassette Sales, this row heading now reads Total Tape Sales.

Now it's time to verify that all the editing changes that you've made to the sales table in the 2005 Sales worksheet have been picked up and applied in the 2006 and 2007 worksheets.

10. Click the 2006 Sales sheet tab and the 2007 Sales sheet tab in succession to verify that all of the editing changes you made to the first worksheet are made as well on the other two worksheets.

Note how much time you saved by making these changes in a group rather than to the individual worksheets.

11. Select cell A1 on the 2005 Sales sheet and then save your edited workbook under the filename **CGMedia 05-07 - groupedit.xlsx** in your Excel 2007 Practice folder before you close the workbook.

Part II
Using Formulas and Functions

The 5th Wave   By Rich Tennant

Spreadsheet
Creation
.50¢ - Min.

In this part . . .

Formulas and spreadsheets go together like cake and ice cream, and the chapters that make up Part II are full of exercises that give you a chance to create formulas of almost every flavor. Here, you get a taste of every kind of function that Excel has to offer. You also have an opportunity to practice building and copying the types of basic formulas that are a sure recipe for success in any spreadsheet you create.

Chapter 6
Building Formulas

*N*o one disputes that formulas are the center of almost every spreadsheet you create. Being able to build formulas (both those that perform simple arithmetic calculations as well as those that perform more sophisticated computations using Excel's built-in functions) is a critical skill. The exercises in this chapter give you a chance to practice building both types of formulas as well as modifying how and when the formulas in the spreadsheet are recalculated.

Building Formulas

All the formulas you build in an Excel spreadsheet, regardless of their function and degree of complexity, have one thing in common: They all begin with one simple character, = (the equal-to sign). Typing an equal-to sign activates the Enter and Cancel buttons on the Formula bar. It also changes the nature of the Name Box drop-down box so that its list displays commonly-used functions rather than the range names assigned to the workbook.

If you forget to type this as your initial character when creating formulas by hand (Excel is always sure to put one in for you when you build formulas with the Insert Function button), the program inserts the string of operands and operators you enter as a text reference.

If you build a legitimate formula, Excel either computes the answer and displays it in the current cell in the worksheet or, if unable to successfully calculate the answer, the program displays one of the following error values in the cell:

- ✓ **#NULL!** appears when your formula specifies an intersection of two ranges that do not, in fact, intersect

- ✓ **#DIV/0!** appears when your formula attempts to divide by zero

- ✓ **#VALUE!** appears when your formula contains some sort of improper argument type or operand (such as a text entry when the operator requires a value)

- ✓ **#REF!** appears when your formula contains an improper cell reference

- ✓ **#NAME?** appears when your formula contains a text reference that Excel doesn't recognize (such as a reference to a range name that no longer exists in the workbook)

- ✓ **#NUM!** appears when your formula contains invalid numeric values (such as a text entry where a number is required)

- ✓ **#N/A** appears when your formula refers to a value that is not available to it

Building formulas by hand

To build a formula by hand, all you have to do is type an = (equal-to) sign and then designate the string of operands and operators that the formula should use in making its calculation(s). Operands can be constants that you type into the formula (such as 5.5 or 100), or they can be cell references (such as B5 or A10:J17) that you point directly to in the worksheet or type.

Table 6-1 shows you a list of all the operators, including their type, character, and operation.

Table 6-1	The Different Types of Operators in Excel Formulas		
Type	*Character*	*Operation*	*Example*
Arithmetic			
	+ (plus sign)	Addition	=A2+B3
	- (minus sign)	Subtraction or negation	=A3-A2 or -C4
	* (asterisk)	Multiplication	=A2*B3
	/	Division	=B3/A2
	%	Percent (dividing by 100)	=B3%
	^	Exponentiation	=A2^3

Type	Character	Operation	Example
Comparison			
	=	Equal to	=A2=B3
	>	Greater than	=B3>A2
	<	Less than	=A2<B3
	>=	Greater than or equal to	=B3>=A2
	<=	Less than or equal to	=A2<=B3
	<>	Not equal to	=A2<>B3
Text			
	&	Concatenates (connects) entries to produce one continuous entry	=A2&" "&B3
Reference			
	: (colon)	Range operator that includes all cells between the colon	=SUM(C4:D17)
	, (comma)	Union operator that combines multiple references into one reference	=SUM(A2,C4:D17,B3)
	(space)	Intersection operator that produces one reference to cells in common with two references	=SUM(C3:C6 C3:E6)

Before you attempt Exercise 6-1, you may want to play the Formulas with Arithmetic Operators.exe demo located in the Excel Feature Demos folder on your workbook CD-ROM. This feature demonstration shows you how to build simple formulas using a range name as well as the addition, subtraction, multiplication, division, and exponentiation operators.

Solve It

Exercise 6-1: Building Simple Arithmetic Formulas

In Exercise 6-1, you get practice building various types of simple arithmetic formulas by hand. In creating these formulas, you get experience building a formula by pointing to its cell references. You also get experience with using a range name as a cell reference and referring to a cell reference in your formulas (the so-called *external* reference).

1. If Excel 2007 is not already running, launch the program.

You'll use the first two blank worksheets of the Book1 workbook as practice worksheets for building your formulas.

Solve It

Exercise 4-7: Printing All the Sheets in a Workbook

In Exercise 4-7, you get practice printing an entire workbook containing worksheets with annual sales data for four years (2005 through 2008) as a single report. This report will contain a single header and footer:

1. Open the *Exercise4-7.xlsx* workbook file in the Chap4 folder of the Excel 2007 Workbook folder.

This worksheet contains four years of CG Media annual sales data that you will print in a single report.

2. Open the Print dialog box (Ctrl+P) and then select the Entire Workbook option button in the Print What section before clicking the Preview button to open the Print Preview window.

Excel displays the first page of a 12-page report in the Print Preview window.

3. Check out all 12 pages of the report in the Print Preview window.

Note that pages 4, 5, 7, and 8 have columns too narrow to print the data (indicated by #####s in their cells). Also, note that the gridlines are turned on in pages 10, 11, and 12 that print the 2005 annual sales data.

4. Click the Show Margins check box in the Print Preview tab to turn on the margin and column markers and then use the column markers to widen the columns that are too narrow to display the sales data on pages 4, 5, 7, and 8.

Next, you need to remove the gridlines from the printed pages for 2005 sales data on pages 10, 11, and 12.

5. Close the Print Preview window and then click the Sales 05 sheet tab to make this worksheet active. Click the Print check box under Gridlines in the Sheet Options group of the Ribbon's Page Layout tab to deselect it.

Now, you need to add a header and footer to each worksheet that identifies it in the printed report. The header will be a custom one that displays the name of the worksheet in the left-hand section and the word, Confidential!, in the right-hand section. The footer will be a standard one that prints the current page number and the total page number as in Page 1 of 12.

6. Click the Sales 08 sheet tab and then click the Page Layout button on the Status bar. Next, click the Click to Add Header text in the header area and then click the left-hand section to select it and click the Sheet Name button to insert &[Tab] code. Next, click the right-hand section and then type the text, **Confidential!,** into this section. Finally, click the Footer button on the Ribbon and click the Page 1 of ? option on its drop-down menu to insert these codes for this prefab footer.

In the custom header for the Sales 08 worksheet at the top of the page, Sales 08 appears aligned with the left margin and Confidential! appears aligned with the right. The prefabricated footer at the bottom reads Page 1 of 3.

2. Change the name of Sheet1 of the worksheet to **Formulas** and that of Sheet2 to **Ext Ref**.

   Next, you'll group the two sheets together (by Shift+clicking the second sheet's tab) so that you can increase the magnification setting for both sheets in a single operation.

3. Group the Formulas and Ext Ref sheets together by Shift+clicking their tabs and then use the Zoom slider on the Status bar to increase the worksheet display magnification percentage for the two sheets to 170%.

   This increased magnification will make it easier to see what you're doing as you build your first formulas.

4. Right-click the Formulas sheet tab and then click the Ungroup Sheets option on its shortcut menu. Then, enter the value **42** in cell A2 of the Formulas worksheet and then name this cell **Source**.

   To give a range name to the current cell, click the Name Box on the Formula Bar, type the range name (with no spaces between letters or words), and then press the Enter key.

5. Select cell A4 in the Formulas worksheet and then type = (equal-to sign) to start a new formula, and click cell A2.

   The formula you're in the process of entering into cell A4 now reads =**Source**, both in the cell and on the Formula bar. A marquee showing the cell named Source is displayed in cell A2.

6. Click the Enter button (the one with the check mark) on the Formula bar to complete the formula entry in cell A4.

   The formula in cell A4 now returns 42 as its answer — this formula consists solely of an external reference to cell A2, the cell you named Source, so whatever value you enter into the source cell is immediately brought forward and *dynamically* copied to cell A4.

7. Update the value in the source cell, A2, from 42 to **128**.

   Because the link between cell A4 and A2 was created by your formula with the external reference, cell A4 of the worksheet now contains 128 as well.

8. Enter the following values into the designated cells of the Formulas worksheet:
   - **34** in cell B4
   - **47.5** in cell B5
   - **2.2** in cell B6
   - **10%** in cell B7
   - **3** in cell B8

9. Create an addition formula in cell C4 that adds the value in cell A4 to that in cell B4 by pointing to these cells:
   - Position the cell cursor in cell C4.
   - Type =.

- Press ← twice to select cell A4 (the first operand).

- Type + (the addition operator).

- Press ← once to select B4 (the second operand).

- If the formula reads =A4+B4, click the Enter button on the Formula bar.

10. Use this same pointing technique to create an addition formula in cell A5 that adds 5 to the value in cell A4 above.

The addition formula in cell A5 should read =A4+5 on the Formula bar and the answer should appear as 133 in the cell.

11. With the cell cursor in cell A5, drag the Fill handle down to the cell range A6:A8.

Excel copies the original formula you entered into cell A5 down to cells A6, A7, and A8, which now contain the calculated values, 138, 143, and 148, respectively.

12. Build the following arithmetic formulas in the designated cells:

- Subtraction formula in cell C5 that subtracts the value in cell B5 from that in cell A5 — remember that - (hyphen or dash) is the subtraction operator in Excel.

- Division formula in cell C6 that divides the value in cell A6 by that in B6 — remember that / (forward slash) is the division operator in Excel.

- Multiplication formula in cell C7 that multiplies the value in cell A7 by that in B7 — remember that * (asterisk) is the multiplication operator in Excel.

- Exponentiation formula in cell C8 that raises the value in cell A8 by that in cell B8 — remember that ^ (caret) is the exponentiation operator in Excel.

13. Use the Side by Side feature to check your formulas against those in the Formulas worksheet in the *Solved6-1.xlsx* workbook in the Chap6 folder of the Excel 2007 Workbook folder.

Make sure that not only your answers in the cells of this worksheet agree, but the contents of the formulas agree, as well.

14. When everything checks out, save the new workbook with the arithmetic formulas you built with the filename **Practice Formulas.xlsx** in your Excel 2007 Practice folder after closing the *Solved6-1.xlsx* file. Leave the *Practice Formulas.xlsx* workbook open with the Formulas worksheet active for the next exercise.

Exercise 6-2: Building Comparative Formulas

Arithmetic formulas in the spreadsheet (when properly formed) always return numeric results. Excel supports another type of formula, known as a comparative formula, which returns only one of two possible results, TRUE or FALSE. In Exercise 6-2, you get practice in creating these types of formulas.

1. Use the Formulas worksheet of the *Practice Formulas.xlsx* workbook that you created in Exercise 6-1 to get some experience with building comparative formulas.

Now you will add comparative formulas to this worksheet that indicate whether different comparisons in the worksheet are true or false.

2. Build a comparative formula in cell D4 that weighs the value in cell A4 against that in B4 and indicates whether they are equal to each other:

   • Type = in cell D4 to begin the formula

   • Press the ← key three times to select cell A4

   • Type = again, this time as the comparative operator

   • Press the ← key twice to select cell B4 so that the formula now reads =A4=B4

   • Click the Enter button on the Formula bar to complete the formula and compute the result (which is FALSE because the values in these two cells are not currently equal to one another)

   When you complete this formula, Excel enters the logical value FALSE into cell D4 because the values currently in cells A4 (128) and B4 (34) are not equal to one another.

3. Build the following comparative formulas in the designated cells:

   • In cell D5, a formula that compares the value in cell A5 to that in cell B5 and indicates whether the one in A5 is larger than the one in B5 — use the > (greater than) symbol as the operator.

   • In cell D6, a formula that compares the value in cell A6 to that in cell B6 and indicates whether the one in A6 is smaller than the one in B6 — use the < (less than) symbol as the operator.

   • In cell D8, a formula that compares the value in cell A8 to that in cell B8 and indicates whether the one in A8 is unequal to the one in B8 — use the <> (less than and greater than back to back) symbols as the operator.

   Then, note that Excel returns TRUE in cell D5 because the value currently in cell A5 (133) is larger than that in cell B5 (47.5). And Excel returns FALSE in cell D6 because the value currently in cell A6 (138) is not less than that in cell B6 (2.2). Finally, Excel returns TRUE in cell D8 because the current values in cells A8 (148) and B8 (3) certainly are unequal to one another.

4. Change the value in the Source cell, A2, from 128 to **34**.

   Check the contents of your formulas against those shown in Figure 6-1.

   Note how Excel immediately updates all the formulas in columns A, C, and D whose computations depend in some way on this value. The answers change from FALSE to TRUE in cell D4 and TRUE to FALSE in cell D5 and remain unchanged in cells D6 and D8.

5. Save your changes to your *Practice Formulas.xlsx* workbook before proceeding on to Exercise 6-3.

Figure 6-1:
The
Formulas
sheet of
*Practice
Formulas
.xlsx* with
all its arith-
metic and
comparative
formulas
displayed in
their cells.

Solve It

Exercise 6-3: Working with Error Values in Formulas

Well-designed spreadsheets contain many dependent formulas like your *Practice Formulas.xls* workbook. The problem comes when any of the formulas on which they depend return one of those dreaded error values covered earlier in this chapter. When that happens, the error values spread like wildfire to all the dependent formulas, making it very difficult, if not impossible, to identify the source of the problem. In Exercise 6-3, you use the formulas in your Formulas sheet of the *Practice Formulas.xlsx* workbook to get some experience with the error values that formulas can return and how they infect all dependent formulas in a spreadsheet.

1. Click the Name Manager button in the Defined Names group on the Ribbon's Formulas tab or press Alt+MN to open the Name Manager dialog box. Click Source to select it in the list box and then click the Delete button at the top of the Name Manager and OK in the alert dialog box before you click the Close button.

As soon as you click Close to close the Name Manager dialog box, most of the cells in this spreadsheet contain the #NAME? error value because every formula you created in this worksheet is dependent in some way upon the *Source* range name, inheriting this error value from the original formula in cell B4 with the external reference the moment you delete its name.

2. Click the Undo button on the Quick Access toolbar or press Ctrl+Z to restore the *Source* range name to the workbook.

You can tell that Excel restored the range name because those awful #NAME? error values all disappear from the Formulas worksheet.

3. Now click cell B6 and press the Delete key to delete the value (2.2) in cell B6.

As soon as you empty cell B6, a #DIV/0! error value is returned by the division formula in cell C6. This is because all empty cells in any Excel worksheet carry the value of zero, and this is why #DIV/0! is the most common type of error value to plague spreadsheets. Often, a template or new spreadsheet you create contains division formulas referring to empty cells for which you do not have or have not yet entered values. These all naturally return #DIV/0! error values (in Chapter 12, you find out how to create formulas that prevent this type of error value by using the IF function).

4. Use Undo to restore the original 2.2 value to cell B6.

The moment you restore the value to cell B6, the #DIV/0! error value disappears from cell C6.

5. In cell B7, replace 10% with the text **ten percent** to see what effect this has on the multiplication formula entered in cell C7.

Although it's possible to build formulas that deal with text, the one in cell C7 is not one of them. When you enter *ten percent* as a text entry in cell B7, its formula essentially chokes, returning the #VALUE! error value to the cell.

6. Use Undo to restore the original 10% value to the cell.

As soon as you restore the original numerical value of 10% to cell B7, Excel removes the #VALUE! error value from cell C7.

7. Leave your *Practice Formulas.xlsx* workbook open for the next exercise on building formulas using a few of Excel's built-in functions.

Building formulas with built-in functions

Excel offers you a wide assortment of built-in functions that can save valuable time in creating the formulas needed in your spreadsheet. In place of the operands and operators of your hand-made formulas, built-in functions use function names and arguments. All the Excel functions follow the general syntax of the SUM function, the most widely used spreadsheet function:

```
=SUM(number1,number2, . . .)
```

Note the following about this syntax in this example:

✔ The function name is always shown in all caps because Excel automatically displays it that way on the Formula bar regardless of what case you use in entering its name. (This means that there are no case restrictions when typing in the function name — you just have to be careful to spell its name correctly.)

✔ The argument(s) used by the function immediately follow the function name and they are enclosed in a balanced pair of parentheses — this means that for every open parenthesis [(], you need a close parenthesis [)].

✔ The functions that require or can take more than a single argument separate the individual arguments within the parentheses with commas.

Even functions such as NOW that take no arguments require the use of a pair of parentheses to finish them off; for example, =NOW(). If you omit the empty pair of parentheses, Excel fails to recognize the function and returns the #NAME? error value to its cell.

Excel classifies each of its built-in functions into one of eleven categories (with a twelfth being custom functions that you define yourself). Six of these functions are available from dedicated command buttons on the Ribbon's Formulas tab, and all of them are available from the Insert Function dialog box, which you open by clicking the Insert Function at the very beginning of the Formulas tab or the Insert Function button right on the Formula bar (both use the *fx* marking).

Building a formula from the Insert Function dialog box carries many benefits. Besides starting your formula by automatically entering the requisite = (equal-to) symbol on the Formula bar for you, this dialog box, shown in Figure 6-2, contains the following features that aid you in locating and using any function:

- ✔ **Search for a Function** enables you to look for a function by entering a brief description of the kind of calculation you want to do.

- ✔ **Or Select a Category** enables you to find a function by selecting a category (Financial, Date & Time, and so on) other than the default Most Recently Used that keeps a record of the most commonly used functions, including the ones you've used most recently.

- ✔ **Select a Function** enables you to display syntax information showing you the arguments plus a short description on any function you select in this list box.

- ✔ **Help on This Function** displays online help (that you can also print) about the usage and arguments required by the function currently selected in the Select a Function list box.

As soon as you select your function in the Insert Function dialog box by selecting it and clicking OK, Excel not only inserts the skeleton of the function on the Formula bar, but also displays a Function Arguments dialog box for the function, which you can use in selecting the cell references and values to be used in the computation.

Figure 6-2:
The Insert Function dialog box directs you in correctly adding any Excel function to a formula in the spreadsheet.

Q. Can I mix built-in functions with hand-made formulas?

A. Yes, most definitely: Excel functions can serve as operands in any formula that you construct manually, as in =SUM(A5:J10)^2 to square the total of the range of values in the cell range A5:J10 of the worksheet returned by the SUM function.

Before you attempt Exercise 6-4, you may want to play the Formulas via AutoSum.exe demo located in the Excel Feature Demos folder on your workbook CD-ROM. This feature demonstration shows you how to build SUM formulas with the AutoSum button on the Home tab and then copy them to new cell ranges.

Exercise 6-4: Building Formulas with the AutoSum Command Button

In Exercise 6-4, use the Formulas worksheet of your *Practice Formulas.xls* workbook to get some experience using the SUM, AVERAGE, and COUNT functions in the spreadsheet. These functions are so frequently used that Excel doesn't even require you to access them from the Insert Function dialog box, making them readily available from the AutoSum command button on the Ribbon's Home tab.

1. Drag through the cell range A4:A8 to select all their values in the Formulas worksheet of your *Practice Formulas.xlsx* workbook.

Note that the Average, Count, and Sum indicators on the Status bar immediately show you that the average of the values selected is 44, the count 5, and the total 220.

2. Click cell A9 in the Formulas worksheet and then click the AutoSum command button in the Editing group at the end of the Home tab (the one with sigma Σ on it — be sure not to click its drop-down button to open its menu).

Excel immediately responds by entering the SUM formula, =SUM(A4:A8), in cell A9. Note that the program also places a marquee bounding box around the cell range A4:A8 in the worksheet as well as selects the argument A4:A8 in the SUM function itself. This enables you to modify the range or ranges of cells to be totaled by the SUM function either by editing its argument in the function or dragging the boundaries of its marquee.

3. Click the Enter button on the Formula bar to complete this formula in cell A9.

Excel enters the formula =SUM(A4:A8) in this cell as shown on the Formula bar and displays the total of the range, 220, in the cell.

4. This time, click the drop-down button attached to the AutoSum command button on the Home tab and select Average on its drop-down list.

Excel now enters the formula =AVERAGE(A4:A8) for your editing or approval in cell A9.

5. Click the Enter button on the Formula bar to enter this formula in the cell.

Excel enters the formula =AVERAGE(A4:A8) in this cell as shown on the Formula bar, and displays the average of the range, 44, in the cell.

6. Click the Undo button on the Quick Access toolbar or press Ctrl+Z to restore the SUM formula in cell A9. Click cell B9 and then select the Count Numbers option on the AutoSum button's drop-down menu before you click the Enter button on the Formula bar to create a formula in cell B9 that returns the number of values in the range B4:B8.

The formula you construct in cell B9 reads =COUNT(B4:B8) and this formula returns 5 as its result.

7. Replace the value 10% in cell B7 with the text entry **ten**.

   Ignoring the reappearance of the #VALUE! error in cell C7 for the moment, note that the result returned to cell B9 changes from 5 to 4, indicating that the COUNT function counts *only* the numeric entries in the cells you include in its argument.

8. Restore 10% to cell B7 with Undo, position the cell cursor in cell C9, and click the Insert Function button on the Formula bar.

   Excel opens the Insert Function dialog box, where you can select any function built into or added to the program.

9. Move the Insert Function dialog box to the right out of the way of the values in your spreadsheet. Select Most Recently Used as the category and then click SUM in the Select a Function list box before you click OK.

   Excel opens the Function Arguments dialog box and supplies what the program finds as the most logical cell range address (C4:C8) in its Number1 Argument text box.

10. Drag through the cell range A4:A8 to replace the default Number1 argument of C4:C8 with this range.

    Note how Excel automatically condenses the Function Arguments dialog box down to just the text box for the Number1 argument as you drag through the cell range and then immediately restores the dialog box the moment you release the mouse button.

11. Press Tab or click the Number2 argument text box and then drag through the cell range B4:B8 to select this range as the second to be included in the total.

    Note that as soon as you select the Number2 argument text box, Excel adds a Number3 text box to the Function Arguments dialog box.

12. Designate the cell range C4:C8 as the third argument in the Number3 argument text box.

    Note that the Function Arguments dialog box shows the subtotals of each of the three ranges you've selected immediately following their respective argument text boxes and that the Formula bar now contains the whole SUM formula ready for insertion into cell C9:

    ```
    =SUM(A4:A8,B4:B8,C4:C8)
    ```

13. Click OK to close the Function Arguments dialog box and enter the SUM formula into cell C9.

    Excel enters the SUM function into cell C9 — the formula with this function appears on the Formula bar and the result of totaling these three cell ranges (157855) appears in cell C9.

14. Save your changes to a workbook named **Practice Formulas – Ex6-4.xlsx** in your Excel 2007 Practice folder and leave the workbook open for the next exercise.

Editing formulas

Editing a formula, especially one that uses a function with multiple arguments, can take a little getting used to. Fortunately, Excel makes formula editing within the cells of the worksheet as easy as it can by isolating the ranges and displaying them in different color bounding boxes when you put the program in Edit mode.

The only problem comes when you're dealing with a formula so complex and long that its contents can't be displayed within the worksheet display. Fortunately, on the rare occasion when this occurs, you can still edit the formula on the Formula bar as it automatically expands its rows to accommodate the extra length.

Solve It

Exercise 6-5: Editing Formulas in a Worksheet

In Exercise 6-5, use the formulas you created in the Formulas worksheet of your *Practice Formulas – Ex6-4.xlsx* workbook to get some experience with formula editing. In this exercise, make changes to the SUM formula you previously constructed in cell C9 that totals the three ranges A4:A8, B4:B8, and C4:C8.

1. If the cell cursor is not already in cell C9, click this cell before you press F2 to put Excel into Edit mode.

Excel responds by displaying the contents of the SUM formula in cell C9 of the worksheet. The addresses of each of the cell ranges in the three arguments of this SUM function appear in a different color and each of these colors corresponds to that of the bounding box that encloses its cell range in the worksheet.

2. Use ← to move the insertion point through the arguments in the SUM function until the insertion point is flashing between the 8 in the A8 and the comma that follows the first A4:A8 argument.

Note as you move the insertion point to the left through the SUM function how the syntax for the SUM function appears right below it and how Excel displays the number3, number2, and finally the number1 argument in bold as the insertion point travels through the cell range in the equivalent argument in the function above.

3. Hold down the Shift key as press the ← key to select and highlight the range A4:A8 (from right to left).

4. Redefine the number1 argument by dragging through the cell range A2:A8 in the worksheet.

A moving marquee appears in the cells you select as you redefine the cell range for the number1 argument in the SUM function.

5. Check the formula on the Formula bar in cell C9 to make sure that cell range for the number1 argument of the SUM function is now A2:A8. Next click the Enter button on the Formula bar to complete the editing of the formula in cell C9.

The result in cell C9 changes from 157855 to 157889 and the edited SUM formula appears on the Formula bar as =SUM(A2:A8,B4:B8,C4:C8).

6. Click the Comma Style button on the Home tab to format the result in cell C9 with this number format.

Excel displays the result as 157,899.20 in cell C9 and automatically widens column C to display the value in the Comma Style format with two decimal places.

7. Save your editing changes to the formula in cell C9 in a workbook file named **Practice Formulas – Ex6-5.xlsx** in your Excel 2007 Practice folder. Leave this file open for the next exercise.

Altering the natural order of operations

When you build a formula that combines different operators, Excel follows the order of precedence shown in Table 6-2. When you use operators that share the same precedence level, the program performs the calculations on the operands in a strictly left-to-right order.

Table 6-2	Natural Order of Operator Precedence in Formulas	
Precedence	*Operator*	*Type/Function*
1	–	Negation
2	%	Percent
3	^	Exponentiation
4	* and /	Multiplication and Division
5	+ and –	Addition and Subtraction
6	&	Concatenation
7	=, <, >, <=, >=, <>	All Comparative Operators

Sometimes, you need to override the natural order of precedence in order to get your formula to return the desired result. To override the natural order, you enclose the operand and operator of the operation you want performed first in parentheses.

For more complicated formulas, you may end up nesting sets of parentheses one within the other in order to obtain the desired computation order. When this is the case, Excel always performs the calculation within the innermost set of parentheses working its way out according to the sequence shown in Table 6-2.

Solve It

Exercise 6-6: Changing the Order in Which Formulas Are Calculated

In Exercise 6-6, use the Formulas sheet of your *Practice Formulas – Ex6-5.xlsx* workbook to construct several new formulas and then experiment with adding parentheses to see what effect they have on the computed results.

1. Enter the following values in designated cells in the Formulas worksheet in your *Practice Formulas - Ex6-5.xlsx* workbook:

   - **100** in cell B11
   - **50** in cell C11
   - **2** in cell D11

2. Position the cell cursor in cell E11 and construct and enter the following formula:

   `=B11+C11/D11`

   Instead of an answer of 75, Excel returns one of 125 because it performs the division between cell C11 and D11 (50/2=25) with its higher level of precedence of 4 before doing the addition between cell B11 and C11 (100+25) with its lower precedence level of 5.

3. With the cell cursor in cell E11, press F2 to put Excel in Edit mode.

4. Press the ← key until the insertion point is located between the = and the B in B11, and then type **(** — a open parenthesis. Then, press the → key until the insertion point is between the second 1 in C11 and the / and then type **)** — a close parenthesis.

   The edited formula should appear as follows in cell C11:

   `=(B11+C11)/D11`

5. Click the Enter button on the Formula bar to complete the edit of the formula in cell E11.

   After the addition of the parentheses, the formula returns the result of 75, showing that it now performed the addition between cell B11 and C11 first (100+50) and then divided that result by the value in D11 (150/2).

6. Enter the following values in designated cells:

   - **300** in cell A13
   - **200** in cell B13
   - **100** in cell C13
   - **2** in cell D13

7. Position the cell cursor in cell E13 and enter the following formula:

   `=A13+B13-C13/D13`

   Note that Excel returns a result of 450 when you enter this formula because, following the natural order of precedence, it performs the computations as follows:

   - C13/D13 or 100/2 = 50 to cell C13
   - A13+B13 or 300 + 200 = 500 to cell B13
   - B13-C13 or 500 – 50 = 450 to cell E13

8. Use pairs of parentheses to alter the computation order in the formula in E13 so that Excel performs the subtraction between cells B13 and C13 first, adds this result to the value in cell A13, and then, finally, divides the result of that addition by the value in D13, giving you a final result of 200.

When editing this formula, begin by enclosing the first operation to be performed inside a pair of parentheses (B13-C13), and then enclose the second operation in a second pair of parentheses, (A13+(B13-C13)) so that edited formula appears as

```
=(A13+(B13-C13))/D13
```

9. With the cell cursor in cell E13, display all the formulas in the cells of the worksheet, widening column E and reducing the display magnification percentage as needed so that you can see all the formulas on your screen. (Check your results against those shown in Figure 6-3 with the Formulas worksheet at 130% of normal magnification.)

   Note that in this display mode, when the cell cursor is in a cell that contains a formula, Excel employs the same type of color coding as it does when you edit a formula in its cell. The colors assigned to the cell references within the formula correspond to that of the bounding box surrounding the actual cell or cell range in the worksheet.

10. Use the arrow keys to move the cell cursor to other cells in this spreadsheet that contain formulas, including cell C9.

11. Turn off the display of the formulas in the worksheet, set the magnification of the Formulas worksheet to 150% of normal, select cell C9, and then save your changes in a workbook named **Practice Formulas – Ex6-6.xlsx** in your Excel 2007 Practice folder. Leave this version of the workbook file open for the next exercise.

Figure 6-3: The Formulas sheet of the revised *Practice Formulas – Ex6-5.xlsx* workbook, with all its formulas displayed in the worksheet.

Using External Reference Links

External references in a formula are those that refer to cells outside of the current worksheet, either on other sheets of the same workbook file or in sheets in other workbook files. Because their cells reside outside of the current worksheet, it isn't sufficient to specify the cell reference only, as you do with purely local cell references.

When you refer to a cell that resides in another worksheet of the same workbook, you preface the cell address with the sheet name separated by an exclamation point (!), following this syntax:

```
Sheet1!A1
```

When you refer to a cell that resides in a sheet in another workbook file, you need to include the filename (enclosed in square brackets) as well as the sheet name (enclosed in a pair of single quotation marks) and cell reference, following this syntax:

```
'[file.xls]Sheet1'!A1
```

Many times, you use external references to create links to values in another sheet that need to be brought forward to the new worksheet. When you set up a link rather than just pasting in a static value, any changes made to the value in the original cell are automatically updated in the linked cell.

The easiest way to create an external reference link is to click the Copy button on the Home tab (Ctrl+C) to copy the cell to the Clipboard. Switch to the cell where you want to set up the link and then paste it with the Paste Link option on the Paste button's drop-down menu (Alt+HVN).

Solve It **Exercise 6-7: Building Formulas with External Links**

In Exercise 6-7, use your *Practice Formulas – Ex6-6.xlsx* workbook to get experience with constructing links using external references.

1. With the cell cursor in cell C9 of the Formulas worksheet that contains the SUM formula totaling the values in the cell ranges A2:A8, B4:B8, and C4:C8, copy the contents of this cell to the Clipboard (Ctrl+C).

   Now, paste a link to this formula in a cell in the second worksheet in your workbook named Ext Ref.

2. Click the Ext Ref sheet tab in the workbook to select this worksheet and then position the cell cursor in cell B3.

   Next, you will paste a link to the formula in cell C9 of the initial Formulas worksheet.

3. Choose Paste | Paste Link in the Clipboard section of the Ribbon's Home tab or press Alt+HVN. Then, use AutoFit to widen column B.

   The value 157889.20 appears in cell B3 of the Ext Ref sheet and the following link formula with the external reference appears on the Formula bar:

   ```
   =Formulas!$C$9
   ```

4. Enter the heading **Formulas Sheet Total** in cell A3 and then widen column A of the Ext Ref sheet sufficiently to display the entire heading.

Next, you will change a value in a cell of the Formulas worksheet that is referenced in the SUM function in the original formula.

5. Switch back to the Formulas worksheet by clicking its sheet tab and then change the value in the source cell A2 of this sheet from 34 to **56**.

Note the effect that increasing this source value has on the total in cell C9 of this Formulas worksheet.

6. Click the Ext Ref sheet tab and verify that cell B3 in this worksheet now contains the same value as C9 in the Formulas worksheet, thanks to the linking formula you created there.

Linking formulas are automatically updated whenever values in the cell they refer to change.

7. Click the New button on the customized Quick Access toolbar or press Ctrl+N to open a new blank workbook.

Excel opens a blank Book2 workbook file.

8. Enter the heading **Practice Formulas Workbook Total** in cell A2, widen column A to display the entire heading, increase the display magnification percentage to 170%, and then save the Book2 workbook file with the filename **External WrkBk Link.xlsx** in your Excel 2007 Practice folder.

Now you will copy a link to the original SUM formula in cell C9 of the Formulas sheet in your *Practice Formulas – Ex6-6.xlsx* workbook file.

9. Click the *Practice Formulas* button on the Windows taskbar to activate this Excel file and then click the Formulas tab to select this worksheet and copy the original formula in cell C9 to the Clipboard (Ctrl+C).

Next, you need to switch over to your *External Wrkbk Link.xlsx* workbook file where you will paste the link.

10. Click the *External WrkBk* button on the Windows taskbar to activate this new Excel file and then select cell B2 of its Sheet1 before you click the Paste Link option on the Paste button's drop-down list or press Alt+HVN. Then, use AutoFit to widen column B to display the contents of cell B2.

The value 439,589.40 appears in cell B2 of the Sheet1 worksheet and the following link formula with the external reference appears on the Formula bar:

```
='[Practice Formulas - Ex6-6.xlsx]Formulas'!$C$9
```

11. Save your changes to the *External WrkBk Link.xlsx* workbook and then close this workbook file.

As soon as you close the *External WrkBk Link.xlsx* file, Excel returns you to the Formulas sheet of your *Practice Formulas – Ex6-6.xlsx* workbook.

12. Select cell A2 in the Formulas sheet and then update the value in this cell from 56 to **72**.

As soon as you enter this new value, Excel automatically updates all the formulas on this worksheet that refer to this cell.

13. Check that the contents in cell B3 of the Ext Ref sheet has been updated to 779,438.27 to reflect the change to the value in cell C9 of the Formulas sheet. Then, switch back to the Formulas sheet, save your changes to this workbook with the same filename, *Practice Formulas – Ex6-6.xlsx,* in your Excel 2007 Practice folder, and close this file.

Now, open the *External WrkBk Link.xlsx* file to see what happens when you open an external workbook file containing a link to a formula or value in another workbook whose result has changed.

14. Open the *External WrkBk Link.xlsx* workbook by selecting it from the Recent Documents list on the Office pull-down menu (Alt+F).

Note the Security Warning banner that appears at the top of the worksheet display when this workbook opens. This warning indicates that Excel has automatically disabled the updating of the links in this file.

15. Click the Options button in the Security Warning banner to open Microsoft Office Security Options dialog box.

This dialog box contains two option buttons:

- **Help Protect Me from Unknown Content (Recommended):** The default option selected to prevent external links from being updated.

- **Enable This Content:** The option to have Excel go ahead and update all the external links in the workbook (select this option only when, as in this case, you know and trust the files to which this workbook is linked).

16. Click the Enable This Content option button in Microsoft Office Security Options dialog box and then click OK.

Excel closes the Microsoft Office Security Options dialog box as well as the Security Warning banner in the worksheet. The program also updates the value in cell B2 of Sheet1 to 779,438.27. Note that the external reference displayed on the Formula bar now contains the entire path name for the workbook file along with its sheet and cell reference.

17. Save this change to the *External WrkBk Link.xlsx* workbook and then close the file.

Controlling When Formulas Are Recalculated

As you've seen in the exercises in this chapter, Excel immediately and automatically recalculates all the formulas in a worksheet the moment you make a change to any cell referred to in its formulas. This automatic recalculation mode is fine as long as your spreadsheet is relatively small and your edits to it are few.

Working in this mode can, however, be a real drag (both literally and figuratively) when the worksheet is large and contains lots and lots of formulas: You may be forced to wait quite a few seconds while Excel recalculates every loving formula before you can do anything more after each and every editing change you make.

To avoid this hassle, change the recalculation mode from automatic to manual on the Calculation Options drop-down menu on the Ribbon's Formula tab (Alt+MXM) so that Excel recalculates the formulas in the worksheet only when you specifically tell it to by selecting the Calculate Now or Calculate Sheet command button on the Formulas tab, press F9, or save changes to the workbook.

Solve It

Exercise 6-8: Controlling When Formulas Are Recalculated

In Exercise 6-8, you get practice in switching to manual recalculation in a workbook and then using the Calculate Now option to update formulas whose input values have changed.

1. Open the *Exercise6-8.xlsx* workbook in the Chap6 subfolder inside the Excel 2007 Workbook folder.

   This workbook contains an earlier version of the now familiar Practice Formulas workbook with its Formulas and Ext Ref sheets.

2. Update the value in cell A2 of the Formulas sheet from 34 to **102**. Then, use AutoFit to widen column C in the Formulas worksheet and column B in the Ext Ref worksheet to display the contents of cells C9 and B3, respectively.

   Verify that Excel has automatically recalculated the formulas in both your Formulas and Ext Ref worksheets and that cell C9 on the Formulas sheet and B3 on the Ext Ref sheet now both contain the same value: 1,816,854.91.

3. Select the Manual option on the Calculation Options button's drop-down menu on the Ribbon's Formulas tab or press Alt+MXM.

   Excel switches the workbook to manual recalculation.

4. Update the value in cell A2 of the Formulas sheet from 102 to **144**.

   Note that none of the calculated values in the Formulas sheet have been updated (C9 still contains 1,816,854.91) and that the Calculate indicator has now appeared on the Status bar.

5. Click the Calculate Sheet command button on the Formulas tab of the Ribbon or press Alt+MJ.

   Note that Excel recalculates the formulas on the Formulas worksheet and that cell C9 now contains the value 4,412,310.20, but that the Calculate indicator has not disappeared from the Status bar. Then, switch to the Ext Ref sheet and note that the linked formula in cell B3 has not been updated and still contains the value 1,816,854.91.

6. Press F9 to have Excel recalculate all the formulas in the entire workbook.

   Note that not only does cell B3 of the Ext Ref worksheet now contain the updated value 4,412,310.20, but that the Calculate indicator has now disappeared from the Status bar.

7. Switch back to the Formulas worksheet, and then update cell A2 to **165.88** before you click the Calculate Now command button on the Ribbon's Formulas tab or press F9.

Check to make sure that all the formulas on both sheets of the workbook have now been updated by verifying that both cells C9 in the Formulas sheet and B3 in the Ext Ref sheet now contain 6,423,962.85.

8. Update cell A2 in the Formulas worksheet to 188 and then save this change to the **Practice Formulas – manrecalc.xlsx** workbook.

Note that Excel not only saves your change to cell A2 in the *Practice Formulas – manrecalc.xlsx* workbook file, but also recalculates the formulas using this new value and then saves these updated values as well.

9. Close the *Practice Formulas – manrecalc.xlsx* workbook file by exiting Excel 2007.

Note that any changes you make to the recalculation mode are saved as part of the workbook file, so that they are in effect the next time anyone opens the file for editing.

Chapter 7

Copying and Correcting Formulas

In This Chapter

▶ Copying formulas with relative cell references

▶ Copying formulas with absolute cell references

▶ Copying formulas with mixed cell references

▶ Using range names in formulas

▶ Creating array formulas

▶ Tracing and eliminating formula errors

▶ Dealing with circular references in a formula

Copying an original formula that you build to all the cells in the worksheet that per-form the same type of computation is one of the more common tasks you perform as part of creating a new spreadsheet. Despite this fact, understanding just how Excel goes about adjusting the cell references when you copy a formula is not widespread among new users. The exercises in this chapter give you a chance to practice copying formulas using all the different types of cell references. In addition, you practice assign-ing range names to the cells that are referenced to in spreadsheet formulas, creating array formulas that do away with the need for making formula copies, as well as tracing and eliminating the source of errors that have spread across the workbook.

Copying Formulas with Relative References

When your original formula uses cell references rather than constant values (as most should), Excel makes copying that formula to every place that requires the same type of computation a complete no-brainer. The program does this by automatically adjusting the cell references in the original formula to suit the position of the copies you make. It does this through a system known as *relative cell addresses*, whereby the column refer-ences in the cell address in the formula change to suit their new column position, and the row references change to suit their new row position.

Excel indicates that a cell reference is relative simply by stating its column letter and row number without preceding either part of the reference with a $ (dollar sign), the symbol denoting an absolute reference, as in A1 or BC457.

Exercise 7-1: Copying Formulas in the R1C1 Reference Style

In Exercise 7-1, you get practice copying an original formula with relative cell references. To help you understand how Excel adjusts cell references in copied formulas, you change the program from the familiar default cell reference system with column letters and row numbers to the R1C1 system, where both the cell's row and column are numbered.

1. If Excel isn't running, launch the program. Open the *Exercise7-1.xlsx* workbook file in your Chap7 folder in the Excel 2007 Workbook folder.

This file contains a copy of the 2008 Production Schedule table without any formulas.

2. Position the cell cursor in cell K3 and click the AutoSum button on the Ribbon's Home tab to create a SUM formula that totals the Part 100s scheduled to be produced over the nine-month period from April to December in row 3. Then, click the Enter button on the Formula bar.

AutoSum enters the following master formula in cell K3:

```
=SUM(B3:J3)
```

3. Use the Fill handle on the cell cursor to copy this formula down column K to the cell range K4:K7.

Excel copies the original formula plus its formatting to the empty cells down the column, automatically adjusting the row reference in each formula copy.

4. Position the white-cross mouse pointer on the Fill handle of the cell cursor and then, when the AutoFill Options drop-down button appears, click it. Select the Fill Without Formatting item at the bottom of the drop-down list that appears.

Selecting the Fill Without Formatting option restores the border along the top edge of cell K7 that Excel took out when copying the formatting from cell K3 to this range. Now, take a moment to examine the copies you made of the original SUM formula in cell K3 by using the arrow keys to move the cell cursor through each cell: K4, K5, K6, and K7. Note how the row number changes in each copy made down the cells in column K.

To help you understand what Excel is really doing when you make copies of a formula containing relative cell references down the rows of a column, turn on the R1C1 Reference system. In this system, both the rows and columns of the worksheet are given numbers so that the cell reference A1, for example, becomes R1C1 (because column A is the first column from the left edge of the worksheet) and cell D6 becomes R6C4 (because column D is the fourth column from the left edge of the worksheet).

5. Click Office button | Excel Options or press Alt+FI, and then click the Formulas tab in the left pane. Click the R1C1 Reference Style check box to select it before you click OK.

You can tell you are "not in Kansas anymore" using the familiar row number, column letter reference type system — all the columns are now numbered from left to right just as the rows are from top down.

6. Position the cell cursor in cell K3 (now called R3C11) and examine the contents of the original SUM formula on the Formula bar.

In R1C1 notation, the formula entered in this cell now reads:

```
=SUM(RC[-9]:RC[-1])
```

The first thing to note about cell references in formulas in R1C1 notation is that they are completely egocentric; always referring to the cell that contains the formula (they could care less about the worksheet at large). This formula says, in essence, "Use the SUM function to total from the cell that is nine columns to the left of the current column through the cell that is one column to left all in the same row." The minus sign in front of the number following the column reference denotes columns to the left of the current one just as the minus in front of a number following a row reference denotes rows above (positive integers in these references denote columns to the right and rows below the current one).

7. Press the ↓ key to move the cell pointer down column K through all the cells, K4, K5, K6, and K7, that contain copies of the formula you constructed in cell K3, noting the contents of each copy on the Formula bar as you move the cursor down a row.

You will note that each and every cell in this column contains the exact same formula:

```
=SUM(RC[-9]:RC[-1])
```

Excel hasn't really adjusted anything in any of the formula copies you made! It's all a convenient fiction (that's fancy talk for a big lie) to say that Excel adjusts the relative row and column references in formula copies because that's the way it *appears* to work when the program is in its normal column letter, row number reference system. (Now that I've let you in on this little secret, just keep it under your hat.)

8. Position the cell cursor in cell R7C2 (erstwhile B7) and use AutoSum to construct a SUM formula that totals the part numbers scheduled to be produced in April of 2008.

This formula in R1C1 notation appears on the Formula bar as follows:

```
=SUM(R[-4]C:R[-1]C)
```

9. Use the Fill handle to copy this formula across the rest of the columns of the table to the range R7C3:R7C10 (C7:J7).

Verify that each of the copies in all these cells contains the identical formula in R1C1 notation as you constructed in cell B7, that is, R7C2.

10. Restore the old tried-and-true row number and column letter notation system by removing the check mark from the R1C1 Reference Style check box on the Formulas tab of the Excel Options dialog box.

The Prod Sched worksheet once again identifies its cell references in the standard column letter and row number notation (as B7).

11. Move the cell cursor across the cell range B7:J7, noting how Excel adjusts the cell reference (in standard notation).

When you make copies of a formula across the columns of a single row using relative references, Excel adjusts only the column letter.

12. Save this workbook with the filename **Production Sch 08 – relref.xlsx** in your Excel 2007 Practice folder and then close the workbook file.

Copying Formulas with Absolute References

Absolute cell references, as their name implies, do not change for nobody or nothing. A truly absolute reference firmly roots both the column and row reference (as opposed to a mixed reference that just plants either the row number or the column letter, but not both). This type of reference comes in handy when you need to refer to a cell that contains a value that acts like a constant that must remain unchanged in all formula copies.

Excel indicates that a cell reference is absolute by preceding both its column letter and row number with a $ (dollar sign), the symbol denoting an absolute reference, as in $A$1 or $BC$457. When building or editing a formula, you can convert a relative cell reference that contains the insertion point simply by pressing the F4 key.

Before you attempt Exercise 7-2, you may want to play the Formulas with Absolute Refs.exe demo located in the Excel Feature Demos folder on your workbook CD-ROM. This feature demonstration shows you how to build a formula containing absolute cell references before you make copies of it.

Exercise 7-2: Copying a Formula with Absolute Cell References

In Exercise 7-2, you get practice creating an original formula that contains an absolute cell reference to prevent Excel from adjusting any part of its cell reference in the formula copies that you make.

1. Open the *Exercise 7-2.xls* workbook file in your Chap7 folder in the Excel 2007 Workbook folder.

This file contains a copy of the 2008 Production Schedule table with all the formulas you created and copied in Exercise 7-1 for totaling the units to be produced by month across the columns and by part down the rows. In this exercise, you add a row of formulas that compute what percentage each monthly production quota represents of the projected nine-month total.

2. Enter the heading **Percent of Total** in cell A9 of the Prod Sched worksheet. Then, click the Wrap Text button in the Alignment group of the Ribbon's Home tab to wrap the row heading on two lines in cell A9.

Next, you'll construct a formula that calculates what percentage each monthly total is of the nine-month grand total in cell K7.

3. Construct a formula in cell B9 that divides the April 2008 quota in cell B7 by the grand total in cell K7 and then format the cell with the Percent Style number format with two decimal places.

The formula in cell B9 should read:

```
=B7/K7
```

To format the result in cell B9 in the Percent Style with two decimal places, click the Percent Style command button in the Number group of the Ribbon's Home tab and then click the Increase Decimal command button (located in the same row of the Number group) twice.

4. Use the Fill handle to copy the original formula you constructed in cell B9 to the cell range C9:J9.

   Something is clearly wrong with the copies as they all contain those dreaded #DIV/0! error values rather than the desired percentages.

5. Position the cell cursor in cell C7 to examine the formula that Excel copied there.

   The formula in this cell reads

   ```
   =C7/L7
   ```

   When Excel made the first copy, the program not only adjusted the column reference for the monthly quota (from B7 to C7) but for the projected total as well (K7 to L7). Because L7 is empty, the copy is, in essence, trying to divide by zero (all empty cells carry a zero value); thus the division error value.

   To prevent this problem with the copies (and to correct it), in the original division formula, the divisor, K7, with the projected total must be an absolute cell reference (as in $K$7), so that it remains constant in all the copies in which Excel naturally adjusts the dividend (that is, the amount to be divided) containing the various monthly production quotas.

6. Position the cell cursor back in cell B9 with the original formula and then press F2 to put Excel in Edit mode.

7. With the insertion point positioned after the cell reference K7 (so that you don't have to move the insertion point in order to convert this cell reference), press F4 to convert the relative K7 cell reference to absolute $K$7 and then click the Enter button on the Formula bar.

   Excel enters the formula =B7/$K$7. Note that this revised formula gives you the same result (11.35%). The question, however, is will it give you the same error value when you make your copies of this formula set.

8. Use the Fill handle to copy this edited version of the original formula in cell B9 to the cell range C9:J9.

   That's more like it! This time all the formula copies return realistic percentages in place of those awful division errors.

9. Position the cell cursor in cell A1 of the Prod Sched worksheet and then save the workbook with the filename **Production Sch 08 – absref.xlsx** in your Excel 2007 Practice folder before you close the workbook.

Copying Formulas with Mixed References

Just as you'd expect, mixed cell references are those that mix relative and absolute references in a cell. A mixed cell reference can either have the row reference absolute and column relative (as in A$3) or the column reference absolute and the row relative (as in $A3).

You can convert a cell reference you're entering or editing in a formula to either type of mixed reference by pressing F4 as follows:

- ✔ **First** time to convert the cell reference from completely relative to completely absolute (C5 to $C$5)

- ✔ **Second** time to convert from completely absolute to a mixed reference with the row absolute and the column relative ($C$5 to C$5)

- ✔ **Third** time to convert from a mixed reference with the row absolute and the column relative to one with the column absolute and row relative (C$5 to $C5)

- ✔ **Fourth** time to convert from a mixed reference with the column absolute and row relative back to a completely relative reference ($C5 to C5)

You only need to resort to mixed cell references in an original formula when you intend to copy this formula to empty cells in two directions; that is, both down the rows and then over the columns to the right or over to columns on the right and then down the rows, *and* need to prevent Excel from adjusting either the column letter or the row number reference in all the copies.

Before you attempt Exercise 7-3, you may want to play the Formulas in Loan Table.exe demo located in the Excel Feature Demos folder on your workbook CD-ROM. This feature demonstration shows you how to construct the same type of loan table by building the original formula with the PMT function using correct cell references and then copying it throughout the table.

Solve It

Exercise 7-3: Creating a Loan Table with Mixed Cell References

Exercise 7-3 gives you practice in constructing a loan payment table that requires the use of mixed and absolute cell references in the original formula as well as two-dimensional formula copying. To create this original formula for the payment table, you use the PMT function, the arguments of which require all the different types of cell references (including both types of mixed cell references) in order for all the copies to refer to the correct cells.

1. Open a new workbook in Excel and use its blank Sheet1 worksheet to create this loan payment table.

This table uses the PMT function to compute the monthly mortgage payments for a sequence of different loan amounts (principals) and interest rates. The PMT function is a Financial function that requires three arguments: *Rate,* which is the interest rate per payment period; *Nper,* which is the number or payment periods for the loan; and *Pv,* which is the present value or loan amount (the function also accepts two other optional arguments that you won't need to use in this exercise).

You begin by entering the table headings and the three initial values (loan amount, term of the loan, and interest rate) to be used to generate the sequence of the different loan amounts and interest rates as well as in the construction of the original PMT formula that you then copy in two dimensions to the rest of table:

2. Enter the following headings in the designated cells and then widen column A to suit with AutoFit:

   - **Loan Payment Table** in cell A1

   - **Principal** in cell A2

   - **Interest** in cell A3

   - **Period** in cell A4

3. Enter the following values in the designated cells and format them as indicated:

   - **435000** in cell B2 formatted with the Accounting number format with zero decimal places

   - **5%** in cell B3 formatted with two decimal places

   - **30** in cell B4

4. Create a formula in cell A7 that dynamically copies the initial principal value entered in cell B2 to this cell.

   To create a dynamic link between the value in one cell and another cell in the same worksheet, type = to start the formula, followed by the reference of the cell with which you want the value linked.

   Cell A7 contains the formula =B2 and displays the initial principal amount $435,000 brought forward from cell B2.

5. Create a formula in cell A8 that adds 500 to the value in cell A7 and then use the Fill handle to copy this formula down the rows to the cell range A9:A17.

   Cell A8 contains the formula =A7+500 and displays the result $435,500.

6. Create a formula in cell B6 that dynamically copies the initial interest rate entered in cell B3 to this cell.

   Cell B6 contains the formula =B3 and displays the initial interest rate amount 5.00%.

7. Create a formula in cell C6 that adds 0.25% to the value in cell B6, and reduce the number of decimal places to two.

   Cell C6 contains the formula =B6+0.25% and displays the result 5.25%.

8. Use the Fill handle to copy this formula across the columns to the cell range D6:J6.

   Now that your range of principals and interest rates are created, you're ready to construct the initial formula using the PMT function that you will copy down to row 17 in column D of the table and then over to column J.

9. Position the cell cursor in cell B7 and then click the Financial command button in the Function Library group of the Ribbon's Formula tab or press Alt+MI before you click PMT on its drop-down menu.

   Excel inserts =PMT() into cell B7 and immediately opens its Function Arguments dialog box.

10. Drag the PMT Function Arguments dialog box to the right so that it's out of the way and no longer hides cell B7 in the worksheet.

The first argument to specify is the Rate argument, for which you will select cell B6 that is linked to the starting interest rate in cell B3. Note that you must consider what part of this cell reference, if any, should be adjusted when you copy this formula down the rows of this table (from 7 through 17) and then across the columns (from B through J) and adjust its reference accordingly.

Note that when you copy the PMT formula down the rows of the table, you definitely do *not* want Excel to adjust the row number because all of the interest rates are in row 6, meaning that this part of the cell reference must be absolute. When you then copy the PMT formula to columns on the right, you do, however, need the column letter to be adjusted in order to pick up the quarter percentage point entered into the succeeding columns in row 6, so you do need to keep this part of the cell reference relative. Therefore, for this argument, you need to convert B6 from its completely relative reference to the mixed cell reference, B$6 (column adjusted but not the row).

Moreover, because the starting interest rate you enter into cell B3 and bring forward to cell B6 is a *yearly* rate and the PMT function calculates the *monthly* payment, you need to divide this yearly interest amount by twelve so that the Rate argument represents a monthly portion.

11. With the insertion point in the Rate text box, click cell B6 to select and enter its reference, then press F4 twice to convert it to the mixed reference, B$6, before you type **/12,** and then press Tab.

B$6/12 now appears in the Rate argument text box and the calculated result 0.004166667 appears to its right.

The Nper argument picks up the single loan period value entered in cell B4. Because this value acts a constant in the table, all the loan payments calculated by the PMT function refer to it. Therefore, this reference has to be completely absolute, $B$4, so that Excel adjusts neither its column letter nor its row number in any of the copies. In addition, because this period is in years (30 years to begin with), you need to multiply it by twelve so that the PMT function is dealing with the total number of months.

12. With the insertion point in the Nper text box, click cell B4, and then press F4 once to convert its reference to $B$4 and type ***12** before you press Tab.

$B$4*12 now appears in the Nper argument text box and the calculated result 360 appears to its right.

The last required argument is the present value or loan amount for which you will select cell A7 that is linked to the initial principal entered into cell B2. When you copy the PMT formula down the rows of column B, you want Excel to adjust the row number so that it picks and uses the increased principals (that increment by $500 in each subsequent row). You do not, however, want Excel to adjust the column letter in this argument when you copy the formula to the columns to the right because all the principals are entered in only one column. Therefore, for this last PMT argument, you need a mixed cell reference of $A7 (with column reference absolute and row reference relative).

13. With the insertion point in the Pv text box, click cell A7, and then press F4 three times to convert it to the mixed reference, $A7.

Check the arguments in your Function Arguments dialog box against those shown in Figure 7-1 and note the Formula result of -2335.17406 near the bottom. When each argument checks out, proceed to Step 14. If you discover that you need to change the type of cell reference in any argument, edit the formula (F2) and then position the blinking cursor in that reference. Press F4 until the correct mixed or absolute reference appears.

14. Select the OK button to close the Function Arguments dialog box and to complete the formula with the PMT function in cell B7, and then use the Fill handle to copy this formula down the rows of column B to cell B17.

Now that you've copied the original formula down column B, you're ready to copy it to the right to column J.

15. While the range B7:B17 is still selected by the cell cursor, use its Fill handle to copy the original PMT formula across the columns of the table to and including column J (the entire cell range B7:J17 is selected when you finish copying the formulas in the second direction across the columns).

Now you need to widen columns C through J to display all the calculated results.

16. Use AutoFit to widen columns C:J sufficiently to displayed their contents.

The results in your loan table should match those shown in Figure 7-2.

17. Change the period from 30 to **15** in cell B4 and note the increase to the monthly payments in the table, and then click the Undo button on the Quick Access toolbar or press Ctrl+Z to return the loan term to its original 30 years.

Note as soon as you change the period Excel immediately recalculates all the PMT formulas in your loan table.

18. Put Excel into manual recalculation mode and then experiment with changing the initial principal in cell B2 to **425000** and a starting interest rate in B3 of **4.00%**. Click the Calculate Now button or Press F9 to update the loan table by recalculating the monthly payments using the new range of principal amounts and interest rates.

Click the Manual option on the Calculation Options button's drop-down menu on the Formulas tab of the Ribbon or press Alt+MXM to put the workbook into manual recalculation mode.

As soon as you change the initial principal amount in cell B2, the Calculate indicator appears on the Status bar, letting you know that the formulas in the loan table are no longer up to date. As soon as you finish entering the new initial interest rate and choose Calculate Now, Excel updates all the formulas and the Calculate indicator disappears.

19. Use Undo to restore the original 435000 and 5% values in cells B2 and B3, respectively, and position the cell cursor in cell B7. Save your Loan Payment Table with the filename **Loan Table – manrecalc.xlsx** in your Excel 2007 Practice folder. Then, close the workbook.

Figure 7-1: The Function Arguments dialog box showing the final arguments for the PMT function.

Figure 7-2: The completed Loan Payment Table after copying the PMT function and widening the columns to suit.

Using Range Names in Formulas

In completing the exercises in Chapter 6, you got experience with assigning a range name to a cell that held a constant (named *Source*) and then using that name in a linking formula. This linking formula supplied the basic value used in most of the hand-made formulas you then constructed on the worksheet.

Instead of assigning range names to constants that you actually enter into particular cells of the worksheet, you can create range names that store constant values not tied to entries in any cell. You can then paste the constant's range name into any formula that needs its value in order to successfully perform its calculations.

Another important use for range names is as identifiers of the cell references used in the operands and arguments of the formulas constructed for a typical data table. In this situation, you have Excel assign the table's row and column headings as the range names for data cells in the corresponding rows and columns. You then have Excel substitute these range names for the cell references in all the formulas in the table that refer to these data cells.

Before you attempt Exercise 7-4, you may want to play the Formulas with Range Names.exe demo located in the Excel Feature Demos folder on your workbook CD-ROM. This feature demonstration shows you how to assign range names to cells in a spreadsheet table and then use these range names in formulas you construct to help document the formulas' functioning.

Exercise 7-4: Creating Ranges Names for Formulas

In Exercise 7-4, you get practice defining range names from the headings in a table and then assigning the names to formulas in a worksheet table.

1. Open the *Exercise7-4.xlsx* file in your Chap7 folder inside your Excel 2007 Workbook folder.

This file contains a variation on the Spring Sale table that you can use to practice assigning a range name to a constant as well as creating range names from a table's row and column headings.

2. Click the Define Name command button on the Ribbon's Formulas tab or press Alt+MMD to open the New Name dialog box, and then type **Discount_rate** (don't forget the underscore) as the range name in the Name text box. (This name replaces the title of the table that automatically appears as the suggested range name because its cell, A1, is selected in the worksheet.)

Note that by default the scope of a range name is the entire workbook. You can, if you want, restrict the scope of the range name you're defining to the current worksheet or another particular sheet in the workbook.

3. Press Tab three times to select `='2008 Spring Sale'!$A$1` in the Refers To text box, and then replace this reference by typing **=15%** and click OK.

Excel now adds a range name called Discount_rate to the workbook that sets the discount percentage equal to a constant 15%. Note, however, that this range name does not refer to any particular cell in the worksheet.

4. Position the cell cursor in cell D3 and there construct a formula that multiplies the retail price of the table with the code number 12-305 in cell C3 by the 15% discount rate. Type =, click cell C3, type *, and then click the Use in Formula button on the Formulas tab and click Discount_rate on its drop-down menu.

The formula in cell D3 now reads

```
=C3*Discount_rate
```

5. Click the Enter button on the Formula bar and then copy this formula down to the cell range D4:D7.

   Note in each of the copies of the formula that although Excel adjusts the row number of each reference to the cell in the Retail Price column, it treats the range name, Discount_rate, as an absolute reference.

6. Create a formula in cell E3 that computes the sale price of the table code numbered 12-305 by subtracting its discount amount from its retail price, as in =C3-D3, and then copy this formula down the cell range E4:E7.

   Next, you're going to have Excel assign range names to the table cells in the range C3:E7 from the row and column headings in row 2 and column B of the Sale Table.

7. Select the cell range B2:E7 that includes the column and row headings and then click the Create from Selection command button on the Formulas tab or press Alt+MC.

   Excel opens the Create Names from Selection dialog box. This dialog box contains four check boxes, Top Row, Left Column, Bottom Row, and Right Column, that you can select to indicate which row and column headings to use in assigning the new range names.

8. If necessary, click the Top Row and Left Column check boxes to select them before you click OK in the Create Names from Selection dialog box.

   Next, you'll create a list of the range names that you defined for this sales table on Sheet2 of the workbook.

9. Double-click Sheet2 and then rename its tab **Range Names**. Increase the magnification to 150%, enter the heading, **Range Name List**, in cell A1 of the Range Names sheet, and position the cell cursor in its cell A2.

   To create a list of the current range names in the workbook, you need to open the Paste Name dialog box and use its Paste List command.

10. Open the Paste Name dialog box by clicking the drop-down button attached to the Use in Formula command button on the Ribbon's Formulas tab and then clicking the Paste Names option at the very bottom of its drop-down menu. Then, click the Paste List command button in Paste Name dialog box.

    Excel pastes an alphabetical list of range names in the cell range A2:B11. Note that this alphabetical listing of the range names in the workbook is static, so you would have to generate it again with the Paste List button if you edit the names in this workbook and then want an up-to-date list.

11. Use AutoFit to widen column A and B of the Range Names sheet so that all the entries in the first and second columns of this list are completely displayed in the worksheet. Right-align the range names in the cell range A2:A11 and then click cell A1.

    Next, you create a new window in the *Exercise7-4.xlsx* workbook that enables you to compare the Sale Table in the 2008 Spring Sale sheet and the Range Name List in the Range Names sheet side by side on your screen.

12. Click View | New Window on the Ribbon or press Alt+WN to create a new window in the workbook named Exercise7-4.xlsx:2. Then, click the Switch Windows button and click the Exercise7-4.xlsx:1 option on its drop-down menu (or press Alt+WW1) to make the first window active. Finally, click the View Side by Side command

button (or press Alt+WB) to display both the Exercise7-4.xlsx:1 and the Exercise7-4.xlsx:2 windows together on the screen, one on top of the other.

After you open new windows on the same workbook, you can display a range of cells on any of its worksheets in the different window panes.

13. Click the 2008 Spring Sale sheet tab in the Exercise7-4.xlsx:1 window on the top to make the sheet with the Sale Table active in the top window. Use the Zoom slider to reduce the magnification display percentage to 100% in the workbook. Then, check your screen against the one shown in Figure 7-3.

Note that both the 2008 Spring Sale worksheet in the top window (Exercise7-4.xlsx:1) and the Range Names sheet in the lower window (Exercise7-4.xlsx:2) are affected equally by the zoom command.

14. Click the View Side by Side button to display only the 2008 Spring Sale worksheet and then increase the screen magnification percentage to 150%.

Now, you're ready to apply the range names listed in the Range Name Listing on the Range Names sheet to the formulas you constructed and copied in the Sale Table in the 2008 Spring Sale worksheet.

15. Select the cell range with the formula D3:E7 in the sales table. Then, click the drop-down button attached to the Define Name button on the Formulas tab and click the Apply Names option on its drop-down menu or press Alt+MMA to open the Apply Names dialog box.

The Apply Names dialog box contains a list with all the range names you've defined in the workbook selected.

16. Select the Options button to expand the Apply Names dialog box, and then deselect the Omit Column Name If Same Column and the Omit Row Name If Same Row check boxes and click OK.

When these check boxes are selected, Excel does not bother to repeat row and column range names in the formulas. As a result, the formulas copied down the rows and across the columns of a table all end up with the same descriptions (which pretty much defeats the purpose of displaying them in the formulas in the first place).

17. Examine the use of the range names created from the row and column headings in all the individual formulas in the cell range D3:E7.

Note that the operand of each formula now includes both the row and the column range name (separated by a space that represents the Intersection operator) created from the cell's row and column heading. For example, the subtraction formula in cell E6 now reads

```
=Buffet Retail_Price-Buffet Discount
```

This identifies the formula as subtracting the value in the cell at the intersection of the Buffet row and Discount column range names from the value in the cell at the intersection of the Buffet row and Retail_Price column range names.

18. Select cell A1 in the 2008 Spring Sale worksheet and then save your changes to this workbook with the filename **Spring Furniture Sale – namedfrmls.xlsx** in your Excel 2007 Practice folder, and then close the workbook.

Figure 7-3:
Exercise7-4
.xlsx work-
book with
the 2008
Spring Sale
sheet active
in the top
window and
the Range
Names
sheet active
in the
bottom one.

Building Array Formulas

Instead of copying a formula to all the cells that perform the same type of calculation, you can build an *array formula* that performs the desired calculation not only in the active cell but in all the other cells to which you would normally copy the formula. An array formula is a special formula that operates on a range of values. If this range is supplied by a cell range (as is often the case), it is referred to as an *array range*. If this range is supplied by a list of numerical values, they are known as an *array constant*.

You are already quite familiar with arrays even though you may not realize it. This is because the Excel worksheet grid with its column-and-row structure naturally organizes your data ranges into one-dimensional and two-dimensional arrays (one-dimensional arrays take up a single row or column, whereas two-dimensional arrays take up multiple rows and columns).

Figure 7-4 illustrates a couple of two-dimensional arrays with numerical entries of two different sizes. The first array is a 3-by-2 array in the cell range B2:C4. This array is a 3-by-2 array because it occupies three rows and two columns. The second array is a 2-by-3 array in the cell range B6:D7. This array is a 2-by-3 array because it uses 2 rows in three columns.

If you were to list the values in the first 3-by-2 array as an array constant in a formula, they would appear as follows:

```
{1,4;2,5;3,6}
```

Here are several things to note in this expression:

- ✔ The array constant is enclosed in a pair of braces ({}).
- ✔ Columns within each row are separated by commas (,) and rows within the array are separated by semicolons (;).
- ✔ Constants in the array are listed across each row and then down each column, *not* down each column and across each row.

The second 2-by-3 array expressed as an array constant appears as follows:

```
{7,8,9;10,11,12}
```

Note again that you list the values across each row and then down each column, separating the values in different columns with commas and the values in different rows with a semicolon.

Figure 7-4:
Worksheet containing a 3-by-2 array in the cell range B2:C4 and a 2-by-3 array in the cell range B6:D7.

Solve It

Exercise 7-5: Constructing Array Formulas

In Exercise 7-5, you get practice creating array formulas for a spreadsheet in cell ranges that need to perform the same type of calculation. This gives you a chance to compare the technique of entering a single array formula into an entire cell range with that of entering an original formula in a single cell that you then copy to the entire range.

1. Open the *Exercise 7-5.xlsx* file in your Chap7 folder inside your Excel 2007 Workbook folder.

This file contains a copy of the February 2008 Hourly Wage spreadsheet that you can use to practice constructing array formulas. This worksheet is designed to compute the bi-weekly wages for each employee by multiplying the hourly rate by the number of hours worked. Rather than create an original formula for each period that computes the wages for the first employee and then copying it down rows for all the others, do this with array formulas.

2. Position the cell cursor in cell R10 and then select the cell range R10:R13.

You are going to construct the following array formula that you then enter as a single entry into the cell range R10:R13 you just selected:

```
={A4:A7*R4:R7}
```

The range A4:A7 contains the hourly rates for all four employees, whereas the range R4:R7 contains the total hours each one worked in the first period.

3. Type = to start the array formula and then select the cell range A4:A7. Type * (asterisk), the multiplication operator, and then select the cell range R4:R7.

To complete an array formula, you must press a very special key combination, Ctrl plus Shift plus Enter. This key combination lets Excel know you're constructing an array formula as well as informs it to enter this array formula into all the cells in the selected range.

4. Press Ctrl+Shift+Enter to complete the array formula and enter it into the selected range R10:R13.

Excel enters the array formula ={A4:A7*R4:R7} in all the cells in the selected range R10:R13.

5. Construct an array formula in the cell range AI10:AI13 that multiplies the hourly rates in the cell range A4:A7 by the second-period hour totals in the cell range AI4:AI7.

The array formula you enter into the cell range AI10:AI13 appears on the Formula bar as follows:

```
={A4:A7*AI4:AI7}
```

6. Construct an array formula in the cell range AJ10:AJ13 that totals the two pay periods for each employee.

The array formula you enter into the cell range AJ10:AJ13 appears as follows on the Formula bar:

```
={R10:R13+AI10:AI13}
```

7. Select cell AJ10 to deselect the cell range and then press the Delete key to remove the addition formula from this cell.

   Excel responds by displaying an alert dialog box informing you that you cannot change part of an array. When editing array formulas, you must work entirely with the ranges specified as the operands.

8. Click OK to close the alert dialog box and now select the range AJ10:AJ13 before you press Delete.

   This time, Excel deletes the array formula from the entire range.

9. Click the Undo button on the Quick Access toolbar or press Ctrl+Z to restore the deleted array formula to the range AJ10:AJ13. Then, select cell A1 and save this workbook with the filename **Feb 08 Wages – arrayfrmls.xlsx** in your Excel 2007 Practice folder before you close the workbook.

Tracing and Eliminating Formula Errors

As you found out firsthand when performing Exercise 6-3 in Chapter 6, an error value returned by a single faulty formula can spread like wildfire to all the cells that refer to its value throughout the entire spreadsheet, making it very difficult to determine its source. Fortunately, Excel offers some very effective tools on its Formula Auditing toolbar that you can use to track down the cell that's causing your error woes by tracing the relationships between the formulas in the cells of your worksheet.

By tracing the relationships, you can test formulas to see which cells, called *direct precedents* in spreadsheet jargon, directly feed the formulas and which cells, called *dependents* (nondeductible, of course), depend upon the results of the formulas. Excel even offers a way to visually backtrack the potential sources of an error value in the formula of a particular cell. To display the precedents and dependents of a formula as well as for tracing the source of errors, you can use the command buttons in the Formula Auditing group of the Ribbon's Formulas tab.

When you click the Trace Precedents and Trace Dependents buttons on the Formulas tab, Excel shows the relationship between a formula and the cells that directly and indirectly feed it as well as those cells that directly and indirectly depend upon its calculation. The program establishes this relationship by drawing arrows from the precedent cells to the active cell and from the active cell to its dependent cells.

If these cells are on the same worksheet, Excel draws solid red or blue arrows extending from each of the precedent cells to the active cell and from the active cell to the dependent cells. If the cells are not located locally on the same worksheet (they may be on another sheet in the same workbook or even on a sheet in a different workbook), Excel draws a black dotted arrow. This arrow comes from or goes to an icon picturing a miniature worksheet that sits to one side, with the direction of the arrowheads indicating whether the cells on the other sheet feed the active formula or are fed by it.

Solve It | **Exercise 7-6: Finding the Source of Error Values in a Spreadsheet**

In Exercise 7-6, you get some practice using Excel's formula auditing features to trace the precedents and dependents of a formula to find the source of error values in a spreadsheet.

1. Open the *Exercise7-6.xlsx* workbook in your Chap7 folder inside your Excel 2007 Workbook folder.

    This workbook contains a copy of the Practice Formulas workbook you created as part of the exercises in Chapter 6. You can use its Formulas and Ext Ref worksheets to practice tracing and eliminating errors:

2. Remove the range name, "Source", given to cell A2 in the Formulas worksheet by clicking the Name Manager button on the Formulas tab (Alt+MN) to open the Name Manager dialog box. Click the Source range name in the list box to select it and then click the Delete button. Click OK in the alert dialog box asking you if you're sure you want to delete the range name and then click the Close button to close the Name Manager.

    As soon as you remove the range name, the spreadsheet on the Formulas worksheet fills with #NAME? error values.

3. Click cell C9 with the SUM function that sums the three cell ranges A2:A8, B4:B8, C4:C8 to select it.

    Now, trace the source of this error value.

4. Click the Error Checking button in the Formula Auditing group of the Ribbon's Formulas tab or press Alt+MKK to open the Error Checking dialog box.

    Excel displays the Error Checking dialog box, which briefly explains that this error value is due to the fact that the formula now contains unrecognized text. This is not something that you can fix by editing the formula on the Formula bar, so, in this case, you need to trace the error.

5. Click the Trace Error button in the Error Checking dialog box.

    Excel draws a diagonal arrow from cell A4 pointing to cell C9, indicating that this is the direct source of the error (if you select the Previous button in the Error Checking dialog box, Excel steps the cell cursor back through each of the cells with the #NAME? error value in the order in which they spread in this spreadsheet).

    In this situation, you need to identify the cell or cells that feed the cells containing the #NAME? error values.

6. Click the Close button (the one with the X) in the Error Checking dialog box and then click the Trace Precedents button in the Formula Auditing group of the Ribbon's Formulas tab or press Alt+MP.

    Excel adds three arrows pointing directly to cell C9, showing the precedents of its error value, the most telling of which is the one drawn from cell A2. If you didn't already know that cell A2 was the culprit causing all these error values (having removed its range name yourself), this precedents diagram would have tipped you off immediately.

7. Click the Trace Precedents button in the Formula Auditing group of the Formulas tab or press Alt+MP a second time.

Clicking the Trace Precedents button a second time (or double-clicking it to begin with) displays all the indirect precedents and dependents of the formula in the current cell. In this case, Excel now shows the flow and direction of all the sum formulas both down the columns and across the rows that contribute both directly and indirectly to its computed value.

8. Click the Remove Arrows button on the Formulas tab (the one with the eraser) or press Alt+MAA.

   Excel removes all arrows from the worksheet display.

9. Position the cell cursor in cell A4, the first one with a #NAME? error value, and then click the Trace Dependents button in the Formula Auditing group of the Formulas tab or press Alt+MD.

   The program draws arrows showing the direct dependents of the formula in this cell, which include the formulas down the column that use its value to compute their own and the formulas across the row in C4 and D4 and, of course, the formula in cell C9.

10. Click the Trace Dependents button on the Formulas tab or press Alt+MD a second time.

    Excel draws arrows showing the indirect dependents of the formula in cell C9. Note that this includes a black dotted arrow line drawn from cell C9 to a graphic showing a tiny worksheet. This is Excel's way of alerting you to the fact that there are cells dependent on this one on other worksheets of the workbook to which its error value has naturally spread.

11. Click the Ext Ref sheet tab to make this worksheet active and note that cell B3 that contains the linking formula also now contains a #NAME? error value. Click cell B3 and then click the Trace Precedents button on the Formulas tab or press Alt+MP.

    Excel draws a black dotted line to cell B3 from a graphic showing a tiny worksheet, indicating that the source of this error value is on another worksheet.

12. Click the Remove Arrows button on the Formulas tab and then click the Formulas sheet tab to switch back to this worksheet. There, reassign the range name, **Source**, to cell A2 by selecting the cell and then typing this range name into the Name Box on the Formula bar before you press Enter.

    Note that the moment you rectify the source of the error (both literally and figuratively), all the nasty #NAME? error values in the spreadsheet immediately disappear along with all the arrows depicting the direct and indirect dependents.

13. Close the *Exercise7-6.xlsx* workbook file without saving your changes.

Dealing with Circular References

A *circular reference* in a formula is one that depends, directly or indirectly, upon its own value. The most common type of circular reference occurs when you mistakenly refer in the formula to the cell in which you're building the formula itself. For example, suppose that cell B10 is active when you build this formula:

```
=A10+B10
```

As soon as you complete this formula entry in cell B10, Excel displays an alert box that says that it cannot calculate the formula due to the circular reference. As soon as you press Enter or click OK to close this alert box, the program displays an Excel Help window with information about circular references. After you close this window, you see that the program also inserts 0 in the cell with the circular reference and the indicator Circular References followed by the cell address with the circular reference appears on the Status bar.

Excel is not able to resolve this example of a circular reference in cell B10 because the formula's calculation depends directly upon the formula's result, creating an endless loop that continuously requires recalculating and can never be resolved.

Not all circular references are impossible for Excel to resolve. Some formulas contain a circular reference that can eventually be resolved after many recalculations of its formula (referred to as *iterations*) because the results get closer and closer to a resolution point with each go-round or iteration of the formula.

Solve It

Exercise 7-7: Solving a Circular Reference in a Formula

In Exercise 7-7, you get practice with a circular reference in a formula that Excel can eventually resolve by doing multiple iterations.

1. Open the *Exercise7-7.xlsx* workbook in your Chap7 folder in your Excel 2007 Workbook folder.

   This workbook contains an income statement spreadsheet with a circular reference in cell B13 that Excel catches the moment you open the file.

2. Read the text of the alert dialog box that appears the moment you open the *Exercise7-7.xlsx* workbook and then click OK to close it.

   The moment you close this alert dialog box, Excel displays an Excel Help window. This particular Help window gives you information either on locating and removing a circular reference or on making a circular reference work by changing the number of times that the program evaluates its formula.

3. Click the Make a Circular Reference Work by Changing the Number of Times that Excel Iterates Formulas link to display its information in the Help window. Look over this information or print it out before you close the Help window.

   Excel draws arrows that point to the cells involved in this circular reference, from the Total Other Income cell B15 to cell B13, which computes the bonuses; from the Income before Taxes cell B17 to cells B15 and B13; and to and from this Income Before Taxes cell B17 to cell B19, which computes the net income.

   These computations constitute a circular reference because the formula in cell B13 computes the amount of the bonuses as a percentage of the net income in cell B19 (=B19*20%), which, in turn, is dependent upon the amount of the bonus as it is included in the other income calculation in cell B15 that is then fed to the total income (loss) calculation in cell B17, which is itself used in calculating the net income in cell B19.

4. Click Office button | Excel Options or press Alt+FI. Click Formulas in the left pane and then click the Enable Iterative Calculation check box before you click OK.

   The moment you click OK to close the Options dialog box and to put this new calculation setting into effect, Excel resolves the circular reference in cell B13 that calculates the bonuses based on the net income and all the arrows showing all the cells involved in this circular reference disappear from the worksheet.

5. Click cell A1 and then save this version of the Income Statement with the filename **Income Statement 08 –circref.xlsx** in your Excel 2007 Practice folder before you close this file.

Chapter 8

Creating Date and Time Formulas

● ●

In This Chapter

▶ Building date and time formulas

▶ Using the Date functions

▶ Using the Time functions

● ●

*F*ormulas that perform calculations between elapsed dates and times are quite common in spreadsheets. The exercises in this chapter give you a chance to build formulas that calculate the difference between starting and ending dates and times as well as to use Excel Date and Time functions to perform a variety of tasks, including returning the current date and time in a spreadsheet, converting text entries to valid date and time numbers, and more.

Constructing Date and Time Formulas

You already have some experience entering dates and times in a worksheet and then changing how they appear by assigning different date and time number formats. Remember that all you need to do when you enter a date or time number in a worksheet is to emulate one of these date or time number formats when making the entry.

The only thing the least little bit baffling about date and time entries in a worksheet is the actual way that Excel stores the date and time numbers into a cell when you make an entry following one of the standard number formats. Behind the scenes (that is, the date or time number formats) lies a serial number. In the case of dates, this serial number represents the number of days that have elapsed between the date you enter and the beginning of the twentieth century (making January 1, 1900 serial date number 1). In the case of time, the serial number is a fraction representing the number of hours, minutes, and seconds that have elapsed since midnight (which is serial number 0.00000000, so that twelve noon is 0.50000000).

To build a simple date formula that calculates the number of days that have elapsed between two dates entered in the worksheet, subtract the cell containing the starting date from the one containing the ending date. Excel then displays the calculated result in a date format, which you then have to reformat with another number format (such as Number with no decimal points) to see the number of days that this "date" actually represents.

To build a simple time formula that calculates the fractional part of the day that has elapsed between two times entered in the worksheet, you subtract the cell containing the starting time from the one containing the ending time. Excel then displays the calculated result as a fraction that you can then convert into hours by multiplying by 24.

When entering times in a spreadsheet that you intend to use in formulas to compute elapsed times, be sure to enter all times after twelve noon either using a twenty-four clock (as in 13:05 for 1:05 PM) or with the PM signifier after the time number. Otherwise, Excel interprets all the times you enter as occurring in the AM.

Before you attempt Exercise 8-1, you may want to play the Formulas Date & Time.exe demo located in the Excel Feature Demos folder on your workbook CD-ROM. This feature demonstration shows you how to build and copy simple formulas that calculate elapsed dates and times.

Solve It

Exercise 8-1: Building Formulas that Calculate Elapsed Dates and Times

In Exercise 8-1, you get practice building simple formulas that calculate the differences between different dates and different times entered into the cells of a worksheet.

1. If Excel isn't running, launch the program and use its Book1 to build some simple formulas that calculate elapsed times and dates. If the program is already running, click the New button on your customized Quick Access toolbar or press Ctrl+N to create a new workbook for this purpose.

You'll start by entering some column headings in row 2 of the new worksheet.

2. Use the Zoom slider to increase the display magnification percentage of the Sheet1 worksheet from 100% to 200% and then enter the following headings in the designated cells:

- **Start** in cell A2
- **End** in cell B2
- **Elapsed** in cell C2

3. Enter the following dates in the designated cells:

- **11-6-07** in cell A3
- **2-15-08** in cell B3

4. Construct a formula in cell C3 that subtracts the starting date from the ending date, that is, =B3-A3.

Excel now displays 101 as the answer in cell C3.

5. Enter the following dates in the designated cells:

- **4-26-04** in cell A4
- **7-21-06** in cell B4
- **11-30-03** in cell A5
- **5-19-06** in cell B5

6. Use the Fill handle to copy the formula in cell C3 down to the range C4:C5.

Excel finds the difference between the dates in cells B4 and A4 to be 816 days and the difference between the dates in cells B5 and A5 to be 901 days.

7. Enter the following times in the designated cells:

   - **8:12 AM** in cell A7

   - **2:15 PM** in cell B7

8. Construct a formula in cell C7 that calculates the difference between the ending time and the starting time, that is, =B7-A7.

   Excel calculates the difference between the two times and returns 6:03 AM to cell C7. You need to convert this time into a simple number by formatting it with the Number format.

9. Click the drop-down button attached to Number Format on the Ribbon's Home tab and then click the Number option on its drop-down menu to format cell C7 with the Number format with two decimal places.

   Excel now displays 0.25 as the answer in cell C7.

10. Convert the fraction of the day into hours by editing the formula in cell C7 so that the program multiplies the difference between the two cells by 24.

    When editing the formula, be sure to enclose the subtraction operation in parentheses so that Excel performs the subtraction first and then multiplies this difference by 24, as in

    ```
    =(B7-A7)*24
    ```

    After you edit the formula, Excel returns 6.05 as the number of hours in cell C7.

11. Enter the following times in the designated cells:

    - **7:35 AM** in cell A8

    - **15:05** in cell B8

    - **9:45** in cell A9

    - **6 PM** in cell B9

12. Use the Fill handle to copy the formula in cell C7 down to the range C8:C9.

    Because you edited the basic formula in cell C7 so that it returns the number of hours elapsed (rather than the fractional part of the day) and formatted the result with the Number format with two decimal places before you copied the formula, the copies in cells C8 and C9 automatically return the number of hours expressed with two decimal places, 7.50 and 8.25, respectively.

13. Position the cell cursor in cell A1 and then save this new workbook with the filename **Date & time frmls.xlsx** in the Excel 2007 Practice folder and then close the workbook.

Working with Simple Date Functions

Excel contains a number of straightforward Date functions that help you work with dates in your spreadsheets. These functions run the gamut from those that return the current date to those that convert text to date serial numbers (so you can use them in formulas that compute the number of days that have elapsed).

Solve It

Exercise 8-2: Using the TODAY, NOW, DATE, and DATEVALUE Date Functions

In Exercise 8-2, you get practice using several of the simple date functions offered on the Date & Time button's drop-down menu on the Ribbon's Formulas tab.

1. Open the *Exercise8-2.xlsx* workbook file in your Chap8 folder in your Excel 2007 Workbook folder.

This workbook contains a Date Formulas worksheet that you can use to practice building formulas with several of Excel's Date functions.

2. With cell cursor in cell B1, click the Date & Time button on the Ribbon's Formulas tab or press Alt+ME and then click TODAY on its drop-down menu.

Excel inserts the =TODAY() formula in cell B1 and displays its Function Arguments dialog box. This dialog box explains that this particular function takes no arguments.

3. Click OK in the Function Arguments dialog box or press Enter.

Excel enters the current date into cell B1 formatted as 4/5/2008.

4. Click cell D1 in the Date Formulas worksheet, and then select the NOW function on the Date & Time button's drop-down menu and click OK in its Function Arguments dialog box.

Excel inserts the current date and time in cell D1 in the format 4/5/2008 9:10.

5. Press Ctrl+1 to open the Format Cells dialog box. Then, click Time in the Category pane and click the 1:30 PM sample in the Type list box before you click OK.

Excel formats the current date and time in cell D1 so that only the time is displayed, as in 9:10 AM.

6. Click cell D3, and then select the DATE function on the Date & Time button's drop-down menu. Next, designate the numeric entries in cells A3, B3, and C3 of the worksheet as the Date function's arguments in its Function Arguments dialog box in the following order:

• Click cell C3 when the insertion point is in the Year argument text box

• Press Tab and then click cell A3 for the Month argument

• Press Tab and then click cell B3 for the Day argument and then click OK

When you click OK to close the Function Arguments dialog box, Excel returns the date 2/15/1949 to cell D3.

7. Use the Fill handle on cell D3 to copy its formula with the DATE function down to the cell range D4:D8.

Note that contents of the cell range D3:D8 is composed of DATE function formulas rather than date serial numbers. To convert these formulas to their calculated date values, you'll copy them to the Clipboard and then paste their values in column E to the right, using the Paste Values option on the Paste button's drop-down menu.

8. Leave the cell range D3:D8 selected and then press Ctrl+C to copy this range to the Clipboard.

Excel places a marquee around the cell range D3:D8.

9. Click cell E3 and then press Alt+HVV to select the Paste Values option on the Home tab's Paste button's drop-down menu.

Excel copies the date serial numbers into the range E3:E8. Note that the date serial numbers copied into this cell range are completely static: Unlike the DATE function formulas in the cell range D3:D8, revising the numeric entries made in the cells in the range A3:C8 would have no effect on them.

10. Use the Format Cells dialog box (Ctrl+1) to format these date serial numbers in cell range E3:E8 with the Date number format that uses the sample 14-Mar-01.

Next, you'll use the DATEVALUE function to convert the date entries in the cell range A10:A14 of the Date Formulas worksheet that have been entered as text (prefaced with an apostrophe) to their corresponding date serial numbers.

11. Click cell B10 and then select the DATEVALUE function on the Date & Time button's drop-down menu. Click cell A10 to enter this cell address as the Date_Text argument in the Function Arguments dialog box and click OK.

Excel displays the calculated date serial number 32546 in cell B10.

12. Use the Fill handle to copy this DATEVALUE formula in cell B10 down to the cell range B11:B14 and then use Format Cells dialog box (Ctrl+1) to format these date serial numbers with the Date number format that uses the sample 14-Mar-01.

Now, you're ready to save your work in the Date Formulas worksheet.

13. Position the cell cursor in cell F3 of the Date Formulas sheet and save a copy of the workbook with the filename **Date Function Practice.xlsx** in your Excel 2007 Practice folder, and leave the workbook open for Exercise 8-3.

Working with Excel's More Sophisticated Date Functions

In addition to the straightforward Date functions such as TODAY, NOW, DATE, and DATE-VALUE, Excels includes a bunch of more sophisticated and powerful Date functions that you can use to calculate elapsed dates, future dates, days of the week, weeks of the year, and the like. These more sophisticated Date function are all available on the Date & Time button's drop-down menu and take an array of different required and optional arguments. Among the most important of these Date functions on this drop-down menu are

- ✔ **EDATE(*start_date,months*)** calculates the elapsed date so many months ahead (positive months argument) or behind (negative months argument) the start_date argument you specify.

- ✔ **EOMONTH(*start_date,months*)** calculates the last day of the month so many months ahead (positive months argument) or behind (negative months argument) the start_date argument you specify.

- ✔ **NETWORKDAYS(*start_date.end_date,[holidays]*)** calculates the number of work days between the start_date and end_date arguments — the optional holidays argument can specify a range of holiday dates to be excluded from the workday total.

✔ WEEKDAY(*serial_number*,[*return_type*]) calculates a number indicating the day of the week specified by the serial_number argument — the optional return_type argument can be the number 1, 2, or 3 where 1 (or no return_type argument specified) starts the week on Sunday (1) and ends it on Saturday (7), 2 starts the week on Monday (1) and ends it on Sunday (7), and 3 starts the week on Monday (0) and ends it on Sunday (6).

✔ WEEKNUM(*serial_number*,[*return_type*]) calculates a number indicating where the week in the date specified by the serial_number argument falls within the year — the optional return_type argument can be the number 1 or 2, where 1 (or no return_type argument specified) starts the week on Sunday (1) and ends it on Saturday (7) and 2 starts the week on Monday (1) and ends it on Sunday (7).

✔ WORKDAY(*start_date*,*days*,[*holidays*]) calculates the work date that is so many days ahead (positive days argument) or behind (negative days argument) the start_date argument you specify — the optional holidays argument can specify a range of holiday dates to be excluded from the calculation.

✔ YEARFRAC(*start_date*,*end_date*,[*basis*]) calculates the fraction of the year between the start_date and end_date arguments you specify — the optional basis argument can be a number between 0 and 4 that signifies the following:

  • **0** (or no basis argument) bases the year fraction on the U.S. (NASD) method of 30/360 (whereby if the starting date is equal to the 31st of the month, it becomes equal to the 30th; if the ending date is equal to the 31st of the month, the ending date becomes the 1st of the following month).

  • **1** bases the year fraction on the actual days divided by the actual days.

  • **2** bases the year fraction on the actual days divided by 360.

  • **3** bases the year fraction on the actual days divided by 365.

  • **4** bases the year fraction on the European method of 30/360 (whereby starting and ending dates that fall on the 31st of the month are made equal to the 30th of the same month).

Solve It

Exercise 8-3: Using the WEEKDAY, WEEKNUM, and YEARFRAC Date Functions

In Exercise 8-3, you get practice using a few of Excel's more sophisticated Date functions, WEEKDAY, WEEKNUM, and YEARFRAC on the Date & Time button's drop-down menu.

1. Use the Date Formulas worksheet in *Date Function Practice.xlsx* workbook file you created when doing the previous exercise.

You'll start by creating a formula in cell F3 that uses the WEEKDAY function to return the day of week of the date entered in cell E3.

2. With the cell cursor in cell F3, select the WEEKDAY function on the Date & Time button's drop-down menu. Then, click cell E3 to enter this cell address in the Serial_number argument text box and press Tab to select the Return_type text box. Then, type **2** in this text box and click OK to close the WEEKDAY Function Arguments dialog box.

Excel returns 2 to cell F3, indicating that this date in 1949 fell on a Tuesday (when you select 2 as the return_type, 1 is Monday, 2 is Tuesday, 3 is Wednesday, 4 is Thursday, 5 is Friday, 6 is Saturday, and 7 is Sunday).

3. Use the Fill handle to copy this formula with the WEEKDAY function down to the cell range F4:F8.

   Next, you'll use the WEEKNUM Date function to determine the number of the week of each date entered in the range B10:B14.

4. Click cell C10 and then select the WEEKNUM function on the Date & Time button's drop-down menu. Click cell B10 to enter this address in the Serial_number text box and press Tab and type **2** in the Return_type text box before you click OK to close the WEEKNUM's Function Arguments dialog box.

   Excel returns 7 to cell C10, indicating that February 7th fell in the 7th week of 1989 when you designate Monday as the first day of the week.

5. Copy the WEEKNUM formula in cell C10 down to the cell range C11:C14.

   Next, you'll use the YEARFRAC Date function to determine what fractional part of a year the number of days elapsed between two dates represents.

6. Click C17 and select the YEARFRAC function at the very bottom of the Date & Time button's drop-down menu. Click cell A17 to enter this address in the Start_date text box. Then, press Tab and click cell B17 to enter its address in the End_date text box. Finally, press Tab and then type **3** in the Basis text box before you click OK to close the WEEKNUM's Function Arguments dialog box.

   Excel returns 0.2 to cell C17.

7. Format the result in cell C17 with the Number format on the drop-down menu attached to the Number Format command button on the Ribbon's Home tab. Use the Fill handle to copy this formula down to the cell range C18:C19.

   Now you're ready to check your formulas and their answers before you save your work.

8. Check your answers against those shown in the Date Formulas sheet in the *Solved8-3.xlsx* workbook file in your Chap8 subfolder in the Excel 2007 Workbook folder. When everything checks out, save your changes to the *Date Function Practice.xlsx* workbook (Ctrl+S) and then close the workbook.

Working with the Time Functions

Excel's Time functions are a smaller subset of the Date functions. They include the NOW function, which returns the current date and time; TIME, which creates a time fraction from values representing the hour, minutes, and seconds; and TIMEVALUE, which converts a time entered or imported into the worksheet as text so that you can use it in formulas that calculate elapsed times.

Exercise 8-4: Building Formulas with Common Time Functions

In Exercise 8-4, you get practice using a few of Excel's Time functions. These Time functions, like the Date functions you used in Exercises 8-2 and 8-3, are available on the Date & Time button's drop-down menu on the Ribbon's Formulas tab.

1. Open the *Exercise8-4.xlsx* file located in your Chap8 folder in the Excel 2007 Workbook folder on your hard disk.

   The file contains a Time Formulas worksheet that you can use to practice using some of the Time functions.

2. Display the current time in cell B1 using the NOW function — format the result with the 1:30 PM Time format.

   Next, you'll use the TIME function to create various times using the hour, minutes, and seconds entered into the cell range A3:C8.

3. Click cell D3 and then select the TIME function on the Date & Time button's drop-down menu. Then, click A3 to enter its address in the Hour text box; press Tab and click cell B3 to enter its address in the Minute text box; and press Tab and click C3 to enter its address in the Second text box. Finally, click OK to close the TIME Function Arguments dialog box.

   Excel enters the time formatted as 1:10 AM in cell D3.

4. Open the Format Cells dialog box (Ctrl+1) and then format this cell with the Time type 1:30:55 PM sample before you use the Fill handle to copy the formula down to the cell range D4:D7.

   Excel displays the times with hours, minutes, and seconds displayed in this cell range.

5. Widen column D to display all the times. Then, copy the times calculated in the cell range D3:D7 and then paste their fractional values in the range E3:E7.

   To copy only the values from a cell range, paste them into place using the Paste Values option on the Paste button's drop-down menu on the Ribbon's Home tab (Alt+HVV).

6. In cell B10, select the TIMEVALUE function on the Date & Time button's drop-down menu to convert the text entry in cell A10 to a bona fide time.

   Excel returns the fractional time value 0.52083 to cell B10.

7. Open the Format Cells dialog box (Ctrl+1) and format the result in this cell with the 13:30:55 type time format and then copy this formula down to the cell range B11:B14.

   Now you're ready to check your time formulas and their answers before you save your work.

8. Use the Side by Side feature to check your answers against those shown in the Time Formulas sheet in the *Solved8-4.xlsx* workbook file in your Chap8 folder inside your Excel 2007 Workbook folder. When everything checks out, click cell B1 in your Time Formulas worksheet and save it in a new workbook named **Time Function Practice.xlsx** inside your Excel 2007 Practice folder. Then exit Excel.

Chapter 9

Financial Formulas and Functions

• •

• •

*A*s the old song says, "Money makes the world go round" and to that end, Excel supplies you with plenty of built-in functions for getting the latest spin on how much you're making and spending. In this chapter, you get the chance to practice using some of the basic investment, depreciation, and currency conversion functions that make up a part of the program's financial group.

Working with Financial Functions

Excel offers a fair number of sophisticated financial functions for determining such things as the present, future, or net present value of an investment; the payment, number of periods, or the principal or interest part of a payment on an amortized loan; the rate of return on an investment; and the depreciation of your favorite assets.

The key to using many of Excel's financial functions is in understanding the terminology used by their arguments. Many of the most common financial functions such as PV (Present Value), NPV (Net Present Value), FV (Future Value), and PMT (Payment) take similar arguments:

✔ **Pv** is the present value that is the principal amount of the annuity.

✔ **Fv** is the future value that represents the principal plus interest on the annuity.

✔ **Pmt** is the payment made each period in the annuity. Normally, the payment is set over the life of the annuity and includes principal plus interest without any other fees.

✔ **Rate** is the interest rate per period. Normally, the rate is expressed as an annual percentage.

✔ **Nper** is the total number of payment periods in the life of the annuity. It is calculated by taking the Term (the amount of time that interest is paid) and multiplying it by the Period (the point in time when interest is paid or earned) so that a loan with a three-year term with 12 monthly interest payments has 3 x 12, or 36, payment periods.

When using financial functions, keep in mind that the fv, pv, or pmt arguments can be positive or negative, depending on whether you're receiving the money (as in the case of an investment) or paying out the money (as in the case of a loan). Also keep in mind that you want to express the rate argument in the same units as the nper argument. For example, if you make monthly payments on a loan and you express the nper as the total number of monthly payments (as in 360 (30 x 12) for 30-year mortgage), you need to express the annual interest rate in monthly terms as well. So if, for example, you pay an annual interest rate of 7.5% on the loan, you express the rate argument as 0.075/12 so that it is monthly as well.

Using the Basic Investment Functions

The following six functions form the core Excel financial functions for determining whether a particular investment is worthwhile:

- **FV(*rate,nper,pmt,[pv],[type]*)** — Future Value — calculates the future value of an investment, assuming a constant interest rate and constant payments on a periodic basis.

- **PV(*rate,nper,pmt,[fv],[type]*)** — Present Value — calculates the present value of an investment; that is, the total amount that a series of future payments is worth now.

- **PMT(*rate,nper,pv,[fv],[type]*)** — Payment — calculates the payment for a loan, assuming a constant interest rate and stream of payments.

- **RATE(*nper,pmt,pv,[fv],[type]*)** calculates the interest rate for any type of annuity.

- **NPER(*rate,pmt,pv,[fv],[type]*)** — Number of Periods — calculates how many periods are required for an investment, assuming a constant interest rate and constant payments on a periodic basis.

- **NPV(*rate,value1,[value2],[...]*)** — Net Present Value — calculates the present value of an investment by using a discount rate and a series of future payments (negative values) and income (positive values).

As you can see in this list, the syntax of these functions is similar, requiring, with the exception of NPV, their own particular combination of the standard rate, nper, pmt, and pv arguments discussed in the previous section. You will also note that the functions that use these combination take the following optional arguments (indicated in the square brackets):

- **[*Pv*]** optional argument in the FV function is the present value or lump-sum amount for which you wish to calculate the future value: If you omit the pv argument, Excel assumes a present value of zero (0).

- **[*Fv*]** optional argument in the PV, PMT, RATE, and NPER functions represents the future value or cash balance you want to have after making your last payment: If you omit the fv argument, Excel assumes a future value of zero (0).

- **[*Type*]** optional argument in the FV, PV, PMT, RATE, and NPER functions indicates whether the payment is made at the beginning or the end of the period — enter 0 (or omit the type argument) when the payment is made at the end of the period and use 1 when it is made at the beginning of the period.

✔ **[Guess]** optional argument for the RATE function indicates the estimated rate percentage (assumed to be 10 percent if this optional argument is omitted). Note that this optional argument does *not* appear in the Function Arguments dialog box for the RATE function; therefore, you can only add this optional argument to the RATE function when you manually enter it into a cell's formula.

Exercise 9-1: Building Formulas with the FV, PV, PMT, RATE, and NPER Functions

In Exercise 9-1, you get a chance to practice using the FV, PV, PMT, RATE, and NPER financial functions to solve a series of seven real-world problems found on the four worksheets (FV, PV, PMT, and NPER) in the *Exercise9-1.xlsx* workbook file.

1. If Excel is not currently running, launch the program and then open the *Exercise9-1.xlsx* workbook file inside your Chap9 folder in the Excel 2007 Workbook folder.

Use the problems found on the FV, PV, PMT, and NPER worksheets in this workbook to practice creating financial formulas using the FV, PV, PMT, RATE, and NPER functions.

2. Position the cell cursor in cell C4 of the FV worksheet, the answer cell for Question 1, and then click the FV option on the Financial button's drop-down menu on the Ribbon's Formulas tab. Then, use the Hint cells in the range C7:C11 to construct the appropriate arguments for the FV function.

When defining the arguments for your FV function in its Function Arguments dialog box, move the dialog box out of the way of the cell range B7:C11 and then click the appropriate cell in this range to define the three required (Rate, Nper, and Pmt) and two optional arguments (PV and Type) when the insertion point is located in its argument text box.

Excel returns a future value of $5,938.43 in the answer cell C4 of the FV worksheet.

3. Position the cell cursor in cell C15 of the FV worksheet, the answer cell for Question 2, and select the FV option on the Financial button's drop-down menu to construct a formula using the FV financial function (with the appropriate cells in the range B18:C22 as its arguments) that calculates the total amount of money that you pay on the loan.

Excel returns a future value of -$14,519.23 in the answer cell C15 of the FV worksheet.

Now, switch to the PV worksheet and get some practice creating formulas that use the Present Value financial function.

4. Click cell C4 of the PV worksheet, the answer cell for Question 3, and then select the PV option on the Financial button's drop-down to construct a formula using the PV financial function (with the appropriate cells in the range B7:C11 as its arguments) that calculates the amount of money you should pay for the property.

Excel returns a present value of -$718,227.17 in the answer cell C4 of the PV worksheet.

5. Position the cell cursor in cell C15 of the PV worksheet, the answer cell for Question 4, and select the RATE option on the Financial button's drop-down menu to construct a formula using the RATE financial function (with the appropriate cells in the range B7:C11 as its arguments) and your answer to Question 3 in cell C4 to check the interest rate.

Excel returns an interest rate of 6.50% in the answer cell C15 of the PV worksheet (same as the rate entered into cell C7 of this worksheet).

6. Click cell C4 of the PMT worksheet, the answer cell for Question 5, and then select the PMT function on the Financial button's drop-down menu to construct a formula using the PMT financial function (with the appropriate cells in the range B7:C11 as its arguments) that calculates your monthly loan payment.

Be sure that you convert the rate argument and the nper argument for the PMT function you construct to the equivalent months by entering the appropriate calculations to their cell references in the Rate and Nper argument text boxes of the Function Arguments dialog box for the PMT function. In that way, the annual interest rate in C7 is divided by 12 and the number of years in C8 is multiplied by 12.

Excel returns a payment of -$3,987.02 to the answer cell C4 of the PMT worksheet.

7. Click cell C15 of the PMT worksheet, the answer cell for Question 6, and there construct a formula using the PV financial function with the appropriate cells in the range B7:C11 as its arguments to check the loan amount you used in Question 5.

The formula with the PV in cell C15 should compute the same $465,000 amount entered in cell C9 that you used as the PV argument of the PMT function in cell C4.

8. Click C4 of the NPER worksheet, the answer cell for Question 7, and then select the NPER function on the Financial button's drop-down button to construct a formula using the NPER financial function (with the appropriate cells in the range B7:C11 as its arguments) that calculates how long it will take you to pay off your loan.

Be sure that you convert the answer returned by the NPER function in months to the equivalent years.

Excel returns -13.64 years to the answer cell C4 of the NPER worksheet (after you divide the -163.71 months returned by the NPER function by 12).

9. Check your answers against those in the equivalent worksheets in the *Solved9-1.xlsx* workbook located in your Chap9 folder in the Excel 2007 Workbook folder.

After you check your financial formulas and answers, you're ready to save your work in a new practice workbook.

10. Click cell A1 of the FV worksheet and save your work in a new workbook file named **Financial Function Practice.xlsx** in your Excel 2007 Practice folder. Close this new workbook.

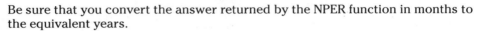

Exercise 9-2: Building Formulas with the IRR and NPV Functions

The NPV function returns the sum of any series of cash flows, discounted to the present day, using a particular discount rate. The cash flows tracked by the NPV function are either income (money you make) indicated by positive numbers in the function's values argument, or payments (money you pay out) indicated by specifying negative numbers.

When using the NPV function to determine the wisdom of an investment, you keep in mind that this function assumes that the cash flows (be they income or payments) specified by the values argument(s) are all made at the end of the first period. As this assumption does not conform to the understanding of net present value in standard accounting, when using this function, you always need to include a Time 0 (even if its value is $0) in order for your answer to be in accord with the accepted definition of NPV.

In Exercise 9-2, you get an opportunity to practice using both the NPV and IRR functions (Internal Rate of Return) to determine the advisability of making certain capital expenditures in the form of equipment purchases. The IRR function returns the interest rate received for an investment consisting of cash flows (income and payments) made at regular intervals. Note that unlike when using the RATE function, the cash flows do not have to be equal, although they must be made regularly on a periodic basis (monthly, quarterly, annually, and the like).

The IRR function computes its result using an iterative process (similar to that used to resolve certain circular references like the one you encountered in Chapter 7). For this reason, the function takes an optional guess argument, where you may specify your best guess or target percentage. If you don't specify a guess argument for an IRR function, Excel automatically uses 10% as its target.

1. Open the *Exercise9-2.xlsx* workbook file inside your Chap9 folder in the Excel 2007 Workbook folder.

   In this exercise, you finish the model constructed on its NPV & IRR worksheet. In doing so, you get practice using the NPV and IRR functions to determine the financial wisdom of making capital expenditures in the form of purchased equipment, given the level of anticipated income resulting from the asset acquisition, the anticipated taxes on that extra income, and the depreciation of those assets over their three year life.

2. Select the cell range B3:C7 and then click the Create from Selection button on the Formulas tab or press Alt+MC to open Create Names from Selection dialog box. Make sure that only the Left Column check box is selected in this dialog box before you click OK.

   Excel assigns the row headings in B3:B7 to the cells in C3:C7.

3. Make the following entries in the designated cells:

   - **38000** in cell C3
   - **1500** in cell C4
   - **15000** in cell C5
   - **6%** in cell C6
   - **27%** in cell C7

4. Click cell H10 and type = - (an equal to sign followed by a minus sign with no spaces) and then click cell C3 and then click the Enter button on the Formula bar.

   Cell H10 contains the formula =-Initial_Cost and returns the value -38,000 to the cell in the worksheet.

5. Click cell C11 and type = (an equal to sign) and then click cell C5 before you click the Enter button on the Formula bar.

   Cell C11 contains the formula =Expected_Income and returns 15,000 to the cell in the worksheet.

6. Click cell D11 and then select the SLN (Straight Line depreciatioN) function on the Financial button's drop-down menu.

The SLN function takes three arguments; cost, with the initial cost of your asset; salvage, with the value of the asset at the end of its useful life; and life, which indicates the number of years that the asset is expected to be in use.

7. While the insertion point is in the Cost argument text box, click cell C3 in the worksheet to insert the range name Initial_Cost in this box. Then, press Tab and click cell C4 to insert the range name Salvage_Value in the Salvage argument text box. Finally, press Tab again and type **3** in the Life argument text box and then click OK.

Excel inserts an SLN function in cell D11 and returns the answer 12,167 to its cell in the worksheet.

8. Click cell E11 and construct a formula that subtracts the first-year depreciation amount in cell D11 from the pre-taxable income in cell C11.

Excel returns 2,833 to cell E11.

9. Click cell F11 and construct a formula that deducts the estimated taxes using the tax rate percentage in cell C7 from the taxable income in cell E11.

The standard way to construct this type of formula is to multiply the taxable income by 1 minus the tax rate. In this particular case, this formula in F11 would appear as

```
=E11*(1-Tax_Rate)
```

Excel returns an after-tax amount of 2,068 to cell F11.

10. Click cell H11 and there construct a SUM formula that adds the depreciation value in cell D11 to the after-tax income in cell F11 to the salvage value in cell G11. (I explain more about depreciation and salvage values in the next section of this chapter.)

Excel inserts the formula =SUM(D11,F11,G11) in cell H11 and returns a sum of 14,235 to the cell in the worksheet.

11. Use the Fill handle to copy the entries in the cell range C11:H11 down to the range C12:H13.

Now, you're ready to build the formula that brings the salvage value in cell C4 to cell G13 in the table.

12. Click cell G13 and construct a formula with a reference to the Salvage_Value cell C4.

This formula in cell G13 appears as

```
=Salvage_Value
```

13. Click cell F2 and type = (equal to sign), and then click cell H10 in the worksheet to select it before you type + (plus sign).

The formula in the cell and on the Formula bar in F2 now reads

```
=H10+
```

14. Click the Financial button on the Formulas tab; then click the NPV option on its drop-down menu to insert NPV() into the formula. Click cell C6 to insert the Interest_Rate range name in the Rate argument text box. Press Tab and then select the cell range H11:H13 in the worksheet to insert this range address in the Value1 text box and then click OK.

Excel inserts the following formula in cell F2 that computes the net present value of the investment in cell F2 as $1,310:

```
=H10+NPV(Interest_Rate,H11:H13)
```

15. Click cell H2 and then select the IRR option on the Financial button's drop-down menu. Select the cell range H10:H13 in the worksheet to insert this range address in the Values argument text box and then click OK.

    Excel computes an 8% internal rate of return on this investment, which is certainly acceptable.

16. Check your model against the one in the NPV & IRR worksheet in the *Solved9-2.xlsx* workbook in your Chap9 folder of your Excel 2007 Workbook folder.

    If everything checks out, proceed to the next step, where you change some of the basic assumptions of your model.

17. Change the following values in the designated cells:

    • **1000** in the Salvage_Value cell C4

    • **12000** in the Expected_Income cell C5

    Note that at this salvage value and anticipated income amount, the net present value is a loss of $4,884 and the internal rate of return has now sunk to a dismal =1% — with these figures, the capital investment is decidedly not a wise one.

18. Click the Undo button on the Quick Access toolbar or press Ctrl+Z until you have restored the original salvage value and expected income figures to the spreadsheet.

    Now you're ready to save your work.

19. Click cell A1 and then save your work in a new workbook named **NPV & IRR Function Practice.xlsx** in your Excel 2007 Practice folder and then close this new workbook.

Figuring the Depreciation of an Asset

The moment you put an asset you purchase into service, it begins to depreciate (lose value). Excel lets you choose between four different Depreciation functions, each of which uses a slightly different method for depreciating an asset over time. These built-in Depreciation functions include

✔ **SLN** to calculate straight-line depreciation

✔ **SYD** to calculate sum-of-years-digits depreciation

✔ **DB** to calculate declining balance depreciation

✔ **DDB** to calculate double-declining balance depreciation

All four depreciation functions require the following cost, salvage, and life arguments, and in addition, all except the SLN function require the period argument:

- ✔ Cost, indicating the initial cost of the asset that you're depreciating.

- ✔ Salvage, indicating the value of the asset at the end of the depreciation (also known as the salvage value of the asset).

- ✔ Life, indicating the number of periods over which the asset is depreciated (also known as the useful life of the asset).

- ✔ Period, indicating the period over which the asset is being depreciated — note that the units you use in the period argument must be the same as those used in the life argument of the Depreciation function. For example, if you express the life argument in years, you must also express the period argument in years.

Note that DB function accepts an optional month argument. This argument is the number of months the asset is in use in the first year. If you omit this optional argument from your DB function, Excel assumes the number of months of service to be 12. Also, when using the DDB function, you can add an optional factor argument. This argument is the rate at which the balance declines in the depreciation schedule. If you omit this optional argument, Excel assumes the rate to be 2 (thus, the name *double-declining balance*).

The following exercise gives you an opportunity to practice using all four types of depreciation in a partially completed Depreciation Table that then enables you to compare the amount of depresication each year in the useful life of an asset.

Solve It | Exercise 9-3: Building Formulas with the SLN, SYD, DB, and DDB Depreciation Functions

In Exercise 9-3, you get practice creating a depreciation table that uses all four types of depreciation functions: SLN, SYD, DB, and DDB.

1. Open the *Exercise9-3.xlsx* workbook file inside your Chap9 folder in the Excel 2007 Workbook folder.

   This workbook contains a Depreciation worksheet with a Depreciation Table comparing the four depreciation methods side by side that you will complete.

2. Select the cell range B3:C6 and then click the Create from Selection button on the Ribbon's Formulas tab or press Alt+MC to open the Create Names from Selection dialog box. Make sure that only the Left Column check box is selected in this dialog box and then click OK.

   Excel assigns the row headings in the range B3:B6 to the cells C3:C6 in the Depreciation worksheet.

3. Make the following entries in the designated cells:

   - **Office Furniture** in the Type_of_Asset cell, C3

   - **50000** in the Cost cell, C4

   - **10** in the Life_in_years cell, C5

   - **1000** in the Salvage cell, C6

4. Click cell C9 and construct a formula that references the Cost cell, C4, and then use the Fill handle to copy this formula across the row to the cell range D9:F9.

   Now you're ready to build a formula that deducts the straight-line depreciation for the first year in cell C10.

5. Click cell C10; there, type = (an equal sign) and then click cell C9 before you type – (minus sign).

   The formula in the cell and on the Formula bar now reads

   ```
   =C9-
   ```

6. Click the SLN option on Financial button's drop-down menu. Then, click C4 to insert the Cost range name in the Function Arguments Cost text box. Press Tab and then click C6 to insert the Salvage range name in the Salvage text box. Finally, press Tab and click cell C5 to insert the range name Life__in_years cell (C5) in the Life text box before you click OK.

   Excel inserts the formula =C9-SLN(Cost,Salvage,Life_in_years) and returns $45,100 in cell C10 in the worksheet.

7. Copy the formula in cell C10 down to the cell range C11:C19.

   Next, you need to construct a formula that calculates the first-year depreciation using the sum-of-years-digits method.

8. Click cell D10 and construct a formula that subtracts the cost amount in D9 from the first-year depreciation returned by the SYD function using the following arguments:

   - Cost cell in the Cost text box
   - Salvage cell in the Salvage text box
   - Life_in_years cell in the Life text box
   - Cell B10 in the Per text box

9. Copy the formula in cell D10 down the cell range D11:D19.

   Now, you're ready to construct a formula that calculates the first-year depreciation using the declining balance method.

10. Click cell E10 and construct a formula that subtracts the cost amount in E9 from the first-year depreciation returned by the DB function using the following arguments:

    - Cost cell in the Cost text box
    - Salvage cell in the Salvage text box
    - Life_in_years cell in the Life text box
    - Cell B10 in the Period text box

11. Copy the formula in cell E10 down the cell range E11:E19.

    Next, you construct the formula that calculates the first-year depreciation using the double-declining balance method.

12. Click cell F10 and construct a formula that subtracts the cost amount in F9 from the first-year depreciation returned by the DDB function using the following arguments:

- Cost cell in the Cost text box

- Salvage cell in the Salvage text box

- Life_in_years cell in the Life text box

- Cell B10 in the Period text box

13. Copy the formula in cell F10 down the cell range F11:F19.

Now your depreciation table is complete. All you have to do is check your table against the one in the Depreciation worksheet in the *Solved9-3.xlsx* workbook.

14. Check the formulas in your Depreciation worksheet against those in the *Solved9-3.xlsx* workbook file in your Chap9 folder in your Excel 2007 Workbook folder.

When everything checks out, proceed to Step 15.

15. Make the following updates in the designated cells:

- **25000** in the Cost Cell (C4)

- **5** in the Life_in_years cell (C5)

- **500** in the Salvage cell (C6)

Note that when Excel finishes recalculating the Depreciation Table using your new inputs, the depreciation formulas in the Straight Line column (C) return negative values to all the rows below Year 5 and #NUM! error values to the SYD, Declining Balance, and Double-declining Balance columns.

16. Click the Undo button on the Quick Access toolbar or press Ctrl+Z until you have restored the original Cost, Life_in_years, and Salvage values to cells C4, C5, and C6 in the table. Next save your work in a workbook file named **Depreciation Function Practice.xlsx** in your Excel 2007 Practice folder before you close the file.

Chapter 10

Using Math Functions

● ●

In This Chapter

▶ Rounding off numbers in a spreadsheet

▶ Using functions for calculating products, powers, and square roots

▶ Summing the products in cells ranges or arrays

▶ Doing conditional summing

● ●

*T*he Math & Trig group of functions includes a wide variety of mathematical functions for computing new values as well as for controlling the results of calculations. This group also includes a large assortment of trigonometric functions most often needed in engineering and scientific endeavors. In this chapter, you get a chance to practice using some of the math functions more commonly needed in spreadsheets for business applications.

Rounding Off Values

Rounding off numbers that have fractions is one of the more frequent tasks you may undertake in Excel. Excel includes three functions in the Math & Trig category that you can use for rounding off the numbers in a worksheet:

✔ **ROUND(*number,num_digits*)** to round the value specified by the number argument to the number of digits specified by the num_digits argument

✔ **ROUNDUP(*number,num_digits*)** to round up the value away from 0 (zero) that is specified by the number argument to the number of digits specified by the num_digits argument

✔ **ROUNDDOWN(*number,num_digits*)** to round down the value toward 0 (zero) that is specified by the number argument to the number of digits specified by the num_digits argument

Q. What's the difference between using one of Excel's rounding functions to round off values to a particular decimal place and using a number format to control how many decimal places are displayed?

A. Formatting a number only changes the way the value appears in the cell, whereas rounding off a number with one of the Excel functions actually changes the number of digits in the value entered in that cell.

Solve It

Exercise 10-1: Building Formulas with the ROUND, ROUNDUP, and ROUNDDOWN Functions

In Exercise 10-1, you get practice using the ROUND, ROUNDUP, and ROUNDDOWN Math functions to change the precision of various values in a worksheet.

1. If Excel isn't running, launch the program and then open the *Exercise10-1.xlsx* workbook file in your Chap10 folder in the Excel 2007 Workbook folder.

This file contains a Rounding Functions worksheet, where you can practice using the ROUND, ROUNDUP, and ROUNDDOWN functions on the value of the mathematical constant pi, accurate to nine decimal places, returned by the PI function to cell A3.

2. Click cell B3 and then click the ROUND option on the Math & Trig button's drop-down menu on the Ribbon's Formulas tab. Then, click cell A3 to insert its address in the Number text box of the Function Arguments dialog box. Finally, press Tab and then type 0 in the Num_digits text box before you click OK to close the ROUND Function Arguments dialog box.

B3 contains the formula =ROUND(A3,0) and displays 3 in its cell.

3. In cell B4, construct a formula with the ROUND function that rounds off the value of pi in cell A3 to one decimal place.

Because all the rounding formulas you're going to create for this exercise use the same value in cell A3, you can save time by making copies of the original ROUND formula and then editing the function name and/or the num_digits argument in the copies as needed. To do this, however, you must remember to convert the reference to cell A3 from relative to absolute when constructing the formula with the Insert Function feature.

B4 contains the formula =ROUND(A3,1) and displays 3.1 in its cell.

4. In cell B5, construct a formula with the ROUND function that rounds off the value of pi in cell A3 to two decimal places.

B5 contains the formula =ROUND(A3,2) and displays 3.14 in its cell.

5. In cell B6, construct a formula with the ROUND function that rounds off the value of pi in cell A3 to three decimal places.

B6 contains the formula =ROUND(A3,3) and displays 3.142 in its cell.

6. Click cell B7 and then click the ROUNDUP option on the Math & Trig button's drop-down menu. Click cell A3 to insert its address into the Number text box of the

Function Arguments dialog box. Then, press Tab and type **2** in the Num_digits text box before you click OK to close the ROUNDUP Function Arguments dialog box.

B7 contains the formula =ROUNDUP(A3,2) and displays 3.15 in its cell.

7. In cell B8, construct a formula with the ROUNDUP function that rounds up the value of pi in cell A3 to four decimal places.

B8 contains the formula =ROUNDUP(A3,4) and displays 3.1416 in its cell.

8. Click cell B9 and then click the ROUNDDOWN option on the Math & Trig button's drop-down menu. Click cell A3 to insert its address into the Number text box of the Function Arguments dialog box. Then, press Tab and type **2** in the Num_digits text box before you click OK to close the ROUNDDOWN Function Arguments dialog box.

B9 contains the formula =ROUNDDOWN(A3,2) and displays 3.14 in its cell.

9. In cell B10, construct a formula with the ROUNDDOWN function that rounds down the value of pi in cell A3 to four decimal places.

B10 contains the formula =ROUNDDOWN(A3,4) and displays 3.1415 in its cell display. Compare your spreadsheet to one shown in Figure 10-1. If everything checks out, proceed to Step 10.

10. Save your workbook file in your Excel 2007 Practice folder with the filename **Round Off Practice.xlsx** and then close the workbook.

Figure 10-1: The Round Off Practice .xlsx workbook with its ROUND, ROUNDUP, and ROUNDDOWN formulas.

Finding Products, Powers, and Square Roots

Although you can create formulas that multiply values using the asterisk (*) operator as well as those that raise a number to a particular power by using the caret (^), Excel also includes PRODUCT and POWER functions that perform these types of calculations for you. And for those times when you need to find the square root of a value, the program includes a SQRT function. These three Math functions work with the following arguments:

- ✔ **PRODUCT(*number1,number2,* . . .)** where the number1 and number2 arguments are the values you want to multiply with one another

- ✔ **POWER(*number,power*)** where the number argument is the value you want to raise to the power specified by the power argument

- ✔ **SQRT(*number*)** where the number argument is the value for which you want the square root

---

Solve It

Exercise 10-2: Building Formulas with PRODUCT, POWER, and SQRT

In Exercise 10-2, you get practice using the Math & Trig PRODUCT function to calculate the product of a range of values, the POWER function to square and cube values, and the SQRT function to find the square root of values.

1. Open the *Exercise10-2.xlsx* workbook file in your Chap10 folder in the Excel 2007 Workbook folder.

   This file contains a Misc. Math Functions worksheet where you can practice using the PRODUCT, POWER, and SQRT functions in a couple of tables.

2. Click cell D3 and then click the PRODUCT option on the Math & Trig button's drop-down menu. Drag through cells B3 and C3 to insert the range B3:C3 in the Number1 text box of the PRODUCT Function Arguments dialog box before you click OK.

   D3 contains the formulas =PRODUCT(B3:C3) and displays 46 in its cell.

3. Format the computed amount in cell D3 with the Accounting Number Format button in the Number group of the Ribbon's Home tab and then copy this formula down to the cell range D4:D5.

   Next, you'll use the POWER function to square and cube values in the worksheet.

4. Click cell B9 and then click the POWER option on the Math & Trig button's drop-down menu. Then, click A9 to insert its address in the Number text box of the Function Arguments dialog box. Press Tab and then type **2** in Power text box before you click OK. Then, copy this POWER formula down to the cell range B10:B11.

   Next, create a formula using the POWER function that cubes a value by raising the number to the power of 3.

5. In cell C9, construct a formula with the POWER function that cubes the value in cell A9 and then copy this POWER formula down to the cell range C10:C11.

   Now you'll use the SQRT function to find the square roots of values in the worksheet.

6. Click cell D9 and then click the SQRT option on the Math & Trig button's drop-down menu. Then click cell A9 to insert its address into the Number text box of the SQRT Function Arguments dialog box and click OK. Then, copy this SQRT formula down to the cell range D10:D11.

Cell D11 returns a #NUM! error value in the cell because the SQRT function cannot compute square roots for negative numbers (multiplying one negative number by another always results in a positive product).

To avoid the #NUM! error in this formula, you can nest the ABS function that returns the absolute value of cell A11 (which is always positive) inside the SQRT function as follows:

```
=SQRT(ABS(A11))
```

7. Edit the original formula in cell D9 by positioning the insertion point between the T in SQRT and the open parenthesis. Type **(ABS** and then position the insertion point between 9 in A9 and the close parenthesis, and then type another close parenthesis before clicking the Enter button on the Formula bar.

The edited formula should appear on the Formula bar as follows:

```
=SQRT(ABS(A9))
```

8. Copy this edited version of the SQRT formula with the nested ABS function over the original formula copies in the cell range D10:D11.

Check your results against those shown in Figure 10-2. If everything checks out, proceed to Step 9.

9. Save your workbook file in the Excel 2007 Practice folder with the filename **Prod Power Sqrt Practice.xlsx** and then close the workbook.

Figure 10-2:
The Prod Power Sqrt Practice.xlsx workbook with its PRODUCT, POWER, and SQRT formulas.

	A	B	C	D
2	Code	Price	Qty	Total Price
3	908978	$ 23.00	2	$ 46.00
4	456078	$ 45.00	3	$ 135.00
5	234478	$ 67.00	4	$ 268.00
8	Value	Squared	Cubed	Square Root
9	24	576	13824	4.898979486
10	35	1225	42875	5.916079783
11	-9	81	-729	3

D11 =SQRT(ABS(A11))

Doing Fancier Sums

Without any doubt, SUM is the preeminent function in the Math & Trig category. This function is so central to spreadsheet formula making that the Home tab of the Ribbon contains its own AutoSum button to facilitate the construction of all your SUM formulas.

The SUM function is not the only function in the Math & Trig category capable of computing totals. In addition, the program offers more specialized summing functions for use when you need to total the products or squares of the values in a range or total values only when a particular condition is met.

Summing products, squares, and their differences

You can use the SUMPRODUCT function to have Excel total the products returned by multiplying the values in corresponding arrays. For one array to correspond to another, each must consist of the same number of rows and columns.

For example, suppose you have a spreadsheet with a 2 x1 array in the cell range B2:B3 that contains the values 4 and 5 (expressed as {4;5}), and another 2 x 1 array in the cell range D2:D3 that contains the values 6 and 3 (expressed {6;3}) — see Chapter 7 for a quick refresher on arrays. Because both these arrays have the same number of rows (2) and columns (1), they correspond and can be used as arguments in the SUMPRODUCT function.

The SUMPRODUCT function uses the following syntax:

```
SUMPRODUCT(array1,array2, . . .)
```

Note that the SUMPRODUCT function accepts up to a maximum of 30 array arguments. The SUMPRODUCT function is not the only summing function to use these arguments. The following summing functions also follow the same syntax as SUMPRODUCT:

- ✔ **SUMX2MY2** (SUM X squared minus Y squared) to sum the difference between the squares of two corresponding arrays

- ✔ **SUMX2PY2** (SUM X squared plus Y squared) to return the grand total of the sums of the squares in two corresponding arrays

- ✔ **SUMXMY2** (SUM X minus Y squared) to sum the squares of the differences in two corresponding arrays

The SUMSQ function that totals the squares of the arguments is similar to these summing functions except that you can use individual numbers as well arrays for its arguments.

Solve It

Exercise 10-3: Building Formulas with the SUMPRODUCT, SUMSQ, and SUMX2MY2 Functions

In Exercise 10-3, you get practice using the Math functions SUMPRODUCT, SUMSQ, and SUMX2MY2 to calculate products and square roots in arrays that you've entered into a worksheet.

1. Open the *Exercise10-3.xlsx* workbook file in your Chap10 folder in the Excel 2007 Workbook folder.

   This file contains a SUM Functions worksheet with two 2 x 1 arrays, the first in light yellow in the cell range B2:B3 and the second in light green in the cell range D2:D3. You will use these arrays to practice using the SUMPRODUCT, SUMSQ, and SUMX2PY2 functions.

2. Click cell F6 and then click the SUMPRODUCT option on the Math & Trig button's drop-down menu. Drag through cells B2 and B3 to enter the range address B2:B3 in the Array1 text box of the Function Arguments dialog box. Then, press Tab and drag through cells D2 and D3 to insert the range address D2:D3 in the Array2 text box before you click OK.

   Excel inserts the formula =SUMPRODUCT(B2:B3,D2:D3) into cell F6 and returns a result of 39 as the sum of the products of the two arrays.

3. Verify the calculated result returned by the SUMPRODUCT formula in cell F6 by constructing the following simple formulas in the designated cells that replicate the computation made by the SUMPRODUCT function:

   - Formula in cell C6 that multiplies the value in B2 by that in D2

   - Formula in cell D6 that multiplies the value in B3 by that in D3

   - Formula in cell E6 that adds the value in C6 to that in D6

   The calculated total returned to cell E6 should be 39, just like one in cell F6 next door.

4. Click cell G8 and then select the SUMSQ option on the Math & Trig button's drop-down menu. Then, select cell B2 in the worksheet as the Number1 argument and cell D2 as the Number2 argument in the SUMSQ Function Arguments dialog box before you click OK.

   Excel returns a total of 52 to cell G8.

5. Verify the calculated result returned by the SUMSQ formula in cell G8 by constructing the following simple formulas in the designated cells that replicate its computation:

   - Formula in cell D8 that squares the value in B2

   - Formula in cell E8 that squares the value in D2

   - Formula in cell F8 that adds the value in D8 to that in E8

 To square a value in a cell with a simple formula, insert the cell reference followed by the caret (^) operator and 2 (for example, =B2^2 to square the value in B2). To square a value with a function, select the POWER option on the Math & Trig button's drop-down menu and then select B2 as the Number argument and type **2** as the Power argument.

   The calculated total returned to cell F8 should also be 52, matching the one in cell G8 next door.

6. Click cell G10 and then click the SUMSQ option on the Math & Trig button's drop-down menu. Then, select the cell range B2:B3 as the Number1 argument and cell range D2:D3 as the Number2 argument before you click OK.

   Excel inserts the formula =SUMSQ(B2:B3,D2:D3) in cell G10 and returns a sum of 86.

7. Verify the calculated result returned by the SUMSQ formula in cell G10 by constructing the following simple formulas in the designated cells that replicate its computation:

   - Formula in cell B10 that squares the value in B2

   - Formula in cell C10 that squares the value in B3

   - Formula in cell D10 that squares the value in D2

   - Formula in cell E10 that squares the value in D3

   - Formula in cell F10 that sums the values in cell range B10:E10

   The calculated total returned to cell F10 should now be 86, matching the one in cell G10.

8. Click cell G12 and then click the SUMX2MY2 option on the Math & Trig button's drop-down menu. Then, select the cell range B2:B3 as the Array_x argument and cell range D2:D3 as the Array_y argument before you click OK.

   Excel inserts the formula =SUMX2MY2(B2:B3,D2:D3) in cell G12 and returns a sum of -4.

9. Verify the calculated result returned by the SUMX2MY2 formula in cell G10 by constructing the following simple formulas in the designated cells that replicate its computation:

   - Formula in cell B12 that squares the value in B2

   - Formula in cell C12 that squares the value in B3

   - Formula in cell D12 that squares the value in D2

   - Formula in cell E12 that squares the value in D3

   - Formula in cell F12 that subtracts the sum of D12 plus E12 from the sum of B12 plus C12

When constructing the formula in cell F12 that subtracts the sum of D12 plus E12 from that of B12 plus C12, be sure to enclose the values to be summed (B12+C12) and (D12+E12) in parentheses.

The calculated total -4 returned to cell F12 should now match the one in cell G12.

10. Open the *Solved10-3.xlsx* workbook in the Chap10 folder in the Excel 2007 Workbook folder and check the results in your SUM formulas sheet against its formulas. If everything checks out, save your work in a workbook in your Excel 2007 Practice folder with the filename **SumProd-Sq-Diff Practice.xlsx** and then close this workbook.

Conditional totals

All the variations of the SUM function you've used up to now calculate their totals come rain or shine. The SUMIF function, however, is a little different: It only sums its designated values when a particular condition is true. The SUMIF function, although located in the Math & Trig category, could have just as easily been classified as one of the Logical functions (see Chapter 13) because it basically works only when its comparative condition returns the logical value TRUE (refer back to Chapter 6 for a refresher on creating comparative formulas that return TRUE or FALSE as their answers).

The syntax of the SUMIF function includes the following arguments:

```
SUMIF(range,criteria,[sum_range])
```

The range argument specifies the cells that you want Excel to evaluate using the condition or conditions specified by the criteria argument. The optional sum_range argument specifies the cells you want Excel to sum when the condition in the criteria argument is found TRUE. You only need to specify a sum_range argument when the cell range to be summed is not the same as the one whose values are evaluated as to whether they meet the condition set up the criteria argument.

To get some practice using the SUMIF function, you will work with the Jan-06 Sales worksheet in the workbook containing the data list of the January 2006 sales for the fictitious company, Chris's Cookies. This data list tracks the sales by store location, the type of baked item sold (lemon tarts, blueberry muffins, Lots of Chips cookies, and strawberry pie), the date of sale, the number of dozens sold, the price per dozen, and the daily sales total. Most of these fields tracked in the data list have range names assigned to their data (Store_name to the data in the Store field, Date_sold to the data in the Date field, Item_sold to data in the Item field, and Daily_sales to the data in the Daily Sales field) that you can refer to in place of cell ranges in the formulas you construct using the SUMIF function.

Solve It

Exercise 10-4: Using the SUMIF Function

In Exercise 10-4, you get practice using the SUMIF function to calculate different totals depending upon conditions you specify.

1. Open the *Exercise10-4.xlsx* workbook file in your Chap10 folder in Excel 2007 Workbook folder.

Use its Jan-08 Sales worksheet to practice using the SUMIF function by constructing a formula that uses this function to total the daily sales for all lemon tarts sold in the month of January, 2008.

2. Click cell I3 to select it, type **=sum** into the cell, and then double-click SUMIF on the drop-down menu that appears to select this function.

Excel inserts =SUMIF(in cell CI3 and displays the arguments used by this function as a ScreenTip beneath the cell. This SUMIF function uses the Item_sold range as its range argument and the Daily_sales range as its sum_range argument. The condition for the criteria argument is where the item sold is equal to lemon tarts, which is expressed as follows:

```
"=lemon tarts"
```

Note that because you are evaluating a text string in this comparative expression that contains a space, you must enclose the entire criteria argument inside double quotation marks.

3. With the insertion point just inside the open parenthesis of the SUMIF function, click the Use in Formula button on the Formulas tab and then click Item_sold on its drop-down menu.

Excel inserts this range name as the range argument so that the formula in cell I3 now reads

```
=SUMIF(Item_sold
```

4. With the insertion point at the end of the Item_sold range name, type a comma (,) and then type **"=lemon tarts"** followed by another comma (,).

The formula in cell I3 now reads

```
=SUMIF(Item_sold,"=lemon tarts",
```

5. With the insertion point after the comma following the criteria argument in the SUMIF function, click the Use in Formula button on the Formulas tab and then click Daily_sales on its drop-down menu. Then, type **)** (a close parenthesis) to finish off the formula and click the Enter button on the Formula bar to insert into cell I3.

The completed formula in cell I3 now reads

```
=SUMIF(Item_sold,"=lemon tarts",Daily_sales)
```

and the formula returns $815.00 to the cell.

6. Use the same technique to construct on your own a SUMIF function in cell I4 that totals the daily sales for just blueberry muffins.

Be sure the criteria argument for this SUMIF function includes the quotation marks:

```
"=blueberry muffins"
```

Cell I4 contains the formula =SUMIF(Item_sold,"=blueberry muffins",Daily_sales) and the formula returns $1,305.00 to the cell.

7. Construct a SUMIF function in cell I5 that totals the daily sales for just Lots of Chips cookies.

Cell I5 contains the formula =SUMIF(Item_sold,"=lots of chips cookies",Daily_sales) and the formula returns $771.12 to the cell.

8. Construct a SUMIF function in cell I6 that totals the daily sales for just strawberry pie.

Cell I6 contains the formula =SUMIF(Item_sold,"=strawberry pie",Daily_sales) and the formula returns $2,256.49 to the cell.

9. Construct a SUMIF function in cell I8 that totals the daily sales for all items except for strawberry pie.

Use the <> operator with strawberry pie to have Excel exclude it from the total, while at the same time summing the daily sales for all the other baked items:

```
"<>Strawberry pie"
```

Cell I8 contains the formula =SUMIF(Item_sold,"<>strawberry pie",Daily_sales) and the formula returns $2,891.12 to the cell.

10. Click cell I10 and then save your work in your Excel 2007 Practice folder with the filename **SumIf Function Practice.xlsx** and leave this workbook open to use in completing Exercise 10-5 on using the Conditional Sum Wizard.

Solve It

Exercise 10-5: Using the Conditional Sum Wizard

The SUMIF function works great when you only have only one criterion that you want to apply in doing the summing. It does not, however, work when you have multiple criteria that you need to use in determining which numbers get added to the total and which don't. For those situations, you have to turn to the Conditional Sum Wizard, a nifty little Excel add-in tool that walks you through the steps of building more complex SUM formulas that utilize IF conditions that can include multiple criteria.

In Exercise 10-5, you use the Conditional Sum Wizard to construct a formula using the Chris's Cookies monthly sales list in the Jan-08 Sales worksheet that sums the daily sales made at the Anderson Rd. store location for all baked items except for strawberry pie after the date of January 1, 2008.

1. Use the *SumIf Function Practice.xlsx* workbook in your Excel 2007 Practice folder that you created in Exercise 10-4 to complete this exercise.

   Before you can use the Conditional Sum Wizard, you need to activate this add-in program.

2. Click Office button I Excel Options or press Alt+FI to open the Excel Options dialog box. Then, click Add-ins in the left pane and click the Go button to the right of Manage Excel Add-ins to open the Add-ins dialog box. Click the Conditional Sum Wizard check box and then click OK.

   If the Conditional Sum Wizard has not yet been installed, Excel displays an alert dialog box asking you if you want to install it now. Click the Yes button or press OK to install this add-in program.

   After you activate the Conditional Sum Wizard, Excel adds a Conditional Sum button to a new Solutions group at the very end of the Ribbon's Formulas tab.

3. With the cell cursor in cell I10, click the Conditional Sum button on the Formulas tab or press Alt+MY to open the Step 1 of 4 Conditional Sum Wizard dialog box.

   In this dialog box, you indicate the entire range of the data list, including its column labels (field names). In this case, you need to select the cell range of the entire data list A2:G62.

4. Drag the cell cursor through the cell range A2:G62.

   The text box in the Step 1 of 4 dialog box now contains the range 'Jan-08 Sales'!$A$2:$G$62.

5. Click the Next button to proceed to the Step 2 of 4 Conditional Sum Wizard dialog box.

   In the Step 2 of 4 dialog box, you indicate the column to sum as well as the column(s) to evaluate and the condition(s) to be used.

6. Leave Daily Sales in the Column to Sum text box, select Date in the Column drop-down list box below, > (greater than) in the Is drop-down list box, and leave 1/1/2008 selected in This Value drop-down list box before you select the Add Condition button.

   The Add Condition list box now contains the condition Date>1/1/2008.

7. Using these drop-down list boxes and the Add Condition button, add a second condition where the Item is not equal to (<>) strawberry pie.

   The condition Item<>Strawberry pie now appears on top of the Date>1/1/2008 condition in the Add Condition list box.

8. Add a third and final condition with these controls where the store is equal to (=) Anderson Rd.

   The condition Store=Anderson Rd. now appears above the Item<>Strawberry pie and Date>1/1/2008 conditions in the Add Condition list box.

9. With these three conditions defined, click the Next button to open the Step 3 of 4 Conditional Sum Wizard dialog box. There, leave the Copy Just the Formula to a Single Cell option button selected and then click the Next button.

   If you were to select the Copy Formula and Conditional Values, the Wizard would then prompt you for cell references for each column used in a condition and its associated SUMIF formula.

10. In the Step4 of 4 Conditional Sum Wizard dialog box, click cell I10 in the worksheet to insert the reference 'Jan-08 Sales'!$I$10 in its text box and then select the Finish button.

    Excel then inserts a long SUM function containing several nested IF conditions in cell I10 and returns $717.17 to the cell.

11. Open the *Solved10-5.xlsx* workbook in your Chap10 folder in the Excel 2007 Workbook folder and then check the SUMIF formulas and SUM formula with nested IF functions in your workbook against those found in this workbook file. If everything checks out OK, save you changes to the **SumIf Function Practice.xlsx** workbook (click Yes when asked to replace the original) and then close both the workbook files as you exit Excel.

Chapter 11

Using Common Statistical Functions

*E*xcel includes one of the most complete sets of statistical functions available outside of a dedicated statistics software program. These functions run the gamut from the more mundane AVERAGE, MAX, and MIN functions to the more exotic and much more specialized CHITEST, POISSON, and PERCENTILE statistical functions. In addition, the program offers an assortment of counting functions that enable you to count the number of cells that contain values, are nonblank (and thus contain entries of some kind), or count only the cells in a cell range that meet the criteria you specify. In this chapter, you get a chance to practice working with the most commonly used statistical functions, AVERAGE, MAX, and MIN, as well as the different counting functions.

Computing Averages

The average is the arithmetic mean computed by summing all the values to be averaged and then dividing this total by the number of values. Excel's AVERAGE function, which calculates the average of a range or series of values, uses the following syntax:

```
AVERAGE(number1,[number2],[. . .])
```

One way to understand the workings of the AVERAGE function is to display the corresponding SUM and COUNT formulas that return the exact same result. For example, suppose you want to find the average of the values in the cell range D4:D8 in your spreadsheet by entering the following formula in a cell:

```
=AVERAGE(D4:D8)
```

In place of this AVERAGE function, you could obtain the same result by entering the following formula:

```
=SUM(D4:D8)/COUNT(D4:D8)
```

Note that the COUNT function shown as the divisor in this equivalent formula returns the number of cells in the specified range that contain numeric entries (see Exercise 11-3 later in this chapter for practice in using COUNT).

Note that if the values in the number arguments of the AVERAGE function contain cells with text entries, logical values (TRUE or FALSE), or that are blank, Excel ignores them in the counting calculation (they are naturally ignored in the summing). However, if the cells in the number arguments contain 0 (zero) values, they are used in the counting calculation (even though they add nothing to the sum).

In addition to the AVERAGE function used to calculate the arithmetic mean in a range or series of values, Excel also includes a MEDIAN function, which takes the same kind of arguments. Instead of the arithmetic mean, the MEDIAN function returns the value that lies precisely in the middle of those in the range or series specified as its arguments, with half greater and half less.

Solve It

Exercise 11-1: Building Formulas with the AVERAGE and MEDIAN Functions

In Exercise 11-1, you get practice using the AVERAGE function to calculate the statistical average value in a range of values and the MEDIAN function to calculate the middle value in a range.

1. If Excel is not currently running, launch the program. Then, open the *Exercise11-1.xlsx* workbook file in your Chap11 folder inside the Excel 2007 Workbook folder.

This workbook contains a Home Sales-08 worksheet with a concise data table showing the recent house sales in a small subdivision during April and May. You can use the sampling in this sales table to practice using the AVERAGE and MEDIAN functions.

2. Select the cell range D4:D8 in the Home Sales-08 worksheet. Click the Name box, type the range name, **Selling_price**, and press the Enter key.

You will use the range name Selling_price as the argument of the AVERAGE and MEDIAN functions in the formulas you now add to the Home Sales-08 worksheet.

3. Click cell D10, type **=av**, and then double-click AVERAGE on the Function drop-down menu. Then, click the Selling_price on the Use in Formula button's drop-down menu on the Formulas tab. Finally, type **)** — the close parenthesis — to complete the formula and then click the Enter button on the Formula bar to insert it in cell D10.

Cell D10 contains the formula =AVERAGE(Selling_price) and returns $743,500 to the cell.

4. Enter the following formula in cell E10:

```
=SUM(Selling_price)/COUNT(Selling_price)
```

As you can see, this division formula using the SUM and COUNT functions in cell E10 returns the same value as the AVERAGE function in D10.

5. Delete the formula in cell E10. Click cell D12 and then click the More Functions button on the Ribbon's Formulas tab. Then, highlight Statistical on its drop-down menu and click the MEDIAN option on continuation menu. Then drag through the cell range D4:D8 in the worksheet to insert the range name Selling_price in the Number1 text box of the MEDIAN Function Arguments dialog box before you click OK.

D12 contains the formula =MEDIAN(Selling_price) and returns $645,000 to the cell. Note the difference between the average and the median sales price as computed by Excel in cells D10 and D12. The average selling price for a home in the sample shown in this table is nearly $100,000 more than the median.

6. Save your work in a new workbook file in your Excel 2007 Practice folder. Name the file **Stat Function Practice.xlsx** and leave this file open in Excel for the next exercise.

Finding the Highest and Lowest Values

The MAX and MIN functions compute the highest and lowest values in a cell range or series, respectively. They take the same type of arguments as the AVERAGE and MEDIAN statistical functions. Although they may not seem very powerful when using them on very small samples (such as the selling prices in the Home Sales-08 worksheet you used in Exercise 11-1), where you can visually pick out the highest and lowest selling prices in an instant, they come in quite handy when dealing with large data sets, where it would take a long time to locate these key values.

Solve It | ## Exercise 11-2: Building Formulas with the MAX and MIN Functions

In Exercise 11-2, you get practice using the MAX Statistical function to return the highest value in a range and the MIN function to return the lowest value.

1. Use the *Stat Function Practice.xlsx* workbook you saved in your Excel 2007 Practice folder at the end of Exercise 11-1 to practice adding MAX and MIN functions to the spreadsheet table located on the Home Sales-08 worksheet.

   Begin by creating a formula in cell D14 that calculates the highest selling price in the Selling_price range (D4:D8).

2. Locate the cell cursor in cell D14 in the Home Sales-08 worksheet and construct a formula using the MAX function with the range name Selling_price (assigned in Exercise 11-1) as its argument to find the largest selling price in the range.

   Cell D14 contains the formula =MAX(Selling_price) and Excel returns $1,085,000 to the cell as the highest selling price in this range.

3. Construct a formula in cell D16 using the MIN function with Selling_price as its argument to find the lowest selling price in the range.

   Cell D16 contains the formula =MIN(Selling_price) and Excel returns $550,000 as the lowest selling price in the range.

4. Insert two new rows into the sales table immediately above the row containing the sales data for 566 Elm Street in the cell range B7:D7.

   To insert two rows of blank cells in this table, select the cell range B7:D8 and then click the Insert command button in Cells group of the Ribbon's Home tab.

5. Update the sales table by making the following data entries into the newly inserted blank rows of cells:

- **211 River Road** in cell B7, **5/15/08** in cell C7, and **495000** in cell D7
- **8989 King Place** in cell B8, **5/23/08** in cell C8, and **1,500,000** in cell D8

Note the effect that your table edits have on the average price, high price, and low price cells in the spreadsheet as calculated by the AVERAGE, MAX, and MIN functions, respectively.

6. Save your changes and then close this workbook file.

Counting Cells

Excel includes three counting functions, COUNTA, COUNT, and COUNTBLANK. You can use these functions to build formulas that compute the number of cells in a particular region or worksheet that are occupied, contain numeric entries, or are blank. The syntax of these functions is as follows:

- ✔ **COUNTA(***number1*, *[number2]*, *[. . .]***)** to return the number of nonblank cells in the number argument(s)
- ✔ **COUNT(***number1*, *[number2]*,*[. . .]***)** to return the number of cells containing numeric entries in the number argument(s)
- ✔ **COUNTBLANK(***range***)** to return the number of blank cells in the range argument

In addition to these standard counting functions, the program includes a COUNTIF function that works much like the SUMIF function you encountered in Chapter 10. You can use this function to return the count in a cell range of only those cells whose entries meet the condition you set up in its criteria argument. This function uses the following syntax:

```
COUNTIF(range,criteria)
```

When specifying a number for the criteria argument of the COUNTIF function, you simply enter the number or the reference to the cell that contains the number. When specifying a comparative expression or text for the criteria argument, you must remember to enclose the argument in a set of double quotation marks. For example, to use COUNTIF to find the number of cells in the range E15:E45 that contain the number 50, you would enter the following formula:

```
=COUNTIF(E15:E45,50)
```

If, however, you want to know the number of cells in this range that contain values greater than or equal to 50, you would enter this formula:

```
=COUNTIF(E15:E45,">=50")
```

Further, suppose that cell D10 contains the numeric entry 50 and you want to construct the COUNTIF formula using this cell reference in the criteria argument rather than the number itself. You would have to enter this version of the formula as

```
=COUNTIF(E15:E45,">="&D10)
```

Remember from Table 6-1 that the & (ampersand) acts as the concatenation text operator that connects text to another entry (in this case, it connects the text ">=" to the cell reference, D10) to produce one continuous entry.

If you enclose a cell reference (such as D10 in the previous example) inside quotation marks in the COUNTIF criteria argument, Excel interprets the cell address as a text string to locate in the entries in the function's range argument.

Solve It

Exercise 11-3: Building Formulas with the COUNT, COUNTBLANK, COUNTA, and COUNTIF Functions

In Exercise 11-3, you get practice using the various COUNT Statistical functions to calculate the number of entries in a range of cells.

1. Open the *Exercise11-3.xlsx* workbook file in your Chap11 folder in the Excel 2007 Workbook folder.

This workbook contains a version of the Home Sales-08 worksheet that you can use to practice using the counting functions.

2. Select the cell range B1:D8 in the Home Sales-08 worksheet. Click the Name box on the Formula Bar, type **Sales_table**, and then press Enter.

Excel assigns the range name Sales_table to the cell range B1:D8 so that you can use this range name as the argument of your formulas using the COUNT functions.

3. Click D12 and construct a formula using the COUNTA statistical function with Sales_table as its argument that returns the number of cells with entries of any kind in this range.

Cell D12 contains the formula =COUNTA(Sales_table) and returns 19 to the cell.

4. Position the cell cursor in D14 and construct a formula using the COUNT function with Sales_table as its argument that returns the number of cells with numeric entries in this range.

Cell D14 contains the formula =COUNT(Sales_table) and returns 10 to the cell.

5. Position the cell cursor in D16 and construct a formula using the COUNTBLANK function with Sales_table as its argument that returns the number of empty cells in this range.

Cell D16 contains the formula =COUNTBLANK(Sales_table) and returns 5 to the cell.

6. Position the cell cursor in cell D10 and construct a formula that computes the total number of cells in the Sales_table range.

   The total number of cells in the Sales_table range is equal to the number of occupied cells returned by the COUNTA function in cell D12 plus the number of empty cells returned by the COUNTBLANK function in cell D16.

   Cell D10 contains the formula =D12+D16 and returns 24 to the cell.

7. Position the cell cursor in cell D18 and create a formula with the COUNTIF function that returns the number of addresses in the cell range B4:B8 of the Sales table that have the word *Street* in them.

   When specifying text in the criteria argument of the COUNTIF function, you can use the * (asterisk) as the wildcard character to stand in for multiple, unnamed characters or the ? (question mark) to stand in for individual characters. For example, use "*Street" to find addresses of any length that end with the word Street.

   Cell D18 contains the formula =COUNTIF(Sales_table,"*Street") and returns 2 to the cell.

8. Position the cell cursor in cell D20 and create a formula with the COUNTIF function that returns the number of selling prices in the cell range D4:D8 of the Sales table that are above $600,000.

   Don't forget to enclose the criteria argument with the > (greater than) operator in a set of double quotation marks.

   Cell D20 contains the formula =COUNTIF(Sales_table,">600000") and returns 3 to the cell.

9. Enter the value 400000 in cell F3 and then format it with Accounting Number format with no decimal places.

   You will now edit the formula with the COUNTIF function in cell D20 so that it refers to the contents of cell F3 rather than the static amount 600000.

10. Edit the formula in cell D20 so that the criteria argument immediately following the ">" (greater than) operator refers to contents in cell F3 rather than the static value of 600000.

    When referring to a cell reference in the criteria argument of the COUNTIF function, don't omit the & (ampersand) text operator immediately following the ">" (greater than) operator and immediately preceding the reference to cell F3.

    Cell D20 now contains the edited formula =COUNTIF(Sales_table,">"&F3) that returns 5 to the cell.

11. Replace the $400,000 entered into cell F3 with **$700,000**.

    Note that the COUNTIF function immediately updates the result in cell D20 from 5 to 2 (only two entries in the range D4:D8, cells D4 and D8, have selling prices over $700,000).

    Next, convert the label in cell C20 into a text formula (see Chapter 14 for details) that will reflect whatever value you happen to enter into cell F3.

12. Edit the contents of cell C20, Number of Selling Prices over $600,000, as follows:

```
="Number of Selling Prices over $"&F3
```

Start by pressing F2 and then the Home key to put the insertion point at the beginning of the text entry. Then, type = (equal sign) followed by "(double quote). Next, delete 600,000 at the end of the cell entry and then type a second " (double quote) followed by & (ampersand). Finally, click cell F3 and then click the Enter button on the Formula bar.

After you click the Enter button, the label, Number of Selling Prices over $70000, appears at the bottom of the Home Sales-08 worksheet to the left of the value 2 in cell D20.

13. Change the value in F3 from 700000 to 500000.

Cell D20 now contains 5 again and the label in C20 to the left reads Number of Selling Prices over $500000.

14. Use Excel's Side by Side feature to check your Home Sales-08 worksheet against the one shown in the *Solved11-3.xlsx* workbook in the Chap11 subfolder of your Excel 2007 Workbook folder. When everything checks out, save your workbook as a new file named **Count Function Practice.xlsx** in your Excel 2007 Practice folder on your hard disk and then close the file.

Using the Statistical Functions in Analysis ToolPak Add-in

For you serious statisticians out there, the Analysis ToolPak add-in — which you first encountered in Chapter 10 if you completed its exercises — contains a whole bunch of extra statistical functions that may come in handy in your work. Before you can access these supplementary statistical functions, you must install and activate the Analysis ToolPak by clicking Office Button | Excel Options or press Alt+FI to open the Excel Options dialog box. Then, click Add-ins in the left pane and click the Go button to the right of Manage Excel Add-ins to open the Add-ins dialog box. Click the first Analysis ToolPak check box (the one without the VBA designation) in the Add-Ins Available list box and then click OK.

If the Analysis ToolPak has not yet been installed, Excel displays an alert dialog box asking you if you want to install it now. Click the Yes button to install this add-in program.

After you activate the Analysis ToolPak add-in, Excel adds their specialized statistical functions to the Statistical category both in the Insert Function dialog box and on the drop-down menu that appears when you highlight More Functions | Statistical on the Ribbon's Formulas tab.

Chapter 12

Using Lookup Functions

*T*he Lookup functions in the Lookup & Reference category of Excel functions are designed to automate the process of matching values in two separate lists or tables in a workbook and then returning a related value. For example, you can set up a price lookup table in a worksheet where you store and update the prices for all the items your company sells. After that, you construct formulas in a sales table using the appropriate lookup function that match an item number entered into a field in the sales table with an item number entered into the price lookup table. When the function finds a match between these item numbers, Excel then copies the price associated with that item number in the price lookup table and pastes it into the appropriate field in the sales table.

The Reference functions are primarily designed to return specific types of information about particular cells or regions of a worksheet. This part of the Lookup & Reference category also includes functions that create hyperlinks to different worksheets and documents and that transpose the data in a table so that data that originally ran across the rows now runs down the columns, and vice versa.

In this chapter, you get a chance to practice creating formulas that automate table lookup, including looking up a single value, either across a row of a lookup data table or down one of its columns, as well as using the Lookup Wizard to perform a lookup that uses two values to find the matching data in a lookup data table.

Returning Single Values from a Lookup Table

The most popular of the Lookup & Reference functions are the HLOOKUP (for Horizontal Lookup) and VLOOKUP (for Vertical Lookup) functions. The VLOOKUP function searches vertically (top to bottom) the leftmost column of a lookup table until the program locates a value that matches or exceeds the one you are looking up. The HLOOKUP function searches horizontally (left to right) the topmost row of a lookup table until it locates a value that matches or exceeds the one you're looking up.

The VLOOKUP function uses the following syntax:

```
VLOOKUP(lookup_value,table_array,col_index_num,[range_lookup])
```

The HLOOKUP follows the nearly identical syntax:

```
HLOOKUP(lookup_value,table_array,row_index_num,[range_lookup])
```

The arguments of these two Lookup functions can be explained as follows:

- ✔ The lookup_value argument designates the range that contains the values or text to be looked up in the table.

- ✔ The table_array argument designates the range with the data table you want looked up in the lookup table as well as the data you want returned from the lookup table.

- ✔ The col_index_num argument in the VLOOKUP function designates the number of the column in the lookup table (starting with 1 for the leftmost column and increasing one each column to the right) that contains the data you want returned to the data table.

- ✔ The row_index_num argument in the HLOOKUP function designates the number of the row in the lookup table (starting with 1 for the topmost row and increasing one down each row) that contains the data you want returned to the data table.

- ✔ The optional range_lookup argument is a TRUE or FALSE value that indicates whether you want Excel to find an approximate (TRUE or argument omitted) or exact match (FALSE) to numerical entries in the range designated by the function's lookup_value argument.

When using the VLOOKUP and HLOOKUP functions, the text or numeric entries in the lookup column or row (that is, the leftmost column of a vertical lookup table or the top row of a horizontal lookup table) must all be unique (no duplicates allowed). These entries must also be arranged or sorted in ascending order; that is, alphabetical order for text entries, lowest-to-highest order for numeric entries. (See Chapter 17 for exercises on sorting data in a list or table.)

Performing a horizontal lookup

You use the HLOOKUP function when you're dealing with a lookup table where the data to look up is entered in the first (top) row, arranged sequentially (that is, alphabetically for text entries and from smallest to largest in the case of numeric entries) by columns from left to right. Figure 12-1 shows just such a lookup table at the top of the Jan-08 Sales worksheet — the Price Lookup table in the cell range C3:F4.

Figure 12-1:
The Jan-08 Sales worksheet showing the Price Lookup table immediately above the Daily Sales spreadsheet.

First off, note that bakery items listed in the top, lookup row of this Price Lookup table are text values arranged in alphabetical order from left to right as follows:

✔ Blueberry muffins in cell C3

✔ Lemon tarts in cell D3

✔ Lots of Chips cookies in cell E3

✔ Strawberry pie in cell F3

Second, note that the price per dozen for each bakery item is listed in a corresponding column immediately below in the second row of the table (cell range, C4:F4). The order of the values in the cells in this row is dictated entirely by the order of their associated bakery items in the row above.

Before you attempt Exercise 12-1, you may want to play the Formulas with the HLOOKUP Function.exe demo located in the Excel Feature Demos folder on your workbook CD-ROM. This feature demonstration shows you how to complete this exercise, including adding the range names to the lookup table and constructing and copying the formula using the HLOOKUP function in the sales table.

Exercise 12-1: Building Formulas that Perform Horizontal Lookups in a Table

In Exercise 12-1, you use the information kept in this Price Lookup table to supply the missing information to the Price/Doz column in the Daily Sales data list below it. To do this, you construct a formula using the HLOOKUP function that matches the bakery item listed as sold in the Item column of the data list (C7:C66) against the items shown in the top row of the Price Lookup table. It then returns the price per dozen for the matched item to the appropriate cell in the Price/Doz column in the data list (F7:F66).

1. If Excel is not currently running, launch the program. Then, open the *Exercise12-1.xlsx* workbook file in your Chap12 folder in the Excel 2007 Workbook folder on your hard disk.

   This workbook contains the Jan-08 Sales worksheet with the Price Lookup table and the Daily Sales data list you need to practice using the HLOOKUP function.

2. Using the Name Box on the Formula bar, assign the following range names to the designated cell ranges:

   • **Item_match** to cell range C7:C66

   • **Price_info** to cell range C3:F4

3. Click cell F7 and then click the HLOOKUP option on the Lookup & Reference button's drop-down menu. Then, click and drag through the cell range C7:C66 to insert the range name Item_match into the Lookup_value text box. Press Tab, and then drag through the cell range C3:F4 to insert the Price_info range name into the Table_array text box. Then press Tab and then type **2** into the Row_index_num argument text box. Finally, press Tab and enter **FALSE** in the Range_lookup argument text box before you press OK to close the HLOOKUP Function Arguments dialog box.

   Note that you enter 2 as the Row_index_num argument because you want Excel to return the appropriate prices from the second row (as you count down) of the Price_info range. You enter FALSE into the Range_lookup argument text box because you only want exact matches between the bakery items entered into the Item_match range (C7:C66) and the bakery items entered into the top row of the Price_info range.

   Cell F7 now contains the formula =HLOOKUP(Item_match,Price_info,2,FALSE) and returns 2.50 to the cell.

4. Use the Fill handle on the cell cursor to copy this formula down to the cell range F8:F66.

   Check the prices returned by the copies of the original HLOOKUP formula in the top rows of the Daily Sales data list against those shown for the various bakery items in the Price Lookup table. The price per dozen for the blueberry muffins should be returned as 3.75, strawberry pie as 8.99, and Lots of Chips cookies as 1.89.

5. Increase the price per dozen for Lots of Chips cookies in cell E4 of the Price Lookup table from 1.89 to 3.89.

   Note that this change to the basic price is immediately updated in all the sales of Lots of Chips cookies in the Daily Sales data list. By using a lookup table to supply the basic price per dozen data to this list, you only need make a single change to a price in the Price Lookup table in order to update every single sale of that item in the entire data list.

6. Save your work in a new workbook named **HLookup Function Practice.xlsx** in your Excel 2007 Practice folder and then close this workbook file.

Performing a vertical lookup

You use the VLOOKUP function when the data to look up is entered in the first (leftmost) column, arranged sequentially (that is, alphabetically for text entries and from smallest to largest in the case of numeric entries) by rows from top to bottom. Figure 12-2 shows you just such a vertical lookup table in the form of its Tip Schedule in the cell range B4:C103 (of which only the first twenty-some rows are visible in the figure).

The Tip Schedule in the Tip Lookup worksheet is arranged in two columns: Pretax Total and Tip Amount. Because the Pretax Total column is the first or leftmost column in this table, it contains the data to lookup and match against the Food Total entered in cell F2 of this spreadsheet. As B is the lookup column, you note that its values are arranged in numerical order from smallest to largest.

Figure 12-2:
The Tip Lookup worksheet with Tip Schedule for looking up the tip amount based on the pretax food total.

Solve It

Exercise 12-2: Building Formulas that Perform Vertical Lookups in a Table

In Exercise 12-2, you construct a formula using the VLOOKUP function that returns the tip amount to cell F3 from the Tip Amount column of the Tip Schedule table based on the Food Total entered into cell F2 and matched against the amounts listed in the Pretax Total column. Note that this represents a situation where you do *not* want Excel to use exact matching because the amount entered into the Food Total cell can often fall between the whole dollar amounts listed in the Pretax Total column of the Tip Schedule. When this happens (and you don't specify FALSE as the optional range_lookup argument in the VLOOKUP function), Excel returns the amount from the row above.

1. Open the *Exercise12-2.xlsx* workbook file in your Chap12 folder in the Excel 2007 Workbook folder on your hard disk.

   This workbook contains the Tip Lookup worksheet with the Tip Schedule that you need to practice using the VLOOKUP function.

2. Assign the following range names to the designated cells and cell ranges:

   - **Food_total** to cell F2
   - **Tip_table** to the cell range B4:C103

   When naming the Tip_table range, try using the AutoSelect feature to select the cell range B4:C103 in a couple of clicks.

3. Click cell F3 and then click the VLOOKUP option on the Lookup & Reference button's drop-down menu. Then, click cell F2 in the worksheet to insert the range name **Food_total** into the Lookup_value argument text box. Press Tab and type **tip_table** in the Table_array argument text box. Finally, press Tab and then type **2** into the Row_index_num argument text box and then click OK to close the VLOOKUP Function Arguments dialog box.

   Cell F3 contains the formula =VLOOKUP(Food_total,Tip_table,2) and returns $1.35 to the cell.

   Note that you enter 2 into the Col_index_num argument text box because you want Excel to return the appropriate tip amounts from the second column (as you count from left to right) of the Tip_table range. Note that you omit the optional Range_lookup argument for this particular VLOOKUP function because you want Excel to return a tip amount even when the program doesn't find an exact match between the amount in the Food_total cell and the whole dollar amounts listed in the Pretax Total column.

   The Formula result shown at the bottom of the Function Arguments dialog box is a perfect example of this situation. Currently, the Food_total cell F2 contains $9.33. When Excel matches this in the Pretax Total column of the Tip Schedule, it does not find an exact match. In this case, it returns 1.35 as the formula result, the tip amount for a pretax total of 9.00 in row 13 of the Tip Schedule.

   When you don't use exact matching for numerical values, Excel always selects the value from the row in the table_array argument in a VLOOKUP function or the column in an HLOOKUP function whose value is closest but doesn't exceed the value specified by the lookup_value argument.

4. Change the Food Total value in cell F2 from $9.33 to **$87.20**.

The moment you complete the edit in this cell, Excel returns a new tip amount of $13.05 to cell F2 (this tip amount is 15% of 87.00, the nearest value in the Tip Schedule that does not exceed the Food Total value).

5. Save your changes to the Tip Lookup worksheet in a new workbook in your Excel 2007 Practice folder. Name the workbook **VLookup Function Practice.xlsx** and then close the workbook file.

Using the Lookup Wizard

The HLOOKUP and VLOOKUP functions are just fine when you only need Excel to look up a single value in a horizontal or vertical lookup table and then return the nearest or exact match based on that single value. Sometimes, however, you need Excel to perform a two-way lookup (as shown in Figure 12-3), whereby the program returns a value from a data table based on both a lookup value in its top row as well as a lookup value in its leftmost column.

When such a need arises, it's time to call upon the Lookup Wizard. This nifty add-in enables you to perform two-way lookups in a table without having to worry about constructing the final complex formula with its required INDEX and MATCH Reference functions.

Figure 12-3: Performing a two-way lookup in the Production Schedule table.

Solve It

Exercise 12-3: Using the Lookup Wizard to Build Formulas that Perform Two-Way Lookups in a Table

Figure 12-3 shows you a situation where you need to look up two values, the Part Number and the Date, in order to return the Quota from the 2008 Production Schedule table. You will use the Lookup Wizard add-in in Exercise 12-3 to return the production quota from this table based on these two lookups.

1. Open the *Exercise 12-3.xlsx* workbook file in your Chap12 folder in your Excel 2007 Workbook folder.

This workbook contains the Production-08 worksheet with the 2008 Production Schedule you need to practice performing a two-way lookup using the Lookup Wizard add-in.

Before you can use the Lookup Wizard, you need to activate this add-in program.

2. Click Office Button | Excel Options or press Alt+FI to open the Excel Options dialog box. Then, click Add-ins in the left pane and click the Go button to the right of Manage Excel Add-ins to open the Add-ins dialog box. Click the Lookup Wizard check box and then click OK.

If the Lookup Wizard has not yet been installed, Excel displays an alert dialog box asking you if you want to install it now. Click the Yes button to install this add-in program.

After you activate the Lookup Wizard, Excel adds a Lookup button to the Solutions group at the very end of the Ribbon's Formulas tab.

3. Click the Lookup button in the Solutions group of the Formulas tab.

Excel opens the Lookup Wizard - Step 1 of 4 dialog box that prompts you to indicate the cell range to search including its row and column labels. In this case, you must select the range B3:K7.

4. Drag through the cell range B3:K7 in the Production-08 worksheet.

'Production-08'!$B$3:$K$7 appears in the text box.

5. Click Next to open the Lookup Wizard - Step 2 of 4 dialog box.

The Step 2 of 4 dialog asks you to identify by its heading the column and the row that contains the data to look up.

6. Leave Apr-08 selected in the Column Label drop-down list box and Part 100 selected in the Row Label drop-down list box and then click the Next button.

The Lookup Wizard - Step 3 of 4 dialog box now appears, asking you to select the form in which the Wizard displays the result. By default, Excel just copies the formula to a cell in the worksheet, but you can also have the program copy the lookup parameters; that is, the column lookup value and the row lookup value along with the lookup formula it constructs.

In this case, this latter option is exactly the one you want to use because it enables you to change these lookup parameters in the worksheet later on and have the lookup formula find a new result based on these new values.

7. Click the Copy the Formula and Lookup Parameters option button to select it and then click the Next button.

   Excel displays the Lookup Wizard - Step 4 of 6 dialog box, asking you to identify the cell where you want to copy the date, 4/1/2008.

8. Click cell C12 in the Production-08 worksheet.

   'Production-08'!$C$12 appears in the text box.

9. Click the Next button.

   Excel displays the Lookup Wizard - Step 5 of 6 dialog box, asking you to identify the cell where you want to copy the part number, Part 100.

10. Click cell C11 in the Production-08 worksheet.

    'Production-08'!$C$11 appears in the text box.

11. Click the Next button.

    Excel displays the Lookup Wizard - Step 6 of 6 dialog box, asking you to identify the cell where you want to copy the lookup formula.

12. Click cell C13 in the Production-08 worksheet.

    'Production-08'!$C$13 appears in the text box.

13. Click the Finish button to close the Lookup Wizard - Step 6 of 6 dialog box.

    Excel returns the result 500 to the Quota cell, C13.

14. Position the cell cursor in cell C13 and then examine the formula Excel entered there on the Formula bar.

    Note that Excel has constructed a formula using an INDEX function with two nested MATCH functions as its arguments. Both of these Reference functions are needed in order to perform a two-way lookup in a table.

15. Change the Part Number in cell C11 to **Part 102**.

    As soon as you change the Part Number to Part 102, Excel recalculates its lookup formula and returns 350 to the Quota cell, C13. (You can check that this is the correct value in the 2008 Production Schedule table above.)

16. Change the Date in cell C12 by entering **9/1/08** in this cell.

    As soon as you change the Date Number to Sep-08 in this cell, Excel recalculates its lookup formula and returns 378 to the Quota cell, C13.

17. Save your changes in a new workbook named **Lookup Wizard Practice.xlsx** in the Excel 2007 Practice folder and then close this workbook file by exiting Excel.

Chapter 13

Using Logical Functions

*T*he Logical function category is a small but powerful group of six functions (TRUE, FALSE, IF, AND, OR, and NOT) that you can use in decision-making formulas. (A *decision-making formula* is one where one set of values should be used or action taken when a particular condition is met and another when it is not.) You can also combine them with certain Information functions (such as ISBLANK, ISNUMBER, ISTEXT, and ISERROR) to create error-trapping formulas that prevent Excel error values (especially #DIV/0!, #NUM!, and #VALUE! errors) from spreading to other dependent formulas in the spreadsheet.

In this chapter, you get a chance to practice using the Logical functions in spreadsheets to create both decision-making and error-trapping formulas.

Working with the Logical Functions

The Logical functions, as their name implies, deal exclusively with the Logical values of TRUE and FALSE. With the exception of the TRUE, FALSE, and NOT functions (whose only purpose is to enter the Logical values, TRUE, FALSE, and its opposite into a cell of the worksheet), the other three Logical functions, IF, AND, and OR, evaluate expressions entered as their arguments as either TRUE or FALSE.

The granddaddy of all the Logical functions is the IF function, which follows this syntax:

```
IF(logical_test,value_if_true,value_if_false)
```

The IF function works by evaluating a comparative expression that you enter as its logical_test argument as being either TRUE or FALSE. If the expression is found to be TRUE, Excel then uses the value or text or executes the expression you enter as the value_if_true argument of the function. If the expression is found to be FALSE, the program uses the value or text or executes the expression you enter as the value_if_false argument.

When entering a number or reference to a cell that contains a number or formula that returns a number for the value_if_true and value_if_false arguments, you simply enter the value or cell address. When entering text for these arguments, you need to enclose the text in a set of double quotation marks. And when entering an expression, you enter the operands and operator or function name and arguments as you would in any formula.

Constructing Decision-Making Formulas

The biggest use for the IF function is performing conditional operations in a formula: one set of operations when the IF condition expressed by its logical_test argument is found to be TRUE and another when it is not. These decision-making formulas can be one of two types: those formulas that perform their computations using alternate values depending upon the outcome of the condition, or those that perform alternate calculations based on the outcome.

Choosing between alternate values

Figure 13-1 shows an example of the first type of decision-making formula, where alternate values can be put to good use. The spreadsheet shown in this figure contains a variation of the Tip Lookup worksheet you encountered in Chapter 12. In this version, the Tip Schedule contains tip amounts for alternate tip percentages (15% in column C and 20% in column D), and the input section of the spreadsheet contains a Tip Percentage cell (G2), where the user can specify either 15 or 20 percent as the tip percentage.

Figure 13-1:
The Tip Schedule with alternate 15% and 20% tip percentages.

To take advantage of the alternate percentages in this revised Tip Schedule in the following exercise, you need to nest an IF function inside the VLOOKUP function as its col_index_num argument. This IF function then selects the appropriate column of the Tip Schedule to use (2 for the 15% Tip amount in column C or 3 for the 20% Tip amount in column D), depending upon whether the Tip Percentage cell, G2, contains 15% or 20% as its data entry.

Exercise 13-1: Using the IF Function to Build Formulas that Select Alternate Values

In Exercise 13-1, you get practice using the IF function with a VLOOKUP function to decide whether to give a 15% or 20% tip based on the amount of the food total.

1. If Excel is not currently running, launch the program and open the *Exercise13-1.xlsx* workbook file in your Chap13 folder in the Excel 2007 Workbook folder on your hard disk.

You will use this expanded version of the Tip Lookup worksheet to practice adding the IF function to a VLOOKUP function that selects between the 15% or 20% column of the Tip Schedule, depending upon which percentage is entered into the Tip Percentage cell, G2:

2. Click cell G2 to select it.

This Tip Percentage cell can contain only one of two entries: 15% or 20%. Use Excel's Data Validation feature in this cell to ensure that it can contain no other data entry.

3. Click Data | Data Validation on the Ribbon or press Alt+AVV to open the Data Validation dialog box.

The Data Validation dialog box contains three tabs: Settings that enables you to define what data is allowed in a cell; Input Message that enables you to define a ScreenTip message indicating what type of data is allowed; and an Error Alert tab that enables you to define an error message that appears when a user tries to make an entry that is not allowed.

4. Click the List option in the Allow drop-down button on the Settings tab. Then, enter 15% and 20% in the Source text box separated by a comma (with no spaces, as in **15%,20%**) before you click OK.

When you select the List as the Data Validation option, you can either select the cell range that contains the allowable data entries in the Source text box or type in the allowable entries.

Note when you close the Data Validation dialog box, Excel adds a drop-down button to cell G2. When you click this button, the drop-down list contains the only two allowed values for this cell: 15% or 20%.

5. Click the drop-down button that now appears on the right side of the Tip Percentage cell, G2, and then select 20% on its drop-down menu.

Next, you need to assign some range names that you will use in defining the arguments for the formula with your VLOOKUP function.

6. Assign the following range names to the designated cells or cell ranges:

- **Tip_percent** to cell G2

- **Food_total** to cell G3

- **Tip_table** to the cell range B4:D103

7. Click cell G4 and then type **=vl**. Next, double-click VLOOKUP that appears in the drop-down menu beneath cell G4 to display =VLOOKUP(in the cell with a list of VLOOKUP arguments appearing beneath it.

As you may remember from Exercise 12-2, the VLOOKUP function takes the following arguments:

- *Lookup_value:* Specifies the cell containing the value you want looked up in the first column of the vertical lookup table (the cell named Food_total, in this case).

- *Table_array:* Specifies the cell range containing the values in the lookup table (the cell range named Tip_table, in this case).

- *Col_index_num:* Specifies the number of the column, counting from left to right, that contains the values you want returned from the lookup table (in this case, that number is 2 when the Tip Percentage is 15% or 3 when the Tip Percentage is 20%).

8. Click Food_total on the Use in Formula button's drop-down menu on the Formulas tab to paste the range named Food_total in the formula as the lookup_value argument. Then type a comma (,) and click Tip_table on the Use in Formula button's drop-down menu to paste Tip_table into the formulas as the table_array argument. Finally, type a second comma (,) in preparation for entering the col_index_num argument.

Now all you need is to construct a formula using the IF function for the col_index_num text argument. The IF function inserts 2 as the column index number when the cell named Tip_percent contains 15% as its entry; otherwise, it inserts 3. This is how this function should appear in the col_index_num argument text box:

```
IF(Tip_percent=15%,2,3)
```

9. With the insertion point immediately following the second comma (separating the table_array and col_index_num arguments), click the IF option on Logical button's drop-down menu on the Formulas tab. Click cell G2 to insert the Tip_percent range name in the Logical_test argument text box and then type **=15%**. Then, press Tab and then type **2** in the Value_if_true argument text box. Finally, press Tab again and then type **3** in the Value_if_false argument text box before you click OK.

Excel displays an alert dialog box indicating that the formula that you're trying to enter in cell G4 contains an error (the formula needs a second close parenthesis to close off the arguments for the VLOOKUP function). This dialog box also suggests fixing this error by adding the second close parenthesis so that both the parentheses enclosing the arguments for both IF and VLOOKUP functions are balanced.

10. Click the Yes button or press Enter to have Excel correct the formula by adding a second close parenthesis to close off the IF function nested as the col_index_num argument of the VLOOKUP function.

    Cell G4 contains the formula

    ```
    =VLOOKUP(Food_total,Tip_table,IF(Tip_percent=15%,2,3))
    ```

    and this formula returns the value $1.80 (the tip amount for a food total of $9.33 at 20%). If this checks out, proceed to Step 11.

11. Change the Tip Percentage from 20% to 15% by positioning the cell cursor in cell G2 and then selecting 15% on its drop-down list.

    Excel immediately decreases the tip amount in cell G4 from $1.80 to $1.35.

12. Increase the food total in cell G3 to 75.50.

    Excel increases the tip amount in cell G4 from $1.35 to $11.25.

13. Type **17** in the Tip Percentage cell and then click the Enter button on the Formula bar.

    Excel beeps at you and displays an error dialog box with the message, "The value you entered is not valid."

14. Click the Cancel button and then open the Data Validation dialog box again (choose Data | Data Validation on the Ribbon or press Alt+AVV).

    Now, you'll create an input message that the user sees whenever he selects the cell.

15. Click the Input Message tab and then, in the Input Message text box, type **Click this drop-down button and then select 15% or 20% on its drop-down list**.

    Next, create an error message that is displayed whenever a user tries to enter a value that is no longer allowed.

16. Click the Error Alert tab and then, in the Error Message text box, type **The entry in this cell is limited to 15% or 20% only! Click Cancel and then select 15% or 20% on the cell's drop-down list.** Then, click OK to close Data Validation dialog box.

    A text box with your input message now appears next to the lower-right of cell G2.

17. Click the text box with your input message and drag it up until the top of the message box is even with the top of the Tip Percentage cell, G2, and position its left edge so that it's now touching the cell's drop-down button without obscuring any part of it.

18. Type **12** in the Tip Percentage cell, G2, and then press Enter.

    This time, Excel displays your custom error message in its error alert dialog box.

19. Select the Cancel button in the error alert dialog box to close it and restore the current 15% entry to the cell.

20. Click cell A1 and then save your work in a new workbook called **Alt VLookup Practice.xlsx** in your Excel 2007 Practice folder on your hard disk and then close the workbook file.

Selecting between alternate calculations

In addition to selecting alternate values, you can use IF functions to perform alternate calculations depending upon the outcome of the condition stated by its logical_test argument. A common situation is to have Excel perform the calculation only when the IF condition is TRUE and perform no computation when it is FALSE.

Figure 13-2 shows you an example of this situation. Here, you see a slightly different version of the Spring Sale worksheet that you use in earlier exercises. This table contains a Discounted column, which determines whether a furniture item is to be discounted based on its suggested retail price listed in the Retail Price column. It also contains a Discount Amount column, which computes the amount of the discount only if the Discounted column indicates that the furniture item is eligible for a discount.

Before you attempt Exercise 13-2, you may want to play the Formulas with the IF Function.exe demo located in the Excel Feature Demos folder on your CD-ROM. This feature demonstration shows you how to build formulas with IF functions that perform alternate calculations based on the particular values entered into the spreadsheet table.

Figure 13-2: The Spring Sale worksheet with Discounted and Discount Amount columns.

Spring Sale Furniture Prices

Code	Description	Retail Price	Discounted	Discount Amount	Sales Price
02-305	36-inch round table	1,250.00			$ 1,250.00
02-240	72-inch dining table	1,400.00			$ 1,400.00
04-356	Hutch	2,500.00			$ 2,500.00
01-234	Side chair	350.00			$ 350.00
03-003	Arm chair	500.00			$ 500.00
01-240	Armoire	1,750.00			$ 1,750.00

Solve It

Exercise 13-2: Using the IF Function to Build Formulas that Perform Alternate Calculations

In Exercise 13-2, you will construct the necessary formulas with IF functions for this version of the Spring Sale worksheet — one set to determine whether the furniture item should be discounted and another set to compute the discount amount only when the item is eligible for the discount.

1. Open the *Exercise13-2.xlsx* workbook file in your Chap13 folder in the Excel 2007 Workbook folder.

You will use this expanded version of the Spring Sale worksheet to practice constructing the formulas with IF functions needed to determine whether a furniture item is eligible for a discount. If it is, you create formulas to compute the discount amount and sale price.

2. Position the cell cursor in cell D4, where you build the formula that determines whether the 36-inch round table is to be discounted.

The determinant for eligibility for a discount is whether the suggested retail price is greater than or equal to $1,000. In terms of the Logical_test argument text box, you need to create this type of comparative expression using cell C4, as in

```
C4>=1000
```

3. Click the IF option on the Logical button's drop-down menu. Then, click cell C4 in the worksheet to insert its address in the Logical_test argument text box and type **>=1000** before pressing Tab. Then, type **"Yes"** (and be sure to enclose Yes in the pair of double quotation marks) in the Value_if_true argument text box before you press Tab again. Finally, type **"No"** (and be sure to enclose No in the pair of double quotation marks) in the Value_if_false argument text box and then click OK.

Cell D4 contains the formula

```
=IF(C4>=1000,"Yes","No")
```

and the formula returns Yes to the cell because the value currently entered into cell C4 is indeed greater than 1000.

4. Use the Fill handle to copy this formula in D4 down to the cell range D5:D9.

Now, you need to create a formula using the IF function that checks whether the cell in the Discounted column contains "Yes" or "No" and then calculates the discounted amount accordingly.

5. Click cell E4 and then click the IF option on the Logical button's drop-down menu on the Ribbon's Formulas tab to open its Function Arguments dialog box. Then, fill in the three argument text boxes in this dialog box with the following values:

- D4="Yes" in the Logical_test argument text box

- C4*20% in the Value_if_true argument text box

- 0 in the Value_if_false argument text box

When you click OK in the Function Arguments dialog box, cell E4 contains the formula

```
=IF(D4="Yes",C4*20%,0)
```

and the formula returns 250.00 to the cell because cell D4 contains Yes (because the value in C4 is greater than 1,000). Therefore, the formula calculates a discount of 20% (1250 × 0.20=250).

6. Use the Fill handle to copy this formula in cell E4 down to the cell range E5:E9.

   In the final table, all the furniture items except for the Side chair and Arm chair should be discounted and have discounted amounts computed in column E.

7. Use Excel's Side by Side feature to check your final results against those shown in the *Solved13-2.xlsx* workbook file in your Chap13 folder. If everything checks out, click cell A1 and then save your changes to a new workbook named **If Function Practice.xlsx** in your Excel 2007 Practice folder and leave this file open for Exercise 13-3.

Nesting IF functions

IF functions in decision-making formulas are great when you're dealing with situations that only require two alternatives — one that comes into play when a certain condition exists, and the other that comes into play when it does not. But what about a situation where you have more than two alternatives?

For example, in the Spring Sale worksheet you used in the previous IF function exercise, suppose you still only want to discount furniture that retails over $1,000, but want to use two different discount amounts as well: 15% for suggested retail prices that are equal to or lower than $1,500, and 20% for suggested retail prices that are above $1,500.

To accommodate such a case, you would have to nest a second IF function within the original one, making the second nested IF function either the value_if_true or value_if_false argument of the original. Specifically, in the Spring Sale worksheet example, you would nest the second IF function as the value_if_true argument of the original IF function. The first IF condition then tests if the furniture item is to be discounted (indicated by a Yes in the Discounted column, meaning that the item's retail is above $1,000). If this item is found to be eligible for a discount, the second value_if_true argument IF function determines whether it receives a 20- or 15% discount.

Solve It

Exercise 13-3: Building Formulas with Nested IF Functions

In Exercise 13-3, you get practice nesting IF functions in a single formula so that you can add more conditions that automatically determine what calculations are performed.

1. Use the *If Function Practice.xlsx* workbook file you created in Exercise13-2 (if you don't have access to this file, open the *Solved13-2.xlsx* workbook in your Chap13 folder in the Excel 2007 Workbook folder on your hard disk).

   You will use this version of the Spring Sale worksheet with the completed formulas in the Discounted and Discount Amount columns to practice using one IF function as an argument of another.

2. Select cell E4. On the Formula bar, place the insertion point immediately in front of the C in C4 in the value_if_true argument of the IF function in this cell.

   You will now edit the formula by inserting another, nested IF function.

3. Type **IF(** — open parenthesis — and then click cell C4 in the worksheet.

   The edited formula on the Formula bar should now read:

   ```
   =IF(D4="Yes",IF(C4C4*20%,0)
   ```

4. Type **>=1500,** — a greater than and equal sign, 1500, and a comma — to complete the value_if_true argument for the new nested IF function.

   The edited formula on the Formula bar should now read

   ```
   =IF(D4="Yes",IF(C4>=1500,C4*20%,0)
   ```

5. Click the I-beam mouse pointer to position the insertion point between the % (percent sign) and the comma (,) immediately preceding 0 in this formula — be sure not to press the → key.

6. Type a comma (,) and then click cell C4 in the worksheet.

   The edited formula on the Formula bar should now read

   ```
   =IF(D4="Yes",IF(C4>=1500,C4*20%,C4,0)
   ```

7. Type ***15%)** — that is, an asterisk, 15%, and a close parenthesis — to complete the value_if_false argument for the nested IF function.

   The final edited formula on the Formula bar should now read

   ```
   =IF(D4="Yes",IF(C4>=1500,C4*20%,C4*15%),0)
   ```

   In essence, this edited form of the formula with nested IF function in the value_if_true argument of the original IF function is saying

   - Evaluate the contents of cell D4 and, if Excel finds that this cell contains Yes as its entry, the program evaluates the contents of cell C4; otherwise, it just enters 0 (zero) in the current cell.

   - If Excel does end up evaluating the contents of cell C4, the program checks to see if this cell contains a value greater than or equal to 1,500. If the cell does, it then multiplies this value by 20%; otherwise, the program multiplies the value in C4 by 15%.

8. Click the Enter button on the Formula bar and then copy this edited formula down to the cell range E5:E9.

   In this version of the Spring Sale table, the Hutch and Armoire are now discounted 20%, the 36-inch round table and 72-inch dining table are both discounted 15%, and the Side and Arm chairs still receive no discount at all.

9. Use Excel's Side by Side feature to check your final results against those shown in the *Solved13-3.xlsx* workbook file in your Chap13 folder inside your Excel 2007 Workbook folder. If everything checks out, click cell A1 and then save your changes in the **If Function Practice.xlsx** workbook and then close this file.

Constructing Error-Trapping Formulas

Sometimes, you know ahead of time that certain error values are unavoidable in a worksheet as long as certain data entries are missing. The most common error value that gets you into this kind of trouble is the #DIV/0! error value. This error value appears not only when the divisor in a division formula is actually 0 (zero) but also when the divisor refers to an empty cell (which carries the numerical equivalent) in which you haven't yet had an opportunity to make any data entry (as when generating a new workbook from an Excel template file).

Fortunately, you can use the IF function to suppress the appearance of such error values in formulas. When you do this, you not only get the benefit of not having to look at them (there is, after all, nothing subtle about them), but you also ensure that they don't spread to any other parts of the spreadsheet containing dependent formulas. This means that in suppressing the display of error values in their original formulas, you also end up trapping them in their original cells.

When using IF functions in the construction of error-trapping formulas, you often use them in combination with some of the functions in the Information category, the most versatile of which is the ISERROR function. This nifty little function evaluates the cell reference you specify as its value argument and returns TRUE if the cell contains any of those pesky error values (#N/A, #VALUE!, #REF!, #DIV/0!, #NUM!, #NAME?, and #NULL!) and FALSE if it contains any other kind of entry. You can use its little brother function, ISERR, to test for all error values in a cell, excluding #N/A, for Not Available, which some users do not consider an error value per se.

Figure 13-3 shows a situation where you need to construct an error-trapping formula. Here, you see an empty version of the Production Schedule worksheet that is on its way to being saved as an Excel template file. Before that can happen, however, you would need to suppress all those #DIV/0! error values in the cell range B9:J9 until you begin entering the production quota figures for the particular months. (The error values appear because cell K7 with the grand total that it used as the divisor in their formulas contains 0 (zero).) The way to do that, as you will see in Exercise 13-4, is by constructing a formula that traps this error in the original formula and all its copies.

Figure 13-3:
Empty Production Schedule worksheet containing #DIV/0! error values due to the 0 (zero) in the grand total in cell K7.

Exercise 13-4: Building Formulas that Trap Errors

In Exercise 13-4, you get practice creating formulas with IF functions that trap #DIV/0! error values in the worksheet by replacing them with zeros so that they don't spread throughout the spreadsheet.

> **1.** Open the *Exercise13-4.xlsx* workbook in your Chap13 folder in the Excel 2007 Workbook folder on your hard disk.
>
> You will use this empty version of the Production Schedule worksheet to practice constructing error-trapping formulas using the IF function.
>
> **2.** Click cell B9 that contains the original division formula.
>
> You need to edit this formula by adding an IF function that inserts 0 (zero) rather than the #DIV/0! error value in the cell if cell K7 is empty or contains 0 (zero) as is currently the case.
>
> **3.** Press F2 to place Excel in Edit mode and then press the ← key to position the insertion point between = (equal to sign) and the B in B7. Then, type **IF(** — open parenthesis — and then select cell K7.
>
> The edited formula in the cell and on the Formula bar should now read:
>
> ```
> =IF(K7B7/$K$7
> ```
>
> **4.** Press F4 one time to convert the relative cell reference, K7, to the absolute reference, $K$7. Then, type **=0,0,** (that is, the equal-to sign followed by zero, a comma, and then another zero and comma). Finally, click the I-beam mouse pointer at the very end of the formula, after the 7 in the final $K$7 cell reference to position the insertion point there and then type **)** — close parenthesis.
>
> The final, edited formula in the cell and on the Formula bar should now read
>
> ```
> =IF($K$7=0,0,B7/$K$7)
> ```
>
> **5.** Click the Enter button on the Formula bar to complete this edit and enter the edited formula with the IF function into cell B9.
>
> In place of that ugly #DIV/0! error value in cell B9, the benevolent 0.00% should now appear.
>
> **6.** Copy the edited formula in cell B9 to the right to the cell range C9:J9.
>
> Now all the #DIV/0! error values are gone from the Production Schedule worksheet, replaced by 0.00% entries.
>
> **7.** Position the cell cursor in cell B3 and enter the #N/A value using the NA function in the Information function category from the More Functions drop-down menu on the Formulas tab.
>
> The NA function is one of those few Excel functions that doesn't require any arguments; therefore, you can use this function to enter the #N/A error value into the current cell simply by entering **=NA()** and clicking the Enter button.
>
> Note that the moment you enter the #N/A value into B3, this error value spreads to the subtotal cells, K3 and B7, and from there to the grand total in cell K7, and from there to all the division formulas that use its value as their divisor.

To trap this in cell K7 and prevent its spread to the cell range B9:J9, you need to edit the original formula in cell B9 by adding the ISERROR function and then copy this version across the columns of this row.

8. Position the cell cursor in cell B9 and then edit the IF function in this cell's formula by replacing the logical_test argument, $K$7=0, with **ISERROR($K$7)**.

Don't forget to enclose the $K$7 as the value argument of the ISERROR function in its own pair of open and close parentheses nested within the IF function's pair of open and close parentheses.

The final, edited formula in the cell and on the Formula bar should now read

```
=IF(ISERROR($K$7),0,B7/$K$7)
```

9. Copy this new version of the error-trapping formula to the cell range C9:J9.

As soon as you finish copying this revised error-trapping formula, Excel replaces all the #N/A values in this % of Total cell range with 0.00%, restricting the #N/A values to the production table itself without enabling these values to spread beyond it.

10. Position the cell cursor in the Home cell, A1, and then save your work in a new workbook file named **Error Trap Practice.xlsx** in your Excel 2007 Practice folder and then close this file.

Chapter 14

Text Formulas and Functions

· ·

In This Chapter

▶ Understanding how to construct text in formulas

▶ Creating formulas that combine text entries stored in different cells

▶ Changing the case of text entries using the Text functions

· ·

*A*t first, thinking about text formulas and functions in spreadsheets may seem strange, accustomed as we all are to thinking of spreadsheets as number crunchers. Nevertheless, not only can you construct formulas that use text as operands with the special concatenation or linking operator, but you can also build formulas using any number of Text functions that require text exclusively in their arguments.

In this chapter, you get a chance to practice building text formulas that link together separate text cell entries whose text should be entered together in the same cell. You also get a chance to use Text functions to convert text entries to the proper upper- and lowercase letters.

Constructing Text Formulas

Simple text formulas (that is, those that don't rely on any Text functions) merely join pieces of text together using the & (ampersand) operator. It's the so-called *concatenation* operator, which means to join or string together in a series. Here are a couple of caveats to keep in mind about text formulas:

   ✔ The text operands must be enclosed in sets of quotation marks.

   ✔ Spaces must be included in the operands (and within the quotes) if you don't want the text to glom together as a single illegible clump of letters.

For example, if you want to create a text formula in cell B2 that joins the word *Summary* to the text entry *Order*, entered in cell A2, and you enter the following formula in this cell:

```
=A2&Summary
```

Excel returns the #NAME? error value because you didn't enclose the text *Summary* in quotation marks. Note that this is necessary even when the text you're entering is just a single word with no spaces.

Also, suppose you have the first name *Keith* entered in cell A3, and the last name *Smith* entered next door in cell B3, and you enter the following text formula in cell C3:

```
=A3&B3
```

Excel returns to cell C3 the following glommed-together text:

```
KeithSmith
```

To have the text formula return the first and last name separated by the customary space, you need to enter this version of the text formula in cell C3:

```
=A3&" "&B3
```

Note that in this version, the invisible-to-the-eye space (entered by pressing the space-bar) is enclosed in quotation marks, although there are no spaces between these quotation marks and the & (ampersand) concatenation operators.

Q. When would I typically need to create text formulas in a spreadsheet?

A. You may often work with data lists where pieces of information such as the first, middle, and last name as well as the person's title along with his street, city, state, and ZIP code are all stored in separate cells (for purposes of sorting). Text formulas that join these separate pieces of information can save hours of retyping when you need to reassemble this disparate information in mailing lists.

Solve It

Exercise 14-1: Building Simple Text Formulas that Join Data Entries

In Exercise 14-1, you get practice building text formulas that join pieces of text entered into different cells of a worksheet together as a long string in other cells.

1. If Excel is not currently running, launch the program and then open the *Exercise14-1.xlsx* workbook file in the Chap14 folder in the Excel 2007 Workbook folder on your hard disk.

You use the entries in the Client Addresses list in its Text Formulas worksheet to practice creating simple text formulas.

2. Position the cell cursor in cell G1 and construct a text formula that joins the text entry *Client* in cell B1 with the text entry *Addresses* in cell C1.

Add a space enclosed inside quotation marks and sandwiched between & (ampersand) operators in the middle of the cell references to prevent the two text entries from being joined into ClientAddresses in the cell.

Cell G1 contains the formula

```
=B1&" "&C1
```

and the formula returns Client Addresses to the cell.

3. Click the Copy button in the Clipboard group of the Home tab or press Ctrl+C to copy the formula in cell G1 to the Clipboard. Click cell B1 and then click the Paste Values option on the Paste button's drop-down menu.

Excel pastes the text and not the formula on top of the Client entry in cell B1.

Note the repetition of Addresses in G1, which still contains the formula that combines the text in B1 (Client Addresses) with the text entry in C1 (Addresses) so that it now reads Client Addresses Addresses.

4. Delete the Addresses entry in cell C1.

Note that both B1 and G1 now show Client Addresses. In cell B1, this is the result of a text entry created from a copy of the original text formula; whereas in G1, it is the result of the original text formula you constructed.

5. Position the cell cursor in cell G3 and construct a new text formula that joins the house number in cell A3 with the street name in B3.

The text formula you enter in cell G3 should appear on the Formula bar as

```
=A3&" "&B3
```

Note that the entry in cell A3 is the number *123* (not entered as a text with a preceding quotation mark nor formatted with the Text format), yet Excel has no problem joining this value to the obvious text entry in cell B3 using the concatenation operator.

6. Copy the text formula in cell G3 down to the cell range G4:G17 and then use AutoFit to widen column G as needed to display all the conjoined street addresses.

7. Position the cell cursor in cell H3 and construct a text formula that combines the city name in cell C3 with the state abbreviation in cell D3 and the ZIP code in cell E3, making sure that there is a comma and a space immediately following the city and a space between the state and ZIP code.

Don't forget to enclose the comma and the trailing space after the reference to cell C3 with the city in quotation marks, as in

```
=C3&", "&
```

Cell H3 contains the formula

```
=C3&", "&D3&" "&E3
```

and the formula returns Centerville, IL 60789 to the cell.

8. Copy the text formula in cell H3 down to the cell range H4:H17 and then use AutoFit to widen columns as needed.

Now you're ready to construct a text formula that combines the concatenated text in cell G3 with that in H3 to make one long text entry.

9. Position the cell cursor in cell I3 and construct a formula the joins the text in cell G3 with that in cell H3: Make sure that this formula inserts a comma and a trailing space between the street address in cell G3 and the city, state, and ZIP in cell H3.

Cell I3 contains the formula

```
=G3&", "&H3
```

and the formula returns 123 Niles Avenue, Centerville, IL 60789 to the cell.

10. Copy the text formula in cell I3 down to the cell range I4:I17 and then use AutoFit to widen column I to suit (you may also have to scroll the screen to the right to display all the data).

Finally, you need to sort these addresses.

11. While the cell range I3:I17 still selected, click the Sort A to Z option on the Sort & Filter button's drop-down menu in the Editing group of the Ribbon's Home tab or press Alt+HSS. When the Sort Warning dialog box appears, select the Continue with the Current Selection option button before you select its Sort button. (Excel is concerned that you forgot to include data that needs sorting in the cell range G3:H17.)

    Note that nothing changes in the order of the addresses in the selected range when you finish the Sort. This is because the cells contain text formulas rather than the actual text entries you see displayed. If you want to be able to find and sort text entries that you create in a spreadsheet with text formulas, you need to replace the formulas with their values. In this particular case, you copy the value on top of the formulas, thereby replacing them.

12. While the cell range I3:I17 still selected, click the Copy button in the Clipboard group on the Home tab or press Ctrl+C and then (without doing a thing to the cell selection) click the Paste Values option on the Paste button's drop-down menu or press Alt+HVV.

    Excel replaces the formulas with their calculated values in the same range. (You can verify this because the contents of the Formula bar now reads 123 Niles Avenue, Centerville, IL 60789, instead of =G3&", "&H3.)

13. Click the Sort A to Z option on the Sort & Filter button's drop-down menu on the Home tab or press Alt+HSS again and then click the Continue with the Current Selection option button before you click its Sort button.

    Note how, at the time you use the Sort A to Z option, Excel rearranges the text in the cell selection.

14. Click the Sort Z to A option on the Sort & Filter button's drop-down menu or press Alt+HSO. Click the Continue with the Current Selection option button before you select the Sort button when the Sort Warning dialog box appears.

    This time, Excel arranges the addresses in descending order (following the street number — for more on how Excel sorts values, see Chapter 17).

15. Position the cell cursor in cell A1 and then save your work with the filename **Text Frmls Practice.xlsx** in your Excel 2007 Practice folder and leave the workbook open as you will need it to complete Exercise 14-2.

Using Text Functions

Excel's Text functions offer a wide variety of methods for searching and manipulating text entries in a spreadsheet. These functions include the CONCATENATE function for joining together strings of text (specified as its *text* arguments) — just like the & (ampersand) operator in the handmade formulas you constructed in Exercise 14-1 — and, perhaps even more useful to most, the UPPER, LOWER, and PROPER functions for changing the capitalization of text entries in the spreadsheet. (Most of the other Text functions are seldom required outside of macros and specialized VBA programming applications.)

Figure 14-1 shows you an example of a spreadsheet that is in desperate need of the PROPER function, which changes the case of the text specified as its sole argument to Title case, where only the first letter in each word is uppercase.

Figure 14-1:
Client List
spreadsheet
with the
names in
all capital
letters.

As you can see in this figure, both the first and last names of each of the clients in the list are all uppercase letters and need to be converted to the Title case. This is a situation that you sometimes encounter when using data lists stored in text files that you import with the Text Import Wizard into an Excel worksheet. (This wizard opens automatically when you try to open a text file.)

Solve It

Exercise 14-2: Building Formulas with Text Functions that Join Data Entries and Change Their Case

Exercise 14-2 shows you how easy it is to take care of problems in a worksheet using the PROPER function. Knowing how to convert text entries to the desired case in a spreadsheet is very important because it can literally save you from hours of text editing, not to mention retyping, both of which are a colossal waste of your time.

1. Open the *Exercise14-2.xlsx* workbook file in your Chap14 folder in the Excel 2007 Workbook folder on your hard disk .

You will use the uppercase first and last name text entries in the Client List in its Text Functions worksheet to practice using a couple of Excel's Text functions.

2. Click cell C3 and then click the PROPER option on the Text button's drop-down menu on the Ribbon's Formulas tab. Click cell A3 in the worksheet to enter its cell reference into the Text Argument text box in the Function Arguments dialog box and then click OK.

Cell C3 contains the formula =PROPER(A3) and this formula returns Aiken to the cell.

3. Use the Fill handle to copy this formula with the PROPER function down to the cell range C4:C17 and then over to the cell range D3:D17.

   Note that all the first and last name entries are now correct with the exception of *Mcavoy* (which should be *McAvoy*) in cell C11 and *Mcclinton* in cell C12 (which should be *McClinton*). You will have to manually edit these entries later on as the PROPER function is only able to deal with the first letters in words.

4. Click cell E3 and then click the CONCATENATE option on the Text button's drop-down menu. Then, click cell D3 in the worksheet to enter its cell reference in the Text1 Argument text box and then press Tab. Type " (a double quotation mark), press the spacebar, and then type " (a double quotation mark) to insert a blank space in the Text2 Function Argument text box before you press Tab. Finally, click cell C3 in the worksheet to enter its cell reference in the Text3 Argument text box and click OK.

   Cell E3 contains the formula = CONCATENATE(D3," ",C3) and this formula returns the text Christopher Aiken to the cell.

5. Copy the formula in cell E3 down to the cell range E4:E17 and then use AutoFit to widen column E.

   Now, you need to replace the text formulas with the CONCATENATE functions with their text so that you can edit and sort the names in this list.

6. Replace the CONCATENATE formulas in the selected cell range E3:E17 by copying their values on top of their formulas using the Paste Values option on the Paste button's drop-down menu.

   Remember you must first copy the cell selection E3:E17 with Ctrl+C (indicated by the marquee around the range) before you select the Paste Values option.

7. Edit the entries in E11 and E12, changing *Mcavoy* in cell E11 to *McAvoy* and *Mcclinton* in cell E12 to *McClinton*.

   Now open a new window to display your *Text Frmls Practice.xlsx* workbook on the screen.

8. Choose View | Arrange All on the Ribbon or press Alt+WA to open the Arrange Windows dialog box and then click the Vertical option button before you click OK.

   Excel now displays windows with parts of the *Exercise14-2.xlsx* workbook and *Text Frmls Practice.xlsx* workbook side by side.

9. Scroll the Text Functions worksheet in the *Exercise14-2.xlsx* workbook so that column F is visible in the window.

   Now, you'll get ready to copy the addresses from the Text Formulas sheet of the *Text Frmls Practice.xlsx* workbook to the Text Functions sheet of the *Exercise14-2.xlsx* workbook.

10. Click a cell in the Text Formulas worksheet in the *Text Frmls Practice.xlsx* workbook to make it active and then scroll column I into view and select the cell range I3:I17 (containing the joined addresses).

    Now, you'll use drag-and-drop to copy the addresses in the cell range I3:I17 on the Text Formulas worksheet to the Text Functions worksheet

11. Hold down the Ctrl key and position the mouse pointer somewhere along the bottom edge of the cell selection. Drag the outline of the selection from the Text Formulas worksheet in the *Text Frmls Practice.xlsx* workbook to the cell range F3:F17 in the Text Functions worksheet in the *Exercise 14-2.xlsx* workbook. When the outline fills the cell range F3:F17 in this worksheet, release the mouse button.

Excel copies the addresses into the cell range F3:F17 in the Text Functions worksheet.

12. Click the Close button in the upper-right corner of the *Text Frmls Practice.xlsx* workbook window.

Now, make maximize the Text Functions worksheet of the *Exercise 14-2.xlsx* workbook so that it fills the Worksheet area.

13. Click the Maximize button in the upper-right corner of the *Exercise 14-2.xlsx* workbook window.

Next, widen column F in the Text Functions worksheet so that all the copied addresses fit within it.

14. Use the AutoFit feature to widen column F in Text Functions worksheet.

15. In cell G3, create a formula using the CONCATENATE Text function that joins the first and last name in cell E3 with the address information in cell F3, making sure to add a comma and trailing space after the last name.

Cell G3 contains the formula

```
=CONCATENATE(E3,",  "&F3)
```

and the formula returns Christopher Aiken, 788 Rincon Road, Bend, OR 97700 to the cell.

16. Copy the formula in cell G3 down to the cell range G4:G17 and then widen column G and scroll the worksheet as needed to completely display the names and addresses in this range on your screen.

Next, you want to replace the Text formulas with their text so that you can sort them in alphabetical order.

17. Replace the formulas in the cell range G3:G17 with their text values and then sort the selection with the Sort A to Z option on the Sort & Filter button's drop-down menu on the Editing group of the Ribbon's Home tab.

Check your results against those shown in Figure 14-2. If they match, proceed to the final step.

18. Select cell A1 and then save your work in a new workbook named **Text Func Practice.xlsx** in your Excel 2007 Practice folder. Then, close the workbook file as you exit Excel.

Figure 14-2:
The Text Functions worksheet after sorting the names and addresses in the cell range G3:G17 alphabetically by first name.

Part III
Working with Graphics

The 5th Wave   By Rich Tennant

"No, it's not a pie chart, it's just a corn chip that got scanned into the document."

In this part...

Part III is living proof that there is indeed life beyond number-crunching in the Excel spreadsheet. Here, you have an opportunity to tap into your more "artistic" side as you get practice in creating and gussying up charts of various types, as well as experience in adding and using graphics in your spreadsheets.

Chapter 15

Charting Spreadsheet Data

• •

In This Chapter

▶ Understanding how Excel charts spreadsheet data

▶ Creating a chart from the Insert tab of the Ribbon

▶ Creating a chart on a separate chart sheet

▶ Formatting the basic chart

▶ Editing a chart

• •

*B*esides the actual data entry and building the formulas for a spreadsheet, charting the data may well be one of the most essential tasks you perform in Excel. By presenting spreadsheet data in a visual form, relationships between the data that were not apparent in numerical form often become quite obvious. Fortunately, Excel offers you a wealth of different types of charts with which to depict these relationships. Half the fun of charting is selecting the most appropriate chart type and customizing it to your needs.

In this chapter, you get a chance to practice charting spreadsheet data, both in the worksheet and on separate chart sheets. You also get practice with customizing the various parts of the basic chart so that they present the data in the clearest possible way.

Understanding Excel Charts

Excel charts are directly tied to the spreadsheet data they represent in the worksheet. As a result, the editing changes you make to the underlying data have a direct and immediate effect on their contents (somewhat analogous to the way that changes you make to data entries referred to in a formula immediately affect the calculated result when Automatic Recalculation is in effect).

Figure 15-1 shows you a typical clustered column chart created as part of a worksheet from the data in a spreadsheet table (not currently visible). As you see in this figure, a typical Excel chart contains a variety of distinct elements (explained in Table 15-1). It's important that you become familiar with these elements: Each is an editable part of the chart that you're often required to modify after construction of the basic chart.

Figure 15-1: A typical clustered column chart containing a variety of standard chart elements.

Table 15-1	Typical Chart Elements
Element	**Description**
Chart	Everything inside the chart window including all parts of the chart (labels, axes, data markers, tick marks, and other elements in this table).
Data marker	A symbol on the chart, such as a bar in a bar chart, a pie in a pie chart, or a line on a line chart that represents a single value in the spreadsheet. Data markers with the same shape, pattern, or color represent a single data series in the chart.
Chart data series	A group of related values, such as all the values in a single row in the worksheet — all the production numbers for Part 100 in the sample chart, for example. A chart can have just one data series (shown in a single bar or line), but it usually has several.
Series formula	A formula describing a given data series. The formula includes a reference to the cell that contains the data series name (such as the name Jan-92), references to worksheet cells containing the categories and values plotted in the chart, and the plot order of the series. The series formula can also have the actual data used to plot the chart. You can edit a series formula and control the plot order.

Element	Description
Axis	A line that serves as a major reference for plotting data in a chart. In two-dimensional charts, there are two axes — the x (horizontal) axis and the y (vertical) axis. In most two-dimensional charts (except, notably, bar charts), Excel plots categories (labels) along the x-axis and values (numbers) along the y-axis. Bar charts reverse the scheme, plotting values along the y-axis. Pie charts have no axes. Three-dimensional charts have an x-axis, a y-axis, and a z-axis. The x- and y-axes delineate the horizontal surface of the chart. The z axis is the vertical axis, showing the depth of the third dimension in the chart.
Tick mark	A small line intersecting an axis. A tick mark indicates a category, scale, or chart data series. A tick mark can have a label attached.
Plot area	Area where Excel plots your data, including the axes and all markers that represent data points.
Gridlines	Optional lines extending from the tick marks across the plot area, making it easier to view the data values represented by the tick marks.
Titles	Labels you add to identify the chart. You can add a chart title to iden-tify the entire chart, a horizontal axis title to identify the data on the x- or category axis, and a vertical axis title to identify the data (and units) on the y- or value axis.
Legend	A key that identifies patterns, colors, or symbols associated with the markers of a chart data series. The legend shows the data series name corresponding to each data marker (such as the name of the red columns in a column chart).

Excel not only offers you a wide array of basic chart types from which to choose, but it also enables you to decide where you want to place the chart — either in the worksheet along with the data it represents graphically or on a separate chart sheet in the workbook.

A chart like the one shown in Figure 15-1 that is placed on the worksheet is referred to as an *embedded chart* (although it's not so embedded that you can't still move and resize it on the worksheet as needed). Figure 15-2, on the other hand, shows you this same clus-tered column chart now on its own chart sheet.

You select and manipulate a chart sheet in the Excel workbook via its sheet tab, just the same as you do with a regular worksheet.

Figure 15-2:
Typical
clustered
column
chart from
Figure 15-1
placed on a
separate
chart sheet.

Q. What benefits do I get from placing a chart on its own chart sheet rather than embedding it in the worksheet?

A. Charts that you place on their own chart sheets generally print larger and are easier to print — all you have to do is select the chart sheet before you open the Print dialog box (Office button | Print). In addition, you may find it somewhat easier to edit a chart that you place in its own sheet because you don't have worry about inadvertently selecting the chart area when you intend to select the chart title or legend for editing.

Solve It

Exercise 15-1: Modifying an Existing Embedded Chart

In Exercise 15-1, you get practice working with an embedded clustered bar chart that has already been added to a worksheet to visually represent the number of parts produced each month for the year 2008.

1. If Excel 2007 is not currently running, launch the program and then open the *Exercise15-1.xlsx* workbook file in your Chap15 folder in the Excel 2007 Workbook folder on your hard disk.

You will use the embedded clustered column chart in the Sched-08 worksheet to practice selecting different parts of the chart and switching the chart placement between embedding in the worksheet and placing it on a separate chart sheet.

2. Click anywhere on the embedded clustered column chart right below the 2008 Production Schedule table to select this chart.

   Eight sizing handles (those clusters of three little dots) appear around the perimeter of the embedded Clustered Column chart indicating that it is now selected. In addition, the Chart Tools contextual tab with its three Design, Layout, and Format tabs appears at the end of the Ribbon and the spreadsheet data used in creating the chart is indicated by different colored bounding boxes surrounding the row and column heads as well as the data entries.

3. Position the mouse pointer on the sizing handle that's located in the middle on the right edge. When the mouse pointer changes to a double-headed arrow, drag the thin black outline of the chart area until its right edge is flush with the right edge of column J in the worksheet. Release the mouse button.

   Note that Excel redraws the clustered column chart to fit in the new width. Now the horizontal axis titles along the x axis (the ones that show the month and year under each cluster of columns in the chart) are no longer displayed on the bias on a 45-degree angle.

4. Click the Design tab under Chart Tools to display its tools.

   The Design tab contains buttons that enable you to change the chart type, layout, and style.

5. Click the More button in the lower-right corner of the Chart Styles group on the right side of the Design tab to display all the style thumbnails in this palette. Then, click the Style 42 thumbnail in the second column of the last row.

   Excel assigns this style (with its multi-colored data series outlined against a black background) to the clustered column chart and displays the other colors that use this same type of outlining on the Chart Styles group of the Design tab.

6. Click the chart title, Scheduled Production - 2008.

   Four round sizing handles appear on the perimeter of a box drawn around the text in the Chart Title, indicating that you can now move or resize the title in the chart area.

7. Position the I-beam mouse pointer after the dash in the title and then click the mouse to place the insertion point. Press the Backspace key to delete the dash and then type **for** so that the Chart Title reads, *Scheduled Production for 2008*. Click outside the Chart Title text box in an empty place in the chart area to deselect the chart title and set your edit.

   Now, try making some changes to a few of the worksheet values represented in the chart.

8. Make the following editing changes to entries in the designated cells, noting the change in the column of the chart representing the data point you're changing:

   - **353** in cell D4 containing the scheduled production of Part 101 for June 2008

   - **660** in cell E3 containing the scheduled production of Part 100 for July 2008

   - **475** in cell H5 containing the scheduled production of Part 102 for October 2008

Each time you change a value that's represented graphically in the chart, its data marker changes.

9. Click anywhere on the embedded clustered column chart to select it and then click the Move Chart button in the Location group on the Design tab under the Chart Tools contextual tab or press Alt+JCM to open the Move Chart dialog box.

   The Move Chart dialog box contains two options: New Sheet and Object In (currently selected).

10. Select the New Sheet option button and then replace the generic Chart1 name in the associated text box with **Sched-08 Chart** before you click OK.

    Excel inserts a new chart sheet named Sched-08 Chart as the first sheet in your *Exercise15-1.xlsx* workbook in front of the Sched-08 sheet. This new chart sheet contains the erstwhile embedded clustered column chart.

11. Reposition the Sched-08 Chart sheet so that it's located immediately after the Sched-08 worksheet in the workbook by dragging its sheet tab.

    Next, see how the chart on its own sheet will print.

12. With the Sched-08 Chart sheet selected, click the Print Preview button on your customized Quick Access toolbar.

    Note that Excel automatically selects the landscape orientation for the chart in the Print Preview window to print it full size on the page.

13. Click the Close Print Preview button on the Print Preview tab to return to the Normal view of the Sched-08 Chart sheet.

    Now, move the clustered column chart back to the Sched-08 worksheet as an embedded object.

14. Move the clustered column chart back to the Sched-08 sheet and then move the chart object so that the top edge of the chart area is flush with the bottom edge of row 9 and the left edge is flush with the left edge of column B. Then, resize the chart so that the bottom edge of the chart is flush with the top edge of row 27 and the right edge of the chart is flush with the right edge of column I.

    Now you're ready to save your changes in a new Excel workbook.

15. Position the cell cursor in cell A1 and then save your work in a new workbook named **Production Sch 08 – embedchrt.xlsx** in your Excel 2007 Practice folder. Close the workbook file.

Creating Charts

Creating a new embedded chart in Excel 2007 couldn't be easier:

1. Simply select the data and headings in the worksheet that you want represented in the new chart.

2. Click the Insert button on the Ribbon and then select the type of chart to create by clicking the button for the general type of chart (Column, Line, Pie, Bar, and so on) and then clicking the thumbnail of the subtype you want to use on the button's drop-down gallery.

3. Refine the new chart as needed using the command buttons on the Design, Layout, and Format tabs under the Chart Tools contextual tab on the Ribbon.

Q. Do I have to select the data I want to graph before I select the type of chart on the Ribbon's Insert tab?

A. No, as long as the cell cursor is located in one of the cells of the table of data you want to chart, you can have Excel make a guess as to the data range to be graphed (which you can refine, if the program leaves out necessary data or includes extraneous data).

Before you attempt Exercise 15-2, you may want to play the Chart Creation.exe demo located in the Excel Feature Demos folder on your CD-ROM. This feature demonstration shows you how to create a new chart on the same worksheet as the data it represents.

Solve It Exercise 15-2: Creating a New Embedded Chart

In Exercise 15-2, you get practice creating and formatting a new embedded chart that represents only the quarterly sales data in two sales categories that are contained in a much larger, more detailed sales table.

1. Open the *Exercise15-2.xlsx* workbook file in your Chap15 folder in the Excel 2007 Workbook folder on your hard disk.

   This workbook contains a Sales-08 worksheet with the CG Media - 2008 Sales table showing only the quarterly subtotals and the 2008 annual total (the columns with the supporting monthly data are currently hidden). You will use this quarterly sales data to practice creating a new embedded chart.

2. Without moving the cell cursor out of cell A1, click the Insert | Column on the Ribbon or press Alt+NC to display the Column chart drop-down gallery. Then, click the Clustered Column thumbnail at the beginning in the first column of the first row of this gallery.

   Excel inserts a new embedded clustered column chart in the Sales-08 worksheet shown in Figure 15-3. Note that this initial chart contains more data than you want represented (you don't need the annual totals or the total sales for both the CDs and tapes to be represented in this chart).

3. Move the new chart so that its top edge is flush with the top edge of row 17 and its left edge is flush with the left edge of column E. Then, resize the embedded chart so that its bottom edge is flush with the top edge of row 36 and its right edge flush with the left edge of column S.

Next, you need to remove the annual total and total sales for CDs and tapes from the clustered column chart. Begin by removing the Annual Total data markers from the chart.

4. Click the Select Data command button on the Design tab under the Chart Tools contextual tab on the Ribbon or press Alt+JCE to open the Select Data Source dialog box.

If the Chart Tools contextual tab with its Design, Layout, and Format tab doesn't appear on your Ribbon, this means that the new clustered column chart you created is not currently selected. To make the Chart Tools contextual tab appear on your Ribbon, click an empty space in the clustered column chart area to select it.

The Select Data Source dialog box contains two columns: Legend Entries (Series) on the left side and the Horizontal (Category) Axis Labels on the right. Each column currently contains the names of the entries that appear in the legend and on the x-axis of the chart.

To remove the Annual Total from the chart, you need to temporarily switch the rows and columns of this chart so that the annual sales appear on the legend.

5. Click the Switch Row/Column button in the Select Data Source dialog box.

Excel switches the chart so that there are data series for each of four quarters plus the annual total in the clustered bars arranged by type of sales.

6. Click CG Media – 2008 Sales by Category and Date Annual Total at the bottom of the Legend Entries (Series) column and then click the Remove button at the top of the column.

Excel removes the data series for the Annual Total from the body of the chart and from the legend.

7. Click the Switch Row/Column button again to return the four quarters to the category x-axis of the chart and the types to the legend.

Now, you need to delete the empty Compact Discs and Cassettes series from the chart and legend along with Total Sales data series.

8. Click Compact Discs at the top of the Legend Entries (Series) column and then click the Remove button.

Excel removes this empty heading that did not represent any charted data from the legend.

9. Repeat this procedure to remove Cassettes (another empty label) and Total Sales from the legend. Then, click OK to close the Select Data Source dialog box.

Now, the chart represents only two data series, Total CD Sales and Total Tape Sales, listed in the legend.

10. Save your work in a new workbook file named **CG Media 08 – embedchrt.xlsx** in your Excel 2007 Practice folder on your hard disk and then leave the workbook file open for Exercise 15-3.

Figure 15-3: The new embedded clustered column chart immediately after creation.

Formatting Charts

Many times you find that you have to finesse the formatting of elements in the particular chart that the Excel initially produces for you. You can make short work of making large and small formatting changes using the command buttons found on the three tabs under the Chart Tools contextual tab:

- ✔ **Design tab** to change the basic type, layout, or style of the chart
- ✔ **Layout tab** to change the positioning and content of a particular chart element
- ✔ **Format tab** to change the font, line, or fill of a particular chart element

Before you attempt Exercise 15-3, you may want to play the Chart Formatting.exe demo located in the Excel Feature Demos folder on your workbook CD-ROM. This feature demonstration shows you how to make various formatting changes to an existing embedded chart using options on the Format tab that appears under the Chart Tools contextual tab.

Solve It

Exercise 15-3: Making Formatting Changes to a Chart

In Exercise 15-3, you get practice making formatting changes to the clustered column chart you created in the previous exercise. This exercise gives you practice selecting a new chart style as well as making formatting changes to particular elements of the chart, including the chart area, titles, and axes.

1. Use the clustered column chart in your *CG Media 08 – embedchrt.xlsx* workbook that you created in the previous exercise to practice making formatting changes to a finished chart.

This chart represents the correct data in the Sales-08 worksheet but still lacks any titles.

2. If your clustered column chart is not already selected, click somewhere on a blank space in the chart area to select this object. Then, scroll up the rows of the worksheet so that the entire clustered column chart is visible on your computer screen.

Clicking somewhere on the embedded chart not only selects this graphic object, but also adds the Chart Tools contextual tab with its Design, Layout, and Format tabs to the end of the Ribbon.

3. Click the Design tab and then click the More button in Chart Layouts group or press Alt+JCL to open the Chart Layouts drop-down gallery. Then, click the Layout 1 thumbnail (first row down in first column) in this drop-down gallery.

Excel adds a temporary title to the chart (Chart Title) that is centered over the Plot Area that you will shortly replace with your own text.

4. Click the More button in the Chart Styles group or press Alt+JCS to open the Chart Styles drop-down gallery. Then, click the Style 26 thumbnail (fourth row down in second column) in this drop-down gallery.

Excel applies the 3-D multicolor style to the clustered columns in your chart.

5. Click the Layout tab under Chart Tools and then click the Gridlines button or press Alt+JAG to display its drop-down menu. Then, highlight Primary Vertical Gridlines or type **V** before you the click Major Gridlines option on its submenu.

Excel adds major vertical gridlines to your clustered column chart.

6. Click the Format tab under Chart Tools and then click Colored Outline – Dark 1 thumbnail (the very first one) in the row of the Shape Styles gallery displayed on the Ribbon.

Note that the moment you highlight this thumbnail in the Shape Styles group, Live Preview displays this outline around the entire chart (because Chart Area is currently selected in the Chart Elements combo box in the Current Selection group on the Format tab) even before you set it by clicking this thumbnail.

7. Click the drop-down button attached to the Chart Elements combo box in the Current Selection group of the Format tab and then click the Chart Title option on its drop-down menu.

Excel selects the Chart Title in your clustered column chart (indicated in the chart area by the appearance of its text box with sizing handles).

8. Click the More button on the WordArt Styles gallery to open this gallery and then click the Gradient Fill – Accent 4, Reflection thumbnail (the purple A with a reflection located in the fourth row down in the fifth column).

   Excel displays the CHART TITLE in all caps using this gradient style.

9. Use the I-beam mouse pointer to drag through CHART TITLE and then replace this dummy text with **CG MEDIA QUARTERLY SALES FOR 2008**. Click somewhere in a blank space in the chart area to deselect the Chart Title.

   Next, you'll assign a gradient fill to the interior of the chart area using the Shape Fill button.

10. Click the Shape Fill button in the Shape Styles group and press and then highlight Gradient on its drop-down menu Alt+JOSFG. Then, click the From Center thumbnail on its gallery (second row in the second column of the Variations section).

    Now, you'll assign a glow shape effect to the border of the chart area using the Shape Effects button.

11. Click the Shape Effects button in the Shape Styles group or press and then highlight Glow on its drop-down menu Alt+JOSEG. Then, click the Accent color 4, 18 pt glow thumbnail on its gallery (fourth row in the fourth column of the Glow Variations section).

    Excel displays a glow effect around the black border of the selected clustered column chart.

12. Click the Vertical (Value) Axis option on Chart Elements drop-down button's menu in the Current Selection group of the Format tab.

    Excel selects the vertical axis of your clustered column chart (indicated by the text box with sizing handles around the vertical axis and values on the left side of the chart).

13. Click the Format Selection button (right below the Chart Elements combo box) to open the Format Axis dialog box with its Axis Options tab selected. Then, click the Fixed option button to the right of the Minimum heading at the top of Axis Options and type **0.01** in its text box. Click Thousands on the Display Units button's drop-down menu.

    Excel divides the displayed values on the y-axis by a thousand and adds the Thousands label to this axis. All that remains for you to do is to remove the display of the two decimal places from the values that appear along this axis.

14. Click the Number tab in the Format Axis dialog box and then click the Decimal Places text box and replace 2 with **0** before you click Close. Then, click somewhere in a cell in the worksheet to deselect the chart.

    Check your formatted chart against the one shown in Figure 15-4. When everything checks out, go on to Step 15.

15. Use the Zoom slider to reduce the magnification percentage until the entire worksheet table and chart are displayed on your screen, and then click cell A1 and save your work in a new file named **CG Media 08 – fmtclscolchrt.xlsx** in your Excel 2007 Practice folder. Leave the workbook open for Exercise 15-4.

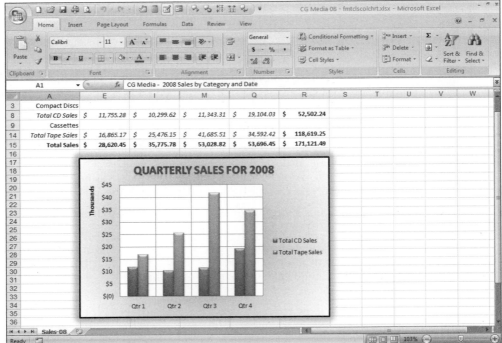

Figure 15-4:
The
embedded
clustered
column
chart after
formatting.

Editing Charts

Excel makes it easy to edit any chart you create. All you have to do is click somewhere in a blank area of the chart in the worksheet if the chart's embedded or its chart sheet if it's not. Excel then selects the chart area and activates the Chart Tools contextual menu. You can then use the command buttons on its Design, Layout, and Format tabs to make all the necessary changes.

Solve It

Exercise 15-4: Editing the Chart Type, Layout, and Style

In Exercise 15-4, you get practice changing the type of an existing chart, its layout, and its basic style.

1. Use the *CG Media 08 – fmtclscolchrt.xlsx* workbook file with the embedded clustered column chart you formatted on its Sales-08 worksheet in the previous exercise to practice making editing changes to a finished chart.

   Begin by changing the type of chart from clustered column to a 3-D stacked bar chart.

2. Click somewhere on a blank space in the chart area of your clustered column chart to select the object and then click the Change Chart Type button in the Type group at the very beginning of the Design tab or press Alt+JCC to open the Change Chart Type dialog box.

The Change Chart Type dialog box is divided into two columns: The name of chart types from Column to Radar appear beneath the Templates option in the left column and thumbnails of the subtypes available for each type appear in rows and columns on the right.

3. Click Bar in the left column of the Change Chart Type dialog box and then click the thumbnail of the Stacked Bar in 3-D subtype on the right side (the fifth one in the first row of the Bar section) before you click OK.

   Excel redraws your embedded chart as a 3-D stacked bar chart.

4. Click the Layout 2 thumbnail (the second one in the currently displayed row) in the Chart Layout gallery.

   In this new layout, Excel displays the chart's legend at the top of the clustered bar chart right below the chart's title. This new layout also displays the quarterly totals for each type of sale (CD or tape) on the appropriate section of the bars in the chart.

5. Click the Layout tab and then click the Gridlines button in the Axes group and then highlight the Primary Vertical Gridlines option on the drop-down menu or press Alt+JAGV. Then, click the Major & Minor Gridlines option on the Vertical Primary Gridlines submenu.

   Excel redraws the 3-D chart with major and minor vertical gridlines down its back and bottom walls.

6. Click the Gridlines button in the Axes group again and then highlight the Primary Horizontal Gridlines option on the drop-down menu or press Alt+JAGH. Then, click the Major & Minor Gridlines option on the Primary Horizontal Gridlines submenu.

   Excel now adds major and minor horizontal gridlines to the back and side walls of the chart.

7. Click the Format tab and then click the Shape Fill button in the Shape Styles group or press Alt+JOSF to open its drop-down menu. Click the White, Background 1 square (in the first row of the first column of the Themes palette).

   Excel removes the gradient from the background of your 3-D stacked bar chart.

8. Click the Shape Effects button in the Shape Styles group or press Alt+JOSE to open its drop-down menu. Highlight the Glow option and then click the No Glow thumbnail in its submenu.

   Excel removes the glow effect from the borders of your 3-D stacked bar chart.

9. Click the drop-down button attached to the Chart Elements button in the Current Selection group and then click the Vertical (Category) Axis option on its drop-down menu.

   Excel selects the category labels Qtr 4 through Qtr 1 on the left side of the 3-D stacked bar chart (indicated by the text box with its sizing handles).

10. Use the command buttons in the Font group of the Ribbon's Home tab to select 12 points as the font size for the quarterly category labels and make their text bold.

    The category titles along the vertical axis at the left end of the stacked bar chart are now much easier to read.

11. Click the legend area in the 3-D stacked bar chart to select Total CD Sales and Total Tape Sales and their markers and use the command buttons in the Font group to make their text 11-point, bold italic. Then, click cell A1 to deselect your 3-D stacked bar chart.

Now check your final 3-D stacked bar chart against the one shown in Figure 15-5. If everything checks out, move on to Step 12.

12. Save your 3-D stacked bar chart in a new workbook file named **GC Media 08 –3dstckbrchrt.xlsx** in your Excel 2007 Practice folder and then close it by exiting Excel.

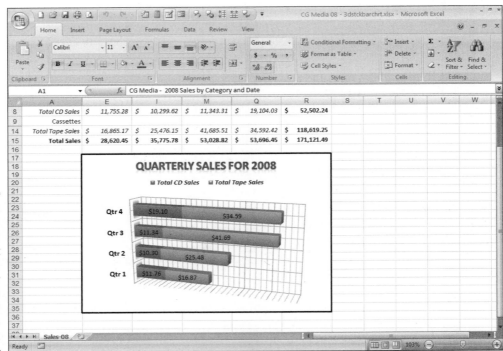

Figure 15-5: The final 3-D stacked bar chart created from your original clustered column chart.

Chapter 16

Adding Graphics to Spreadsheets

. . . .

In This Chapter

▶ Understanding what graphic objects are and how Excel treats them

▶ Adding clip art to the spreadsheet

▶ Importing graphics files into the spreadsheet

▶ Adding graphic shapes and text boxes to the spreadsheet

▶ Constructing WordArt, organizational charts, and other diagrams

. . . .

As you discovered in Chapter 15, the embedded charts you add to a spreadsheet are actually graphic objects that you can move and resize as needed. Embedded charts are by no means the only graphic objects you can have in your worksheet. Excel also enables you to add graphic objects you create yourself as well as those you import from Clip Art and other kinds of graphics files.

In this chapter, you get a chance to practice using all these different types of graphic objects to improve the overall look of your spreadsheets and make their data and charts even more interesting and legible to the user.

Understanding Graphic Objects

The most important thing to remember about graphic objects is that they are distinct objects separate from the cells of the worksheet that float above on their own layers. Because they are distinct objects, you can select them for moving and resizing as you did your embedded chart in Exercise 15-1 in Chapter 15. Because graphic objects remain on separate layers, you can move them one on top of the other, with the object on the topmost layer obscuring parts of the objects on layers below.

To select a graphic object, you must click some part of it (which can sometimes be a bit tricky when different objects overlap each other). As Figure 16-1 demonstrates, when you select a graphic object, Excel displays the name of the object in the Name box on the Formula bar (Right Arrow 1, in this case) while at the same time displaying white circular sizing handles around the perimeter of its shape and a green circular rotation handle at the top. (You can use the Rotation handle to change the orientation of the object by rotating it to any desired angle.) Some graphic objects, such as the block arrow shown selected in Figure 16-1, also display a shaping handle that you can use to modify the basic shape (in this case, the thickness of the body of the arrow in relation to its arrowhead).

Shaping Handles

Figure 16-1:
When you select a graphic object, its name appears in the Name box on the Formula bar along with various handles for manipulating it.

Rotation Handle   Sizing Handles

To move the selected graphic object, position the mouse pointer somewhere inside the object's perimeter. Then, when the pointer becomes an arrowhead with a double cross at its point, drag the object to its new position within the worksheet. To copy the selected object, hold down the Ctrl key as you drag the graphic (when you press the Ctrl key, a plus sign, indicating that the object is being copied, appears above the arrowhead pointer).

You can "nudge" a selected graphic object into its desired position by pressing the arrow keys, ⇧Up, ⇩Down, ⇦Left, or ⇨Right. When you press an arrow, Excel moves the object just a very little bit in that direction. Nudging is very useful when you have an object that's almost in place and requires very little handling to get it into just the right position.

When graphic objects overlay each other, you can move an object that is on higher levels to lower levels by clicking the object to select it and, at the same time, display the Format tab under the Drawing Tools contextual tab, where you select the Send Backward option on the Send to Back button's drop-down menu (Alt+JDAEB). To move an object that's on a lower level up towards the top, you repeat this procedure, this time selecting the Bring Forward option on the Bring to Front button's drop-down menu (Alt+JDAFF).

Excel also makes it possible to group different graphic objects together to create a single composite graphic object by selecting the individual objects (by Ctrl+clicking them) and then selecting the Group option on the Group button's drop-down menu on this Format tab (Alt+JDAGG). Excel indicates that the selected graphics are now grouped (and for all intents and purposes, a single graphic object) by placing a single set of sizing handles around the perimeter formed by all the former separate graphics. You can then manipulate the grouped graphic as a single entity, moving, sizing, rotating, and so on as you would any other object.

The great thing about grouping a bunch of different objects is that Excel never forgets that they were once separate objects that you could independently manipulate. That means that you can always turn them back into separate graphics by ungrouping them. To do this, click the composite graphic object and then choose the Ungroup option on the Group button's drop-down menu on its Format tab (Alt+JDAGU).

Exercise 16-1: Manipulating the Graphic Objects in a Worksheet

In Exercise 16-1, you get practice working with graphic objects by repositioning two existing objects so they overlap one another. You then get practice grouping them together as a single object and using the controls in the Selection and Visibility Task pane to hide and redisplay them in the worksheet.

1. If Excel 2007 is not currently running, launch the program and then open the *Exercise16-1.xlsx* workbook file in your Excel 2007 Workbook folder on your hard disk.

 The Graphic Objects worksheet in this workbook contains the block arrow and "This way to success!" WordArt graphic object that you see in Figure 16-1. You use these two shapes to practice manipulating graphic objects, including moving and resizing them, sending them to different layers, and finally grouping them together as one composite graphic.

2. Click the blue right arrow to select its shape.

 Excel displays the sizing, shaping, and rotation handles in the object's bounding box and the Drawing Tools contextual tab with its single Format tab appears at the end of the Ribbon. In addition, the name of the graphic shape, Right Arrow 1, appears in the Name box on the Formula bar.

 Note that the right arrow graphic object contains two shaping handles: one on the shaft or body of the arrow that you can drag up and down to widen and narrow the arrow shaft, and one on the arrowhead that you can drag to the left and right to widen and flatten the head of the arrow.

3. Drag the shape handle attached to the shaft of the arrow downward to narrow the body of the arrowhead until it's just slightly wider than the text, "This way to" in the WordArt graphic object. Then, drag the shape handle attached to the arrowhead to the right to reduce the width of the arrow so that it's about half as wide as before.

 Note that Excel shows you the outline of the shaft and arrowhead as you drag the respective shaping handle so that you can visualize the new shape before you release the mouse button.

4. Drag the right arrow's rotation handle downward to the left to until its arrowhead is rotated counterclockwise so that it is pointed up approximately at a forty-five degree angle.

   Note that Excel shows you the outline of the entire right arrow shape as you drag the rotation handle so that you can visualize its new angle when you release the mouse button.

5. Click somewhere on the WordArt graphic object to select it.

   Note that selecting this object causes Excel to display its name, Rectangle 2, in the Name box on the Formula bar and the Format tab under the Drawing Tools contextual tab continues to appear at the end of the Ribbon.

6. Position the mouse pointer somewhere on the border of the shape's outline and then, when the four-headed arrow appears at the tip of the arrowhead, drag the WordArt graphic object until the left end of its outline overlays the end of the shaft of the right arrow.

   Now you need to rotate the WordArt object counterclockwise to match the basic angle of the right arrow.

7. Use the rotation handle on the WordArt object to rotate its text counterclockwise to match the basic angle of the right arrow object. Then reposition the WordArt object and continue to adjust its angle so that the first three words, "This way to" overlay the right arrow below.

   At this point, your overlaid arrow and WordArt graphic objects should match those shown in Figure 16-2.

Figure 16-2: The right arrow and WordArt graphic objects after overlaying and rotating.

8. Click a cell in the worksheet to deselect the WordArt object. Then, position the four-headed arrow mouse pointer somewhere on the right arrow shape and click to select the object. Then, click the Format tab followed by the Bring to Front button in the Arrange group or press Alt+JDAFR.

Excel positions the right arrow shape on top of the WordArt graphic object, obscuring most of its text.

9. Click the Send to Back button in the Arrange group on the Format tab or press Alt+JDAEK.

Excel returns the right arrow to its original position beneath the WordArt object.

10. Ctrl-click the WordArt graphic object so that both the right arrow shape and the WordArt object are selected. Then, click Group on the Group button's drop-down menu or press Alt+JDAGG.

Excel replaces the two bounding boxes with a single rectangular bounding box that encompasses all of the right arrow and most of the WordArt text.

11. Click the Selection Pane button in the Arrange group on the Format tab or press Alt+JDAP.

Excel opens the Selection and Visibility Task pane on the right side of the Excel screen. This pane displays the names of the three objects in the Graphic Objects worksheet: Group 3, the name given to the grouped object, Rectangle 2, and Right Arrow 1. Note that Excel shows that the Rectangle 2 and Right Arrow 1 graphic objects are grouped together to make up the Group 3 object by indenting their names under Group 3 in this pane.

12. Click the eye icon that appears to the right of the Right Arrow 1 object in the Selection and Visibility pane.

Excel temporarily hides the Right Arrow 1 graphic object in the worksheet (although its name continues to appear in the Selection and Visibility Task pane).

13. Click the Right Arrow 1 object's eye icon again in the Selection and Visibility Task pane to redisplay the image in the worksheet. Then, click Ungroup on the Group button's drop-down menu on the Format tab or press Alt+JDAGU.

Excel removes the Group 3 name from the Selection and Visibility pane and bounding boxes appear around both the Right Arrow 1 and Rectangle 2 objects in the worksheet.

14. Click cell A1 in the worksheet.

Excel deselects both the graphic objects in the sheet and the Drawing Tools contextual tab disappears from the Ribbon.

15. Click the Rectangle 2 name in the Selection and Visibility pane.

Excel selects the WordArt object in the worksheet.

If you have difficulty selecting individual graphic objects that overlay each other in the worksheet, select them by clicking their names in the Selection and Visibility Task pane. To select multiple objects, hold down the Ctrl key as you click the individual object names.

16. Regroup the Rectangle 2 and Right Arrow 1 objects and then close the Selection and Visibility Task pane.

Now all that's left is to save your changes in a new workbook file.

17. Click cell A1 and then save your work as a new workbook with the filename **Graphic Objects Practice.xlsx** in your Excel 2007 Practice folder. Close the workbook.

Adding Various Types of Graphic Objects

The Illustrations and Text groups of Excel's Insert tab are packed with great tools for creating and adding all types of graphic objects. These graphics include clip art and images from other graphics files (including digital photos) that you import into Excel, as well as graphic shapes and SmartArt graphics that you create yourself.

Inserting clip art

Microsoft includes a wide variety of ready-to-use clip art images that you can easily insert in your worksheets. To make it easy to do this, Excel 2007 includes a Clip Art Task pane from which you can conduct word searches for the types of images you want to use. To choose a clip to paste into a worksheet, click the Clip Art button on the Insert tab of the Ribbon or press Alt+NF. Doing this opens the Clip Art Task pane, where you can search for the type of clips you want to use.

Before you attempt Exercises 16-2 and 16-3, you may want to play the Graphics Clip Art & Photos.exe demo located in the Excel Feature Demos folder on the CD-ROM. This feature demonstration shows you how to import clip art images and graphic files into your worksheets and then resize, reposition, and format them.

Solve It **Exercise 16-2: Adding Clip Art to a Spreadsheet**

In Exercise 16-2, you get practice finding the appropriate clip art image to add to an invoice spreadsheet that you will convert into a template file (for generating the real invoices you fill out). You also get practice correctly sizing and positioning the selected image in the invoice header.

1. Open the *Exercise16-2.xlsx* workbook file in the Chap16 folder in your Excel 2007 Workbook folder on your hard disk.

This workbook contains the ITB Invoice worksheet with a copy of an invoice template for a store called Into the Blue that sells kites and accessories. In this exercise, you get to practice finding and adding clip art by sprucing up the otherwise dull invoice heading with an image of a kite.

2. Click the Clip Art button in the Illustrations group of the Insert tab or press Alt+NF.

Excel displays the Clip Art Task pane on the right side of the Excel screen.

3. Enter **kite** as the search text in the Search For text box at the top of the Clip Art Task pane and then select the Go button.

   If you have not previously specified that you want to include online collections in your clip art searches, Excel displays the Microsoft Clip Organizer dialog box that asks you if you want to include the clip art images and digital photos from the Microsoft Office online Web site in the search.

4. Click the Yes button in the Microsoft Clip Organizer dialog box if it appears.

   After finishing the initial image search, Excel returns thumbnails of all the kite images it can locate online to the Clip Art Task pane.

5. Scroll down the images in the Clip Art Task pane until you find the kite image with the spool of string shown selected in the Clip Art Task pane in Figure 16-3. Then, click the image to insert it into the ITB Invoice worksheet.

   Excel inserts a large version of the kite-attached-to-a-spool-of-string image that obscures much of the cells of the invoice. The program also adds the Picture Tools contextual tab to the end of the Ribbon and selects its sole Format tab.

6. Use the sizing handles to substantially resize the kite graphic so that the height of its outline is essentially the same as that of the invoice header.

   Note that selected clip art images have only sizing handles — these images do not offer a rotation handle for changing the orientation or a shaping handle for manipulating the shape. Be sure to drag one of the corner sizing handles diagonally to resize the image without distorting it.

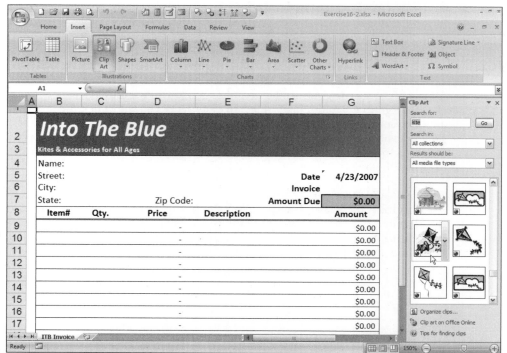

Figure 16-3:
Selecting the kite clip art image to insert into the invoice header.

7. Drag the resized kite clip art image so that the outline of its right edge is flush with the right edge of the invoice header.

   Now, enlarge and distort the kite image so that it's left edge is flush with the column F's left edge.

8. Drag the sizing handle in the center of the left edge of the selected kite clip art image to the left until the image's left edge is roughly flush with the column F's left edge.

   Now, all that remains is to save your worksheet as a template file.

9. Close the Clip Art task pane and select cell A1. Save your work as a new template with the filename **ITB Invoice.xltx** in your Excel 2007 Practice folder and then close the workbook.

   Remember that you must change the file type by selecting Excel Template (*.xltx) in the Save As Type drop-down menu of the Save As dialog box as well as change the filename before clicking the Save button.

Importing graphics files

In addition to the clip art images stored on your computer system, you can also insert graphic files that you keep in any folder containing your artwork and digital photographs, such as My Pictures in My Documents on Windows XP or Pictures in the Documents folder on Windows Vista.

To insert a picture into the worksheet, click the Picture button on the Insert tab of the Ribbon. Doing this opens the Insert Picture dialog box. This dialog box works just like the Open dialog box except that it's set to display only the graphics files that Excel can import, and it automatically looks in the My Pictures folder on your hard disk (which you can change by selecting another folder in the Look In drop-down list box).

After you locate the graphics file with the image you want to insert in the worksheet, click its thumbnail in the Insert Picture dialog box and then click the Insert button to import it into the current worksheet. Excel then displays the image from the file you selected with sizing handles around the perimeter and a rotation handle connected to the sizing handle in the middle at the top of the image. You can then reposition, resize, or rotate the image as needed.

Excel also adds the Picture Tools contextual tab to the end of the Ribbon with its sole Format tab. You can also use the command buttons in the Adjust and Size groups in this Format tab to edit the selected photo. Among other things, these tools make it possible to heighten or lessen the brightness or contrast of the image, crop out unwanted areas around the edges, and compress the image so that it doesn't bulk up the size of your workbook (as only high resolution images can).

Exercise 16-3: Adding Images from Graphic Files to a Spreadsheet

In Exercise 16-3, you get practice adding digital photos to a spreadsheet that you then resize and reposition.

1. Open the *Exercise16-3.xlsx* workbook file in your Chap16 folder in the Excel 2007 Workbook folder.

   This workbook contains a copy of the Home Sales 2008 worksheet that you worked with earlier. You will add a new worksheet to use this copy of the workbook for the 905 Hudson Lane listing in which you will add a couple of digital photos.

2. Insert a new worksheet into the *Exercise16-3.xlsx* workbook after the Home Sales 2008 worksheet that you name **905 Hudson Ln**.

   To insert the new worksheet, click the Insert Worksheet button that appears immediately following the Home Sales 2008 sheet tab.

3. Copy the street address in cell A8 of the Home Sales 2008 worksheet to cell A1 of the 905 Hudson Ln worksheet. Make its font bold, increase its font size to 14 points, and then use AutoFit to resize column A.

   Remember that the easiest way to copy entries between worksheets is to use the copy (Ctrl+C) and paste (Enter or Ctrl+V) method.

4. Make the following entries in the designated cells of the 905 Hudson Ln worksheet:

   • **Sold** in cell in cell A2

   • **Sales Price** in cell A3

   Then, use the appropriate buttons in the Font and Alignment groups of the Home tab to format the entries in cells A2 and A3 so that they are bold and right-aligned in their cells.

   Next, you need to copy the date value in cell B8 of the Home Sales 2008 sheet to cell B2 of the 905 Hudson Ln worksheet.

5. Use the copy and paste method to copy the date in cell B8 in the Home Sales 2008 worksheet to cell B2 in the 905 Hudson Ln worksheet. Then, widen column B in the 905 Hudson Ln sheet to display the entire date.

   Next, copy a link to the sales prices in cell C8 of the Home Sales 2008 worksheet to cell B3 of the 905 Hudson Ln sheet.

6. Use the Copy and Paste Link method to paste an external link to the sales prices in C8 in the Home Sales 2008 worksheet into cell B3 in the 905 Hudson Ln sheet. Then, widen column B to display the entire sales price value.

   The easiest way to do this is to position the cell cursor in cell C8 of the Home Sales 2008 sheet and then click the Copy button on the Home tab before you switch to the 905 Hudson Ln worksheet. Then, click cell B3 before you click the Paste Link option on the Paste button's drop-down menu on Home tab (Alt+HVN).

   Cell B3 now contains the formula =`'Home Sales 2008'!$C$8` and returns $1,085,000 to the cell.

7. Position the cell cursor in cell A5 of the 905 Hudson Ln worksheet and then click the Picture button on the Insert tab or press Alt+NP.

Excel opens the Insert Picture dialog box in the My Pictures folder (Windows XP) or Pictures folder (Vista) on your computer. The photos you want to insert are located in the Graphics subfolder inside the Chap16 subfolder in your Excel 2007 Workbook folder.

8. Select My Documents (XP) or Documents (Vista) in the left pane, and then double-click the Excel 2007 Workbook folder icon, followed by the Chap16 folder icon, followed by the Graphics folder icon.

This folder contains three graphics files: two digital photos saved in the JPEG graphics format and one company logo graphic saved in the GIF graphics format. Note that the Files of Type drop-down list box is automatically set to display all the graphic file formats that Excel supports. Also note that Excel automatically displays thumbnails of each of these graphics files along with their filenames.

9. Click the *Hudson Lane Exterior.jpg* thumbnail to select it and then select the Insert button to bring it into the 905 Hudson Ln worksheet.

Excel inserts the selected photo complete with sizing and rotation handles, while at the same time displaying the Picture Tools contextual tab on the Ribbon.

10. Move the photo so that its left edge is flush with the left edge of column B and its top edge is flush with the top of row 6; resize the graphic so that its bottom edge is flush with the bottom of row 19 (and its right edge nearly extends to the right edge of column G).

Next, use the Contrast and Brightness command buttons in the Adjust group of the Format tab under the Picture Tools contextual tab to increase the contrast in this photo and decrease its brightness.

11. Click the Contrast button and then click the +20% option on its drop-down menu. Click the Brightness button and then click the -10% option on its drop-down menu.

Now put a border around the imported photo.

12. Click the More button in the Picture Styles group on the Picture Tools contextual tab and then click the Double Frame, Black thumbnail in the Picture Styles drop-down gallery.

Excel draws a thick black border with a thinner white border within it (like a matte) around the selected home photo.

13. Click cell I6 to position the cell cursor in this cell, and then import the *Hudson Lane Interior.jpg* file into the worksheet, resizing it so that its left edge is flush with the left edge of column I and its bottom edge is flush with the bottom of row 19. Then format this interior photo with the same Double Frame, Black border and increase its contrast 20% (without changing its brightness).

Next, you're going to get the new worksheet ready for printing.

14. Click cell A1 in the 905 Hudson Ln worksheet and then click the Page Layout button on the Status bar. Then, click the Landscape option on the Orientation button on the Ribbon's Page Layout tab.

Note that even in landscape mode, Excel is not able to print both photos on the same page.

15. Click the 1 Page option on the Width button's drop-down menu in the Scale to Fit group on the Page Layout tab. Then, widen column B so that the date is displayed and widen column P just enough so that the right edge of the double frame is displayed.

Now add a custom header to the page.

16. Click the Click to Add Header text at the top of the page in Page Layout mode and then click the Picture button in the Header & Footer Elements group of the Design tab under the Header & Footer Tools contextual tab.

Excel opens the Insert Picture dialog box.

17. Double-click the thumbnail of the *momtrdmk.gif* file with the Mind Over Media, Inc. logo in the Graphics subfolder in the Insert Picture dialog box.

Excel closes the Insert Picture dialog box and then inserts an &[Picture] code in the Right section.

18. Click the Format Picture button on the Design tab and then enter **75%** in the Height text box in the Scale section of the Size tab in the Format Picture dialog box before you click OK.

Next, you'll add a footer to the bottom of the printed page.

19. Scroll down the page and then click the Click to Add Footer text at the bottom of the page. Then, click the 905 Hudson Ln, Page 1 option on the Footer button's drop-down menu.

905 Hudson Ln appears centered in the middle section of the footer and Page 1 appears flush right in the right section of the footer.

20. Open the Print Preview window by clicking the Print Preview button on your customized Quick Access toolbar or by pressing Ctrl+F2.

The Print Preview window now displays Page 1 of the report in landscape mode with both the entire exterior and interior photos together on the page, the Mind Over Media, Inc. logo centered in the top margin, and the sheet name centered and the page number right-aligned in the bottom margin as shown in Figure 16-4.

21. Click the Close Print Preview button to exit Print Preview, click the Normal button on the Status bar, and then select cell A1 of the Home Sales 2008 worksheet before you save the workbook in a new file named **Home Sales 08 – photos.xlsx** in your Excel 2007 Practice folder. Then close the file.

Figure 16-4:
Finished
worksheet
page show-
ing the
two photos
and header
and footer
in the Print
Preview
window.

Adding graphic shapes and text boxes

The Shapes button in the Illustrations group of the Ribbon's Insert tab enables you to manually construct a bunch of different graphics from straight lines, lines with arrow-heads (simply referred to as arrows), rectangular and square shapes, to oval and circular shapes, to name but a few. To draw these shapes, you click the appropriate thumbnail that appears on the Shapes button's drop-down gallery and then drag the thin, black cross pointer to draw its outline. When drawing a line or arrow, Excel draws the line from the place where you originally click the mouse button to the place where you release it.

When drawing a rectangle or an oval, you can constrain the tool to draw a square or circle by holding down the Shift key as you drag the mouse. Note that when drawing a two-dimensional shape such as a rectangle, square, oval, or circle, Excel automatically draws the shape with a blue color fill that obscures any data or graphic objects that are beneath the shape on layers below.

Text boxes are a special type of graphic object that combines text with a rectangular graphic shape. They're great for calling attention to significant trends or special features in the charts that you create. To create a text box, you click the Text Box button in the Text group on the Insert tab or press Alt+NX and then drag the mouse pointer to draw the outline of the box. As soon as you release the mouse button, Excel places the inser-tion point in the upper-left corner of the box.

You can then start typing the text you want displayed in the text box. When the text you type reaches the right edge of the text box, Excel automatically starts a new line. If you reach the end of the text box and keep typing, Excel enters the text outside the bottom dotted line that indicates the bottom border of the box. You then have to resize the text box to display all the text you've entered within its borders. If you want to break the line before it reaches the right edge of the text box, you press the Enter key. When you finish entering the text, click anywhere on the screen outside of the text box to deselect.

Like other graphic objects in Excel, when you select text boxes, they display sizing handles along with a rotation handle. Text boxes also display two different border patterns when you select them:

- ✔ Dotted line outline when you click inside the text box, enabling you to format and edit the text (including deleting individual text characters)

- ✔ Solid thin line outline when you click the border of the text box, indicating that you can reposition and resize the box itself

Keep in mind that text boxes are similar to the comments you created in Exercise 5-10 in Chapter 5 in the sense that they also display the text that you enter in a rectangular box. Text boxes differ from comments, however, in that they are *not* attached to particular cells and *are* always displayed in the worksheet so long as you don't click their eye icons in the Selection and Visibility Task pane (Alt+JDAP) to temporarily hide them in the sheet.

Before you attempt Exercises 16-4 and 16-5, you may want to play the Graphics Shapes & WordArt.exe demo located in the Excel Feature Demos folder on your workbook CD-ROM. This feature demonstration shows you how to add a graphic shape to a worksheet and annotate the shape with WordArt text you add to it.

Exercise 16-4: Adding Graphic Shapes and Text Boxes to Annotate a Chart

In Exercise 16-4, you get practice annotating an existing embedded chart through the addition of graphic shapes and text boxes.

1. Open the *Exercise16-4.xlsx* workbook file in your Chap16 folder in the Excel 2007 Workbook folder on your hard disk.

This workbook contains a 3-D Clustered Column chart on its own chart sheet called 3-D Clstrd Col immediately following the initial Sales-08 worksheet with the table showing the CG Media quarterly subtotals. You will use this 3-D chart to practice drawing graphic shapes and text boxes.

2. Click the 3-D Clstrd Col sheet to make this worksheet active and then click somewhere on the Chart Area to make the chart active. Next, click the Shapes button on the Ribbon's Insert tab and then click the Oval thumbnail in the Basic Shapes section (the one in the second column of the first row of this section).

The mouse pointer becomes a thin black cross. You will use this pointer to draw an oval shape around the third-quarter column in the chart representing that quarter's total tape sales (the tallest purple column in the chart) that will call attention to this chart column.

3. Position the black-cross mouse pointer slightly above and to the left of this tallest purple column representing the total third quarter tape sales and then drag this pointer down and to the right until the outline of the oval shape entirely encloses this chart column. Then release the mouse button.

   As soon as you release the mouse button, Excel draws a long blue oval on top of the column that entirely obscures it. The program also displays the buttons on the Format tab under the Drawing Tools contextual tab on the Ribbon.

4. Click the Shape Fill button in the Shape Styles group of the Format tab and then click the No Fill option on its drop-down menu.

   Excel removes the blue fill color from the long oval so that you can now see the chart column within it.

5. Click the Shape Outline button in the Shape Styles group and then click the red color square in the Standard Colors section of its drop-down palette menu. Click the Shape Outline button again, this time highlighting the Weight Option. Then, click the 3 pt option on the continuation menu that appears to increase the thickness of the red outline.

   The oval surrounding the third-quarter tape sales column in the chart now calls attention to this column with its 3-point red line.

6. Click the Text Box button in the Insert Shapes group at the very beginning of the Format tab. Position the mouse pointer in the blank area in the upper-right section of the chart area and drag the mouse pointer down diagonally to draw a rectangle (use Figure 16-5 as a guide) and then release the mouse button.

   When you release the mouse button, Excel draws the text box outline with dotted lines with the insertion point positioned at the beginning of the first line in this box.

7. Type **Summer Blow-Out Sale** in the text box. Then, drag with the insertion point to select this text.

   Note that Excel automatically selects the Home tab on the Ribbon as soon as you start typing.

8. Use the command buttons in the Font and Alignment groups of the Home tab to make the following changes to the selected text:

   - On the Font Color drop-down menu, change the text color to red

   - On the Font Size drop-down menu, increase the point size of the text to 14 points

   - Use the Bold and Italic buttons in the Font group to make the text bold and italic

   - Use the Center and Middle Align buttons in the Alignment group to center the text horizontally and vertically within the text box

   The Summer Blow-Out Sale text is now centered in the text box.

9. Click somewhere on the dotted-line border of the text box to select it.

   The text box outline changes from a dotted to a solid line.

10. Click the Format tab to make its buttons active and then click the More button in the Shape Styles gallery to open it. Then, click the Subtle Effect - Accent 1 thumbnail (the blue one in the second column of the fourth row).

Excel fills the text box with the blue gradient used by this shape style.

Next, you need to draw an arrow from the text box to the oval outline surrounding the purple column representing total third-quarter tape sales.

11. Click the Arrow thumbnail in the first row of the Shapes gallery displayed in the Insert Shapes group of the Format tab under the Drawing Tools contextual tab. Then, position the thin black-cross mouse pointer on the sizing handle in the lower-left corner of the text box and drag it diagonally down and to the left until the arrowhead touches somewhere on the red oval outline. Release the mouse button.

As soon as you do, Excel draws an arrow with the arrow pointing to and touching the red oval outlining the tape sales third-quarter column.

12. Click the Shape Outline button in the Shape Styles group on the Format tab and then highlight the Weight option on its drop-down menu. Then click the 3 pt option on its continuation menu.

Excel increases the line weight of the arrow to 3 points.

13. Click somewhere in a blank space in the Chart Area to deselect the arrow. Make sure that your chart annotation matches that shown Figure 16-5. Then, save your work in a new workbook called **CG Media 08 – graphics.xlsx** in your Excel 2007 Practice folder. Leave this workbook file open for Exercise 16-5.

Figure 16-5: Finished 3-D clustered column chart with oval-shaped callout and text box with arrow annotations.

Constructing WordArt

The WordArt button in the Text group on the Ribbon's Insert tab enables you to insert super-fancy text in your worksheets. You can combine WordArt with other graphic shapes to produce some really great effects.

To insert a WordArt graphic object in your worksheet, you first click the WordArt button on the Insert tab to open the drop-down WordArt gallery. This gallery contains a wide variety of different text styles illustrated by rows and columns of letter-A thumbnails.

After selecting a WordArt style by clicking its A-thumbnail in the WordArt drop-down gallery, Excel adds an outlined shape to the worksheet containing the dummy text Your Text Here that you then replace with the words or phrase that you want presented in the WordArt style you just selected in the drop-down gallery. You can then use the buttons in the WordArt Styles group on the Format tab under Drawing Tools to further enhance your WordArt graphic.

Solve It

Exercise 16-5: Using WordArt to Annotate a Chart

In Exercise 16-5, you get practice using WordArt to annotate your 3-D clustered column chart on its own chart sheet.

1. Make sure that the *CG Media 08 – graphics.xlsx* workbook that you created in the last exercise is open and its 3-D Clstrd Col chart sheet is active.

   You will now add a WordArt graphic with the name of the company in the upper-left corner of the 3-D clustered column chart showing the quarterly totals for CD and tape sales in 2008.

2. Click somewhere on the blank space in the 3-D clustered column's chart area and then click the WordArt button on the Ribbon's Insert tab or press Alt+NW to open the drop-down WordArt Gallery. Then, click the Fill - Accent 2, Matte Bevel thumbnail (the red one in third column of the sixth and last row).

   Excel inserts a text box using the Fill - Accent 2, Matte Bevel style with the text, Your Text Here, in the middle of the 3-D clustered column chart.

3. Replace the Your Text Here placeholder by typing **CG Media** and then move the text box containing your new text to the blank area in upper-left corner of the 3-D clustered column's Chart Area.

   Next, you'll change the shape of the WordArt text to make it curve down.

4. Click the Text Effects button in the WordArt Styles group of the Format tab to open its drop-down menu. Then, highlight the Transform option at the bottom of this menu to display its continuation menu. Finally, click the Curve Down thumbnail (in the second column of the fourth row of the Warp section) on this menu.

   Excel warps the CG Media WordArt text so that its text curves down and to the right.

5. Move the curved CG Media WordArt so that its fits better in the blank space in the upper-left of the Chart Area and does not obscure any part of the 3-D chart or its title. Then, click somewhere in the blank space of the chart to de-select the WordArt object.

   Check your results against those shown in Figure 16-6.

6. Click the Format tab under the Chart Tools contextual tab and then click the Selection Pane button or press Alt+JOAP to open the Selection and Visibility Task pane on the right side of the Excel screen.

   Note that the Selection and Visibility Task pane lists Chart 1 as the only graphic: the program does not recognize the oval and arrow graphic shapes, text box, and WordArt as graphic objects separate from the 3-D clustered column chart and all its elements. This would not be the case if you added these shapes to an embedded chart in a worksheet.

7. Click the Sales-08 sheet tab. Select the cell ranges E2:Q2 and E15:Q15 containing the quarterly labels and sales totals (for both CDs and tapes) and then click the Pie button on the Ribbon's Insert tab. Finally, click the Exploded Pie in 3-D thumbnail (the second one in the 3-D Pie section) on the Pie drop-down gallery.

   Excel draws the 3-D exploded pie chart in your worksheet with each of the quarterly sales totals depicted in a different color by a separated pie slice.

8. Move the embedded pie chart so that its top edge is flush with the top of row 18 and its right edge is flush with the right edge of column V.

   Now modify the chart style and add a title to it.

9. Click the Layout 2 thumbnail displayed in the Chart Layouts gallery on the Design tab under the Chart Tools contextual tab. Then, click the Chart Title and replace this text with Quarterly Sales for 2008.

   Now, add a text box with the Summer Blow-Out Sale that calls attention to and explains the reason for the large size of the third-quarter pie slice.

10. Click cell A17 in the Sales-08 worksheet and then click the Text Box button on the Insert tab or press Alt+NX. Then, position the thin black-cross pointer in the upper-left corner of cell E19 and drag the pointer down diagonally until it's in the lower-right corner of cell I24. Release the mouse button.

    Excel draws a text box the covers the cell range E19:I24 in the worksheet.

11. Type **Summer Blow-Out Sale** in the new text box and then format its text and box so that it matches the one you created on the 3-D Clstrd Col chart sheet (refer back to Steps 8 through 10 in Exercise 16-4 if you forget what specific enhancements you need to make).

    Now, all that you need to do is to add an arrow that points from the formatted text box to the third-quarter pie slice.

12. Click the Elbow Arrow Connector thumbnail in the Insert Shapes drop-down gallery on the Format tab under Drawing Tools (this is the fifth one from the left in the Lines section). Position the mouse pointer on the sizing handle in the middle of the text box's right edge and drag the mouse over and down until the arrow touches somewhere on the third quarter pie slice (use Figure 16-7 as a guide). Use the Shape Outline button to increase the weight of the arrow to 3 points and then click cell A1.

    Note that you can use the shaping handle on the elbow arrow connecter to move the vertical section of the arrow to the left or right (so that it doesn't overlap the left border of the embedded chart). Also, note that the Selection and Visibility Task pane lists three discrete graphic objects as existing on the Sales-08 worksheet.

13. Close the Selection and Visibility Task pane and then you save your changes to the workbook file (Ctrl+S) before you close this workbook file by exiting Excel.

Figure 16-6:
The 3-D clustered column chart with final WordArt graphic added to it.

Figure 16-7:
The embedded 3-D exploded pie chart with text box and elbow arrow connecter added.

Constructing SmartArt

SmartArt represents a completely new breed of graphic object in Excel that gives you the ability to quickly and easily construct fancy graphical lists and diagrams in your worksheet. SmartArt lists and diagrams come in a wide array of configurations that includes a variety of organizational charts and flow diagrams that enable you to add your own text to predefined graphic shapes.

To insert a SmartArt list or diagram into the worksheet, click the SmartArt button on the Insert tab or press Alt+NM. Excel then opens the Choose a SmartArt Graphic dialog box (shown in Figure 16-8) when you select the category in the navigation pane on the left followed by the list's or diagram's thumbnail in the center section before you click OK.

Excel then inserts the basic structure of the list or diagram into your worksheet along with a text pane (with "Type Your Text Here" on its title bar) containing a text outline to its immediate left. Here's where you enter the text for the various parts of the list or diagram. At the same time, the Design tab of the SmartArt Tools contextual tab appears on the Ribbon with Layouts and Quick Styles galleries for the particular type of SmartArt list or diagram you originally selected.

Figure 16-8:
The Choose a SmartArt Graphic dialog box.

Before you attempt Exercise 16-6, you may want to play the Graphics SmartArt.exe demo located in the Excel Feature Demos folder on this book's CD-ROM. This feature demonstration shows you how to use Excel's SmartArt feature to create and format an organization chart structured as a horizontal hierarchy.

Solve It

Exercise 16-6: Adding a SmartArt Organizational Chart to a Spreadsheet

In Exercise 16-6, you get practice using SmartArt by creating a very basic organization chart in a new worksheet.

1. Launch Excel and then with Sheet1 of the Book1 workbook displayed on-screen, click the SmartArt button on the Ribbon's Insert tab or press Alt+NM to open the Choose a SmartArt Graphic dialog box.

   The Choose a SmartArt Graphic dialog box offers a choice between many different types of lists and diagrams.

2. Click the Hierarchy category in the left pane and then click the Horizontal Hierarchy thumbnail (the first one in the second row) before you click OK.

   Excel inserts a blank organization chart into the Sheet1 worksheet: This chart is divided into a Type Your Text Here section that you can use to enter the text for the new organizational chart and the chart section itself that contains the various boxes (all of which contain the word "Text") with the lines between them.

   Note that if the Type Your Text Here section doesn't appear in the blank Horizontal Hierarchy organizational chart in your worksheet, you can display this section by clicking the button that appears on the left edge of the new organization chart containing two black triangles pointing right and left.

3. Type **CEO Harvey** in the line of the outline displayed in the Type Your Text Here section. Then, click the bulleted and indented [Text] item on the second line in the outline displayed in the Type Your Text Here section.

   Excel displays this title and name both in the outline and the organizational chart itself. Note that when you click the second [Text] item in the outline in the section on the left note that Excel selects the box in the chart in the section on the right where the text you type next will go.

4. Type **President Peters** and then click the bulleted and further indented [Text] item on the third line in the outline displayed in the Type Your Text Here section.

   Excel inserts the name of the president of the company into the top box in the second column of the organizational chart.

5. Type **VP Personnel Jones** and then click the bulleted [Text] item at the same level on the fourth line in the outline displayed in the Type Your Text Here section.

   Excel inserts the name and title of this vice president into the top box in the third column of the organizational chart.

6. Type **VP Planning Arrowsmith** and then click the bulleted [Text] item at the previously indented level on the fifth line in the outline displayed in the Type Your Text Here section.

   Excel inserts the title and name of this vice president into the second box in the third column of the organizational chart.

7. Type **CFO Harris** and then click the bulleted and last [Text] item on the sixth line in the outline displayed in the Type Your Text Here section.

   Excel inserts the name and title of this officer of the corporation into the lower text box in the second column.

8. Type **VP Marketing Smith** and then press Enter.

   Excel inserts the name and title of this vice president into the text box in the third row of the third column of the organizational chart. In addition, because you pressed Enter after making this text entry, Excel has added a new item (at the same outline level) to the Type Your Text Here section and the organizational chart as well.

   Complete the entry by pressing the Enter key whenever you need to insert an item at the same level into a diagram or list. Press the Insert key if you need to indent this new level or press Shift+Tab if you need to move the item to a previous level in the hierarchy.

9. Type **VP Sales Brown** as the last entry in the seventh line of the Type Your Text Here section.

Now that you have the text entered for your new organization chart, you're ready to modify some of its formatting.

10. Click the Close box in the upper-right corner to hide the Type Your Text Here section of the diagram. Then, click the Change Colors button on the Design tab under the SmartArt Tools contextual tab. Click the Colorful Range – Accent Colors 3 to 4 thumbnail (the one in the third column of the Colorful section) on its drop-down gallery.

Excel assigns different colors to each of three levels in this organizational chart, while displaying all items on the same level in the same color.

11. Click the Intense Effect thumbnail in the SmartArt Styles group (the one fifth from the left in the row of thumbnails currently displayed in the gallery in this group of the Design tab).

Excel adds this 3-D effect to all the boxes in the organizational chart.

12. Click the Table Hierarchy thumbnail in the Layouts group of the Design tab.

Now you're ready to move the chart into its final position and resize it.

13. Move the organizational chart so its top border is flush with the top of row 4 and its left edge is flush with the right edge of column B. Resize the chart so that its bottom edge is flush with row 19 and its right edge with the right edge of column I. Then remove the gridlines from the worksheet and rename the sheet Org Chart.

Your finished organizational chart should now look like the one shown in Figure 16-9.

14. Click cell A1 and then save your work in your Excel 2007 Practice folder under the name of **SmartArt Practice.xlsx** before you exit the program.

Figure 16-9:
The finished organizational chart in the Table Hierarchy layout formatted with a colorful and intense 3-D effect.

Part IV
Managing and Securing Data

The 5th Wave   By Rich Tennant

"My girlfriend ran a spreadsheet of my life, and generated this chart. My best hope is that she'll change her major from 'Computer Sciences' to 'Rehabilitative Services'."

In this part...

Part IV offers what you'd call a mixed bag of tricks. Here, you not only get a chance to work with all the basic aspects of creating, maintaining, and querying data lists (also known as database tables), but you also practice the various techniques for securing just that kind of data from any unwanted and unintended changes.

Chapter 17

Building and Maintaining Data Lists

In This Chapter

▶ Creating and editing data lists

▶ Sorting the records in a data list

▶ Subtotaling values in a data list

▶ Filtering out unwanted data in data lists

▶ Querying data in external database tables

*I*n addition to its considerable computational abilities, Excel is also very accomplished at maintaining vast collections of related data in what are referred to as *data lists* or *database tables*. This chapter gives you a chance to practice all the basic aspects of creating and maintaining data lists in Excel, including building the list, adding and editing its data, filtering the list to temporarily remove unwanted data, subtotaling values in a data list, and creating lists from data external to the worksheet.

Creating a Data List

In Excel, a data list or database table is a table of worksheet data with a special structure. Unlike the other types of data tables that you might create in Excel, a data list uses *only* column headings (technically known as *field names*) to identify the different kinds of items the data list tracks. Each column in the data list contains information for each item you track in the database, such as the client's company name or telephone number (technically known as a *field* of the data list). Each row in the data list contains complete information about each entity that you track in the data list, such as ABC Corporation or National Industries (technically known as a *record* of the data list).

All you have to do to start a new data list in a worksheet is to enter the names of the fields that you want to track in the top row of the worksheet and then enter the first record of data beneath. When entering the field names (as column headings), be sure each field name in the data list is unique and, whenever possible, keep the field name short. When naming fields, you can align the field name in the cell so that its text wraps to a new line (by pressing Alt+Enter). Also, you should *not* use numbers or formulas that return values as field names. (You can, however use formulas that return text, such as a formula that concatenates labels entered in different cells.)

When deciding on what fields to create, you need to think of how you'll be using the data that you store in your data list. For example, in a client data list, you split the client's name into separate first name, middle initial, and last name fields if you intend to use this information in generating form letters and mailing labels with your word processor. That way, you are able to address the person by his or her first name (as in *Dear John*) in the opening of the form letter you create, as well as by his or her full name and title (as in *Dr. John Smith*) in the mailing label you generate.

Likewise, you split up the client's address into separate street address, city, state, and ZIP code fields when you intend to use the client data list in generating form letters and you want to be able to sort the records in descending order by ZIP code, say, or send letters only to clients located in certain states. By keeping discrete pieces of information in separate fields, you are assured that you can use that field in finding particular records and retrieving information from the data list, such as finding all the records where the state is California, or the ZIP code is between 94105 and 95101.

When entering the row with the first data record, be sure to format all the cells the way you want the entries in that field to appear in all the subsequent data records in the data list. For example, if you have a salary field in the data list, and you want the salaries formatted with the Currency style number format without any decimal places, be sure to format the salary entry in the first record in this manner. That way, all subsequent records pick up that same formatting for the salary field when you enter them with Excel's data form.

Adding records to a new data list

After entering the row of field names and the first record, you can then append additional records to the list using the data form that Excel generates for the table or directly in the worksheet cells of the list itself (after formatting the list as an Excel data table). Note, however, that the data form is only available when you add the Form button to the Quick Access toolbar as outlined in Exercise 1-4.

Solve It

Exercise 17-1: Constructing a New Data List and Adding Records with the Data Form

In Exercise 17-1, you get practice setting up a new data list by entering its field names and the first record. You then get practice adding a second record to the list using the data form that Excel generates. You also get practice formatting your data list as an Excel table and, after adding a third record directly in the list, filtering and sorting its records using the table's drop-down Filter buttons.

1. If Excel is not currently running, launch the program. Use the Sheet1 worksheet of the new Book1 workbook to practice creating a new data list and then adding and editing its data with the data form by entering the following field names for your new Employee Data List:

- **ID No** in cell A1
- **First Name** in cell B1

- **Last Name** in cell C1
- **Gender** in cell D1
- **Dept** in cell E1
- **Salary** in cell F1
- **Location** in cell G1
- **Date Hired** in cell H1
- **Years of Service** in cell I1
- **Profit Sharing** in cell J1

Then, after entering these field names in row 1, widen their columns to 15, center their entries in their cells, and make these cells bold.

Now that your new data list has its field names in the top row, you're ready to add the first record in the list in row 2 immediately below.

2. Make the following data entries in the designated cells in row 2 as the first record in your new data list:

- **'000928** in cell A2
- **Joy** in cell B2
- **Adamson** in cell C2
- **F** in cell D2
- **Accounting** in cell E2
- **$34,400** in cell F2
- **Boston** in cell G2
- **10-21-87** in cell H2
- **Yes** in cell J2

You skipped the entry in the Years of Service field in cell I2 because this is a calculated field that requires a formula that you must now construct.

3. Create the following formula in cell I2 using the YEAR and TODAY functions, and then format the cell with the Number format using no decimal places:

```
=YEAR(TODAY())-YEAR(H2)
```

This formula calculate the years of service by taking the current year as returned by the TODAY function and subtracting it from the year entered in the Date Hired field.

4. Rename Sheet1 **Employee Data List** and then click the Form button on your customized Quick Access toolbar to open the data form for the Employee Data List.

Excel creates the data form for the Employee Data List, which it displays in a dialog box containing a list of the data list fields along with a number of command buttons that you can use to add to and maintain the data list records.

5. Click the New button to start a new record and then enter the following entries into the designated fields (press Tab to move the insertion point to the next field and Shift+Tab to move it back to the previous field):

   - '**000634** in the ID No field

   - **Gene** in the First Name field

   - **Poole** in the Last Name field

   - **M** in the Gender field

   - **Engineering** in the Dept field

   - **75000** in the Salary field

   - **Chicago** in the Location field

   - **9-15-2000** in the Date Hired field

   - **No** in the Profit Sharing field

   After entering all the new information in the appropriate fields of the new record, you still have to enter this record into the data list.

6. Press the Enter key to insert Gene Poole's record into the data list.

   Excel responds by clearing the fields in the data form so you can enter the next (third) record, while at the same time entering the data entries you made in the Data Form into the appropriate columns in the second row of the data list itself.

   Note that you don't have to use the data form to enter records for your data list. If you prefer, you can make entries in the appropriate cells in the data list itself. Adding records via the Data Form does, however, offer the advantage of automatically formatting the new entries to match the others in that field (column) as well as copying any formulas needed to produce the correct results in calculated fields (as in the Years of Service field in the Employee Data List).

7. Select the Close button in Employee Data List data form, position the cell cursor in cell A1, and then click the Format As Table button in the Styles group of the Ribbon's Home tab (Alt+HT). Click the Table Style Light 2 thumbnail in the drop-down gallery (the one in the second column of the first row of the Light section at the top of the gallery). Click the OK button in the Format As Table dialog box asking you to confirm $A$1:$J$3 as the data for your table with the assumption that this table range has a header row at the top.

   Excel formats your employee data list with this light-blue banded formatting. The program also adds drop-down Filter buttons to each of the field names in row 1 of the data list.

8. Click cell A4 and then enter the third record of your employee data list right in the worksheet without the help of the data form. Use the → key to complete each field entry until you reach cell J4, where you can complete the entry by clicking the Enter button on the Formula bar:

   - '**000262** in the ID No field in cell A4

   - **Lance** in the First Name field in cell B4

- **Bird** in the Last Name field in cell C4

- **M** in the Gender field in cell D4

- **Human Resources** in the Dept field in cell E4 and then widen the column with AutoFit

- **21100** in the Salary field in cell F4

- **Boston** in the Location field in cell G4

- **8-13-97** in the Date Hired field in cell H4

- **Yes** in the Profit Sharing field in J4

Note how Excel automatically formats your field entries in Lance Bird's record as you make them using the table format you assigned to the employee data list table.

9. Click the drop-down Filter button on the Location field in cell G1 and then click the (Select All) check box to remove its check mark. Then, click the Boston check box before you click OK.

Excel filters your data list by hiding Gene Poole's record because his location is Chicago rather than Boston. Note that Excel adds a filter cone icon to the Location field's drop-down button to indicate that the data list is currently filtered (and therefore not showing all its records) using values in this particular field.

10. Click the Location field's Filter button again and then click the (Select All) check box to restore its check mark before you click OK.

Excel removes the filtering from this data list by displaying all three of its records. The program also removes the filter cone icon from the field's drop-down button.

11. Click cell A1 and then save your new employee data list in a new workbook named **Data List Practice.xlsx** in your Excel 2007 Practice folder before you close the workbook file.

Editing records in the data form

The data form is not only useful for appending new records to a data list but also for editing field entries in existing records or even deleting entire records from the data list. You can use the Criteria button in the data form to quickly find the records that need editing (this is especially helpful in longer data lists where it is no longer practical to search the records manually). When you click the Criteria button in the data form, Excel clears all the field text boxes so that you can enter the criteria to search for in the record that needs editing.

When entering the criteria for locating matching records in the data form, you can use the question mark (?) and the asterisk (*) wildcard characters just as you do when using the Excel Find feature to locate cells with particular entries (see Chapter 5).

When using the Criteria button in the data form to find records, you can use the following comparative operators when entering search criteria in fields that use numbers or dates:

- ✔ Equal to (=) for finding records with the same text, value, or date you enter

- ✔ Greater than (>) for finding records after the text characters (in the alphabet) or the date, or larger than the value you enter

- ✔ Greater than or equal to (>=) for finding records the same as the text characters, date, or value you enter or after the characters (in the alphabet), after the date, or larger than or equal to the value you enter

- ✔ Less than (<) for finding records before the text characters (in the alphabet) or date or smaller than the value you enter

- ✔ Less than or equal to (<=) for finding records the same as the text characters, date, or value you enter or before the characters (in the alphabet) or the date, or larger than or equal to the value you enter

- ✔ Unequal to (<>) to find records not the same as the text, value, or date you enter

For example, to find all the records where the employee's annual salary is $50,000, you can enter **=50000** or simply **50000** in the Salary field text box. However, to find all the records for employees whose annual salaries are less than or equal to $35,000, you enter **<=35000** in the Salary field text box. To find all the records for employees with salaries greater than $45,000, you would enter **>45000** in the Salary field text box instead. If you wanted to find all of the records where the employees are female *and* make more than $35,000, you would enter **F** in the Gender field text box and **>35000** in the Salary field text box in the same Criteria data form.

Solve It

Exercise 17-2: Finding and Editing Records with the Data Form

In Exercise 17-2, you get practice using the data form generated for an Excel data list to find and edit particular records in the list.

1. Open the *Exercise17-2.xlsx* file in the Chap17 folder in your Excel 2007 Workbook folder.

   This workbook contains a much more complete version of the Employee Data List you created in the previous exercise. You use this version of the Employee Data List worksheet to practice using the data form to find records that need editing.

2. Click the Form button on your customized Quick Access toolbar to open the data form for the Employee Data List and then click the form's Criteria button.

   Excel displays a blank data form where you can enter the search criteria in the appropriate fields.

   You need to find Sherry Caulfield's record in the data list to edit it. Unfortunately, you don't remember how she spells her last name, only that it begins with a C (and not a K) and that she works in the Boston office.

3. Enter **C*** in the Last Name field and **Boston** in the Location field.

   The wildcard character (the asterisk) you entered after the C stands for all the other missing letters in her name.

4. Click the Find Next button in the data form.

The first record that Excel finds where the last name begins with the letter C and the office location is Boston is that of William Cobb.

5. Click the Find Next button a second time.

This time, Excel locates Sherry Caulfield's record, the 25th record of the 32 total.

6. Change Sherry's profit sharing status from no to yes by replacing No with **Yes** in the Profit Sharing field in the data form. Click the Criteria button.

Next, find Charles Smith's record in the Employee Data List, an employee in the Administration department.

7. Select the Clear button to clear the previous search criteria and then enter **Smith** in the Last Name field and **Administration** in the Dept field. Then, click the Find Next button.

Excel finds the record for Steven Smith in Administration.

8. Click the Find Next button a second time.

This time, Excel locates Charles Smith's record, the 29th record of the 32 total.

9. Change Charles Smith's location from San Francisco to **Chicago**. Click the Close button to make the change and, at the same time, close the data form.

10. Save your changes to the Employee Data List worksheet in a new workbook named **Employee List - edited.xlsx** in the Excel 2007 Practice folder. Leave the workbook file open for the next exercise.

Sorting Lists

Excel's Sorting feature makes it easy to rearrange the records or even the fields in your data list. You sort the records in your data list by sorting by rows, whereas you sort the fields in the data list by sorting by columns.

In sorting, you can specify either ascending or descending sort order for your data. When you specify ascending order (which is the default), Excel arranges text in A-to-Z order and values from smallest to largest. When you specify descending order, Excel reverses this order and arranges text in Z-to-A order and values range from largest to smallest. When sorting on a date field, keep in mind that ascending order puts the records in least-recent-to-most-recent date order, whereas descending order gives you the records in most-recent-to-least-recent date order.

When you choose the ascending sort order for a field that contains many different kinds of entries, Excel places numbers (from smallest to largest) before text (in alphabetical order) followed by Logical values (TRUE and FALSE), Error values, and, finally, blank cells. When using the descending sort order, the program uses the same general arrangement for the different types of entries, but numbers go from largest to smallest, text runs from Z to A, and the FALSE logical value precedes the TRUE logical value.

Using sorting keys

To sort your data, Excel uses *sorting keys* to determine how the records or fields should be reordered in the data list. When sorting records, you indicate by cell address which field (that is, column) contains the first or *primary* sorting key. When sorting fields, you indicate which record (row) contains the primary sorting key. Excel then applies the selected sort (ascending or descending) to the data in the key field or row to determine how the records or fields will be reordered during sorting.

When a key field contains duplicates entries, Excel simply lists these records in the order in which they were entered in the data list. To indicate how Excel should order records with duplicates in the primary key, you define a secondary key. For example, if, when organizing the data list in alphabetical order by the Last Name field, you have several records where the last name is Smith, you can have Excel order the Smiths' records in alphabetical order by first name by defining the First Name field as the secondary key. If the secondary key contains duplicates (say you have two John Smiths in your company), you can define a third key field (the Middle Name field, if your data list has one) that determines how the duplicate John Smith records are arranged when the data list is sorted.

Keep in mind that although sorting is most often applied to rearranging and maintaining data list records and fields, you can use the sort command to reorder data in any worksheet table, whether or not the table follows the strict data list structure.

Before you attempt Exercise 17-3, you may want to play the Data Sorting.exe demo located in the Excel Feature Demos folder on your workbook CD-ROM. This feature demonstration shows you how to sort the records of a data list on various fields in the list using the columns' AutoFilter buttons and the Custom Sort dialog box.

Solve It

Exercise 17-3: Sorting the Records in a Data List

In Exercise 17-3, you get practice sorting records in the employee data list you edited in the previous exercise, using various fields as the sorting keys.

1. With the Employee Data List worksheet active in the *Employee List - edited.xlsx* file, click the Last Name field's drop-down Filter button in cell C1 and then click the Sort A to Z option on its drop-down menu.

Excel sorts all the records in the employee data list so that they are in alphabetical order by last name. Note that the program indicates that the list has been sorted in ascending order using the values in the Last Name field by displaying an arrow pointing upward on this field's Filter drop-down button.

2. Click the Salary field's Filter button in cell F1 and then click the Sort Largest to Smallest on its drop-down menu.

Excel sorts all the records in the employee data list so that they are in numerical order from largest to smallest by last salary. This time, the program indicates that the list has been sorted in descending order using the values in the Salary field by displaying an arrow pointing downward on this field's Filter button.

3. Click the Custom Sort option on the Sort & Filter button on the Ribbon's Home tab or press Alt+HSU.

   The Sort dialog box appears and Excel selects all of the records in your data list (omitting the field names in the first row with the field names). The Sort dialog box enables you to add multiple levels of sorting keys to be used in the sort operation.

   Begin by sorting the records in the data list so that they are in alphabetical order by department and then in descending order by salary.

4. Click the Sort By drop-down list button and then click Dept on its list field in the Sort By drop-down list box and then click the A to Z option in the Order column. Then, click the Add Level button and select the Salary field in the Then By drop-down list box. Select the Largest to Smallest option in its Order drop-down list before you click OK.

   Excel reorders the records in the employee data list so that first they are in alphabetical order by department (Accounting, Administration, Engineering, and so on) and then within each department in order from highest to lowest salary ($38,000, $34,400, $29,000 and so on).

   Next sort the records in the data list alphabetically by department, location, and then last name. To perform this sort operation, you need to define three keys all using the A to Z Order option.

5. Open the Sort dialog box and then define the Dept field as the Sort By key, the Location field as the first Then By key, and the Last Name field as the second Then By key (added by clicking the Add Level button), each with its A to Z Order option selected, before you click OK.

   Excel reorders the records in the Employee Data List so that first they are in alphabetical order by department (Accounting, Administration, Engineering, and so on), and then within each department in order by location (Boston, Detroit, San Francisco, and so on), and finally in order by Last Name (Edwards, Percival, Savage, and so on).

6. Close the **Employee List - edited.xlsx** workbook file without saving your changes to the file.

Sorting a list on multiple keys

Sometimes, you may need to sort on more than three fields as you practiced in the previous exercise. For example, suppose you are working with a personnel data list and you want to organize the records in alphabetical order first by department, and then by supervisor, and finally by last name, first name, and middle name. To sort the records in this data list by these five fields, you have to define the following five keys in the Sort dialog box:

✔ Sort by Department in A to Z order

✔ Then by Supervisor in A to Z order

✔ Then by Last Name in A to Z order

✔ Then by First Name in A to Z order

✔ Then by Middle Name in A to Z order

Exercise 17-4: Sorting a Data List on Five Keys

In Exercise 17-4, you get practice sorting the data in a sample personnel data list on five sorting keys:

1. Open the *Exercise17-4.xlsx* file in the Chap17 folder in your Excel 2007 Workbook folder on your hard disk.

    This workbook contains a copy of the personnel data list that you will sort in alphabetical order first by the department name, and then by the supervisor's name, and finally by the employee's last, first, and middle name.

2. Open the Sort dialog box (Alt+HSU) and then define the five keys (Department, Supervisor, Last Name, First Name, and Middle Name) using the A to Z Order option before you click OK.

    Check the Department and Supervisor fields in the re-sorted data list and verify that they are now in alphabetical order first by department name and then by supervisor name. Note in the case of supervisor Johnson in the Administration department that the name of his two William Smith employees are in order by their middle names (William Dennis Smith before William Mathew Smith).

3. Save your sorted personnel data list worksheet in a new workbook file named **Pers Data List – 5keysort.xlsx** in your Excel 2007 Practice folder and leave the workbook file open for the next exercise.

Sorting the fields (columns) in a data list

You can use Excel's column sorting capability to change the order of the fields in a data list without having to resort to cutting and pasting various columns. To sort the fields in a data list, add a row at the top of the list containing numbers from 1 to the number of the last field in the data list (these numbers indicate the desired order of the fields). You then sort the list by column using this row as the sole sorting key.

When sorting the columns in a data list, you must remember to click the Options button and select the Sort Left to Right option button in the Orientation section of the Sort Options dialog box. Otherwise, Excel sorts your records instead of your columns and, in the process, the row of field names become sorted in with the other data records in your list!

To see how to go about sorting the columns of a list, sort the columns of the Personnel Data List you worked with in the previous exercise so that the fields appear in the following order: SSN, Department, Supervisor, First Name, Middle Name, Last Name, Title, Salary.

Exercise 17-5: Sorting the Fields in a Data List

In Exercise 17-5, you get practice sorting the fields to change the order of the fields in an existing data list.

1. With the Personnel Data List worksheet active in the *Pers Data List – 5keysort.xlsx* workbook file whose records you sorted in the previous exercise, select row 1 in the worksheet and then click the Insert button on the Ribbon's Home tab.

Excel inserts a blank row at the top of the Personnel Data List worksheet.

2. Make the following numerical entries in the designated cells of the new, blank row 1:

- **1** in cell A1
- **6** in cell B1
- **4** in cell C1
- **5** in cell D1
- **2** in cell E1
- **3** in cell F1
- **7** in cell G1
- **8** in cell H1

You will now use the values you entered into the cells in row 1 to sort the columns of the table. However, before you can do that you must convert the table with its filter buttons to a normal cell range.

3. Click cell A2 and then click the Design tab under the Table Tools contextual tab. Then, click the Convert to Range button and click Yes in the alert dialog box asking if you want to convert the table into a normal cell range.

Now you're ready to open the Sort dialog box so that you can sort the columns of the table.

4. Select the cell range A1:H20 and then click the Custom Sort option on the Sort & Filter button on the Home tab or press Alt+HSU to open the Sort dialog box.

The first thing to do is to change the options so that Excel sorts the columns from left to right rather than the rows from top to bottom.

5. Click the Options button to open the Sort Options dialog box and there click the Sort Left to Right option button in the Orientation section before you click OK.

Now you're ready to define row 1 as the sole sorting key.

6. Click Row 1 in the Sort By drop-down list and leave the default Smallest to Largest option selected before you click OK.

The fields of the Personnel Data List are now arranged in this order: SSN, Department, Supervisor, First Name, Middle Name, Last Name, Title, and Salary.

7. Delete the top row of the Personnel Data List by clicking the row's header on the left edge of the worksheet and then clicking the Delete button on the Cells group of the Home tab.

   Excel removes the row with the column numbers used in sorting the fields of the data list.

8. Click cell A1 and then click the Format As Table button in the Styles group of the Home tab. Then, click the Table Style Light 15 thumbnail in the drop-down gallery and click OK in the Format As Table dialog box asking you to confirm $A$1:$H$19 as the table range with row 1 containing its headers.

   Excel reapplies the table formatting, adding the filter buttons to each of the field names in row 1.

9. Click cell A1 and then save the Personnel Data List worksheet with the sorted fields and records in a new workbook named **Pers Data List – fieldsort.xlsx** in your Excel 2007 Practice folder and then close the workbook file.

Subtotaling a List

You can use Excel's Subtotals feature to subtotal data in a sorted data list. To subtotal a data list, you first sort the records in the list on the field you want subtotaled and then designate the field that contains the values you want totaled. (These don't necessarily have to be the same fields in the data list.)

When you use the Subtotals feature, you aren't restricted to having the values in the designated field added together with the SUM function. You can instead have Excel return the number of entries with the COUNT function, the average of the entries with the AVERAGE function, the highest entry with the MAXIMUM function, the lowest entry with the MINIMUM function, or even the product of the entries with the PRODUCT function.

Solve It

Exercise 17-6: Subtotaling the Records in a Data List

In Exercise 17-6, you get practice adding subtotals and grand totals to fields in a version of the employee data list.

1. Open the *Exercise17-6.xlsx* file in your Chap17 folder in the Excel 2007 Workbook folder on your hard disk.

   This workbook contains a copy of the employee data list that you can use to practice using Excel's Subtotal feature.

2. Sort the employee data list, first alphabetically by department, and then numerically, from highest-to-lowest order by salary.

   Be sure to select the Largest to Smallest Order option after selecting Salary as the Then By key in the Sort dialog box (Alt+HSU).

   You sort the records in the data list by the Dept field and then the Salary field because you want Excel to subtotal the salaries in each department. The Dept field provides what is referred to as the *break* in the subtotals report because each time the department entry changes, Excel computes a subtotal (in this case, a subtotal of the values entered in the Salary field).

However, before you can subtotal the data list, you must convert its table into a normal range of cells.

3. Click the Design tab under the Table Tools contextual tab. Then, click the Convert to Range button and click Yes in the alert dialog box asking you to confirm converting the table into a normal cell range.

Excel removes the filter buttons from the data list.

4. Click cell A2 in the data list cell range and then click the Subtotal button on the Ribbon's Data tab or press Alt+AB to open the Subtotal dialog box.

You must supply at least three pieces of information in the Subtotal dialog box:

- Field at which the subtotals break in the At Each Change In drop-down list box

- Function to use in computing the subtotals (Sum is the default, but you can also select Count, Average, Max, Min, or Product) in the Use Function drop-down list box

- Field(s) whose values are to be subtotaled by selecting the check box in front of the field name in the Add Subtotal To list box

5. Click the Dept option on the At Each Change In drop-down list box. Then, click Sum on the Use Function drop-down list box. Finally, put a check mark in the Salary check box in the Add Subtotal To list box and remove the check marks in any other check boxes in this list before you click OK.

Excel subtotals the salaries in Employee Data List by department, while at the same time adding outline buttons to the rows (Figure 17-1 shows how the first part of this data list should now appear in your Employee Data List in Excel).

You can use these outline buttons to collapse and expand the subtotals in the data list.

6. Click the number 1 button at the top of the row header to collapse the subtotals down to the grand total of all the salaries for all departments in row 39 and then widen column F, if necessary, to display its grand total.

The first level of the outlined rows shows only the grand total. Next, display the subtotals for each of the departments in the data list.

7. Click the number 2 button at the top of the row header.

Excel now displays the rows with the salary totals for Accounting in row 7, Administration in row 13, Engineering in row 26, Human Resources in row 33, and Information Services in row 38, along with the grand total of all salaries in row 39.

8. Click the number 3 button at the top of the row header to redisplay the rows with all the records in the data list along with the Salaries Department subtotals and Salary grand total. Press Ctrl+8 to hide the outline buttons.

Ctrl+8 is a shortcut key combination that you can use to hide and then redisplay the buttons and other controls in any spreadsheet you've outlined.

9. Click cell A1 and then save the employee data list with the subtotals in a new workbook file named **Employee List – subtotal.xlsx** in your Excel 2007 Practice folder and then close the workbook file.

Figure 17-1:
The first
part of the
Employee
Data List
after
subtotaling
its salaries
by
department.

Filtering a List

It is one thing to set up a data list and load it with tons of data, but it's quite another to get just the information you need out of the list. The procedure for specifying what data you want displayed in an Excel data list is called *filtering* the data list or database. The procedure for extracting only the data you want from the database table or data list is called *querying* the database.

At the most basic level, Excel enables you to filter out all but the information you need with its AutoFilter feature that temporarily hides the display of unwanted records. To filter a data list, you must display the Filter drop-down buttons in the row of cells containing the fields for the list. You can do this in one of two ways:

✔ Position the cell cursor in one of the cells of the data list and then format the range of data as a table using the Format As Table button in the Styles group on the Home tab or press Alt+HT and then selecting one of the styles to apply to the list.

✔ Position the cell cursor in one of the cells in the row containing the field names for a data list and then click the Filter option on the Sort & Filter button's drop-down menu or press Alt+HSF or Ctrl+Shift+L.

Either way you do it, the program then adds drop-down buttons to each of the field names in the top row of the list. When you click a field's Filter drop-down button, its drop-down menu contains a (Select All) check box item (selected by default) at the top of a list of check box items for all the individual items in that field. When you de-select the (Select All) check box, all the check boxes for all the individual entries are all automatically de-selected. You can then filter the list to just those records containing particular entries by selecting their individual check boxes.

In addition, the drop-down menu contains one of the following three menu items, depending upon the type of entries in that field, each attached to its own continuation menu of criteria options:

- ✔ **Text Filters** for text fields to filter the records of the data list using particular text criteria such as Begins With, Ends With, Contains, and Does Not Contain and the like

- ✔ **Date Filters** for date fields to filter the records of the data list using particular date criteria such as Today, Tomorrow, This Week, Last Week, This Month, Last Month, and so on

- ✔ **Number Filters** for calculated fields or fields with numeric entries to filter the records of the data list using particular numerical criteria such as Equals, Does Not Equal, Greater Than, Less Than, Top 10, Above Average, and so forth

In addition, the continuation menus attached to each of the three options, Text Filters, Date Filters, and Number Filters contain a Custom Filter option that you can select to open the Custom AutoFilter dialog box. The Custom AutoFilter dialog box enables you to use more complex filtering criteria by designating the type of operator (AND or OR) to use in evaluating the first and the second condition in the top and bottom drop-down list boxes; you can specify the values to be evaluated in the first and second condition in the associated combo boxes. You also specify the type of relationship between the two conditions with the AND or OR option buttons (the AND option button is selected by default).

When selecting the operator for the first and second condition in the leftmost drop-down list boxes at the top and bottom of the Custom AutoFilter dialog box, you have the following choices:

- ✔ Equals
- ✔ Does not equal
- ✔ Is greater than
- ✔ Is greater than or equal to
- ✔ Is less than
- ✔ Is less than or equal to
- ✔ Begins with
- ✔ Does not begin with
- ✔ Ends with
- ✔ Does not end with
- ✔ Contains
- ✔ Does not contain

Note that you can use the Begins with, Ends with, and Contains operators and their negative counterparts when filtering a text field — you can also use the question mark (?) and asterisk (*) wildcard characters when entering the values for use with these operators. (The question mark wildcard stands for individual characters and the asterisk for one or more characters.) You use the other logical operators when dealing with numeric and date fields.

When specifying the values to evaluate in the associated combo boxes on the right side of the Custom AutoFilter dialog box, you can type in the text, number, or date, or you can select an existing field entry by clicking the box's drop-down list button and then clicking the entry on the pop-up menu.

Before you attempt Exercise 17-7, you may want to play the Data Filtering.exe demo located in the Excel Feature Demos folder on your workbook CD-ROM. This feature demonstration shows you how to filter the records of a data list by selecting items on a field's AutoFilter drop-down list along with using a field's Top 10 AutoFilter and Custom AutoFilter options.

Solve It

Exercise 17-7: Filtering Records in a Data List

In Exercise 17-7, you get practice filtering the records in the now-familiar employee data list using a number of different criteria.

1. Open the *Exercise17-7.xlsx* file in your Chap17 folder in the Excel 2007 Workbook folder on your hard disk.

   This workbook contains a copy of the employee data list that you can use to practice querying a data list by filtering out all records except for those that contain the data with which you want to work.

2. Click the Filter option on the Sort & Filter button's drop-down menu on the Home tab or press Ctrl+Shift+L.

   Excel responds by adding filter drop-down list boxes to each of the field names in row 1 of the employee data list.

   Start by filtering the data list to include just the records where the employee is part of the profit-sharing plan.

3. Click the filter drop-down list box in the Profit Sharing field name and then select No on the drop-down list to remove its check mark as well as the check mark in the (Select All) check box. Click OK.

   Excel hides all the records where the Profit Sharing is No, leaving displayed only those where the Profit Sharing entry is Yes.

4. Click Clear Filter from the "Profit Sharing" option on the Profit Sharing field's drop-down list to redisplay all the records in the data list.

   When you filter the records in a data list, Excel simply temporarily hides the records.

5. Click the Years of Service filter drop-down button, highlight the Number Filters option, and then click Top 10 on the continuation menu to open the Top 10 AutoFilter dialog box, where you click OK.

The Top 10 AutoFilter dialog box enables you to display only the records with the top or bottom 10 (more or less) values (by selecting Items in the rightmost drop-down list box) or percentage (by selecting Percent in this drop-down list box) in the selected field.

6. Click the Sort Largest to Smallest option on the Years of Service drop-down list to sort the filtered records so that they are displayed in order from the longest to shortest top ten years of service.

Excel reorders the filtered records so that they are now in descending order according to the number of years of employment.

7. Redisplay all the records in the data list and then click the Salary filter button. Highlight the Number Filters option and then click Custom Filter on the continuation menu to open the Custom AutoFilter dialog box.

Use the Custom AutoFilter dialog box to filter out all the records except for those where the annual salary is between $40,000 and $75,000.

8. Select Is Greater Than or Equal To in the first drop-down list box and then click the second combo box to its immediate right and type **40000**. Select Is Less Than or Equal To in the second drop-down list box below the AND and OR option buttons (the AND should be selected). Type **75000** in the combo box to its immediate right before you click OK.

Excel filters out all the records in the data list except for those where the annual salary is equal to $40,000 or more and $75,000 or less.

9. Sort the filtered records so that they are displayed in descending order by salary (largest to smallest).

Because the AutoFilter only temporarily hides the display of the records in a data list, you need to copy the filtered records to a new part of the worksheet or to a new worksheet when you want to retain the subset for future reference and use.

10. Copy the filtered and sorted records currently displayed in the cell range A1:J33 (including the field names in row 1) on the Employee Data List worksheet to the same range on the Sheet2 worksheet. Widen Columns E and G of Sheet2 with AutoFit to display all the entries in this table. Rename the Sheet2 worksheet **Salary Subset** and then click the Employee Data List worksheet to reselect it.

11. Redisplay all the records in the data list on the Employee Data List worksheet. Use the Custom AutoFilter dialog box to filter the list so that only the records where the department is either Engineering or Information Services are displayed and the records are sorted in ascending (A to Z) order by department name.

Be sure to select the OR option button in the Custom AutoFilter dialog box. Note that you can select the department names, Engineering and Information Services, from the two Combo boxes after selecting the Equals or Contains operator in the associated drop-down list boxes in this dialog box.

12. Copy the filtered and sorted records (including the field names to the equivalent cell range in Sheet3) and then rename Sheet3 to **Dept Subset**.

You now have filtered and sorted subsets of the larger employee data list on separate worksheets where you can more easily work with their data.

13. Redisplay all the records in the data list on the Employee Data List worksheet, position the cell cursor in cell A1, and then save your work in a new workbook called **Employee List – fltrd.xlsx** in your Excel 2007 Practice folder and close the workbook file as you exit Excel.

Querying External Database Tables

Excel makes it possible to query other external databases to which you have access and then extract the data that you're interested in into your worksheet for further manipulation and analysis. The external databases that you can query can be as simple as those you maintain with a dedicated database management program such as Microsoft Access all the way up to and including the corporate database itself.

To create a query that acquires data from an external database, you must complete two basic procedures:

✔ Define the data source; that is, the external database that contains the data you want to query

✔ Specify the query itself, including all the columns of data that you want extracted along with the criteria for selecting them

Solve It

Exercise 17-8: Importing a Data Table from an Access Database

In Exercise 17-8, you get practice importing the Products data table from the Northwind database that accompanies Microsoft Access 2007, and then sorting and filtering the records in this data table.

1. If Excel's not currently running, launch the program. If the program is running and a blank workbook is not displayed in it, open a new workbook (Ctrl+N). Then, click the From Access button in the Get External Data group on the Ribbon's Data tab or press Alt+AFA.

Excel opens the Select Data Source dialog box where you specify the Access database to query.

2. Select the *Northwind.mdb* file inside the Chap17 folder inside the Excel 2007 Workbook folder on your hard disk and then click the Open button.

Excel opens the Select Table dialog box listing all the data tables and queries defined for the Northwind database. Enlarge this dialog box as needed to see more of the many tables and queries created for this sample data base.

3. Click Products listed near the bottom of the list in the Select Table dialog box and then click OK.

   Excel opens the Import Data dialog box, where you specify whether to import the data as a regular data list using the Table (default) option, a pivot table (see Chapter 20) using the PivotTable Report option, or a pivot chart using the PivotChart and PivotTable Report option. You can also choose between importing the Access data table data in a particular cell range in the current worksheet or on a new worksheet added to a new workbook file.

4. Leave the Table and Existing Worksheet options selected (with cell $A$1 designated as the first cell into which to import the data) and click OK.

   Excel imports all the data in the Product data table into the Sheet1 worksheet of your new workbook. When the program imports this data into your worksheet, it automatically formats it as a table using Table Style Medium 9 table style.

5. Assign the Table Style Light 8 style to the product table and then rename the Sheet1 **NW Prd Tbl.**

   In this lighter table style, the data records are somewhat easier to read.

6. Sort this product table in Smallest to Largest order on the UnitsInStock field and then filter the records so that only those for products that have *not* been discontinued are displayed.

   Sort the table by selecting the Sort Smallest to Largest option on the UnitsInStock field's filter button's drop-down menu and then filter the records by selecting only the FALSE option in the Discontinued field's filter button's drop-down menu.

7. Save the new workbook with the NW Prod Tbl worksheet containing the Products data table in your Excel 2007 Practice folder under the filename **NWdb Query Practice.xlsx** and then leave the workbook open for the next exercise.

Solve It   ## Exercise 17-9: Querying Data in a Data Table in an Access Database

Instead of importing all the fields and all the records in a data table in an external database into an Excel worksheet as you did in the previous exercise, you can create a query that brings in only the fields you want and the records that meet the criteria you set. In Exercise 17-9, you get practice setting up such a query that imports just the fields in a sample Microsoft Access database table that meet the criteria you set up.

1. With the *NWdb Query Practice.xlsx* file that you created in Exercise 17-8 open in Excel, click the Sheet2 tab and then rename Sheet2 **NW Prd Qry.** Then, click the From Other Sources button on the Data tab (or press Alt+AFO) and then click the From Microsoft Query option at the bottom of the drop-down menu.

   The Choose Data Source dialog box opens, where you indicate the particular source (database, query, or cube) that holds the data you want to import.

2. Click the MS Access Database option on the Databases tab in the Choose Data Source dialog box and then click OK.

   The Select Database dialog box opens where you select the Access .mdb file to use (*Northwind.mdb* in the Chap17 folder inside your Excel 2007 Workbook folder, in this case).

3. If necessary, double-click My Documents (or Documents on Vista) in the Directories list box and then double-click the Excel 2007 Workbook folder followed by the Chap17 folder. Finally, click Northwind.mdb in the Database Name list box and click OK.

   The Query Wizard dialog box opens where you select the tables and the fields (columns) from those tables that you want to include in the query.

4. Scroll down the Available Tables and Columns list box on the left until you locate Products. Then, click the Expand button (+) to display the names of its fields. Add the following five fields to the Columns in the Your Query list box on the right side of the dialog box by clicking their field names in the Available Tables and Columns list box and then clicking the > button in succession:

   - ProductName
   - QuantityPerUnit
   - UnitPrice
   - UnitsInStock
   - Discontinued

   The Columns in the Your Query list box now displays the names of these five fields in the order in which you added them.

5. Click the Next button to display the Query Wizard – Filter Data dialog box. Then, click UnitPrice in the Column to Filter list box and set up a condition where only records in which the products cost between $10.00 and $25.00 are queried.

   In the Only Include Rows Where list box, set up an AND condition where UnitPrice is greater than or equal to 10 and is less than or equal to 25.

6. Click Discontinued in the Column to Filter list box and then set up a condition where only records in which the items that have not been discontinued are queried.

   In the Only Include Rows Where list box, set up the condition, Discontinued equals 0 (the equivalent of FALSE).

7. Click the Next button to open the Query Wizard – Sort Order dialog box. Then, click ProductName in the Sort By drop-down list, leave the Ascending option button selected, and then click Next.

   The Query Wizard – Finish dialog box appears. Here, you choose between viewing the data and editing the query in Microsoft Query or returning the data to Excel. In addition, you can save the query for re-use at a later time.

8. Click the Save Query button to open the Save As dialog box. Then replace the default filename, Query from MS Access Database.dqy with **NWdb Products in Stock.dqy** and then click Save.

   The Save As dialog box closes and you return to the Query Wizard – Finish dialog box, where the Return Data to Microsoft Office Excel option button is selected.

9. Click the Finish button to close the Query Wizard dialog box. Then, if cell $A$1 of Sheet2 in your NWdb Query Practice workbook is selected, click OK in the Import Data dialog box to import the queried data from the Northwind Products data table into Excel.

Excel imports the records that meet your filtering criteria (unit price between $10 and $25 and not discontinued) sorted by product name. Note, however, that these filtered records only include entries for the ProductName, QuantityPerUnit, UnitsInStock, and Discontinued fields of the Products data table.

10. Assign the Table Style Light 8 style to the queried Product table on Sheet2 of your workbook and then rename Sheet2 to NW Prd Qry.

Now you will insert a new column in the queried Product table that will calculate the extended price by multiplying the unit price in column C by the number of units in stock in column D.

11. Insert a new column between columns D and E in the queried Product table and then rename this column in cell E1 from Column1 **Extended Price**. Then, create a formula in cell E2 that multiples the value in C2 by that in D2.

Note that as soon as you create this formula =C2*D2 (which appears a lot longer on the Formula bar because it uses references to the original Products data table in the Northwind database) in cell C2, Excel instantly copies it to all the other rows of the table in the Extended Priced column (the real benefit of formatting a data list as an Excel table).

One of the real beauties of saving a query as you did in Step 8 of this exercise is that you can import data using its criteria and conditions without having to go through the trouble of redefining which fields to include and the criteria on which to filter and sort the data. As you see in the next step, all you have to do is select the name of the query and indicate where to import the data.

12. Click Sheet3 in the workbook and then with cell A1 of this worksheet selected, click the Existing Connections button on the Data tab or press Alt+AX to open the Existing Connections dialog box. Then, click NWdb Products in Stock in the Connections in this Workbook section of the Select a Connection list box and click Open.

Excel closes the Existing Connections dialog box and opens the Import Data dialog box.

13. Click OK in the Import Data dialog box to import the queried data into Sheet3 beginning at cell A1. Then, compare the data in the imported table on Sheet3 with that imported on your NW Prd Qry worksheet.

Excel repeats the query, importing the same data as originally imported on the NW Prd Qry worksheet. Note, however, that had someone made changes to the records of the Products table in Microsoft Access, the results returned by running the query on Sheet3 could have been quite different, although they used the same criteria and conditions.

14. Click NW Prd Tbl worksheet and then save the changes you've made before you exit Excel.

Chapter 18

Protecting the Spreadsheet

. . . .

In This Chapter

▶ Assigning a password to open a workbook

▶ Assigning a password to make editing changes in a workbook

▶ Protecting a worksheet and determining which actions are enabled

▶ Protecting the entire workbook

▶ Doing data entry in the unlocked cells of a protected worksheet

. . . .

*E*xcel enables you to secure your work on two levels:

✔ Protect the workbook file so that only the people you entrust with the password can open the file to view, print, or edit the data

✔ Protect the worksheets in a workbook from unwarranted changes so that only people with that password can modify the contents and design of the spreadsheet

In this chapter, you get the chance to practice securing your Excel workbooks and worksheets on both these levels. In addition, you get the opportunity to experience doing data entry in a protected spreadsheet in which all your movements and edits are automatically restricted to the unlocked cells where such changes are allowed.

Password-Protecting the Workbook

By password-protecting the workbook, you can prevent unauthorized users from opening the workbook and editing it. You set a password for opening the workbook file when it contains spreadsheets whose data are of a sufficiently sensitive nature that only a certain group of people in the company should have access to them (such as spreadsheets dealing with personnel information and salaries). Of course, after you set a password for opening a workbook, you must supply this password to those people who need access to it in order for them to be able to open the file.

You set a password for modifying the workbook when you you're dealing with spreadsheets whose data needs to be viewed and printed by different users, none of whom are authorized to make changes to any of the entries. For example, after a workbook has been through a complete editing and review cycle and all of the suggested changes have been merged, you might assign a password for modifying it to those who have the authority to do so before distributing it company-wide.

When you're dealing with a spreadsheet whose data is of a sensitive nature and should not be modified by *any* of those authorized to open it, you need to set both a password for opening and a password for modifying the workbook file. You assign either one or both of these types of passwords to a workbook file at the time you save it with the Office button | Save As command on the Office menu.

A password-protected workbook file for which you can't reproduce the correct password is the ultimate nightmare (especially if you're talking about a really important spreadsheet with loads and loads of vital data), so, for heaven's sake, don't forget your password or you'll be stuck. Excel does not provide any sort of command for overriding the password and opening a protected workbook, nor does Microsoft offer any such utility. If you think that you might forget the workbook's password, be sure to write it down somewhere and keep that piece of paper in a secure place (preferably under lock and key). It's always better to be safe than sorry when it comes to passwords for opening files.

Exercise 18-1: Assigning a Password for Opening and Editing a Workbook

In Exercise 18-1, you get practice assigning passwords that are required to open and to edit the contents of an Excel workbook file.

1. If Excel is not currently running, launch the program and then open *Exercise18-1.xlsx* in your Chap18 folder in the Excel 2007 Workbook folder on your hard disk.

   This workbook contains three worksheets: Employee Data List, Salary Subset, and Department Subset. Use this sample workbook file to practice assigning a password for opening the workbook and another for editing its worksheets.

2. Click Office button | Save As or press F12 or Alt+FA to open the Save As Dialog box. Then, open the Excel 2007 Practice folder and replace the filename *Exercise18-1.xlsx* with **Employee List – protected.xlsx** in the File Name text box, but don't click the Save button quite yet.

   To assign a password for opening and/or for editing the workbook, you need to open the General Options dialog box.

3. Click the Tools button and then click General Options on its drop-down list to open the General Options dialog box.

   The General Options dialog box contains a Password to Open and a Password to Modify text box where you can enter these passwords. In addition, this dialog box contains an Always Create Backup check box that, when checked, tells Excel to automatically make a backup copy of the workbook you're saving to disk (that you can use in the event that the original file is corrupted and becomes inoperable). The Read-Only Recommended check box, when checked, assigns read-only status to the workbook you're saving (preventing you from saving changes to the file without either changing its filename or the folder in which it is located).

4. Type **opensesame** (all lowercase letters) as the password in the Password to Open text box and then click the Password to Modify text box.

Note that Excel automatically masks each character as you type it by replacing it with a dot. Keep in mind that all passwords are case-sensitive; for example, the passwords *opensesame*, *Opensesame*, and *OpenSesame* are three different passwords.

5. Type **abracadabra** in the Password to Modify text box and then click OK.

Excel displays the Confirm Password dialog box, where you must reenter the *opensesame* password for opening the *Employee List - protected.xlsx* workbook file.

6. Type **opensesame** in the Reenter Password to Proceed text box and then click OK.

A second Confirm Password dialog box appears, where you must reenter the *abracadabra* password for modifying the *Employee List - protected.xlsx* workbook file.

7. Type **abracadabra** in the Reenter Password to Modify text box and then select OK.

Assuming that you were able to faithfully and exactly reproduce the *opensesame* password to open and *abracadabra* password to modify, Excel displays no more Confirm Password dialog boxes, returning you to the Save As dialog box.

8. Click the Save button to save the *Employee List - protected.xlsx* with the password to open and password to modify the workbook. Then close the workbook (Ctrl+W).

Now try reopening the password-protected workbook file.

9. Click the Office button and then click *Employee List – protected.xlsx* at the top of the Recent Documents list or press Alt+F and type 1.

Excel displays a Password dialog box, informing you that the *Employee List –protected.xlsx* file is protected.

10. Type the password to open the file, **opensesame**, in the Password text box and then click OK.

As soon as you click OK to close the first Password dialog box where you entered the password to open the workbook file, a second one appears prompting you to enter the password for write access to the file. Note that if you are unable to provide this password, Excel opens the workbook file in read-only mode (so that changes to the file can only be saved in a copy of the file).

11. Type the password to modify, **abracadabra**, in the second Password text box and then click OK.

As soon as you correctly enter the second password, Excel opens the *Employee List - protected.xlsx* workbook for editing or printing just as it would a non-protected workbook.

Go ahead and remove the password to modify the workbook as this kind of protection amounts to little more than saving the workbook file as a read-only file.

12. Click Office button | Save As or press F12 and then open the General Options dialog box by clicking the Tools drop-down button and selecting General Options on its drop-down list.

To remove a password from a file, all you have to do is to delete it from the Password to Open or Password to Modify text box in the General Options dialog box.

13. Select all the masked characters in the Password to Modify text box and then press the Delete key to remove them before you click OK.

14. Click the Save button in the Save As dialog box, and then click Yes in the confirmation alert dialog box to save the *Employee List - protected.xlsx* workbook without a write-access password.

15. Close the *Employee List - protected.xlsx* workbook and then try reopening it again.

    This time, you only need to reproduce the *opensesame* password to open the workbook file.

16. Close the *Employee List - protected.xlsx* workbook a last time without saving any further changes to it.

Protecting the Worksheet

After you've got your spreadsheet the way you want it, you are very wise to use Excel's Protection feature to keep it that way: Nothing is quite as bad as having an inexperienced data entry operator doing major damage to the formulas and functions that you've worked so hard to construct and validate. To keep the formulas and standard text in a spreadsheet safe from all unwarranted changes, you need to protect its worksheet.

All cells in the workbook can have one of two different protection formats: locked or unlocked and hidden or unhidden. Whenever you begin a new spreadsheet, all of the cells in the workbook have the locked and unhidden status. However, this status in and of itself means nothing until you turn on protection in the worksheet. At that time, you are then prevented from making any editing changes to all locked cells and from viewing the contents of all hidden cells on the Formula bar when they contain the cell cursor.

What this means in practice is that prior to turning on worksheet protection, you go through the spreadsheet removing the Locked protection format from all the cell ranges where you or your users still need to be able to do data entry and editing even when the worksheet is protected. You also assign the Hidden protection format to all cell ranges in the spreadsheet where you don't want the contents of the cell to be displayed when protection is turned on in the worksheet. Then, after activating protection, the user can make changes only to the unlocked cells and display on the Formula bar the contents of the unhidden cells in the sheet.

When setting up you own spreadsheet templates, you will want to unlock all the cells where users need to input new data and keep locked all the cells that contain headings and formulas that never change. You may also want to hide cells with formulas if you're concerned that their display might tempt the users to waste time trying to fiddle with or finesse them. Then, turn on worksheet protection prior to saving the file in the template file format. You are then assured that all spreadsheets generated from that template automatically inherit the same level and type of protection as you assigned in the original spreadsheet.

When you open the Protect Sheet dialog box (Review | Protect Sheet or Alt+RPS) to turn on protection, Excel gives you an opportunity to assign a password to remove the protection from the sheet (a wise move in most cases). This dialog box also contains the following list of check box options that enable you to specify what particular editing actions users of the worksheet are still allowed to perform:

- ✓ **Select Locked Cells** to enable the user to still be able to move the cell cursor into the locked cells of the worksheet even when he can't change their contents — note that this check box is selected by default but you can deselect it when you want to restrict movement to just the cells containing the unlocked protection format that allow data entry.

- ✓ **Select Unlocked Cells** to enable the user to be able to move the cell cursor into the unlocked cells of the worksheet so that he can make changes to them — note that deselecting this check box automatically deselects the Select Locked Cells check box as well, making it impossible to move the cell cursor to any cells in the worksheet and subsequently make any type of editing changes in the worksheet, which is very rarely your intention.

- ✓ **Format Cells** to enable the formatting of cells (with the exception of changing the locked and hidden status on the Protection tab of the Format Cells dialog box).

- ✓ **Format Columns** to enable formatting so that users can modify the column widths and hide and unhide columns.

- ✓ **Format Rows** to enable formatting so that users can modify the row heights and hide and unhide rows.

- ✓ **Insert Columns** to enable the insertion of new columns in the worksheet.

- ✓ **Insert Rows** to enable the insertion of new rows in the worksheet.

- ✓ **Insert Hyperlinks** to enable the insertion of new hyperlinks to other documents, both local and on the Web.

- ✓ **Delete Columns** to enable the deletion of columns in the worksheet.

- ✓ **Delete Rows** to enable the deletion of rows in the worksheet.

- ✓ **Sort** to enable the sorting of data in unlocked cells in the worksheet (see Chapter 17).

- ✓ **Use AutoFilter** to enable the filtering of data in the worksheet (see Chapter 17).

- ✓ **Use Pivot Table Reports** to enable the manipulation of pivot tables in the worksheet (see Chapter 20).

- ✓ **Edit Objects** to enable the editing of graphic objects such as text boxes, embedded images, and the like, in the worksheet (see Chapter 16).

- ✓ **Edit Scenarios** to enable the editing of what-if scenarios, including modifying and deleting them (see Chapter 19).

Before you attempt Exercise 18-2, you may want to play the Protecting the Worksheet.exe demo located in the Excel Feature Demos folder on your workbook CD-ROM. This feature demonstration shows you how to password-protect a worksheet so that the spreadsheet user can make changes only in a range of cells specified for data entry.

Exercise 18-2: Protecting a Worksheet

In Exercise 18-2, you get practice password-protecting a worksheet so that further modifications are restricted to a single range of data-entry cells.

1. Open *Exercise18-2.xlsx* in your Chap18 folder in the Excel 2007 Workbook folder on your hard disk.

This workbook contains a copy of the Depreciation worksheet that you worked with in Chapter 9. You will use the Depreciation Table on this worksheet to practice unlocking cells before turning on protection in the worksheet.

2. Select the cell range C3:C6 in the Depreciation worksheet and then click the Lock Cell option on the Format button's drop-down menu on the Home tab or press Alt+HOL.

These four cells constitute the input cells for the Depreciation Table where you need to still be able to enter new values even after turning on worksheet protection. By leaving the protection status of the other cells set to locked in the spreadsheet, you ensure that no one can make any changes to the formulas in the table itself, either intentional or otherwise.

3. Click the Protect Sheet button on the Review tab or press Alt+RPS to open the Protect Sheet dialog box (see Figure 18-1).

Figure 18-1:
The Protect Sheet dialog box when it first opens.

When the Protect Sheet dialog box first opens, only the Protect Worksheet and Contents of Locked Cells check box and the Select Locked Cells and Select Unlocked Cells check boxes in the Allow Users of This Worksheet To box are selected.

4. Type **stet** (the Latin command meaning "Let it stand") in all lowercase letters in the Password to Unprotect Sheet text box and then click OK without bothering to deselect any of the three check boxes that are automatically selected.

Now you must re-enter the *stet* password exactly as you entered it the first time to set it in the worksheet.

5. Retype **stet** in the Reenter Password to Proceed text box in the Confirm Password dialog box before clicking OK.

   Now without the *stet* password, users of this worksheet can only make changes in the four cells you unlocked at the beginning of this exercise, although they can still select any cell in the sheet.

6. Make the following changes to the designated cells in the Depreciation worksheet:

   • **35000** in the Cost cell, C4

   • **7** in the Life_in_years cell, C5

   • **5000** in the Salvage cell, C6

   Excel enables you to make these changes because you assigned the unlocked protection formatting to these cells before turning on worksheet protection. Because the worksheet still uses the default automatic recalculation setting, the program recalculates the depreciation values in the Depreciation Table (C9:F19) each time you update an input value.

7. Position the cell cursor in cell D17 containing the first of the #NUM! error values in the table and then press F2 to put Excel in Edit mode.

   Excel beeps at you and displays a warning dialog box indicating that the cell or chart you're trying to change is protected.

8. Click OK and then position the cell cursor in the merged cell B2 and then press the Delete key to remove its contents.

   Again, Excel beeps at you and displays the warning dialog box indicating that the cell or chart you're trying to change is protected.

9. Click OK and then open the Insert and Format buttons' pull-down menus on the Ribbon's Home tab and notice how many of the commands are grayed out, indicating that they are currently unavailable.

   These commands are not available to users unless you specifically enable them when turning on worksheet protection.

10. Click Review | Unprotect Sheet or press Alt+RPS to open the Unprotect Sheet dialog box. Then type **stet** in its Password text box and click OK.

    Excel turns off the worksheet protection, leaving all cell entries in the sheet at risk.

11. Press the Delete key again when the cell cursor is in cell B2.

    This time, Excel gets rid of the heading at the top of this table.

12. Click the Undo button on the Quick Access toolbar or press Ctrl+Z to restore the deleted table heading. Then, click the Protect Sheet button on the Review tab or press Alt+RPS to re-open the Protect Sheet dialog box. This time, click the Format Cells check box (in addition to the Select Locked Cells and Select Unlocked Cells check boxes) before clicking OK (don't bother to assign a password to unprotect this time).

By selecting the Format Cells check box in the Allow Users of This Worksheet To list box before turning on the worksheet protection another time, you enable formatting changes to locked cells in the worksheet, while at the same time denying the ability to make changes to their contents or delete them.

13. While the cell cursor is still located in cell B2, press Ctrl+I to italicize the Depreciation Table heading in this cell with italics. Then, press the Delete key.

This time, Excel allows you to change the formatting of the heading in this cell while still preventing you from deleting its text.

14. Click OK and then position the cell cursor in cell A1. Then, save the protected version of the Depreciation worksheet in a new file named **Depreciation Table – protected.xlsx** in your Excel 2007 Practice folder before you close the workbook.

Doing Data Entry in a Protected Worksheet

When protecting a worksheet, you can easily set it up so that you and your users can jump right to the unlocked cells and avoid ever having to deal with the locked ones (that you can't change anyway) by using the Tab and Shift+Tab keys to navigate the worksheet. All you have to do is format the cells that need changing as unlocked and then remove the check mark from the Select Locked Cells check box in the Protect Sheet dialog box when you turn on the worksheet protection.

When you press the Tab key in such a protected worksheet, Excel jumps the cell pointer to the next unlocked cell to the right of the current one in that same row. When you reach the last unlocked cell in that row, the program then jumps to the first unlocked cell in the rows below. To move back to a previous unlocked cell, press Shift+Tab. When Excel reaches the last unlocked cell in the spreadsheet, it automatically jumps back to the very first unlocked cell on the sheet.

Of course, provided that you haven't changed the After Pressing Enter, Move Selection direction of the Enter key in the Editing Options section of the Advanced tab in the Excel Options dialog box (Alt+FI), you can also use the Enter key to move down the columns instead of across the rows.

Solve It | **Exercise 18-3: Doing Data Entry in a Protected Worksheet**

In Exercise 18-3, you get practice doing data entry in a protected worksheet by first unlocking the cells that require data entry before turning on protection in the worksheet.

1. Open *Exercise18-3.xlsx* in your Chap18 in the Excel 2007 Workbook folder on your hard disk.

This workbook contains a copy of the Spring Sale worksheet that is missing the furniture description and retail price information (all the other data is entered along with the formulas that determine the sale price). Use the sales table in this worksheet to practice doing data entry in a protected worksheet where your movements are restrained to just the unlocked cells in the sheet.

2. Select the cell range C4:D9 in the Spring Sale worksheet and then click the Lock Cell option on the Format button's drop-down menu on the Ribbon's Home tab or press Alt+HOL.

   You unlock these cells because you still need to be able to make data entries in them after you turn on the worksheet protection.

3. Click the Protect Sheet button on the Review tab or press Alt+RPS to open the Protect Sheet dialog box. Then, click the Select Locked Cells check box to deselect this option by removing its check mark before you click OK (don't bother to assign a password to unprotect the worksheet).

   After turning on worksheet protection with this check box unselected, Excel constrains the movement of the cell cursor to just the unlocked cell range C4:D9 in the worksheet.

4. Click cell C4 and then press the Tab key repeatedly until you've moved the cell cursor through each of the cells in the unlocked cell range, C4:D9.

   Excel now restrains the movement of the cell cursor to this range of unlocked cells in the worksheet.

5. Click cell A1 to attempt to locate the cell cursor in the Home cell of the Spring Sale worksheet.

   Note that clicking any cell outside of the unlocked cell range C4:D9 is no longer allowed as long as worksheet protection is in effect.

6. Position the cell cursor in cell C4 and then make the following data entries across the rows of the unlocked cell range in the designated cells by pressing Tab to complete each entry and, at the same time, move the cell cursor to the next cell in the same or next row:

   - **36-inch round table** in cell C4
   - **1250** in cell D4
   - **72-inch dining table** in cell C5
   - **1400** in cell D5
   - **Hutch** in cell C6
   - **2500** in cell D6

   Note that each time you press Tab to complete an entry in the Retail Price column and to move down to the next unlocked cell in row below, Excel calculates the amount of the markdown and the new sales price for that item.

7. While the cell cursor is positioned in cell C7, make the following data entries down the columns of the unlocked cell range in the designated cells by pressing the Enter key to complete each entry and, at the same time, move the cell cursor to the next cell in the same or next column:

   - **Side chair** in cell C7
   - **Arm Chair** in cell C8
   - **Armoire** in cell C9

- **350** in cell D7

- **500** in cell D8

- **1750** in cell D9

8. With the cell pointer back in cell C4, save the protected worksheet version with the completed Spring Sale Furniture Prices table in a new workbook named **Spring Furniture Sale – protectedentry.xlsx** in your Excel 2007 Practice folder and then close the workbook.

Protecting the Entire Workbook

You can apply one last level of protection to your spreadsheet files and that is to protect the entire workbook. When you protect the workbook, you ensure that its users can't change the structure of the file by adding, deleting, or even moving and renaming any of its worksheets.

To protect your workbook, you open the Protect Structure and Windows dialog box (Review | Protect Workbook or Alt+RPW). This dialog box contains two check boxes: Structure (which is automatically checked) and Windows (which is not selected). This dialog box also contains a Password (Optional) text box, where you can enter a password that must be supplied before you can unprotect the workbook.

When you protect a workbook with the Structure check box selected, Excel prevents you or your users from doing any of the following tasks to the file:

- Insert new worksheets
- Delete existing worksheets
- Rename worksheets
- Hide or view hidden worksheets
- Move or copy worksheets to another workbook
- Display the source data for a cell in a pivot table or display a table's page fields on separate worksheets (see Chapter 20)
- Create a summary report with the Scenario Manager (see Chapter 19)

When you turn on protection for a workbook after checking the Windows check box in the Protect Structure and Windows dialog box, Excel prevents you from opening new windows on the same workbook (so that you can compare different sections in one screen) as well as freezing columns and rows in the worksheet.

After you've enabled protection in a workbook, you can then turn it off by choosing Review | Unprotect Workbook on the Ribbon or pressing Alt+RPW. If you've assigned a password to unprotect the workbook, you must accurately reproduce it in the Password text box in the Unprotect Workbook dialog box that then appears.

Exercise 18-4: Protecting the Entire Workbook

In Exercise 18-4, you get practice protecting an entire workbook file while at the same time becoming familiar with the type of editing restrictions this protection entails.

1. Open *Exercise18-4.xlsx* in your Chap18 folder in the Excel 2007 Workbook folder on your hard disk.

This workbook contains a copy of the Employee Data List, Salary Subset, and Department Subset you've worked with in earlier exercises. You will use this file to practice protecting the workbook from further changes.

2. Click the Protect Workbook button on the Ribbon's Review tab or press Alt+RPW.

Excel opens the Protect Structure and Windows dialog box.

3. Click the Windows check box to check this box and leave the Structure check box checked.

By selecting the Windows check box option, you prevent any user not entrusted with the password from making changes to the size and position of the workbook window.

4. Enter **letitbe** as the protect workbook password in the Password (Optional) text box and then click OK. Then, retype **letitbe** in the Reenter Password to Proceed text box in the Confirm Password dialog box that appears and then click its OK button.

Now that you've protected the workbook, see what happens when you try making some routine changes to it.

5. Double-click the sheet tab for the Employee Data List worksheet in an attempt to rename it.

Excel beeps at you and displays an alert box declaring, "Workbook is protected and cannot be changed."

6. Click OK in the alert dialog box and this time attempt to drag the sheet tab for the Employee Data List worksheet to reposition it as the last worksheet in the workbook.

Excel now resists all attempts at reordering the sheets in a workbook: Any attempt to drag any sheet to a new position in the workbook only results in the displaying of the International No symbol (a circle with a backslash in it).

7. Click the View tab on the Ribbon and note that the New Window, View Side by Side, Split, and Freeze Panes buttons are all currently grayed out and unavailable. Click the Hide button in the Window group on the View tab.

Excel displays an 'Exercise18-4.xlsx' is Protected dialog box that prompts you to enter the password.

8. Type **letitbe** in the Password text box and then click OK to hide the *Exercise18-4.xlsx* workbook.

When workbook protection is turned on and a password has been assigned, you must enter that password both to hide and to unhide the workbook.

9. Click the Unhide button on the View tab to open the Unhide dialog box and, with *Exercise 18-4.xlsx* highlighted in the Unhide Workbook list box, click its OK button. Type **letitbe** again in the new Password text box and then click OK to bring back the screen display of the *Exercise 18-4.xlsx* workbook.

Now save this protected version of this sample workbook file under a new filename.

10. Save the protected workbook in a new file named **Employee List – protected-wrkbk.xlsx** in your Excel 2007 Practice folder and then close the workbook as you exit Excel.

Part V
Doing Data Analysis

The 5th Wave · By Rich Tennant

Well, obviously one of the cells in the navigational spreadsheet is corrupt!

In this part . . .

In being able to perform data analysis in your spread-sheets, you begin to tap into the real power of Excel. Part V introduces you to data analysis in two forms: what-if analysis, which enables you to test out different possible outcomes based on different assumptions, and pivot tables, which enable you to summarize large groups of data based on varied criteria that you manipulate on the fly as you will.

Chapter 19

Performing What-If Analysis

. . . .

In This Chapter

▶ Doing what-if analysis with one- and two-variable data tables

▶ Creating and playing with different scenarios

▶ Performing goal seeking

▶ Creating models with the Solver add-in

. . . .

*U*sing what-if analysis in the spreadsheet to project possible future outcomes based on different variables is, to put it mildly, one of Excel's fortes. The program offers you what-if analysis in the form of its one- and two-variable data tables, goal seeking, and Scenario Manager. And if this is not enough, it also includes the Solver add-in utility, which enables you to model more complex problems. In this chapter, you get a chance to practice performing what-if analysis using all of these tools.

Using Data Tables

In the normal Excel spreadsheet, you see the effect of changing an input value on the result returned by a formula as soon as you enter that new input: Each time you change this input value, Excel automatically recalculates the formula and shows you the new result based on the new value. This method is of limited use, however, when you are performing what-if or sensitivity analysis and need to be able to see the range of results produced by using a series of different input values in the same worksheet so that you can compare them to each other.

To perform this type of what-if analysis, you can use Excel's Data Table command. When creating a data table, you enter a series of input values in the worksheet, and Excel then uses each of them in the formula you specify. When Excel finishes computing the data table, you see the results produced by each change in the input values in a single range of the worksheet. You can then save the data table as part of the worksheet if you need to keep a record of the results of a series of input values.

Creating single-variable data tables

In a one-variable data table, Excel substitutes a series of different values for a single input value in a formula. To create a one-variable data table, you need to set up the master formula in your worksheet and then, in a different range of the worksheet, enter the series of different values that you want substituted for a single input value in that formula.

Before you attempt Exercise 19-1, you may want to play the Data Table 1.exe demo located in the Excel Feature Demos folder on your workbook CD-ROM. This demonstration shows you how to perform what-if analysis in a data table in which a series of different values is substituted for a single variable in a formula.

Solve It

Exercise 19-1: Constructing a Single-Variable Data Table in a Worksheet

In Exercise 19-1, you get practice creating a data table with a single variable that changes in each what-if scenario.

1. If Excel is not currently running, launch the program. If the program is already running and no workbook is displayed, create a new workbook (Ctrl+N). Leave the cell cursor in cell A1 of the first worksheet and then rename this sheet from Sheet1 to **Data Table 1**.

You will use this new blank worksheet to practice creating a single-variable data table that computes projected sales growth for 2008 based on various growth rate percentages.

2. Enter the title, **Sales Projections - 2008**, in cell A1, make it bold italic 14 points, and then widen column A to display this entire title and make the following data entries in the designated cells:

- **Sales 2007** in cell A2
- **Growth Rate** in cell A3
- **Projected Sales** in cell A4
- **$875,000** in cell B2
- **2.75%** in cell B3

3. Name the cells in the cell range B2:B4 with the headings you entered in the cell range A2:A4.

Select the entire range A2:B4 and then click the Create from Selection button on the Formulas tab to open the Create Names from Selection dialog box and then be sure that the only the Left Column check box is selected before you click OK.

4. Position the cell cursor in the Projected_Sales cell, B4, and construct the following formula:

```
=Sales_2007+(Sales_2007*Growth_Rate)
```

Note that Excel automatically assigns the range name given to cell B2 rather than the cell address as you build the formula by pointing and selecting its references.

5. Format the cell with the Accounting Number Format button ($) in the Number group of the Home tab and then reduce the decimal places to zero by using the Decrease Decimal button. Then, use the Format Painter button in the Clipboard group of the Home tab to copy this formatting to the Sales_2007 cell (B2).

   Now that you have the input values in place in the spreadsheet, you're ready to build the data table that will test different variables in the basic formula.

6. Paste a link to the Projected_Sales cell, B4, in cell C6 of the worksheet to bring its value forward to this cell.

   Copy the contents of cell B4 into the Clipboard (Ctrl+C) and then paste the link in cell C6 using the Paste Link option on the Paste button's drop-down menu (Alt+HVN). Then, widen column C and press the Esc key to remove the marquee from the Projected_Sales cell, B4.

7. Enter the following potential growth rate percentages in the designated cells:

   - **1.00%** in cell B7

   - **1.50%** in cell B8

8. Use the Fill handle to copy this series of half-percentage point increases down column B to the cell range B7:B17 so that the series ends with a 6.00% growth rate.

   Be sure to select cell B7 and B8 as a range with the cell cursor before you drag the Fill handle down to cell B17.

9. Select the cell range B6:C17. Click the What-If Analysis button on the Ribbon's Data tab and then click Data Table on its drop-down or press Alt+AWT to open the Table dialog box.

   This Table dialog box contains two text boxes: Row Input Cell, where you indicate the variable from the top row of the data table that is to be substituted in the master formula, and Column Input Cell, where you indicate the variable that is to be substituted from its first column.

   Because this one-variable input table contains the substitute values in a single column of the data table (cell range B7:B17), you only need to use the Column Input Cell text box in this case. And because the Growth_Rate cell, B3, contains the original value you want substituted in the master formula in cell B4, you need to enter this cell reference in this text box.

10. Position the cursor in the Column Input Cell text box in the Data Table dialog box, and then click the Growth_Rate cell, B3, in the worksheet before you click OK.

    Excel then fills in the data table, substituting in succession the growth rate percentage entered in the cell range B7:B17 for the Growth_Rate cell in the master formula.

11. Use the Format Painter in the Clipboard group of the Home tab to copy the formatting in cell C6 to the range C7:C17. Check your results against those shown in Figure 19-1.

    Next, examine the formula that Excel used in creating this single-variable data table.

Figure 19-1:
The completed one-variable data table.

12. Position the cell cursor in cell C7 and examine the contents of the formula on the Formula bar.

Excel inserts the following array formula (see Chapter 7) using the TABLE function in the cell range C7:C17 of the data table:

```
{=TABLE(,B3)}
```

The TABLE function can take two arguments, row_ref and column_ref, which represent the row input cell and column input cell for the data table, respectively. In this example, the data table uses only a column input cell, so B3 is the second and only argument of the TABLE function. Because Excel enters the results in a Data table using an array formula, Excel won't allow you to clear individual result cells in its output range. If you try to delete a single result in the data table, Excel displays an alert dialog box telling you that you cannot change part of a table.

13. Increase the value in the original Growth_Rate cell, B3, from 2.75% to **2.875%** and the initial value in the range of variables from 1.00% to **1.25%**.

The moment you enter the new 2.875% growth rate percentage in cell B3, Excel recalculates the values in cells B4 and C6, increasing them from $899,063 to $900,156. And the moment you enter the new initial variable rate of 1.25%, the program recalculates the result in cell C7 of the data table and replaces the original value of $883,750 with $885,938.

You can, however, select the recalculation setting that automatically recalculates all formulas in the worksheet except those in data tables. That way, you can control exactly at what point Excel recalculates your data table using the new variables you've entered.

14. Click the Calculation Options button on the Formulas tab and then click the Automatic Except for Data Tables option on its drop-down menu or press Alt+MXE.

Now that you've put Excel in automatic recalculation except for data tables, see how the program responds when you modify the original growth rate percentage and the initial growth rate variable.

15. Reduce the value in the original Growth_Rate cell, B3 from 2.875% (displayed as 2.88%) to **2.50%** and the initial value in the range of variables from 1.25% to **0.875%** (displayed as 0.88%).

As soon as you reduce the percentage in cell B3, Excel changes the values in cells B4 and C6 from $900,156 to $896,875. However, reducing the initial variable percentage in cell B7 from 1.25% to 0.875% has no immediate effect on the data table cell C7, whose calculated value relies upon this percentage.

The Calculate indicator does *not* appear on the Status bar when you change variables used in the program's data tables after you switch the program's recalculation mode from Automatic to Manual or Automatic Except for Data Tables. This means that when operating in these two recalculation modes, it's entirely up to you to keep track of the changes you make to the variables in the table and whether or not the values in your data tables are up-to-date or are in sore need of manual recalculation before printing or publishing and sharing with your co-workers or clients.

16. Click the Calculate Now button on the Formulas tab or press F9.

As soon as you select this button, Excel reduces the calculated amount in cell C7 from $885,938 to $882, 656.

17. Save your data table on the Data Table 1 worksheet under the filename **Data Table 1 Practice.xlsx** in your Excel 2007 Practice folder and then leave the workbook open for the next exercise with a two-variable data table.

Creating two-variable data tables

In a two-variable data table, Excel substitutes a series of different values for two input values in a formula. When you create a two-variable data table, you enter two ranges of input values to be substituted in the master formula: a single-row range in the first row of the table and a single-column range in the first column of the data table. When you create a two-variable data table, you place a copy of the master formula in the cell at the intersection of this row and column of input values.

Solve It

Exercise 19-2: Constructing a Two-Variable Data Table in a Worksheet

In Exercise 19-2, you get practice constructing a data table that changes two variables as it calculates the possible results for your various what-if scenarios.

1. Use the Data Table 1 worksheet in your *Data Table 1 Practice.xlsx* workbook containing the single-variable data table you constructed in the last exercise.

You will convert the original one-variable data table into a two-variable data table that not only uses a series of growth rate percentages but also a series of projected expenses to sales percentages in calculating possible projected incomes.

2. Select the cell range C6:C17 and then click the Delete button in the Cells group of the Home tab before you rename the Data Table 1 sheet to **Data Table 2**.

   Next, you need to insert blank cells in between row A3:B3 and A4:B4.

3. Select the cell range A4:B4 and then click the Insert button in the Cells group of the Home tab.

   Excel inserts two new blank cells in the range A4:B4, shifting down the existing entries (Projected Sales and the formula =Sales_2007+(Sales_2007*Growth_Rate) with the calculated result $896,875) to the range A5:B5.

4. Make the following data entries in the designated cells:

   - **Expense Rate** in cell A4

   - **3%** in cell B4

5. Assign the range name **Expense_Rate** to cell B4 containing the 3.00% rate of expenses to sales.

   You can assign this range name manually by typing Expense_Rate into the Name box of the Formula bar when cell B4 is selected or with the Create From Selection button on the Formulas tab when the cell range A4:B4 is selected.

6. Edit the formula in cell B5 as follows:

   `=Sales_2007+(Sales_2007*Growth_Rate)-(Sales_2007*Expense_Rate)`

7. Paste a link to the Projected_Sales cell, B5, in cell B7 of the Data Table 2 worksheet.

   When creating a two-variable data table, you place the formula at the intersection of the row and column in the table that contains the series of input values.

8. Make the following data entries in the designated cells:

   - **2%** in cell C7

   - **2.5%** in cell D7

9. Format the cell range C7:D7 with Percent Style number format with 2 decimal places and then use the Fill handle to copy this series of half-percentage point increases across row 7 to the cell range E7:G7 so that the series ends with a 4.00% expense/sales growth rate.

   Be sure to select cells C7 and D7 as a range with the cell cursor before you drag the Fill handle across the row to cell G7.

10. Select the data table's cell range B7:G18 and then click the What-If Analysis button on the Data tab and then click the Data Table option or press Alt+AWT to open the Data Table dialog box.

    To create a two-variable data table, you must specify both the Row Input Cell and the Column Input Cell in the Data Table dialog box.

11. Select the Expense_Rate cell, B4, as the Row Input Cell and the Growth_Rate cell, B3, as the Column Input Cell in the Data Table dialog box and then click OK. Finally, click the Calculate Sheet button on the Formulas tab or press Shift+F9 to calculate the data table.

Excel then fills in the data table, substituting in succession the growth rate percentage entered in the cell range B8:B18 for the Growth_Rate cell in the master formula, and the expense rate percentage entered in the cell range C7:G7 for the Expense_Rate cell.

12. Use the Format Painter to format the cell range C8:G18 with the number formatting used in cell B7; widen the columns of the table with AutoFit as needed.

13. Increase the value in the original Growth_Rate cell, B3, from 2.50% to **2.75%** and the initial value in the range of variables from 0.875% (displayed as 0.88%) to **1.00%**. Then recalculate the worksheet (Shift+F9) and check your results in your data table against those shown in Figure 19-2.

14. Position the cell cursor in cell C8 and examine the contents of the formula on the Formula bar.

Excel inserts the following array formula in the cell range C8:G18 of the data table (note that the TABLE function in this formula uses both the row_ref and column_ref arguments):

```
{=TABLE(B4,B3)}
```

15. Save the Data Table 2 worksheet with your completed two-variable data table in a new workbook with the filename **Data Table 2 Practice.xlsx** in your Excel 2007 Practice folder and then close the workbook.

Figure 19-2: The completed two-variable data table.

Exploring Various Scenarios

Excel enables you to create and save sets of input values that produce different results as *scenarios* using Excel's Scenario Manager. A scenario consists of a group of input values in a worksheet to which you assign a name such as *Best Case, Worst Case, Most Likely Case*, and so on.

Then, to reuse the input data and view the results they produce in the worksheet, you simply select the name of the scenario you want to use and Excel applies the input values stored in that scenario to the appropriate cells in the worksheet. After creating your different scenarios for a worksheet, you can also use the Scenario Manager to create a summary report show you both the input values stored in each scenario as well as key results produced by each.

Solve It

Exercise 19-3: Constructing Various Scenarios for a Spreadsheet

In Exercise 19-3, you get practice using the Scenario Manager to set up a most-likely, best-case, and worst-case scenario for projected sales. You also get practice in creating a summary report that showing you the inputs and results used by each of these scenarios.

1. Open the *Exercise19-3.xlsx* workbook file in the Chap19 folder in your Excel 2007 Workbook folder on your hard disk.

 The Sales Forecast worksheet in this workbook contains the Sales Forecast for 2008 table that you will use to practice creating and using different growth scenarios using different rate of sales growth, COGS (cost of goods sold), and expenses.

2. Select the following changing cells for your scenarios as one cell selection (by holding down the Ctrl key as you click them):

   - Sales_Growth cell, H4
   - COGS cell, H5
   - Expenses cell, H7

3. While cells H4, H5, and H7 are selected, click the What-If Analysis button on the Ribbon's Data tab and then click Scenario Manager on its drop-down menu or press Alt+AWS to open the Scenario Manager dialog box.

 The first time you open the Scenario Manager in a worksheet, there are no scenarios defined. You must use its controls to create the different scenarios that you want to apply to a data table.

4. Click the Add button in this dialog box to open the Add Scenario dialog box and then enter **Most Likely** in its Scenario Name text box before you click OK.

 As soon as you click OK, the Add Scenario dialog box closes and the Scenario Values dialog box opens. Here, you indicate the values to be used by the changing cells in the particular scenario you're building. In this case, Excel picks up the values 0.05, 0.2, and 0.28 for the Sales_Growth, COGS, and Expenses changing cells from the entries made in cells H4, H5, and H7, respectively.

5. Click OK to accept the values in the Scenario Values dialog box picked up from the Sales_Growth, COGS, and Expenses cells in the Sales Forecast table.

   As soon as you click OK, the Scenario Values dialog box closes and the Scenario Manager dialog box reappears.

6. Click the Add button, enter **Worst Case** as the name for a second scenario in the Add Scenario dialog box, and then click OK.

   The Scenario Values dialog box appears again so that you can enter the values for this new scenario.

7. Change the values in the designated changing cells of the Scenario Values dialog box as follows:

   - **0.02** in Sales_Growth
   - **0.3** in COGS
   - **0.3** in Expenses

8. Click OK to return to the Scenario Manager dialog box.

   The dialog box now lists both a Most Likely and a Worst Case scenario.

9. Add a third scenario named Best Case on your own with the following changing values:

   - **0.1** in Sales_Growth
   - **0.05** in COGS
   - **0.1** in Expenses

   When you finish adding this last scenario, the Scenario Manager dialog box lists three scenarios: Most Likely, Worst Case, and Best Case.

10. With Best Case selected in the Scenario Manager dialog box, click the Show button at the bottom of the Scenario Manager dialog box.

    As soon as you click Show, Excel plugs the Best Case scenario's values into the changing cells in the Sales Forecast for 2008 table.

11. Take a look at the Worst Case scenario in the Sales Forecast table by double-clicking Worst Case in the Scenarios list box of the Scenario Manager dialog box.

    Note that you can use the Scenario Manager to quickly and easily plug any number of different scenarios into your data table.

12. Display the Most Likely scenario in the Sales Forecast for 2008 table and then close the Scenario Manager dialog box.

    Next, you'll enter a series of values into the Sales_Growth, COGS, and Expenses cells in the Sales Forecast for 2008 table that are not used by any of your defined scenarios.

13. Enter the following values in the designated changing cells in the Sales Forecast for 2008 table:

   - **17%** in the Sales_Growth cell, H4
   - **25%** in the COGS cell, H5
   - **18%** in the Expenses cell, H7

14. Reopen the Scenario Manager dialog box and then click the Summary button in the Scenario Manager dialog box.

   Excel opens the Scenario Summary dialog box where you define the type of summary report to create (standard table or pivot table) and range of cells containing the formulas into which the various scenario input values are to be applied.

15. Select the cell range B8:G8 in the worksheet table to insert the cell range =$B$8:$G$8 in the Result Cells text box before you click OK.

   As soon as you click OK, Excel inserts a Scenario Summary worksheet in front of the Sales Forecast worksheet in the *Exercise19-3.xlsx* workbook. This worksheet contains an outlined summary table that displays the total projected income for all four quarters along with the values of the Most Likely, Worst Case, and Best Case scenarios used to calculate these totals (as shown in Figure 19-3).

16. Move the Scenario Summary worksheet so that it follows the Sales Forecast worksheet, and then click cell A1 in the Sales Forecast worksheet. Then save your work in a new workbook file named **Scenario Manager Practice.xlsx** in your Excel 2007 Practice folder and close the workbook file.

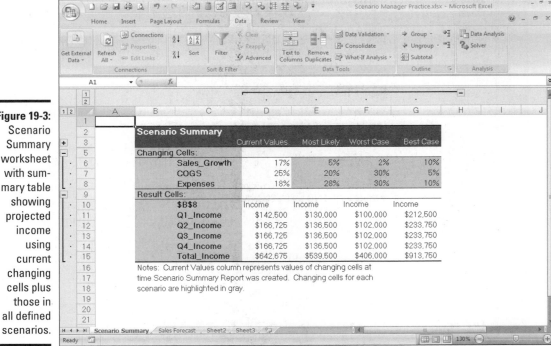

Figure 19-3:
Scenario Summary worksheet with summary table showing projected income using current changing cells plus those in all defined scenarios.

Performing Goal Seeking

Sometimes, you know the outcome that you want to realize in a spreadsheet and you need Excel to help you find the input values necessary to achieve those results. This procedure, which is just the opposite of the what-if analysis you've been doing so far, is referred to as *goal seeking*.

When you only need to find the value for a single variable that will give the desired result in a particular formula, you can perform this simple type of goal seeking with Excel's Goal Seek command. If you have charted the data and created a two-dimensional column, bar, or line chart, you can also perform the goal seeking by directly manipulating the appropriate marker on the chart.

To use the Goal Seek command, you simply select the cell containing the formula that will return the result you are seeking (referred to as the *set cell*), indicate what value you want this formula to return, and then indicate the location of the input value that Excel can change to return the desired result.

Solve It

Exercise 19-4: Doing Goal Seeking in a Spreadsheet

In Exercise 19-4, you get practice using the Goal Seek feature to find out how much the projected sales have to change to reach a particular income target.

1. Open the *Exercise19-4.xlsx* workbook file in the Chap19 folder in your Excel 2007 Workbook folder on your hard disk.

The workbook contains a version of the Sales Forecast for 2008 table that you worked with in the previous exercise with an embedded Clustered Bar chart immediately below it. You will use this table and chart to practice doing goal seeking using both the Goal Seek command and direct manipulation of the data series in the Clustered Bar chart.

2. Position the cell cursor in cell C8 containing the forecasted income for the first quarter of 2008 and then click the Goal Seek option on the What-If Analysis button's drop-down menu on the Data tab (or press Alt+AWG).

Excel opens the Goal Seek dialog box with cell C8 entered in its Set Cell text box. The Goal Seek dialog box also contains a To Value text box, where you enter the target value you're seeking, and a By Changing Cell text box, where you indicate the cell whose value should be changed to reach the target value.

3. Type **500000** in the To Value text box. Then, press Tab to select the By Changing Cell text box and click cell C4 containing the Qtr 1 sales figure in the worksheet to enter its absolute cell reference, $C$4, in this text box before you click OK.

As soon as you click OK closing the Goal Seek dialog box, Excel opens the Goal Seek Status dialog box. In this case, the dialog box indicates that the program has found a solution that increases the income in cell C8 to the target value, $500,000.

Note that not only does Excel update the values in the Sales Forecast for 2008 table to reach the target value, but it also redraws the embedded Clustered Bar chart to suit as well.

4. Click OK to close the Goal Seek Status dialog box. Click the Undo button on the Quick Access toolbar or press Ctrl+Z to restore the original values to the Sales Forecast table and Clustered Bar chart.

Excel restores the original values to the cell range C4:G8 and redraws the embedded clustered bar chart below to suit.

5. Click the Redo button on the Quick Access toolbar or press Ctrl+Y to return to the values entered as the result of your goal seeking.

You can switch between Undo and Redo to your heart's content to compare the two different goal-seeking scenarios.

6. Click cell A1 and save your work in a new workbook file named **Goal Seek Practice.xlsx** in your Excel 2007 Practice folder and then close the workbook file.

Creating Complex Models with Solver

Although the Data Table and Goal Seek commands work just fine for simple problems that require determining the direct relationship between the inputs and results in a formula, you need to use the Solver add-in when dealing with more complex problems. For example, you would use the Solver to find the best solution when you need to change multiple input values in your model and you need to impose constraints on these values or the output value.

The Solver works by applying iterative methods to find the "best" solution given the inputs, desired solution, and the constraints that you impose. During each iteration, the program applies a trial and error method (based on the use of linear or non-linear equations and inequalities) that attempts to get closer to the optimum solution.

When using the Solver, you need to keep in mind that for many problems, especially the more complicated ones, there are many solutions. Although the Solver returns the optimum solution, given the starting values, the variables that can change, and the constraints you define, this solution is often not the only one possible and, in fact, may not be the best solution for you. To be sure that you are finding the best solution, you may want to run the Solver more than once, adjusting the initial values each time you solve the problem.

When setting up the problem in your worksheet model to be solved by the Solver, you define the following items:

- **Target cell**, which is the cell in your worksheet whose value is to be maximized, minimized, or made to reach a particular value

- **Changing cells**, which are the cells in your worksheet whose values are to be adjusted until the answer is found

- **Constraints**, which are the limits you impose on the changing values or the target cell

After you finish defining the problem with these parameters and you have the Solver solve the problem, the program returns the optimum solution by modifying the values in your worksheet. At that point, you can choose to retain the changes in the worksheet or restore the original values to the worksheet. You can also save the solution as a scenario to view later before you restore the original values.

You can use the Solver with the Scenario Manager to help set up a problem to solve or to save a solution so that you can view it at a later date. The changing cells that you define for the Scenario Manager are automatically picked up and used by the Solver when you select this command, and vice versa. Also, you can save the Solver's solution to a problem as a scenario (by clicking the Save Scenario button in the Solver dialog box) that you can then view with the Scenario Manager.

Solve It

Exercise 19-5: Using Solver to Modify Multiple Input Values in a Spreadsheet

In Exercise 19-5, you get practice using the Solver add-in to modify multiple input values in a forecast table.

1. Open the *Exercise19-5.xlsx* workbook file in your Chap19 folder in the Excel 2007 Workbook folder on your hard disk.

The workbook contains a copy of the Sales Forecast worksheet with the Sales Forecast for 2008 table that you will use to practice using the Solver add-in to reach a target income based on changes to multiple parameters.

2. Click Office button | Excel Options or press Alt+FI to open the Excel Options dialog box.

Then, click the Add-Ins tab. Click the Go button with Excel Add-Ins selected on the Manage drop-down list button to open the Add-Ins dialog box.

Finally, click the Solver Add-in check box to put a check mark in it before you click OK.

If the Solver add-in is not currently installed as part of Excel, the program displays an alert dialog box indicating that the feature is not currently installed and prompting you to install it. Go ahead and install Solver by clicking the Yes button in this alert dialog box. After Excel finishes installing the Solver add-in, proceed to Step 3.

3. Position the cell pointer in the Total_Income cell, G8, and then click the Solver button in the Analysis Group on the Ribbon's Data tab to open the Solver Parameters dialog box.

This dialog box displays $G$8 in the Set Target Cell text box. Next, you need to set the target equal to a new value and then indicate the changing cells.

4. Click the Value Of option button to the right of Equal To and then type **650000** in the text box to its immediate right. Next, click the By Changing Cells text box and then click the COGS cell, H5, in the worksheet and Ctrl+click the Expenses cell, H7.

The By Changing Cells text box now contains references to the COGS cell $H$5 and Expenses $H$7 separated by a comma.

5. Click the Solve button in the Solver Parameters dialog box.

As soon as you click the Solve button, Excel closes the Solver Parameters dialog box and then beeps before opening the Solver Results dialog box. In this case, Solver was able to find a solution to the problem by balancing changes to COGS and Expenses that would result in the desired target net income of $650,000.

The Solver Results dialog box gives you a choice between retaining the adjusted values in the Sales Forecast for 2008 table (Keep Solver Solution) and restoring its original values (Restore Original Values). You can also save the solution as a scenario.

6. Click the Save Scenario button to open the Save Scenario dialog box and then type **Optimal** as the name in the Scenario Name text box before you click OK.

As soon as Excel closes the Save Scenario dialog box you are returned to the Solver Results dialog box.

7. Click the Restore Original Values option button in the Solver Results dialog box and then click OK.

Because you saved the Solver's solution with the scenario name, Optimal, you can restore these values to the Sales Forecast table simply by opening the Scenario Manager dialog box and then selecting its name before you click the Show button.

8. Open the Solver Parameters dialog box again.

Note that the Solver Parameters dialog box retains your earlier settings for the target cell, value, and changing cells in their respective use in obtaining the first solution.

9. Click the Add button to the right of the Subject to the Constraints list box to open the Add Constraint dialog box and then click the COGS cell, H5, in the worksheet to insert $H$5 in the Cell Reference text box. Accept the default <= comparative operator. Click the insertion point in the Constraint text box and type **15%** before you click its Add button.

Excel clears the Cell Reference and Constraint text boxes so that you can define a new constraint.

10. This time, click the Expenses cell, H7, in the worksheet to insert $H$7 in the Cell Reference text box, and then click the insertion point in the Constraint text box and type **12%** before you click the OK button.

As soon as you click OK, Excel closes the Add Constraint dialog box and returns you to the Solver Parameters dialog box, where the following comparative expressions now appear in the Subject to the Constraints list box:

- COGS<=15%
- Expenses<=12%

11. Click the Solve button.

This time, when the Solver Results dialog box appears, it indicates that the Solver could not find a feasible solution. When the cost of goods sold and the expenses are kept down to these lower percentages, the projected net income must necessarily exceed the target of $650,000. (Note that the Solver has actually returned $757,375 to the Total_Income cell, G8, using these percentages.)

12. Select the Restore Original Values option button in the Solver Results dialog box and then click OK.

Now save your forecast model under a new filename.

13. Position the cell cursor in cell A1 and then save your work in a new workbook named **Solver Practice.xlsx** in your Excel 2007 Practice folder and then close the workbook file as you exit Excel.

Chapter 20

Generating Pivot Tables

. . . .

In This Chapter

▶ Understanding how pivot tables summarize data and enable you to analyze data lists

▶ Creating a new pivot table

▶ Pivoting the elements in a pivot table

▶ Changing the summary function used in the pivot table

▶ Formatting a pivot table and changing pivot table options

▶ Creating a pivot chart with your pivot table

. . . .

*E*xcel's pivot tables and charts enable you to quickly and extemporaneously summarize vast amounts of spreadsheet data. As such, they're often considered to be the most versatile of the program's many data analysis features, if not its coolest and most powerful. In this chapter, you get the chance to practice creating and using pivot tables and charts to see how they can help reveal complex relationships in the data that might otherwise go completely unnoticed.

Understanding Pivot Tables

Pivot tables are great for summarizing particular values in a data list or database table because they do their magic without requiring you to create formulas to perform their calculations. Unlike the Subtotals feature, another summarizing feature you encountered in Chapter 17, pivot tables let you play around with the arrangement of the summarized data, even after you generate the table. (The Subtotals feature only lets you hide and display different levels of totals in the list.) It's this capability to change the arrangement of the summarized data by rotating row and column headings that gives the pivot table its name.

Pivot tables are also flexible in their ability to summarize data using a variety of summary functions (although totals created with the SUM function will probably remain your old standby). When setting up the original pivot table, you make several decisions: what summary function to use, which columns (fields) the summary function is applied to, and which columns (fields) these computations are tabulated with. You can also use pivot tables to cross-tabulate one set of data in your data list with another. For example, you can use this feature to create a pivot table from an employee database that totals the salaries for each job category cross-tabulated (arranged) by department or job site.

Solve It

Exercise 20-1: Modifying an Existing Pivot Table

In Exercise 20-1, you get practice working with an existing pivot table that summarizes some of the data maintained in the sample employee data list.

1. If Excel is not currently running, launch the program and then open the workbook *Exercise20-1.xlsx* in the Chap20 folder in the Excel 2007 Workbook folder on your hard disk.

   This workbook contains a Employee Data List worksheet with a copy of the employee data list followed by a Employee PvtTbl worksheet that contains a pivot table generated from the data list. You will use this pivot table to practice modifying what data from the employee data list are displayed in the table as well as the manner in which they are displayed.

2. Click the Employee PvtTbl sheet tab and then click B2 to display the PivotTable Tools contextual tab on the Ribbon with its Options and Design tab along with the PivotTable Field List task pane on the right side of the worksheet display.

   The Employee Data List Pivot Table that appears on this worksheet uses the following fields from the Employee Data List:

   - Profit Sharing and Gender fields as the Report Filter fields (in cells B2 and B3, respectively)

   - Dept field as the only Column Labels field (in cell B5)

   - Location field as the only Row Labels field (in cell A6)

   - Salary field as the Value Field for the data items in the body of the pivot table (in the cell range B7:G13) using the SUM function (shown as Sum of Salary in A5)

   Note that the PivotTable Tools contextual tab and the PivotTable Field List task pane appear automatically whenever you position the cell cursor in any cell of the pivot table. They disappear just as automatically when you move the cursor to a cell outside of the cells comprising the pivot table.

3. Click the filter drop-down button attached to the Profit Sharing report filter field in cell B2 and then click the Yes option on its drop-down list. Click OK to display the sum of the salaries in the various departments and locations where the employees do in fact participate in the profit-sharing plan.

   Excel then displays the sum of the salaries according to location and department for those employees who are part of the profit-sharing plan (as indicated by a Yes in the Profit Sharing field in their records within the employee data list).

4. Click the drop-down button attached to the Gender report filter field in cell B3 and then select M on its drop-down list.

   Now the body of the pivot table displays the sum of the salaries in the various departments and locations only where the male employees participate in the profit-sharing plan.

5. Restore the (All) settings to both the Profit Sharing and Gender report filter fields by selecting (All) on their respective drop-down lists and then double-click Sum of Salary in cell A5.

   Excel opens the Value Field Settings dialog box, containing a Summarize By and Show Values As tabs.

6. Click Average in the Summarize Value Field By list box so that the Custom Name text box contains Average of Salary before you click OK.

   The pivot table now displays the averages of the salaries for all the departments and locations in the company regardless of whether the employees are part of profit-sharing or are male or female.

7. With cell A5 still selected in the pivot table, click the Options tab under the PivotTable Tools contextual tab on the Ribbon and then click the Field Settings button or press Alt+JTG to open the Value Field Settings dialog box a second time. Then, select Sum in the Summarize Value By list box again and click OK.

   Excel once again displays the sum of the salaries in the body of the pivot table.

8. Click the Design tab under the PivotTable Tools contextual tab and then click the More button in the PivotTable Styles group or press Alt+JYS to open the PivotTable Styles gallery. Then, click the Pivot Style Medium 2 thumbnail (the one in the second column of the first row of the Medium section of the drop-down gallery).

   Excel now redraws the pivot table using the blue coloring of the Pivot Style Medium 2 table style.

9. Click the Banded Rows and the Banded Columns check box in the PivotTable Style Options group of the Design tab under the PivotTable Tools contextual tab to put check marks in both these check boxes.

   When you select the Banded Rows button and the Pivot Style Medium 2 table style is applied to the table, Excel draws blue borderlines between each of the rows of salary data in the body of the table. When you click the Banded Columns check box, the program draws blue borderlines between each of the columns.

10. Click the Location field's drop-down list button in cell A6 and then click the (Select All) check box to deselect all the check boxes for all the cities. Then, click the check boxes for just Boston, Chicago, San Francisco, and Seattle before you click OK.

    The pivot table now shows the sum of the salaries for all the departments in just the Boston, Chicago, San Francisco, and Seattle locations.

11. Click the (Select All) item at the top of the Location field's drop-down list to reselect the check boxes for all the company locations on its list before you click OK.

    Now save your changes to this pivot table.

12. Select cell A1 on the Employee Data List worksheet and then save your changes in a new workbook named *Pivot Table Practice.xlsx* in your Excel 2007 Practice folder before you close the workbook file.

Creating Pivot Tables

To create a new pivot table, all you need to do is position the cell cursor in one of the cells of the data list whose data is to be summarized in the table and then click the PivotTable button on the Ribbon's Insert tab (Alt+NVT). Excel then selects all the data in the current list and displays the Create PivotTable dialog box, where you specify where to create the new pivot table.

To set up the table, you use the PivotTable Field List task pane to assign fields in the data list to the various parts of the pivot table. You do this by dragging a field name shown in the Choose Fields to Add to Report at the top of the PivotTable Field List task pane into one of the list boxes for the following areas displayed in the Drag Fields Between Areas Below section:

- ✔ **Report Filter:** The fields you drag into this area appear at the top of the pivot table. They function as the fields on whose values you can filter the entire pivot table report.

- ✔ **Column Labels:** The fields you drag into this area appear in the top row of the pivot table. They function as the column headings of the pivot table.

- ✔ **Row Labels:** The fields you drag into this area appear in the first column of the pivot table. They function as the row headings of the pivot table.

- ✔ **Values:** The fields you drag into this area appear in the body of the pivot table. The values in these cells are the ones summarized in the table using various statistical functions: Sum, Count, Average, Max, Min, and so on.

Before you attempt Exercise 20-2, you may want to play the Pivot Table Creation.exe demo located in the Excel Feature Demos folder on your workbook CD-ROM. This feature demonstration shows you how to create a new pivot table that summarizes the data stored in an Excel data list.

Exercise 20-2: Creating a New Pivot Table

In Exercise 20-2, you get practice creating a new pivot table from scratch using the data in a version of the now-familiar employee data list:

1. Open the workbook *Exercise20-2.xlsx* in the Chap20 folder in the Excel 2007 Workbook folder on your hard disk.

   This workbook contains a copy of the Employee Data List worksheet with the data list you will use in creating a new pivot table.

2. Click the PivotTable button in the Tables group of the Ribbon's Insert tab or press Alt+NVT.

   Excel opens the Create PivotTable dialog box while at the same time selecting employee data listed in the cell range A1:J33.

3. Click the Existing Worksheet option button near the bottom of the Create PivotTable dialog box and then click the Sheet2 worksheet tab followed by cell A1 so that the Location text box contains Sheet2!$A$1. Then, click OK to close the Create PivotTable dialog box and rename Sheet2 **Employee PvtTbl**.

Excel displays the blank pivot table framework with instructions in the area of the worksheet you selected and opens the PivotTable Field List task pane on the right side of the worksheet area. In addition, the program selects the Options tab under the PivotTable Tools contextual tab and displays its command buttons on the Ribbon (see Figure 20-1).

4. Drag the Profit Sharing field from the Choose Fields to Add to Report section of the PivotTable Field List and drop it into the Report Filter area. Then drag the following fields and drop them into the following areas:

   • Dept field into the Column Labels area

   • Location field into Row Labels area

   • Salary field into the Values area

Excel builds the basic pivot table shown in Figure 20-2.

5. Save your changes to the Employee PvtTbl worksheet in a new workbook named *Employee List – pvttbl.xlsx* in your Excel 2007 Practice folder and leave the file open for Exercise 20-3.

Figure 20-1: The worksheet with a blank pivot table showing the buttons on the Options tab under the PivotTable Tools contextual tab and the PivotTable Field List task pane.

Figure 20-2:
A new
employee
list pivot
table imme-
diately after
specifying
the data list
fields to use.

Modifying the Pivot Table

The fun just begins with the creation of the basic pivot table. After that, you can refine its look by using the options on the Options tab (as you did in the previous exercise) or the Design tab under the PivotTable Tools contextual tab or by selecting different portions of the table and individually formatting them. You can also show and hide new levels of detail in the table. Perhaps most important, you can modify the structure of the table by pivoting its row, column, and paging fields. Finally, you can change the table's basic summary function as well as add your own calculated fields to the pivot table.

Modifying the table formatting

Modifying the formatting of a new pivot table is a snap with the tools available on the Ribbon's Design tab under the PivotTable Tools contextual tab. You can use the Layout options to change the basic layout of the pivot table as well as the PivotTable Styles gallery and options to quickly transform its look.

Before you attempt Exercises 20-3 and 20-4, you may want to play the Pivot Table Editing.exe demo located in the Excel Feature Demos folder on your workbook CD-ROM. This feature demonstration shows you how to edit an existing pivot table by formatting its values, changing its table style, and pivoting its columns and rows.

Solve It

Exercise 20-3: Modifying the Formatting of a Pivot Table

In Exercise 20-3, you get practice modifying the formatting of the basic pivot table you created in Exercise 20-2.

1. Select a cell in the pivot table you built on the Employee PvtTbl sheet of the *Employee List – pvttbl.xlsx* workbook you created in the previous exercise.

You will use this pivot table to get more practice formatting the table as well as changing what data it summarizes.

2. Assign the Pivot Style Medium 2 style to the pivot table in the PivotTable Styles drop-down gallery and then add borderlines to both the columns and row of the table by selecting the Banded Rows and Banded Columns check boxes.

Next, you need to format the values being summarized in the body of the table.

3. Click cell A3 containing the label, Sum of Salary, in the worksheet and then click Field Settings button on the Options tab under the PivotTable Tools contextual tab on the Ribbon (or press Alt+JTG) to open the Value Field Settings dialog box. Click the Number Format button to open the Format Cells dialog box. Next, click Currency in the Category list box and then enter 0 in the Decimal Places text box before you click OK twice to return to the worksheet.

Excel formats the summed salaries displayed in the body of the pivot table using the Currency number format without any decimal places.

4. Click the drop-down button in cell B1 to the immediate right of the Profit Sharing field heading and then click the Yes option on its drop-down menu before you click OK.

Excel redraws the table showing only the sum of the salaries for employees who are part of the profit-sharing plan.

5. Drag the Gender field from the Choose Fields to Add to Report section of the PivotTable Field List and drop it into the Report Filter area.

Excel adds the Gender field as a second field with which the report can be filtered.

6. Click the drop-down button in cell B2 to the immediate right of the Gender field heading and then click the M option on its drop-down menu before you click OK.

Excel redraws the pivot table, showing only the sum of the salaries for the male employees who are part of the profit-sharing plan.

7. Remove the filters from both the Profit Sharing and Gender report filter fields by clicking the (All) option on their respective drop-down menus.

Now you're ready to save your changes.

8. Click cell B4 in the pivot table containing the heading Column Labels and then save your changes to the workbook file (Ctrl+S) and leave the workbook file open for Exercise 20-4.

Pivoting the table's fields

As the name "pivot" implies, the fun of pivot tables is being able to rotate the data fields used as the rows and columns of tables as well as to change what fields are used and how they're presented. For example, suppose in the employee data list pivot table that, after making the Dept field the pivot table's sole column field and the Location field the sole row field, you now want to see what the table looks like with the Location field as the column field and the Dept field as the row field.

No problem: All you have to do is drag the Dept field label in the PivotTable Field List task pane from the Column Labels area to the Row Labels area and the Location field label from the Row Labels area to the Column Labels area. Voila! Excel rearranges the totaled salaries so that the rows of the pivot table show the departmental grand totals and the columns now show the location grand totals.

Solve It

Exercise 20-4: Modifying the Structure of a Pivot Table

In Exercise 20-4, you get practice modifying the structure of the employee list data table that you built in Exercise 20-2 and completed formatting in Exercise 20-3.

1. With the cell cursor in cell B4 of the Employee PvtTbl worksheet of the *Employee List – pvttbl.xlsx* workbook file, pivot the Dept and Location fields in the table by doing the following:

- Drag the Dept field label from the Column Labels area and drop it into the Row Labels area

- Drag the Location field label from the Row Labels area and drop it into the Column Labels area

Excel pivots the table so that the various office locations now form the columns of the pivot table and the various departments its rows.

2. Drag the Gender field from the Report Filter area and drop it into the Row Labels area underneath the Dept field.

Adding the Gender field in this manner as a second row field makes it into a sub-totaling field so that the pivot table can now display columns with subtotals of the men's and women's salaries as well as a column with their grand total.

Note that Excel also adds Hide buttons (indicated by the minus signs) to each department name that you can click to hide the level of detail and show only the subtotals (after turning on the Subtotals option). These Hide buttons are then replaced with Show buttons (indicated by plus signs) that you can click to display the salary totals for men and women in a particular department.

3. Drag the Profit Sharing field from the Report Filter area and drop it into the Column Labels area underneath the Location field.

Excel makes the employee's profit-sharing status a subtotaling field for the columns of the pivot table.

4. Drag the Years of Service field from the Choose Fields to Add to Report section of the PivotTable Field List task pane and drop it into the Report Filter area in the Drag Fields Between Areas Below section.

Now you can filter the entire pivot table on the seniority of the employees.

5. Click the Subtotals button on the Design tab under the PivotTable Tools contextual tab and then click the Show All Subtotals at Bottom of Group option on the drop-down menu or press Alt+JYTB.

Excel adds a row of totals for each department and a column of totals for each location in the pivot table.

6. Click the Field List button in the Show/Hide group of the Options tab under the PivotTable Tools contextual tab or press Alt+JTL to close the PivotTable Field List task pane.

Next, replace the generic Column Labels and Row Labels in the table with their actual field names.

7. Click the Options button in the PivotTable group at the beginning of the Options tab under the PivotTable Tools contextual tab or press Alt+JTTT to open the PivotTable Options dialog box. Then, click the Display tab in this dialog box and click the Classic PivotTable Layout (Enables Dragging of Fields in the Grid) check box to put a check mark in it before you click OK.

Excel now displays the field names Location and Profit Sharing on the top row of the pivot table and the field names Dept and Gender in the first columns.

8. Click cell C4 with the Location field heading and then click the Collapse Entire Field button in the Active Field group of the Options tab under the PivotTable Tools contextual tab or press Alt+JTP.

Excel collapses the profit-sharing detail, showing only the totals of the salaries for each location.

9. Click A6 with the Dept field heading and then click the Collapse Entire Field button on the Options tab or press Alt+JTP again.

Excel collapses the gender detail, showing only the totals of the salaries for both men and women in each department.

10. Position the cell cursor in cell A4 of the Employee PvtTbl worksheet and then save your modifications to the pivot table (Ctrl+S). Leave the workbook file open for Exercise 20-5.

Changing the table summary function and adding calculated fields

By default, Excel uses the SUM function to total the values in the numeric field(s) that you assign as the data items in the pivot table. Some data summaries require the use of another summary function such as the AVERAGE or COUNT functions. To change the summary function, double-click the label of the field used as a data item or click this label (this label is located at the cell intersection of the first column and row field in a pivot table that has only one data field and uses the default or classic table format). Select Summarize By tab in the Value Field Settings dialog box and select any of the following summary functions in the Summarize Value Field By list box:

- ✔ **Count** to show the count of the records for a particular category (note that Count is the default setting for any text fields that you use as Data Items in a pivot table)

- ✔ **Average** to calculate the average (that is, the arithmetic mean) for the values in the field for the current category and page filter

- ✔ **Max** to display the largest numeric value in that field for the current category and page filter

- ✔ **Min** to display the smallest numeric value in that field for the current category and page filter

- ✔ **Product** to display the product of the numeric values in that field for the current category and page filter (all non-numeric entries are ignored)

- ✔ **Count Numbers** to display the number of numeric values in that field for the current category and page filter (all non-numeric entries are ignored)

- ✔ **StdDev** to display the standard deviation for the sample in that field for the current category and page filter

- ✔ **StdDevp** to display the standard deviation for the population in that field for the current category and page filter

- ✔ **Var** to display the variance for the sample in that field for the current category and page filter

- ✔ **Varp** to display the variance for the population in that field for the current category and page filter

After you select the new summary function to use in the Summarize Value Field By list box in the Value Field Settings dialog box, click the OK button to have Excel apply the new function to the data presented in the body of the pivot table.

In addition to using various summary functions on the data presented in your pivot table, you can create your own calculated fields for the pivot table. Calculated fields are computed by assigning a formula using existing numeric fields in the data source.

After you finish defining a calculated field to a pivot table, Excel automatically adds its name to the PivotTable Field List task pane and assigns it as a Values data item in the data area of the pivot table. The program also adds a new data field and makes it the first column field in the pivot table.

If you want to hide a calculated field from the body of the pivot table, click the check box in front of the calculated data field's name in the Choose Fields to Add to Report section of the Pivot Table Field List pane to remove the check mark. To add the calculated field back into the pivot table, you click the same calculated field's check box again.

Solve It

Exercise 20-5: Modifying the Summary Functions and Adding a Calculated Field to a Pivot Table

In Exercise 20-5, you get practice changing the function used to summarize the data in your employee list pivot table as well as to add a calculated field to it.

1. With the cell cursor in cell A4 of the Employee PvtTbl worksheet of the *Employee List – pvttbl.xlsx* workbook file, click the Field Settings button on the Options tab under the PivotTable Tools contextual tab to open the Value Field Settings dialog box. Then, click Average in the Summarize Value Field By list box on the Summarize By tab before you click OK.

   The body of your pivot table now displays the average salary for each department and location in the company.

2. Open the Value Field Settings dialog box again, this time by double-clicking cell A4, and then use it to change the summary function from AVERAGE to MAX.

   Excel redraws the pivot table so that it shows you the highest salaries for each department and location in the company.

3. Restore SUM as the summary function in the table and then click the Calculated Field option on the Formulas button's drop-down menu on the Options tab or press Alt+JTJF.

   Excel opens the Insert Calculated Field dialog box where you will define the parameters for a Bonus field that calculates bonuses as 2.5% of the employee's salary.

4. Type **Bonus** in the Name text box in the Insert Calculated Field dialog box and then press Tab to select the Formula text box. In this text box, delete the 0 (zero) after the = (equal to) sign (which you want to retain), and then click Salary in the Fields list box followed by the Insert Field button.

   The Formula text box should now read

   ```
   =Salary
   ```

5. Type * (asterisk) followed by **0.025** in the Formula text box.

   The Formula text box should now contain the complete formula

   ```
   =Salary*0.025
   ```

6. Click the Add button and then click OK. Next, click the Field List button in the Show/Hide group of the Options tab or press Alt+JTL to redisplay the PivotTable Field List task pane.

   As soon as the Insert Calculated Field dialog box closes, you see that Excel has added your Bonus field (as Sum of Bonus) as a data item to the body of the pivot table. You also note that Bonus appears at the very bottom of the list box in the PivotTable Field List task pane.

7. Position the cell cursor in cell A1 of the Employee PvtTbl worksheet and then save your changes to the pivot table (Ctrl+S) before you close the workbook file.

Creating Pivot Charts

You can spice up your data summaries quite a bit by generating a pivot chart along with a supporting pivot table. To do this, you follow the same procedure as you do when creating a sole pivot table except that you click the PivotChart option on the PivotTable button's drop-down on the Ribbon's Insert tab (Alt+NVC).

When creating a new pivot chart with a pivot table, Excel embeds the new pivot chart on the same worksheet that contains the new pivot table regardless of whether you place this table on the active worksheet or a new worksheet. After building the pivot table (which simultaneously builds the pivot chart as a clustered column chart), you can use the Move Chart button on the Design tab under the PivotChart Tools contextual tab to move the chart to its own chart sheet.

 Although Excel always chooses the clustered column chart as the basic chart type for each new pivot chart you generate, you can select another chart type for the pivot chart: Simply click the Change Chart Type button on the Design tab under the PivotChart Tools contextual tab and select the new chart type in the Change Chart Type dialog box as you would for any other chart you're creating.

Solve It

Exercise 20-6: Creating a Pivot Chart

In Exercise 20-6, you get practice generating a pivot chart to accompany a new pivot table that you build for the employee data list that you've been using in the exercises in this chapter.

1. Open the workbook *Exercise20-6.xlsx* in the Chap20 folder in your Excel 2007 Workbook folder on your hard disk.

This workbook contains a copy of the Employee Data List worksheet with the data list you will use in creating a new pivot table along with a new pivot chart.

2. Click the Pivot Chart option on the Pivot Table button's drop-down menu on the Ribbon's Insert tab or press Alt+NVC.

Excel opens the Create PivotTable with PivotChart dialog box. Here, you designate the data or table range to be used in creating the pivot table and chart as well as their location in the workbook. Excel displays a marquee around the table range A1:J33 in the worksheet and displays the range name 'Employee Data List'!$A$1:$J$33 in the Table/Range text box.

3. Click the Existing Worksheet option button in the Create PivotTable with PivotChart dialog box and then click the Sheet2 tab in the worksheet followed by cell A1 of this sheet so that Location text field contains Sheet2!$A$1. Click OK.

Excel inserts two blank frameworks in Sheet2 of your *Exercise20-6.xlsx* workbook as shown in Figure 20-3. The program also displays the PivotTable Field List task pane on the right side of the worksheet area and the PivotChart Tools contextual tab with its Design, Layout, Format, and Analyze tabs appears on the Ribbon.

4. Build the pivot table by dragging these fields from the Choose Fields to Add to Report section of the PivotTable Field List task pane to the following areas in the Drag Fields Between Areas Below section:

   • Dept field to the Report Filter area

   • Gender field to the Legend Fields area

   • Location field to the Axis Fields area

   • Salary field to the Values area

   Excel generates an embedded clustered column chart whose columns compare the men's and women's salaries at the various company locations as it builds the underlying pivot table.

   This embedded chart is active in the worksheet indicated by the appearance of the PivotChart Tools contextual tab on the Ribbon and the PivotChart Filter Pane to the side of the embedded chart. You can use the filter buttons in this task pane to filter the data represented in the clustered column chart.

5. Click the Move Chart button at the very end of the Design tab under the PivotChart Tools contextual tab or press Alt+JCM to open the Move Chart dialog box. Then, click the New Sheet option button and replace Chart1 with **Employee PvtCht** before you click OK.

   Excel moves the new clustered column pivot chart to the new Employee PvtCht chart sheet that is inserted in between the Employee Data List and Sheet2 worksheets.

6. Dock the floating PivotChart Filter Pane by dragging its title bar until part of the pane is over the PivotTable Field List task pane and then releasing the mouse button. Then, click the PivotChart Filter button on the Analyze tab under the PivotChart Tools contextual tab or press Alt+JNW to temporarily close the PivotChart Filter pane.

You can use the PivotChart Filter and Field List buttons on the Analyze tab to hide and redisplay these two task panes as needed when working with your pivot chart.

7. Rename the Sheet2 tab **Employee PvtTbl** and then reposition this tab so that is inserted in between the Employee Data List worksheet and the Employee PvtCht chart sheet and then click the Employee PvtCht tab to active the pivot chart sheet.

Next, you'll change the type of chart used by your pivot chart and refine its formatting.

8. Click the Change Chart Type button on the Design tab under the PivotChart Tools contextual tab or press Alt+JCC to open the Change Chart Type dialog box. Click the Clustered Cylinder thumbnail (the one in the first column of the second row in the Column section) and then click OK.

Excel redraws your pivot chart using 3-D cylinders to represent the women's and men's salaries. Now change the chart layout for the clustered column pivot chart.

9. Click the More button in the Chart Layouts group and then click the Layout 5 thumbnail on the drop-down gallery.

Excel redraws the chart, adding a place for a chart and a vertical axis title. The program also adds a data table to the bottom of the chart that includes the legend markers.

10. Make the following formatting changes to the pivot chart:

- Enter **Comparing Women and Men Companywide** as the chart title

- Add horizontal and vertical major and minor gridlines to the chart

- Select thousands as the display units for the vertical axis and then remove the vertical axis title from the chart

- Bold the text along the horizontal and vertical axis and well as in the data table beneath the chart

- Italicize the Thousands label on the vertical axis and the locations along the horizontal axis

Your pivot chart should now look like the one shown in Figure 20-4.

11. Display the PivotChart Filter Pane in the Employee PvtCht sheet and then filter the chart so that only the data for the women's salaries are represented.

Click the Legend Fields (Series) drop-down button in the PivotChart Filter Pane and then click the M check box to remove the check mark from the (Select All) and M check boxes (leaving only the F check box selected) on its drop-down menu before you click OK.

Excel redraws your pivot chart with only the blue cylinders representing the totals of the women's salaries displayed.

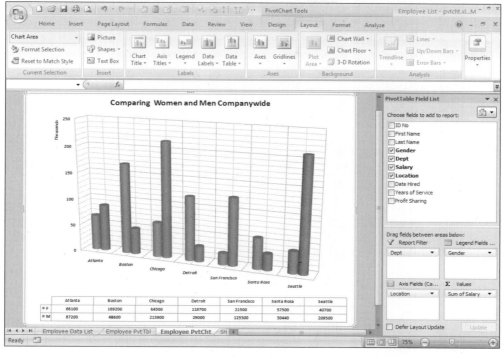

Figure 20-4:
The employee data list clustered cylinder pivot chart after formatting.

12. Restore the men's salaries to the pivot chart and then move the Dept field to the Axis Fields (Categories) area and the Location field to the Report Filter area. Then remove the Sum of Salary field from the Values area and replace this with the Years of Service field.

To remove a field from a pivot chart, drag its field from its area in the Drag Fields Between Areas Below section of the PivotTable Field List task pane and drop it anywhere outside one of the four areas.

Excel redraws your clustered cylinder pivot chart so that it now shows the department names along the horizontal axis and at the top of the data table and compares the women's years of service with that of the men for all office locations.

13. Filter the clustered cylinder chart so that represents the years of service for the men and women in only the Atlanta, Chicago, San Francisco, and Seattle office locations.

Click the Select Multiple Items check box on the Report Filter's drop-down menu and then click the Boston, Detroit, and Santa Rosa check boxes to remove their check marks (leaving the Atlanta, Chicago, San Francisco, and Seattle check boxes selected) before you click OK.

Excel redraws your clustered cylinder pivot chart representing the years of service for women and men in just the Atlanta, Chicago, San Francisco, and Seattle offices.

14. Restore all the locations to the chart by clicking the (All) option on the Report Filter's drop-down menu before you click OK and then hide the display of the PivotChart Filter Pane and the PivotTable Field List by clicking their Close buttons.

    Next, edit the chart title to reflect the data it now represents.

15. Modify the chart title so that it reads, Comparing the Service of Women and Men Companywide.

    Now save your work in a new workbook file.

16. Select cell A1 on the Employee Data List worksheet and then save your work in a new workbook file with the filename **Employee List – pvtcht.xlsx** in your Excel 2007 Practice folder. Close this workbook file as you exit Excel.

Part VI
Macros and Visual Basic for Applications

The 5th Wave   By Rich Tennant

"You know kids — you can't buy them just any spreadsheet creation software."

In this part . . .

Part VI is all about automating routine operations to make your use of the program more efficient. Here, you are introduced to the process of recording sequences of habitual actions in Excel as macros that the program then plays back time and time again in your spreadsheets much more quickly than you can ever hope to do by hand, and without the slightest deviation. You're also introduced to editing macros with Excel's Visual Basic Editor and using the Visual Basic for Applications programming language to extend their functionality.

Chapter 21

Using Macros

*M*acros enable you to automate almost any task that you can undertake in Excel. By using Excel's macro recorder to record tasks that you perform routinely, you not only speed up the procedure considerably (as Excel can play back your keystrokes and mouse actions much faster than you perform them manually), but you are also assured that each step in the task is carried out the same way each and every time you perform the task.

In this chapter, you get a chance to practice recording, testing, and playing back macros that you use to automate repetitive tasks required when building and using your Excel worksheets and charts. You also have the opportunity to practice assigning the macros you record to custom buttons on the Quick Access toolbar.

Creating Macros

You can create macros for your Excel spreadsheets in one of two ways:

✔ Use Excel's macro recorder to record your actions as you undertake them in a worksheet

✔ Enter the instructions that you want followed in VBA code in the Visual Basic Editor

Either way, Excel creates a special *module* sheet that holds the actions and instructions in your macro. The macro instructions in a macro module (whether recorded by Excel or written by you) are stored in the Visual Basic for Applications programming language. You can then study the VBA code that the macro recorder creates and edit this code in the Visual Basic Editor (see Chapter 22).

Using the macro recorder

You can use the macro recorder to create many of the utility-type macros that perform the repetitive tasks necessary for creating and editing your worksheets and charts. When you turn on the macro recorder, it records all of your actions in the active worksheet or chart sheet as you make them.

Note that the macro recorder does not record the keystrokes or mouse actions you take to accomplish an action, but only the VBA code required to perform the action itself. This means that any mistakes that you make while taking an action are not recorded as part of the macro. If, for example, you make a typing error and then edit it while the macro recorder is on, only the corrected entry shows up in the macro without the original mistakes and steps taken to remedy it.

The macros that you create with the macro recorder can be stored either as part of the current workbook, in a new workbook, or in a special, globally available Personal Macro Workbook named *PERSONAL.XLSB* that's stored in a folder called XLSTART on your hard disk. When you record a macro as part of your Personal Macro Workbook, you can run that macro from any workbook that you have open. (This is because the *PERSONAL.XLSB* workbook is secretly opened whenever you launch Excel and, although it remains hidden, its macros are therefore always available.) When you record macros as part of the current workbook or a new workbook, you can run those macros only when the workbook in which they were recorded is open in Excel.

When you create a macro with the macro recorder, you decide not only the workbook in which to store the macro but also what name and shortcut keystrokes to assign to the macro you are creating. When assigning a name for your macro, you use the same guidelines as when assigning a standard range name to a cell range in your worksheet. When assigning a shortcut keystroke to run the macro, you can assign the Ctrl key plus a lowercase letter between a and z as such as Ctrl+q (which is displayed as Ctrl+Q, although you press just Ctrl+q). Alternatively, you can press the Ctrl key plus an uppercase letter between A and Z as in Ctrl+Q (which appears as Ctrl+Shift+Q because you must press all three keys). You cannot, however, assign the Ctrl key plus a punctuation or number key (such as Ctrl+1 or Ctrl+/) to your macro.

Solve It | Exercise 21-1: Recording a New Macro

In Exercise 21-1, you get practice using the macro recorder to record a macro that automatically enters and formats the company name in a cell whenever you play the macro back.

1. If Excel is not currently running, launch the program. If the program is running but no blank workbook is active, create a new workbook (Ctrl+N).

You will use Sheet1 of your new workbook to practice recording and playing back a new macro that enters the Company Name (Mind Over Media, Inc., in this case) in 12-point bold type and then centers the text across columns A through E with the Merge & Center button on the Home tab.

Before you start recording macros in Excel 2007, you're going to display the optional Developer tab on its Ribbon. The Developer tab contains all the command buttons that you need to record, play back, and edit the macros you create.

2. Click Office button | Excel Options or press Alt+FI and then click the Show Developer Tab in the Ribbon check box in the Top Options for Working with Excel section of the Popular tab to put a check mark in it before you click OK.

   Excel adds the Developer tab to the end of the Excel Ribbon. The buttons on this optional tab are divided into three groups: Code, Controls, and XML.

   Note that even when the optional Developer tab is not displayed in Excel, you can still record and view macros using the options attached to the Macros button located at the very end of the Ribbon's View tab (Alt+WM).

3. Click the Record Macro button on the Developer tab or press Alt+LR.

   Excel opens the Record Macro dialog box containing the following four boxes:

   - **Macro Name** text box, where you enter the name for your macro

   - **Shortcut Key** text box, where you define an optional letter (upper- with the Shift key or lowercase) that you want to assign as the shortcut key for playing back the macro you're creating

   - **Store Macro In** combo box, where you choose between This Workbook, New Workbook, and the Personal Macro Workbook as the place in which to record your new macro

   - **Description** text box, where you enter an optional description of the purpose of the macro you're about to create

4. Replace the temporary macro name, Macro1, in the Macro Name text box with **Company_Name** (be sure to enter an underscore character between Company and Name and not a space) and then press Tab to select the Shortcut Key text box.

   Macro names use the same naming rules as when creating ranges names in a worksheet so that you cannot use spaces in their names or begin their names with numbers.

5. In the Shortcut Key text box, type uppercase **C** by pressing Shift+C.

   The Shortcut key appears in the Record Macro dialog box as Ctrl+Shift+C.

6. Click Personal Macro Workbook on the Store Macro In option's drop-down list.

   If you store a macro in the current workbook or a new workbook, you can only use the macro while that particular workbook is open in Excel. When you save a macro in the Personal Macro Workbook, you can use the macro in any workbook you have open.

7. Select the Description text box and then insert the following description: **Enters company name in 12pt bold centered across 5 columns** and then click OK.

   Excel closes the Record Macro dialog box and the Record Macro button on the Developer tab changes to a Stop Recording button.

8. Type **Mind Over Media, Inc.** in cell A1 and then click the Enter button on the Formula bar (be sure that you don't press the Enter key here).

   If you make a typing error while doing this entry, don't worry. Simply delete the incorrect characters and replace them with the correct ones.

9. In the Font group of the Home tab, click the Font Size button to increase the point size to 12 and then click the Bold button to add the boldface attribute to the text. Drag through the cell range A1:E1 to select it and then click the Merge & Center button in the Alignment group.

   Now that you've finished taking the actions you want recorded in your new macro, you need to stop recording.

10. Click the Stop Recording button on the Developer tab of the Ribbon.

    As soon as you click this button, the Recording status indicator disappears from the Status bar.

11. Position the cell cursor in cell A1 of Sheet2 of the workbook and then press Alt+F8 to open the Macro dialog box.

    The Macro dialog box displays a list of all the macros that you defined in the *PERSONAL.XLSB* workbook as well as the current workbook. You can use the controls in this dialog box to run or edit a macro, or even to play the macro back a step at a time. (The latter is especially helpful when a macro does something unintended and you want to find out where exactly it went off track.)

12. Click the PERSONAL.XLSB!Company_Name macro in Macro Name list box before you select the Run button.

    As soon as you select Run, Excel closes the Macro dialog box and runs the Company_Name macro, which enters Mind Over Media, Inc. in cell A1 of Sheet2 centered in 12-point bold text within a merged cell that includes the cell range A1:E1.

13. Select cell G1 in Sheet3 and then run the Company_Name macro using the shortcut key combination, Ctrl+Shift+C, that you assigned to it.

    Excel runs the macro, but this time something unanticipated happens: The program enters the correctly formatted text in cell G1 while still creating the merged cell in the cell range A1:E1 instead of G1:K1 (which would then include the company name).

    Excel does this when you run the Company_Name macro in any cell other than A1 of a worksheet because the macro recorder automatically records the cell references in a macro as absolute rather than relative references (unlike when copying formulas). To fix this macro, you will have to rerecord it with relative references in Exercise 21-2.

14. Exit Excel and select the No button when the alert dialog box appears asking you if you want to save your changes to Book1.

    As soon as you select No in the first alert dialog box, Excel displays a second alert dialog box, this one prompting you to save changes to the Personal Macro Workbook, *PERSONAL.XLSB*, that contains your Company_Name macro. Normally, you would select the Yes button to save your macro for use in other workbooks during other work sessions. However, as you need to rerecord the Company_Name macro using relative references to make it run properly, here you will select No and not bother to save it.

15. Select the No button in the alert dialog box asking if you want to save your changes to the Personal Macro Workbook.

Recording macros with relative cell references

Now you understand why the Code group of the Developer tab contains a Use Relative References button. You need to use this button before you start recording any sequence in a macro that requires relative rather than absolute cell references. Try using this button when rerecording the Company_Name macro in Exercise 21-2 to see what difference it makes when playing the macro back in cells other than A1 in the worksheet.

Solve It

Exercise 21-2: Recording a Macro Using Relative Cell References

In Exercise 21-2, you get practice recording a macro using relative cell references so that it can be played back in cells of a worksheet other than those used in the original recording.

1. Launch Excel and then leave the cell cursor in cell A1 of Sheet1 in the new Book1 workbook.

You will use this new workbook to practice rerecording the Company_Name macro, this time using relative cell references.

2. Click the Record Macro button on the Developer tab or press Alt+LR to open the Record Macro dialog box. Then, fill in its text boxes as follows and then click the OK button:

- **Company_Name** in the Macro Name text box

- Uppercase **C** in the Shortcut Key text box so that the shortcut appears as Ctrl+Shift+C

- Personal Macro Workbook in the Store Macro In combo box

- **Enters company name in 12pt bold** centered across five columns in the Description text box

3. Click the Use Relative References button on the Developer tab or press Alt+LU.

Excel indicates that it is recording relative cell references by highlighting the background of the Use Relative References button on the Developer tab.

4. Rerecord the macro by typing **Mind Over Media, Inc.** in cell A1 and then clicking the Enter button on the Formula bar. Then, use the Font Size button in the Font group on the Home tab to increase the point size to 12 and click the Bold button to add the boldface attribute to the text. Finally, drag through the cell range A1:E1 to select it and then click the Merge & Center button in the Alignment group.

Now you're ready to stop recording the rerecorded macro.

5. Click the Stop Recording button on the Developer tab or press Alt+LR.

Now you're ready to test out your macro recorded with relative cell addresses.

6. Position the cell cursor in cell G1 in Sheet1 and then press Ctrl+Shift+C to test the rerecorded Company_Name macro with relative cell references.

This time, thanks to relative cell references, the macro works as intended by entering the formatted company name, Mind Over Media, Inc., centered across the merged cell in the range G1:K1.

Next, record another macro that enters all twelve months (from January to December) in a single row of the worksheet. This macro enters the names of the months, and then makes their names bold and italic and widens their columns with the AutoFit feature. This Twelve_Months macro also requires relative references during recording to ensure that you can use it to successfully enter the months of the year in any columns of any worksheet.

7. Position the cell cursor in cell A4 of Sheet 1 and then click the Record Macro button on the Developer tab (Alt+LR). Then fill in its text boxes as follows before clicking the OK button:

   - **Twelve_Months** in the Macro Name text box

   - Uppercase **M** in the Shortcut Key text box so that the shortcut appears as Ctrl+Shift+M

   - Personal Macro Workbook in the Store Macro In combo box

   - **Enters the 12 months from Jan to Dec in bold italic** in the Description text box

8. Make sure that Use Relative References button on the Developer tab is still highlighted (if not, press Alt+LU). Then, take the following actions:

   - Type **January** in cell A4 and then click the Enter button on the Formula bar.

   - Drag the Fill handle to the right to extend the range to L4 so that all 12 months from January through December are entered in the range A4:L4.

   - Click the Bold and Italic buttons in the Font group of the Home tab.

   - Click the AutoFit Column Width option on the Format button's drop-down menu in the Cells group of the Home tab.

   - Click cell A4 to deselect the range A4:L4.

   Now you're ready to stop recording the new macro.

9. Click the Stop Recording button on the Developer tab or press Alt+LR.

   Now you're ready to test out your new Twelve_Months macro.

10. Position the cell cursor in cell C8 of Sheet1 and then press Ctrl+Shift+M.

    Excel correctly enters the twelve months of the year in the cell range C8:N8 while at the same time adjusting the widths of columns C to N to suit the length of the month each contains.

11. Exit Excel and select No in the first alert dialog box prompting you to save your changes to the Book1 workbook file. Select the Yes button in the second alert dialog box when prompted to save your macros in the Personal Macro Workbook.

Assigning Macros to the Quick Access Toolbar

Excel enables you to assign macros you create to the custom buttons that you add to the Quick Access toolbar. When you assign a macro to a custom button on the Quick Access toolbar, you can then run the macro simply by clicking its custom button instead of having to open the Macro dialog box or typing its keystroke shortcut.

Solve It

Exercise 21-3: Assigning a Macro to a Custom Button on the Quick Access Toolbar

In Exercise 21-3, you get practice assigning your Company_Name and Twelve_Months macros to custom buttons on the Quick Access toolbar.

1. Launch Excel and leave the cell cursor in cell A1 of Sheet1 in the new Book1 workbook.

You will use this new workbook to practice assigning the two macros that you created in Exercise 21-2 to the Quick Access toolbar.

2. Click the Customize Quick Access Toolbar button at the end of the Quick Access toolbar and then click the More Commands option on its drop-down menu to open the Excel Options dialog box with the Customize tab selected.

To add your macros to custom buttons, you must choose Macros in the Choose Commands From list.

3. Click Popular Commands in the Choose Commands From drop-down box and then click Macros on the drop-down list.

Macros replaces Popular Commands on the drop-down button and Excel displays a list of macros in the list box below.

4. Scroll down the list of macros until you locate your PERSONAL.XLSB!Company_Name and PERSONAL.XLSB!Twelve_Months macros. Then, click <Separator> at the top of the list followed by the Add button. Next, click PERSONAL.XLSB!Company_Name in the list followed by the Add button and then PERSONAL.XLSB!Twelve_Months followed by Add again.

Your two macros now appear at the bottom of the Customize Quick Access Toolbar list box on the right with a <Separator> appearing in between Speak Cells on Enter and PERSONAL.XLSB!Company_Name.

5. Click the OK button to close the Excel Options dialog box.

Your Quick Access toolbar now contains two new buttons at the right end separated from the group of Speak Cells custom buttons by a vertical bar (│). Note that these two new custom buttons use the exactly the same programming icon. The only way to tell them apart is by their ScreenTips.

6. Position the mouse pointer over each of the new custom buttons with the programming icon. When the ScreenTip reads PERSONAL.XLSB!Company_Name, click the button to run the macro.

Excel runs the company name macro by entering the Mind Over Media, Inc. company name in bold in the merged A1:E1 super-cell.

7. Click cell G1 and then click the custom button whose ScreenTip reads PERSONAL.XLSB!Twelve_Months.

Excel runs your Twelve_Months macro, which enters the names of the months January through December in bold italic in the cell range G1:R1 and adjusts their column widths using the AutoFit feature.

8. Exit Excel without saving your changes to the Book1 workbook.

Chapter 22

Using the Visual Basic Editor

In This Chapter

▶ Getting familiar with the Visual Basic Editor

▶ Editing a macro in the Visual Basic Editor

▶ Adding interactivity to a macro with a dialog box that processes user input

▶ Creating and using user-defined functions in the Visual Basic Editor

▶ Saving user-defined functions as Excel add-ins

*V*isual Basic for Applications (usually known simply as VBA) is the official programming language of Excel that you can use to edit as well as to write new macros. The key to editing and writing macros in Visual Basic for Applications is its editing program, the Visual Basic Editor (often abbreviated VBE). The Visual Basic Editor offers a rich environment for coding and debugging VBA code whose interface rivals that of Excel itself in terms of features and complexity.

In this chapter, you get a chance to practice using the Visual Basic Editor to edit macros that you've recorded (see Chapter 21) as well as to enhance their basic functionality through the addition of interactivity. In addition, you get practice using the VBE to create your own custom functions known as *user-defined functions* (often abbreviated UDF).

Using the Visual Basic Editor

You can open the Visual Basic Editor in one of three ways:

✓ Click the Visual Basic button in the Code group at the very beginning of the Developer tab on the Ribbon (Alt+LV).

✓ Press Alt+F11.

✓ Open the Macro dialog box (Alt+F8), select a macro to edit, and then click the Edit button.

Figure 22-1 shows the arrangement of the typical components of the Visual Basic Editor when you first open it. As you can see, this window contains its own menu bar and beneath the menu bar, you find a Visual Basic Editor Standard toolbar, shown in Figure 22-2.

Project Explorer   Code window

Figure 22-1:
The Visual
Basic Editor
window as it
normally
appears
when first
opened.

Properties window

View Microsoft Excel   Design mode Properties window

Save   Find   Break   Toolbox

Copy   Redo   Microsoft Visual Basic Help

Figure 22-2:
The buttons
on the
Standard
toolbar in
the Visual
Basic Editor.

Cut   Object Browser

Insert User Form Paste   Project Explorer

Undo   Reset

Run Sub/User Form

Beneath the Standard toolbar in the Visual Basic Editor, you find a number of tiled windows of various sizes and shapes. Keep in mind that these are the default windows and their default arrangement. They are not the only windows that you can have open in the Visual Basic Editor (as though it weren't crowded and confusing enough as is), and this is not the only way that they can be arranged.

The two most important windows (at least, when you're first starting out using the Visual Basic Editor) are the Project Explorer and the Code window. The Project Explorer window to the immediate left of the Code window (refer to Figure 22-1) shows you all the projects you have open in the Visual Basic Editor and enables you to easily navigate their various parts. Note that in VBA, a *project* consists of all the code and user forms that belong to a particular workbook along with the sheets of the workbook itself.

Editing a recorded macro

The macros that you record in the workbook as well as any you write for it in the Visual Basic Editor are recorded on module sheets to which Excel assigns generic names such as Module1, Module2, and so forth. The actual lines of VBA programming code for the macro stored on a particular module sheet appear in the Code window when you select its module in the Project Explorer (the Code window appears to the immediate right of the Project Explorer).

If you want to rename a module in your VBA project to something a little more descriptive than Module1, Module2, and so on, you can do this in the Properties window that appears immediately below the Project Explorer. Simply click the name (such as Module1) that appears after the label, (Name), on the Alphabetic tab in the Properties window and replace it with a more descriptive name before you press Enter. When renaming a module, remember that you must use the same naming guidelines as when naming a range name in a worksheet: Begin the module name with a letter, not a symbol or number, and don't put any spaces between words (use underscores instead).

After you've created a macro, you don't necessarily have to rerecord it to change the way it behaves. In many cases, you will find it more expedient to change its behavior by simply editing its contents in the Visual Basic Editor. Note that if the macro you want to edit is stored in your Personal Macro Workbook (that *PERSONAL.XLSB* file in the XLSTART folder), it's much easier to edit the macro in the Visual Basic Editor by first un-hiding the Personal Macro Workbook file in Excel.

Keep in mind that Excel automatically hides the Personal Macro Workbook when you exit Excel. This means that you must click the Unhide button on the Ribbon's View tab or press Alt+WU and click OK when PERSONAL.XLSB is selected in the Unhide dialog box to make the *PERSONAL.XLSB* workbook visible if you want to edit its macros directly from this workbook file.

Solve It

Exercise 22-1: Editing a Recorded Macro with the Visual Basic Editor

In Exercise 22-1, you get practice making simple editing changes to the Company_Name macro that you created in your Personal Macro Workbook when doing the exercises in the previous chapter.

   1. Launch Excel 2007 and then click the Unhide button on the View tab or press Alt+WU and then click OK in the Unhide dialog box to unhide the *PERSONAL.XLSB* workbook containing your Company_Name macro.

     The Excel title bar now reads PERSONAL.XLSB.

2. Press Alt+F8 to open the Macro dialog box and then, when Company_Name is highlighted in Macro Name list box, click the Edit button.

   Excel opens the Visual Basic Editor for the Module1 sheet that contains your Company_Name macro. The Code window containing the actual commands in this macro appears less than full size to the right of the Project Explorer and Properties window.

3. Click the Maximize button on the upper-right of the Code window to maximize this window in the Visual Basic Editor.

   In the Code window, note that explanatory comments that are not executed as part of the macro are prefaced with apostrophes and appear in green text, whereas all the VBA commands and properties that are executed at the time you run the macro appear in blue and black text.

4. Position the insertion point after the b in Sub in the first line of code at the very top of the Code window and then press F1 to open a Excel Help window with information on the use of the Sub Statement.

   The Excel Help window opens with information on Sub Statement. You can always get context-sensitive help in the Visual Basic Editor by positioning the insertion point in the command on which you need help and then pressing the F1 Help key.

5. Close the Excel Help window and then replace Calibri with **Times New Roman** in the Name property that is located immediately under the With Selection.Font statement. Make sure to retain the closed pair of double quotation marks around the font name, as in

   ```
   .Name = "Times New Roman"
   ```

6. Increase the font size from 12 to 14 points by changing the Size property, as in

   ```
   .Size = 14
   ```

7. Turn off the ThemeFont property by setting it equal to zero, as in

   ```
   .ThemeFont = 0
   ```

8. Click the View Microsoft Excel button on the Standard toolbar in the Visual Basic Editor (the very first one with the green XL logo).

   Excel returns you to the Personal Macro Workbook, *PERSONAL.XLSB*.

9. Click the Book1 button on the Windows taskbar to switch to this blank workbook and then test out the changes to the Company_Name macro by pressing Ctrl+Shift+C.

   This time, the macro inserts the Mind Over Media, Inc. company name in the merged cell A1:E1 in 14-point bold using Times New Roman as the font.

10. Close the *Book1.xlsx* file without saving your changes and then click the Hide button on the View tab or press Alt+WH to hide the *PERSONAL.XLSB* workbook before you exit Excel. Be sure to click the Yes button this time when prompted to save your changes to the Personal Macro Workbook.

Adding a dialog box that processes user input

One of the biggest problems with recording macros is that any text or values that you have the macro enter for you in a worksheet or chart sheet can never vary thereafter. If you create a macro that enters the heading "Bob's Barbecue Pit" in the current cell of your worksheet, this is the only heading you'll ever get out of that macro. However, you can get around this inflexibility by using the InputBox function. When you run the macro, this Visual Basic function causes Excel to display an input dialog box where you can enter whatever title makes sense for the new worksheet. The macro then puts that text into the current cell and formats this text, if that's what you've trained your macro to do next.

To see how easy it is to use the InputBox function to add interactivity to an otherwise staid macro, follow along with the steps for converting the Company_Name macro that currently inputs the text "Mind Over Media, Inc." to one that actually prompts you for the name you want entered. The InputBox function uses the following syntax:

```
InputBox(prompt[,title][,default][,xpos][,ypos]
        [,helpfile,context])
```

The many arguments of the InputBox function include

- ✔ *Prompt*, which specifies the message (up to 1024 characters) that appears inside the input dialog box, prompting the user to enter a new value (or in this case, a new company name). To have the prompt message appear on different lines inside the dialog box, you enter the functions Chr(13) and Chr(10) in the text (Chr stands for Character and the number codes insert a carriage return to start a new line and a linefeed to position the insertion point at the beginning of the line, respectively).

- ✔ *Title* optional argument, which specifies what text to display in the input dialog box's title bar — if you don't specify a title argument, Excel displays the name of the application on the title bar.

- ✔ *Default* optional argument, which specifies the default response that automatically appears in text box at the bottom of the input dialog box. If you don't specify a default argument, the text box is empty in the input dialog box.

- ✔ *Xpos* and *ypos* optional arguments, which specify the horizontal distance from the left edge of the screen to the left edge of the dialog box and the vertical distance from the top edge of the screen to the top edge of the dialog box. If you don't specify these arguments, Excel centers the input dialog box horizontally and positions its one-third of the way down the screen vertically.

- ✔ *Helpfile* optional argument, which specifies the name of the custom Help file that you make available to the user to explain the workings of the input dialog box as well as the type of data it accepts.

- ✔ *Context* optional argument, which specifies the context number assigned to the help topic — note that when you specify a helpfile and context argument, Excel adds a Help button to the custom input dialog box that users can click to access the custom Help file in the Help window.

Solve It

Exercise 22-2: Making a Recorded Macro Interactive by Adding an Input Dialog Box

In Exercise 22-2, you get practice making your Company_Name macro interactive by adding an input dialog box that prompts the user to enter the name of the company to be inserted into the super-cell it creates.

1. Launch Excel to open a new Book1 workbook in the program. Then unhide the *PERSONAL.XLSB* workbook from Sheet1 of this workbook and open the Company_Name macro that you edited in the previous exercise in the Visual Basic Editor.

   Now, you're ready to add the commands to the Company_Name macro that display a dialog box prompting the user for the worksheet title to enter each time the macro is run.

2. Position the insertion point in the Code window at the beginning of the ActiveCell.FormulaR1C1 statement on line 8 in column 5 and then press Enter to insert a new line. Then, press the ↑ key to move the insertion point up to the beginning of the new blank line 8 in column 5.

   Now you're ready to create the three variables — InputPrompt, InputTitle, and DefaultText — that contain the values you want used as the *Prompt*, *Title*, and *Default* arguments of the InputBox function. You create all variables for the code at the beginning of the macro subroutine by declaring their names and setting them equal to the values you initially want used. Then, when you're ready to enter the InputBox function in the code, all you have to do is enter the variable names in the order of the InputBox arguments. Note that by using variables to supply the *Prompt*, *Title*, and *Default* arguments of the InputBox function, you avoid creating such a long line of code that it is not only hard to read, but hard to edit as well.

3. Type the following code on line 8 to create the InputPrompt variable and then press the Enter key to start a new line 9:

   ```
   InputPrompt = "Enter the title for this spreadsheet in the
           text box below and then click OK:"
   ```

   You have now defined a variable called InputPrompt that you will use as the *prompt* argument of the InputBox function.

4. Type the following code on line 9 to create the InputTitle variable and then press the Enter key to start a new line 10:

   ```
   InputTitle = "Spreadsheet Title"
   ```

   You have now defined a variable called InputTitle that you will use as the optional *Title* argument of the InputBox function.

5. Type the following code on line 10 to create the DefaultText variable and then press the Enter key to start a new line 11:

   ```
   DefaultText = "Mind Over Media, Inc."
   ```

You have now defined a variable called DefaultText that you will use as the optional *Default* argument of the InputBox function.

Next, you define a fourth variable, CompanyName. This variable actually contains the InputBox function using the InputPrompt, InputTitle, and DefaultText variables you just created as its prompt, title, and default arguments.

6. Type the following code on line 11 to create the CompanyName variable that contains the InputBox function:

```
CompanyName = InputBox(InputPrompt, InputTitle, DefaultText)
```

The last step is to replace the value, "Mind Over Media," in the ActiveCell. FormulaR1C1 property with the CompanyName variable (whose value is determined by whatever is input into the Company Name input dialog box), thus effectively replacing this constant in the macro with the means for making this input truly interactive.

7. Select "Mind Over Media, Inc." in line 12 and replace it with the **CompanyName** variable (with no quotation marks) so that this line contains

```
ActiveCell.FormulaR1C1 = CompanyName
```

8. Carefully check your changes to the code of the Company_Name macro against those in the first five lines shown in Figure 22-3. Then, when everything checks out, click File⇨Save PERSONAL.XLSB on the Visual Basic Editor menu bar or press Ctrl+S to save your changes.

Now you're ready to test out the interactive version of your Company_Name macro.

9. Click the View Microsoft Excel button on the Standard toolbar and then activate the Book1 workbook and test out the interactive version of the Company_Name macro by pressing Ctrl+Shift+C.

A Spreadsheet Title dialog box should appear, prompting you for the name of the spreadsheet.

10. Replace Mind Over Media, Inc. in the Spreadsheet Title dialog box with **ABC Corp. Sales** and then select the OK button.

The macro now enters ABC Corp. Sales as the worksheet title in 14-point bold type centered over the merged cell A1:E1 in Sheet1 of Book1.

11. Close the *Book1.xlsx* file without saving your changes, and then hide the *PERSONAL.XLSB* workbook and exit Excel. Be sure that you select the Yes button when prompted to save your changes to the Personal Macro Workbook.

Figure 22-3:
The Visual
Basic
Editor Code
window
after adding
new com-
mands to
make the
Company_
Name macro
interactive.

Creating User-Defined Functions

One of the best uses of Visual Basic for Applications in Excel is to create custom spread-sheet functions, also known as user-defined functions. User-defined functions are great because you don't have to access the Macro dialog box to run them. In fact, you enter them into your spreadsheets just like you do any of the other built-in spreadsheet functions, either with the Insert Function button on the Formula bar or by typing them directly into a cell.

To create a user-defined function, you must do the four following things:

- ✔ Create a new module sheet where the custom function is to be defined in the Visual Basic Editor by selecting its project in the Project Explorer and then choosing Insert⇨Module on the Visual Basic Editor Menu bar.

- ✔ Enter the name of the custom function and specify the names of the arguments that this function takes on the first line in the Code window. Note that you can't duplicate any built-in function names, such as SUM or AVERAGE, and so on, and you must list argument names in the order in which they are processed and enclosed in parentheses.

✔ Enter the formula, or set of formulas, that tells Excel how to calculate the custom function's result using the argument names listed in the Function command with whatever arithmetic operators or built-in functions are required to get the calculation made on the line or lines below.

✔ Indicate that you've finished defining the user-defined function by entering the End Function command on the last line.

To see how this procedure works in action, in the following exercise, you create a user-defined function that calculates the sales commissions for salespeople based on the number of sales they make in a month as well as the total amount of their monthly sales (they sell big-ticket items, such as RVs). Your custom Commission function has two arguments — TotalSales and ItemsSold — so that the first line of code on the module sheet in the Code window is

```
Function Commission(TotalSales,ItemsSold)
```

In determining how the commissions are actually calculated, you base the commission percentage on the number of sales made during the month. For five sales or fewer in a month, you pay a commission rate of 4.5 percent of the salesperson's total monthly sales; for sales of six or more, you pay a commission rate of 5 percent.

To define the formula section of the Commission custom function, you set up an IF construction. This IF construction is similar to the IF function you enter into a worksheet cell except that you use different lines in the macro code for the construction in the custom function. An ELSE statement separates the command that is performed if the expression is True from the command that is performed if the expression is False. The macro code is terminated by an END IF statement. To set the custom function so that your salespeople get 4.5 percent of total sales for five or fewer items sold and 5 percent of total sales for more than five items sold, you enter the following lines of code underneath the line with the Function command:

```
If ItemsSold <= 5 Then
    Commission = TotalSales * 0.045
Else
    Commission = TotalSales * 0.05
End If
```

Solve It

Exercise 22-3: Constructing a Custom Function in the Visual Basic Editor

In Exercise 22-3, you get practice using the Visual Basic Editor to create a custom function that you can then use in your Excel spreadsheets as you do the built-in functions.

1. Open the *Exercise22-3.xlsx* workbook file in the Chap22 folder the Excel 2007 Workbook folder on your hard disk.

This worksheet contains an RV Sales worksheet with the sales for three account representatives, Fred, Holly, and Jack, for which you will create the user-defined Commission function.

2. Unhide the *PERSONAL.XLSB* workbook and then click Visual Basic button on the Developer tab or press Alt+F11 to open the Visual Basic Editor window with a new module sheet from the *PERSONAL.XLSB* workbook.

The Visual Basic Editor opens with the code in the last-accessed module selected.

3. Select Insert⇨Module on the Visual Basic Editor's menu bar to insert a new module into the Visual Basic Editor.

The new module named Module2 is listed in the Project Explorer and Properties windows.

4. Select Module2 following (Name) in the Properties window and then replace Module2 with **Commission_UDF** and press Enter.

Excel renames the Module2 sheet to Commission_UDF and this module name now appears above Module1 in the hierarchy in the Project Explorer window.

5. Click the insertion point in the Code window and then type the following code on Line1:

```
Function Commission(TotalSales, ItemsSold)
```

6. Press Enter to start a new line and Tab to indent; enter the following code on line 2 starting at column 5:

```
If ItemsSold <= 5 Then
```

Excel automatically inserts End Function command in Line 3.

7. Press Enter to start a new line and then Tab again to indent further, and then enter the following indented code on line 3 starting at column 9:

```
Commission = TotalSales * 0.045
```

8. Press Enter to start a new line and then Shift+Tab to outdent; enter the following indented code on line 4 starting at column 5:

```
Else
```

9. Press Enter to start a new line and then Tab to indent; enter the following indented code on line 5 starting at column 9:

```
Commission = TotalSales * 0.05
```

10. Press Enter to start a new line and then Shift+Tab to outdent; enter the following indented code on line 6 starting at column 5:

```
End If
```

Check the lines of code in your custom Commission function against those shown in Figure 22-4. When they check out, proceed to step 11.

11. Choose File⇨Save PERSONAL.XLSB on the Visual Basic Editor menu bar to save your custom function.

Now you're ready to return to your *Exercise22-3.xlsx* workbook where, in the next exercise, you test out your new user-defined Commission function.

12. Click the View Microsoft Excel button on the Standard toolbar in the Visual Basic Editor and then hide the Personal Macro Workbook *PERSONAL.XLSB*.

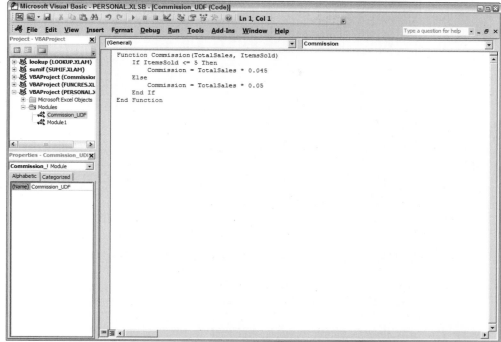

Figure 22-4:
The Visual
Basic Editor
Code
window
after adding
the code
for the
new user-
defined
Commission
function on
its own
module
sheet.

Using a custom function in your spreadsheet

The great thing about custom functions is that they can be inserted into your worksheets with your old friend the Insert Function button on the Excel Formula bar. To find your custom function in the Insert Function dialog box, you just need to select User Defined as the function category.

Solve It | **Exercise 22-4: Constructing Spreadsheet Formulas with a Custom Function**

In Exercise 22-4, you get practice testing out and using the custom Commission function you created in the previous exercise.

1. Make sure that the RV Sales worksheet in your Exercise22-3.xlsx workbook is active. Then click cell E5 in the RV Sales worksheet before you click the Insert Function button on the Formula Bar.

The Insert Function dialog box appears, where you select User Defined as the Function category. Scroll down until you see the name of your custom function as PERSONAL.XLSB!Commission and click its name in the list. Then click OK.

The Function Arguments dialog box for your PERSONAL.XLSB!Commission function appears. This dialog box contains two argument text boxes: TotalSales and ItemsSold.

2. While the insertion point is in the TotalSales argument text box, click cell C4 in the worksheet that contains Fred's total sales and then press Tab to select the ItemsSold argument text box below. Select cell C5 in the worksheet that contains the count of Fred's sales and then click the OK button.

The custom commission function computes Fred's commission as $2,655 (using the 4.5% commission rate because the number of his sales is below five).

3. Use your custom Commission function to compute the sales commissions for Holly in cell E10.

Select cell C9 as the TotalSales argument and cell C10 as the ItemsSold argument for this Commission function.

4. Save your changes to the RV Sales worksheet in a new workbook file named **RV Sales – commissionudf.xlsx** in your Excel 2007 Practice folder and then leave the workbook open for Exercise 22-5.

Saving custom functions in add-in files

The only limitation to the user-defined functions that you save as part of a regular workbook file or the Personal Macro Workbook file is that when you enter them directly into a cell (without the use of the Insert Function dialog box), you must preface their function names with their filenames. So, for example, if you want to type in the custom Commission function that's saved in the Personal Macro Workbook and you enter the following formula:

```
=Commission(C9,C10)
```

(assuming that cell C9 contains the total sales and cell C10 contains the number of items sold), Excel returns the #NAME? error value to the cell. If you then edit the function to include the Personal Macro Workbook's filename as follows:

```
=Personal.xlsb!Commission(C9,C10)
```

Excel then calculates the sales commission based on the TotalSales in C9 and the ItemsSold in C10, returning this calculated value to the cell containing this user-defined function.

To be able to omit the filename from the custom functions you create when you enter them directly into a cell, you need to save the workbook file that contains them as an add-in file (with an .xlam filename extension). Then, after you've saved the workbook with your user-defined functions as an add-in file, you can start entering them into any worksheet without their filename qualifier after activating the add-in in the Add-Ins dialog box.

Solve It

Exercise 22-5: Saving a Custom Function as an Excel Add-In

In Exercise 22-5, you get practice saving your custom Commission function as an Excel add-in that you activate so that you can enter the function directly into a worksheet cell without having to preface the function name with the PERSONAL.XLSB designation.

1. With the *RV Sales – commissionudf.xlsx* workbook you created in Exercise 22-4 open, unhide your *PERSONAL.XLSB* workbook and then open the Visual Basic Editor window.

   Excel opens up the Visual Basic Editor with your Commission_UDF module selected.

2. Choose the Tools⇨VBAProject Properties menu command.

   The Editor opens the VBAProject - Project Properties dialog box containing a General and a Protection tab.

3. Click the Protection tab and then select the Lock Project for Viewing check box.

   Putting a check mark in this check box prevents other users from viewing the custom functions so that they can't make any changes to them. Next, you add a password that prevents them from removing the view protection status.

4. Click the Password text box and enter **cerrado** (Spanish for closed) as the password there. Then click the Confirm Password text box and reenter **cerrado** as the password exactly as you entered it in the text box above before you select OK.

   Now you're ready to return to the worksheet, where you can add a title and description for the new add-in file.

5. Click the View Microsoft Excel button on Visual Basic Editor Standard toolbar.

   Before saving the *PERSONAL.XLSB* workbook as an add-in file, you should add a title and description of the user-defined Commission function it contains (this information then appears in the Add-Ins dialog box whenever you select the add-in file).

6. Activate the PERSONAL.XLSB workbook file and then click Office button | Prepare | Properties or press Alt+FEP to open the Document Properties pane at the top of the worksheet.

   This pane contains seven text boxes: Author, Title, Subject, Keywords, Category, Status, and Comments.

7. Fill in the following information in Document Properties pane before you click the pane's Close button:

   - **Custom Commission Function** in the Title text box

   - **UDF** in the Keywords text box

   - **Add-In** in the Category text box

   - **Computes sales commissions based on the total and number of sales** in the Comments text box

8. Click Office button | Save As or press Alt+FA to open the Save As dialog box. Then, scroll almost all the way to the bottom of the Save as Type drop-down list in the Save As dialog box and click the Excel Add-In (*.xlam) option.

   Doing this selects the AddIns folder in the Save In drop-down list box, showing the names of any add-in files that you've saved there.

9. Click the File Name combo box and change PERSONAL to **Commission** (without changing the .xlam filename extension) before you click the Save button.

   After saving your workbook as an add-in file, you're ready to activate the add-in so that you can enter its user-defined functions in any worksheet.

10. Hide the Personal Macro Workbook, *PERSONAL.XLSB*, to return to your RV Sales worksheet in the *RV Sales – commissionudf.xlsx* workbook. Open the Excel Options dialog box (Alt+FI), click the Add-ins tab and then click the Go button when Excel Add-Ins is selected in the Manage drop-down button.

    Excel opens the Add-Ins dialog box.

11. Click the Custom Commission Function check box to put a check mark in it before you click OK.

    If the name of the Custom Commission Function doesn't automatically appear in the Add-Ins Available list box, click the Browse button. Next, click Commission.xlam file in the AddIns folder in the Browse dialog box and then click OK to add it to the list.

    Excel closes the Add-Ins dialog box and returns you to the RV Sales worksheet where you can test out directly entering the custom Commission function into the formula you're constructing in a cell.

12. Click cell E18 and then type **=commission(**. Then click cell C17 with Jack's totals sales to make it the TotalSales argument for the Commission function. Then, type a **,** (comma) to separate this argument from the next. Click cell C18 with the count of Jack's sales to make it the ItemsSold argument for the Commission function and then type a **)** — close parenthesis.

    The formula in cell E18 and on the Formula bar should now read

    ```
    =commission(C17,C18)
    ```

13. Click the Enter button on the Formula bar.

    Excel accepts the formula `=commission(C17,C18)` — without the PERSONAL.XLSB filename designation — entering it into Formula bar and returning the value $9,100 to the cell.

14. Enter a formula in cell E19 that sums the sales commissions in cells E5, E10, and E18.

    Create a formula that uses the SUM function with these three cell references as its number arguments.

15. Select cell A1 and then save your changes to the RV Sales worksheet(Ctrl+S). Exit Excel, being sure to save your changes to the hidden *PERSONAL.XLSB* workbook file when prompted to do so during the closing of the program.

Part VII
The Part of Tens

The 5th Wave   By Rich Tennant

Oh come on —
how fatal
can it be?

FATAL
ERROR

In this part . . .

The Part of Tens brings together tips to help you apply your workbook experience to your own work in Excel. Here, you get a list of what I consider to be the ten best features in Excel 2007 as well as tips on how to use Excel like a pro. The appendix tells you everything you need to know to get the most out of the material on this book's CD-ROM.

Chapter 23

Top Ten Features in Excel 2007

*I*f you're looking for a quick rundown on what's new and what's cool in Excel 2007, look no further! Here it is — my official Top Ten Features list. Just a cursory glance down the list tells you that the thrust of the features is graphics, graphics, graphics!

The Excel Ribbon

The Ribbon is the heart of the new Excel 2007 user interface. Based on a core of standard tabs, various so-called contextual tabs are added as needed in formatting and editing of specific elements (such as data tables, charts, pivot tables, and graphic objects). The Ribbon brings together almost every command you're going to need when performing particular tasks in Excel. Go to Exercises 1-1 and 1-2 in Chapter 1 for basic practice in locating and selecting commands on the Excel Ribbon.

Conditional Formatting

Technically, conditional formatting is not a new Excel feature, having existed in many of the previous versions. However, the conditional formatting in Excel 2007 is so vastly improved that you might as well considered it to be new. In addition to giving you the ability to define formatting when the values in cells meet certain conditions, you can now instantly apply one of many different Data Bars, Color Scales, and Icon Sets to the cell selection merely by clicking the set's thumbnail in their respective pop-up palettes. When you apply a set of Data Bars to a cell range, the length of each bar in the cell represents its value relative to the others. When you apply a set of Color Scales, each shade of color in the cell represents its value relative to the others. And when you apply one of the Icon Sets, each icon in the cell represents its value relative to the others. See Chapter 3 for details on setting up conditional formatting in your spreadsheets.

Cell Styles

Cell Styles is another feature that, although technically not brand new in Excel 2007, has finally come into its own in this version. In place of the six measly and bland cell styles offered in the previous versions of Excel, Excel 2007 offers more than 40 colorful ready-made styles that offer you a rich and varied choice in formatting that can really spruce up your spreadsheets in very little time.

Moreover, these are styles you can preview in the worksheet with Live Preview (discussed later in this chapter) to see how they look on the data before you apply them and which you apply to the cell selection quickly and easily by clicking its thumbnail in Cell Styles gallery. See Exercise 3-8 in Chapter 3 for practice selecting and applying styles from the new Cell Styles gallery.

Formatting and Editing from the Home Tab

The Home tab of the new Excel Ribbon literally brings home all the commonly-used formatting and editing features. Gone are the days when you had to fish for the right button on some long drawn-out toolbar or on some partially-deployed pull-down menu. Now all you have to do is find the group that holds the command button you need and click it — what could be easier! See Exercises 3-1 through 3-5 and Exercises 3-9 through 3-11 in Chapter 3 for more practice formatting data with command buttons in the Font, Alignment, Number, Styles and Cells groups on the Home tab. See Exercises 5-5, 5-6, and 5-8 in Chapter 5 for practice using the editing commands in the Clipboard, Cells, and Editing groups on this tab.

Charts Directly from the Insert Tab

Charts have been a part of Excel going back more than a decade but it feels like not until Excel 2007 did they come into their own. Excel 2007 retires the Chart Wizard and in its place offers you direct access to all the major types of charts on the Insert tab of the Ribbon. Simply select the data to be charted, click the command button for the chart type on the Insert tab and then select the style you want for that chart type. Presto! You have a really professional chart that, thanks to the many command buttons and galleries on the Design, Layout, and Format tabs, can be completed in no time at all! See Exercises 15-1 through 15-5 in Chapter 15 for practice creating and formatting charts with these Ribbon commands.

Format As Table

This brand new feature is a real keeper. By formatting a table of data with one of the many table styles available on its drop-down gallery, you're assured that all new entries made to the table are going to be formatted in the exactly same manner as others in similar positions in the table and are automatically considered as part of the table when it comes to sorting or filtering the data. (Filtering the data is made easy by the automatic addition of filter buttons to the top row of column headings.) Go to Exercise 3-3 in Chapter 3 for practice on converting a regular cell range into a table and then formatting its data using the Table Styles gallery. See Exercise 17-3 in Chapter 17 for practice using these filter buttons to sort the data in a table and Exercise 17-7 for practice using them to filter its data.

The Zoom Slider on the Status Bar

So, how'd we ever get along without the new Zoom slider that's now always there to use on the Excel 2007 Status bar? Instead of having to select a new magnification percentage for the worksheet from a drop-down menu on some obscure Zoom tool (something you can still do with the Zoom button on the View tab, if you really want to), you can zoom in and out on the spreadsheet in the blink of an eye (actually faster) simply by dragging the Zoom slider right or left. Go to Exercise 5-1 in Chapter 5 for practice using the nifty, new Zoom slider in conjunction with frozen panes and custom views to keep all your spreadsheet data clearly in focus.

Page Layout View

Page Layout View in the Excel worksheet is just what the doctor ordered when it comes to visualizing the paging of printed reports. When you turn on this view by clicking the Page Layout View button on the Status bar, Excel doesn't just show the page breaks as measly dotted lines as in earlier versions but as actual separations. In addition, the program shows the margins for each page including headers and footers defined for the report (which you can both define and edit directly in the margin areas while the program is in this view) and as an extra nice touch throws in a pair of horizontal and vertical rulers to accompany the standard column and row headers. Couple this great feature with the Zoom slider and the Page Break Preview feature and you're going to actually enjoy getting the spreadsheet ready to print. See Exercise 4-1 and 4-3 in Chapter 4 for some hands-on practice using Page Layout view to check out pages and define headers and footers for your printed reports.

Style Galleries

Excel 2007 is jammed full of different style galleries that make it a snap to apply new sophisticated (and, in many cases, very colorful) formatting to tables and lists of data, charts, and various and sundry graphics you add to your worksheets. Coupled with the Live Preview feature (discussed later in this chapter), Excel's style galleries go a long way towards encouraging you to create better looking and a whole lot more colorful and interesting spreadsheets. You get plenty of practice using style galleries in Exercises 3-3 and 3-4 in Chapter 3, Exercises 15-3 and 15-4 in Chapter 15, and Exercises 16-4 through 16-6 in Chapter 16.

Live Preview

You simply can't say enough about Live Preview and how much easier it makes formatting the worksheet. Live Preview works with all the style galleries as well as Font and Font Size pull-down menus in the Font group on the Home tab. It enables you to see how the data in the current cell selection would look with a particular formatting, font, or font size before you actually apply the formatting to the range.

All you have to do is mouse over the thumbnails in the drop-down menu or gallery to see how each of its styles will look on your actual data. As an extra nice feature, many of the larger style galleries sport spinner buttons that enable you to bring new rows of thumbnails in the gallery into view so that you can preview their styles without obscuring any part of the cell selection (as would be the case if you actually open the gallery by clicking its More drop-down button). And when you finally do see the formatting that fits your data to a tee, all you have to do is click its thumbnail to apply it immediately to the selected cell range.

Check out Exercises 3-3 and 3-4 for some practice using Live Preview to apply various font sizes to a table of data before selecting the one to use.

Chapter 24

Top Ten Tips for Using Excel Like a Pro

● ●

In This Chapter

▶ Generating new workbooks from templates

▶ Creating data series with AutoFill

▶ Trapping error values in their original formulas

● ●

*P*erforming the exercises in this workbook gives you an opportunity to work with the most important features of the program, especially those related to building and maintaining spreadsheets. To help you make the most of this hands-on experience, this chapter brings together ten of the most important ways to work efficiently and design the best possible spreadsheets as you start to work on your own.

Generating New Workbooks from Templates

Whenever possible, generate new workbooks from templates that are available for Excel. Don't forget that the program provides you with a whole host of useful templates from Microsoft Office Online in categories ranging from Agendas to Time Sheets that you can start using right out of the box. To do so, just open the New Workbook dialog box by clicking Office button | New or pressing Alt+FN. In addition to the templates listed in the various categories in the New Workbook dialog box, you can search Microsoft Office Online for other templates, which you can then download for use in Excel.

If you can't find a readymade template online that comes close to generating the type of spreadsheet you need, you can create your own template from a sample worksheet that you build from scratch. In this workbook, you enter the formulas along with all standard headings for the data table(s) that the spreadsheet requires, format and secure the tables as needed. Then you save the final workbook as a template file by selecting Excel Template (*.xltx) as the file type in the Save As Type drop-down list in the Save As dialog box (Office button | Save As or Alt+FA).

Organizing Spreadsheet Data on Different Worksheets

As you know, each new workbook that you open contains three identical blank worksheets into which you can enter the data required for your spreadsheet. Unfortunately, too many times, new spreadsheet designers restrict all data entry to the first worksheet so that they end up with one super-colossal spreadsheet with its data spread far and wide all over the entire worksheet. Although some spreadsheets may require the single-sheet treatment, more often than not, the only reason that every bit of data gets put on one sheet is simply that the spreadsheet designer doesn't even stop to consider using a multi-sheet layout.

By utilizing a multi-sheet layout for your workbook, you not only end up with a more manageable worksheet but with one whose data tables and lists are much easier to print individually. Moreover, with just a little forethought, you can set up the data on the successive sheets of the workbook so that when all of them are printed together, the pages of the report naturally present the data and their findings in a clear and cohesive manner.

In designing a spreadsheet that uses a multi-sheet layout, remember that you can add additional worksheets to the workbook (simply click the Insert Worksheet button on the tab following the last sheet in the workbook or press Shift+F11) as needed — the only restriction to the total number of sheets in a workbook is the amount of computer memory available to keep the workbook open. You can also rearrange the sheets in a workbook simply by dragging their sheet tabs to the desired position in the workbook. You can also rename them with much more descriptive names by double-clicking them.

Keep in mind that you can color-code the worksheet tabs in your workbook. To assign a new color to a sheet tab, right-click the tab and then click Tab Color on its shortcut menu. Next, click a color square in either of its two color palettes that appear on the menu's continuation menu to select a standard color or click the More Colors option to open the Custom tab of the Colors dialog box. In the Custom tab, you can assign a custom color by specifying its Red, Green, and Blue values or by dragging the color and intensity sliders before you click OK.

When creating a multi-sheet spreadsheet, consider making the first worksheet a summary worksheet complete with hyperlinks that you or other users of the workbook can use to navigate quickly and directly to important tables and lists on the various worksheets.

Creating Data Series with AutoFill

One of the marks of a true Excel pro is her reliance on the AutoFill feature to quickly generate the data series needed in the spreadsheet. Remember that Excel is capable of creating many series such as months of the year, days of the week, and text with numbers (such as Item 100, Item 101, and the like) simply by entering the first entry in the series in a cell and then dragging the Fill handle down the rows of its column or across the columns of its row to fill out the successive entries in that series (as indicated by the ScreenTip that appears beneath the Fill handle).

Also keep in mind that you can use the Fill handle to generate series that use increments other than 1 (which is the default assumed when you use the Fill handle). All you have to do is make two data entries that indicate the increment that the series should use (such as Monday and Wednesday or 50 and 48), and then select both cells before you drag the Fill handle down or across to create the series.

Further, you can define custom data series whose items don't change by a certain increment (such as a series of company locations like Chicago, Pittsburgh, Dallas, and Boston) and then generate the custom series in a spreadsheet by simply entering its first item in a cell and then dragging the Fill handle as you would with any incremented series.

To create the custom list, you open the Excel Options dialog box (Office button | Excel Options or Alt+FI) and then click the Edit Custom Lists button on its Popular tab to open the Custom Lists dialog box. There, you type the individual items in the series (terminated by the Enter key) in the List Entries list box in the order in which they are to be generated with the Fill handle and then select the Add button. Alternatively, if this custom series already exists in a cell range somewhere in the spreadsheet, select the cell range in the worksheet after selecting the Import List from the Cells text box and then select Import.

Using Range Names

The use of range names in a spreadsheet provides several important benefits; perhaps the most important of which is that you can use the range name to both move and simultaneously select the cell range in a flash no matter where this range is located in the entire workbook. After a range is named, all you have to do to select the range is to choose its range name from the Name box drop-down list on the Formula bar.

This method of selecting cell ranges can be a tremendous time-saver when you're dealing with a table or list of data that you find yourself referring to or editing on a regular basis. This is all the more true if the named range's data tables or lists are located in columns and rows in some distant region of a worksheet.

Remember that you can use range names to select cell ranges with data tables or lists that you print on a regular basis. All you have to do is select the cell range with the Name box, and then open the Print dialog box (Ctrl+P) and select the Selection option button in the Print What section before you select the OK button.

The second important use for range names is to define and name a constant (such as a tax rate or interest percentage) whose value you need to refer to in the formulas you're about to build in a data table or list but which you don't want to enter in the worksheet as a separate cell entry. To do this, open the New Name dialog box (Formulas | Define Name or Alt+MMD) and enter the name for the constant in the Name text box. Next, set the name equal to the value or the formula that calculates the value you want used in the Refers To text box before you select OK. Then, to refer to the constant in a formula you're building, click its name on the drop-down menu that appears when you click the Use in Formula button on the Formulas tab or press Alt+MS.

The final important use for range names is in documenting the functioning of the formulas in your data tables in a spreadsheet. You can do this by having Excel apply the table's row and column headings to the cells of the table. Simply select the table including the cells with the row and column headings before you open the Create Names From Selection dialog box (Formulas | Create From Selection or Alt+MC). Next, select the appropriate check boxes (Top Row, Left Column, Bottom Row, or Right Column) that contain the row and column headings before you select OK. Then, to replace the cell addresses in the formulas in this table with the new range names, click the Apply Names option on the Define Name button's drop-down menu to open the Apply Names dialog box (Alt+MMA). With the Use Row and Column Names check box selected, select the OK button.

Freezing Column and Row Headings

When it comes to the size of your monitor versus the size of your worksheet, your monitor loses hands down every time. This means that in all except the most concise data tables, the column and row headings that identify the entries in its cells soon disappear from view as you make or edit entries in rows lower and columns further to the right than the original screen can contain. To prevent this from happening by keeping a table's or list's headings on the screen at all times no matter how long or wide the table or list becomes, you need to freeze these headings on the screen. To do this, position the cell cursor in the cell located immediately to the right of the column containing the row headings and immediately below the row with the column headings. Then choose View | Freeze Panes | Freeze Panes on the Ribbon (Alt+WFF).

Don't forget that you can save the frozen panes you set up in a spreadsheet as part of a custom view for the worksheet that you can resume at any time simply by selecting its name in the Custom Views dialog box (View | Custom Views or Alt+WC).

Preventing Data Entry Errors with Data Validation

Excel's Data Validation feature makes it easy to prevent users from entering the wrong type of data or invalid values in a particular cell range of the spreadsheet. You can also limit data entry errors by using Data Validation to compel the user to select the entry for a cell from only those values you display on the cell's drop-down list.

To restrict data entry for the selected cell, you select the type of entry that is allowed in the cell on the Allow drop-down list (Whole Number, Decimal, List, Date, Time, Text Length, or Custom) on the Settings tab of the Data Validation dialog box (Data | Data Validation or Alt+AVV). Depending upon the type of entry you allow, you then restrict the range of allowable values. For example, if you select Date as the allowed entry type, you then specify the start and end dates that the cell entry must be between.

By selecting List as the entry type, you're able to create a cell drop-down list that contains the complete list of allowed entries. That way, the spreadsheet user doesn't have to type anything in order to make the cell entry. This type of cell data validation is perfect when its data entry is restricted to a relatively short list whose values must be consistent and spelled correctly (as when sorting or filtering data).

Note, however, that you must enter the list of allowed entries you want to appear on the cell's drop-down list in a cell range somewhere in a worksheet prior to setting up this kind of List entry in the Data Validation dialog box. You then specify the allowable entries for the cell drop-down list by selecting the Source text box on the Settings tab and then selecting the cell range containing the allowed entries in the worksheet.

When setting up Data Validation for a cell, you can also define an input message displayed when the user selects the cell and an error alert message that is displayed when the user attempts to make an invalid data entry. The input message instructs the user on what range of values are allowed in the cell just as the error alert message informs the user why the entry he tried to complete was not allowed.

After setting up Data Validation for a single blank cell, you can then copy the validation settings to an entire range of cells in the spreadsheet using any of the standard copy methods (copy and paste or drag-and-drop).

Trapping Error Values in Their Original Formulas

Error values are not only unsightly but, because they spread so easily to other dependent formulas throughout the spreadsheet, they can be difficult to eradicate. The most professional spreadsheet designers therefore take steps whenever possible to prevent the spread of error values across the spreadsheet by trapping them at their source. The most famous example of where this kind of error trapping is needed occurs in division formulas where the divisor is a cell reference that at times can be blank. As you remember, blank cells as well as cells with text entries carry a zero (0) value as far as formula computations are concerned, so that if they serve as the divisor in a division calculation in a formula, that formula returns the #DIV/0! error value to the cell.

As you found out if you performed Exercise 13-4 in Chapter 13, you can prevent Excel from returning this or any other kind of error value (including #N/A) to the cell by making the division calculation itself the value_if_false argument of an IF function that uses the ISERROR logical function in its logical_test argument to test for the return of an error value, and the value 0 (zero) as its value_if_true argument.

So, for example, if cell K7 is the divisor of a division computation and it could be blank at times, therefore causing the division calculation to return #DIV/0!, you could prevent this and block its spread to other formulas dependent upon its result with the addition of the following IF function:

```
=IF(ISERROR(B7/$K$7),0,B7/$K$7)
```

In this case, Excel returns zero (0) to the cell in place of any error value, performing the actual division only when it's safe to do so.

You can then use Conditional Formatting (see Chapter 3) to flag all error-trapping formulas that return zero (0) — instead of the desired calculated result — with a special type of color or font. Then, you can use the Find feature (see Chapter 5) to locate all the cells in the worksheet that now sport this special formatting when it comes time to fix their cell references so that their formulas return values other than zero.

Saving Memory by Using Array Formulas

In Exercise 7-5 in Chapter 7, you got some experience with constructing array formulas. As you may recall, an *array formula* is one that constructs the same type of calculation in an entire range of cells in a data table at the time you create it. As a result, you don't go through the normal process of first constructing a master formula and then copying to all the other cells in the table that need to perform the same type of calculation.

Array formulas offer two distinct advantages over normal formulas:

- ✔ Array formulas enable you to create all the duplicate formulas needed in the table in a single operation

- ✔ Array formulas require a lot less computer memory to store than individual copies of a single master formula

It is actually the latter, memory-related benefit that makes array formulas so useful. By building array formulas, you can save substantial amounts of computer memory (remember that Excel must be able to load every bit of data in a workbook into memory in order to be able to open the file at all — it does not perform like other programs that can load just parts of a document into memory, switching them out as you work). This memory savings is important in really large workbooks as it enables you to add more data to the spreadsheet as well as keeps Excel from completely bogging down when you open spreadsheets for editing or printing.

Controlling the Display of Data in Tables through Outlines

Many of the spreadsheets you create and maintain in Excel require more columns and rows than can possibly fit on a single screen (even with a really large monitor) unless you select a zoom magnification percentage so small that it's impossible to read its data. In some spreadsheets, such as Regional Income and CG Media Sales tables that you worked with in several different exercises, you can easily reclaim some of this screen estate as well as maintain a great degree of flexibility in how much of the data to display by outlining the tables.

When you outline a typical data table (Data | Group | Auto Outline or Alt+AGA), Excel adds outline buttons to both the rows and columns of the table (that appear in the worksheet's row and column headers). You can then use these outline buttons to control how much of table data is displayed on the screen (accomplished by hiding and unhiding particular rows and columns of the table).

Outlines are perfect for tables such as the Regional Income and CG Media Sales tables, where the monthly income and sales data are naturally summarized by quarterly and annual totals for the various regions and products being tracked. With the help of the level outline buttons, you can quickly collapse the table down to the grand totals or quarterly totals and then just as easily completely expand it to display all the monthly income and sales data as well.

Outlining data tables like these makes it a snap to print and chart just a selected part of their data. For example, to create a chart using only the quarterly totals in the regional income table, all you have to do is use the level outline buttons to display only columns with totals in the data table and then select the quarterly data prior to clicking the desired chart type button on the Ribbon's Insert tab.

Using View Side by Side to Work with Two Workbooks

To be a true Excel pro, you need to be comfortable working not only with the spreadsheet data on different sheets of the same workbook but on sheets of different workbooks as well. One way in which Excel facilitates this is through the program's ability to open side-by-side windows on two different workbooks that you have open at a time.

When you're only dealing with two open workbooks (which is most often the case as any more than two open at a time are pretty hard to keep track of), you can create horizontal windows (one on top of the other), each displaying a part of a different workbook simply by clicking the View Side by Side button on the View tab or pressing Alt+WB.

While the two workbook windows are open in Excel, you can select different worksheets and scroll to different regions in either one by using its sheet tabs and scroll bars that appear at the edge of the window when you make its workbook active (either by clicking the window's title bar or one of the cells of its worksheets).

To move or copy data between the open workbook files, you have a choice between using the drag-and-drop or copy-and-paste method. To use drag-and-drop, select the data to be moved or copied in the worksheet of one window and then drag the outline of the cell selection to the desired cell in the worksheet displayed in the other window. If you want to copy the cell selection, rather than move it, to the workbook in the other window, you must remember to hold down the Ctrl key as you drag its outline to its new position, releasing the Ctrl key only when you're in position and ready to drop the copied data into place.

Appendix

About the CD

*T*he CD-ROM for this book contains practice files that enable you to walk through the exercises in this book yourself, as well as demos that take you through important tasks and Excel features you'll find useful. In this Appendix, I tell you everything you need to know to get the most out of the tools in this CD-ROM.

System Requirements

Make sure that your computer meets the minimum system requirements shown in the following list. If your computer doesn't match up to most of these requirements, you may have problems using the software and files on the CD. For the latest and greatest information, please refer to the ReadMe file located at the root of the CD-ROM.

- A PC with a 500 megahertz (MHz) or faster processor
- Microsoft Windows XP with Service Pack (SP) 2 or Vista
- Microsoft Excel 2007
- At least 256MB of total RAM installed on your computer; for best performance, we recommend at least 1GB
- A CD-ROM drive
- A sound card
- A 1024x768 or higher resolution monitor

If you need more information on the basics, check out these books published by Wiley Publishing, Inc.: *PCs For Dummies*, by Dan Gookin; or *Windows XP For Dummies* and *Microsoft Windows Vista For Dummies*, all by Andy Rathbone.

Using the CD

To install the items from the CD to your hard drive, follow these steps.

1. **Insert the CD into your computer's CD-ROM drive. The license agreement appears.**

    Note to Windows users: The interface won't launch if you have autorun disabled. In that case, click Start➪Run (for Windows Vista, Start➪All Programs ➪Accessories ➪ Run). In the dialog box that appears, type **D:\Start.exe**. (Replace D with the proper letter if your CD drive uses a different letter. If you don't know the letter, see how your CD drive is listed under My Computer.) Click OK.

2. **Read through the license agreement, and then click the Accept button if you want to use the CD.**

    The CD interface appears. The interface allows you to install the exercise Excel workbook files and self-running Essential Technique and Excel Feature Demos on your hard disk with just a click of a button (or two).

What You'll Find on the CD

The following sections are arranged by category and provide a summary of the practice files and self-running demos you'll find on the CD. If you need help with installing the items provided on the CD, refer back to the installation instructions in the preceding section.

The material on the CD-ROM is arranged in three folders:

- ✔ **Excel 2007 Workbook**: This folder contains 20 subfolders (named Chap2, Chap3, and so on) for all of the workbook chapters except for Chapters 1, 21, 23, and 24, which don't require any practice files. These subfolders contain sample Excel workbook files that you use to complete many of the exercises in a particular chapter as well as those that containing completed worksheets that you use to check your work.

- ✔ **Essential Technique Demos**: This folder contains seven self-running demos that show you the Essential Techniques that you need to know in order to perform general tasks involving Excel and Windows, such as opening an existing Excel workbook file for editing, or saving an Excel workbook file with a new filename and in a different folder.

- ✔ **Excel Feature Demos**: This folder contains 30 self-running demos that highlight various features specifically covered in certain exercises in this workbook, such as using the Ribbon interface, copying a formula, creating a chart, and so on.

Workbook Exercise Files

This CD-ROM contains practice files that can be used in conjunction with the exercises. All the practice material for the book is all located in a single Excel 2007 Workbook folder on the CD-ROM. This Excel 2007 Workbook folder contains 20 chapter subfolders (Chap2 through Chap20, and Chap22). These subfolders contain all the practice files you need to complete the exercises in this workbook.

Before you start working through the exercises in this workbook, I suggest that you copy this Excel Workbook folder to the My Documents or Documents folder on your computer's hard drive as follows:

1. Insert the CD-ROM into your computer's CD/DVD drive.

2. Click the Start button on the Windows taskbar and then click My Computer (Windows XP) or Computer (Vista) on the Start menu to open this window in Windows Explorer.

3. Right-click the icon for your CD/DVD drive and select Explore to open its contents in the Windows Explorer window.

4. Click the Excel 2007 Workbook folder icon and then press Ctrl+C.

5. Click the My Documents (Windows XP) or Documents (Vista) link in the left pane of the Windows Explorer window and then press Ctrl+V.

You are now ready to tackle any of the exercises in the workbook using the practice files saved in the particular chapter subfolders within the Excel 2007 Workbook folder inside the My Documents or Documents folder on your hard disk.

When you're finished doing the exercises and no longer need access to the practice files, go ahead and delete the Excel 2007 Workbook folder and all its contents by dropping it in the Recycle bin on the Windows desktop.

Essential Technique Demos

This CD-ROM contains Essential Technique self-running demos that you can play to prepare you for doing the exercises in this workbook. All the Essential Technique demos are located in a single Essential Technique Demos folder on the CD-ROM. You can play these demos on the CD or copy the Essential Technique Demos folder to your hard disk and play them from there.

To play one of these Essential Technique demos, double-click the demo's file icon or right-click it and then click Open on its shortcut menu. Windows then opens the demo in its own window and begins playing. The demo window contains a title bar at the top showing the name of the Essential Technique demo and a playback controller at the bottom of the window. This controller contains buttons that you can click to loop the demo, pause the demo, go forward or backward one frame, turn the audio on or off, turn on or off close captioning, exit the demo, and display general information about the demo.

These Essential Technique demos in the Essential Techniques folder on the CD-ROM include

- ✔ **File Open on Windows Vista.exe:** This demo shows you how to open Excel workbook files when you're running Excel 2007 on the Windows XP operating system.

- ✔ **File Open on Windows XP.exe:** This demo shows you how to open Excel workbook files when you're running Excel 2007 on the Windows Vista operating system.

- ✔ **File Save As on Windows Vista.exe:** This demo shows you how to save existing workbook files under a new filename and folder when you're running Excel 2007 on the Windows XP operating system.

- ✔ **File Save As on Windows XP.exe:** This demo shows you how to save existing workbook files under a new filename and folder when you're running Excel 2007 on the Windows Vista operating system.

- ✔ **File Save on Windows Vista.exe:** This demo shows you how to name and save new workbook files in the proper folder when you're running Excel 2007 on the Windows XP operating system.

- ✔ **File Save on Windows XP.exe:** This demo shows you to name and save new workbook files in the proper folder when you're running Excel 2007 on the Windows Vista operating system.

- ✔ **View Side by Side.exe:** This demo shows you how use Excel's Side by Side feature to compare worksheets in different workbook files in windows one on top of the other. Note that although this demo was created running Excel 2007 on Windows XP, it is fundamentally the same if you're running Excel 2007 on Windows Vista (except that you open your Documents folder in Excel's Open dialog box rather than My Documents).

Excel feature demos

This CD-ROM contains Excel feature self-running feature demos that can be played to prepare you for doing particular exercises. All the Excel feature demonstrations are included in a single Excel Feature Demos folder on the CD-ROM. You can play these demos on the CD or copy the Excel Feature Demos folder to your hard disk and play them from there.

To play one of these Excel feature demos, double-click the demo's file icon or right-click it and then click Open on its shortcut menu. Windows then opens the demo in its own window and begins playing. The demo window contains a title bar at the top that shows you the name of the feature demo and a playback controller at the bottom of the window. This controller contains buttons that you can click to loop the demo, pause the demo, go forward or backward one frame, turn the audio on or off, turn on or off close captioning, exit the demo, and display general information about the demo.

The Excel feature demos in the Excel Feature Demos folder on the CD-ROM include

- ✔ **Cell Ranges Moving & Copying.exe:** This demo shows you how to move and copying cell ranges in a worksheet using the drag-and-drop method and how to move copy ranges in and across worksheets using the cut-and-paste method.

- ✔ **Cell Ranges Selecting.exe:** This demo shows you a number of different methods for selecting a range of cells in a worksheet.

- ✔ **Chart Creation.exe:** This demo shows you how to create a new embedded chart in the same worksheet as the data that you're graphing.

- ✔ **Chart Formatting.exe:** This demo shows you how to format various elements of an existing embedded chart.

- ✔ **Data Filtering.exe:** This demo shows you how to filter a data list in a worksheet so that only the data fitting the criteria you specify is displayed.

- ✔ **Data Series with AutoFill.exe:** This demo shows you how to create various types of sequential data series using Excel's AutoFill feature.

✔ **Data Sort.exe:** This demo shows you how to sort the rows of a data list using different columns of the data list as the sorting keys.

✔ **Data Table 1.exe:** This demo shows you how to perform what-if analysis by constructing a data table that applies different values to a single variable in a particular formula.

✔ **Data Table 2.exe:** This demo shows you how to perform what-if analysis by constructing a data table that applies different values to two variables in a particular formula.

✔ **Formatting Cell Range as Table.exe:** This demo shows you how to format a range of cells in a worksheet as a table in one of the many predefined table styles and then use one of the AutoFilter buttons that the program adds to the table headings to filter the data display.

✔ **Formatting Conditionally.exe:** This demo shows you how to use Excel's Conditionally Formatting feature to add data bars, scales, and icons to various data series in a worksheet.

✔ **Formatting Numbers.exe:** This demo shows you how to format numeric entries in a worksheet using both the buttons in the Number group on the Home tab and the options on the Number tab of the Format Cells dialog box.

✔ **Formulas Date & Time.exe:** This demo shows you how to construct formulas that calculate elapsed dates and times.

✔ **Formulas in Loan Table.exe:** This demo shows you how to construct a loan payment table using the PMT function that compares various monthly payments using a series of loan payments and interest rates.

✔ **Formulas via AutoSum.exe:** This demo shows you how to construct SUM formulas that total a range of cell entries using the AutoSum button in the Editing group on the Home tab.

✔ **Formulas with Absolute Refs.exe:** This demo shows you how to construct and copy a formula that requires an absolute cell reference in such a way as to prevent DIV/0! errors from appearing in the formula's copies.

✔ **Formulas with Arithmetic Operators.exe:** This demo shows you how to construct simple formulas including those that bring a cell value forward to a new cell in the worksheet, as well as those that perform addition, subtraction, division, multiplication, and exponentiation between values entered in different cells.

✔ **Formulas with HLOOKUP Function.exe:** This demo shows you how to use the HLOOKUP (horizontal lookup) function to construct formulas that find matching items in a price lookup table and then return their retail prices to a sales spreadsheet.

✔ **Formulas with IF Function.exe:** This demo shows you how to use the IF function to construct formulas that perform one type of calculation when a particular condition exists in a worksheet table and another type when the condition does not.

✔ **Formulas with Range Names.exe:** This demo shows you how to assign range names to various cells in a worksheet table and then apply these ranges names to some of the table's formulas.

✔ **Graphics Clip Art & Photos.exe:** This demo shows you how to add clip art and photo images saved in separate graphics files to your worksheet.

- ✔ **Graphics Shapes & WordArt.exe:** This demo shows you how to add predefined shapes and WordArt graphics to your worksheet.

- ✔ **Graphics SmartArt.exe:** This demo shows you how to use SmartArt to construct an organizational chart in your worksheet.

- ✔ **Pivot Table Creation.exe:** This demo shows you how to create a new pivot table that summarizes various kinds of data stored in an Excel data list.

- ✔ **Pivot Table Editing.exe:** This demo shows you how to format a new pivot table added to a worksheet as well as modify the data that the table summarizes.

- ✔ **Protecting the Worksheet.exe:** This demo shows you how to protect an existing worksheet from any further changes while at the same time enabling users to add and edit values in the worksheet's specific data entry cells.

- ✔ **Report Headers & Footers.exe:** This demo shows you how to add headers and footers to a report so that their information prints at the top and bottom of each of the report's pages.

- ✔ **Report Page Layout & Breaks.exe:** This demo shows you how to use Excel's Page Layout view to check the paging of a report and how to use the Page Break Preview feature to correct bad page breaks before you send the report to the printer.

- ✔ **Report Print Titles.exe:** This demo shows you how to specify a particular column of a worksheet table as the report's print title so that the row labels in this worksheet column appear on each page of the report, identifying its data.

- ✔ **Using the Ribbon.exe:** This demo explains Excel 2007's Ribbon user interface by documenting its components and then shows you how to select Excel commands on the Ribbon's tabs.

Troubleshooting

I tried my best to compile programs that work on most computers with the minimum system requirements. Alas, your computer may differ, and some programs may not work properly for some reason.

The two likeliest problems are that you don't have enough memory (RAM) for the programs you want to use, or you have other programs running that are affecting installation or running of a program. If you get an error message such as Not Enough Memory or Setup Cannot Continue, try one or more of the following suggestions and then try using the software again:

- ✔ Turn off any antivirus software running on your computer. Installation programs sometimes mimic virus activity and may make your computer incorrectly believe that it's being infected by a virus.

- ✔ Close all running programs. The more programs you have running, the less memory is available to other programs. Installation programs typically update files and programs; so if you keep other programs running, installation may not work properly.

✔ Have your local computer store add more RAM to your computer. This is, admittedly, a drastic and somewhat expensive step. However, adding more memory can really help the speed of your computer and allow more programs to run at the same time.

Customer Care

If you have trouble with the CD-ROM, please call the Wiley Product Technical Support phone number at (800) 762-2974. Outside the United States, call 1 (317) 572-3994. You can also contact Wiley Product Technical Support at `http://support.wiley.com`. John Wiley & Sons will provide technical support only for installation and other general quality-control items. For technical support on the applications themselves, consult the program's vendor or author.

To place additional orders or to request information about other Wiley products, please call (877) 762-2974.

Index

• *D* •

• E •

• *Q* •

• **Z** •

Wiley Publishing, Inc.
End-User License Agreement

READ THIS. You should carefully read these terms and conditions before opening the software packet(s) included with this book "Book". This is a license agreement "Agreement" between you and Wiley Publishing, Inc. "WPI". By opening the accompanying software packet(s), you acknowledge that you have read and accept the following terms and conditions. If you do not agree and do not want to be bound by such terms and conditions, promptly return the Book and the unopened software packet(s) to the place you obtained them for a full refund.

1. **License Grant.** WPI grants to you (either an individual or entity) a nonexclusive license to use one copy of the enclosed software program(s) (collectively, the "Software") solely for your own personal or business purposes on a single computer (whether a standard computer or a workstation component of a multi-user network). The Software is in use on a computer when it is loaded into temporary memory (RAM) or installed into permanent memory (hard disk, CD-ROM, or other storage device). WPI reserves all rights not expressly granted herein.

2. **Ownership.** WPI is the owner of all right, title, and interest, including copyright, in and to the compilation of the Software recorded on the physical packet included with this Book "Software Media". Copyright to the individual programs recorded on the Software Media is owned by the author or other authorized copyright owner of each program. Ownership of the Software and all proprietary rights relating thereto remain with WPI and its licensers.

3. **Restrictions on Use and Transfer.**

   (a) You may only (i) make one copy of the Software for backup or archival purposes, or (ii) transfer the Software to a single hard disk, provided that you keep the original for backup or archival purposes. You may not (i) rent or lease the Software, (ii) copy or reproduce the Software through a LAN or other network system or through any computer subscriber system or bulletin-board system, or (iii) modify, adapt, or create derivative works based on the Software.

   (b) You may not reverse engineer, decompile, or disassemble the Software. You may transfer the Software and user documentation on a permanent basis, provided that the transferee agrees to accept the terms and conditions of this Agreement and you retain no copies. If the Software is an update or has been updated, any transfer must include the most recent update and all prior versions.

4. **Restrictions on Use of Individual Programs.** You must follow the individual requirements and restrictions detailed for each individual program in the "About the CD" appendix of this Book or on the Software Media. These limitations are also contained in the individual license agreements recorded on the Software Media. These limitations may include a requirement that after using the program for a specified period of time, the user must pay a registration fee or discontinue use. By opening the Software packet(s), you agree to abide by the licenses and restrictions for these individual programs that are detailed in the "About the CD" appendix and/or on the Software Media. None of the material on this Software Media or listed in this Book may ever be redistributed, in original or modified form, for commercial purposes.

5. Limited Warranty.

(a) WPI warrants that the Software and Software Media are free from defects in materials and workmanship under normal use for a period of sixty (60) days from the date of purchase of this Book. If WPI receives notification within the warranty period of defects in materials or workmanship, WPI will replace the defective Software Media.

(b) WPI AND THE AUTHOR(S) OF THE BOOK DISCLAIM ALL OTHER WARRANTIES, EXPRESS OR IMPLIED, INCLUDING WITHOUT LIMITATION IMPLIED WARRANTIES OF MERCHANTABILITY AND FITNESS FOR A PARTICULAR PURPOSE, WITH RESPECT TO THE SOFTWARE, THE PROGRAMS, THE SOURCE CODE CONTAINED THEREIN, AND/OR THE TECHNIQUES DESCRIBED IN THIS BOOK. WPI DOES NOT WARRANT THAT THE FUNCTIONS CONTAINED IN THE SOFTWARE WILL MEET YOUR REQUIREMENTS OR THAT THE OPERATION OF THE SOFTWARE WILL BE ERROR FREE.

(c) This limited warranty gives you specific legal rights, and you may have other rights that vary from jurisdiction to jurisdiction.

6. Remedies.

(a) WPI's entire liability and your exclusive remedy for defects in materials and workmanship shall be limited to replacement of the Software Media, which may be returned to WPI with a copy of your receipt at the following address: Software Media Fulfillment Department, Attn.: *Excel 2007 Workbook For Dummies*, Wiley Publishing, Inc., 10475 Crosspoint Blvd., Indianapolis, IN 46256, or call 1-800-762-2974. Please allow four to six weeks for delivery. This Limited Warranty is void if failure of the Software Media has resulted from accident, abuse, or misapplication. Any replacement Software Media will be warranted for the remainder of the original warranty period or thirty (30) days, whichever is longer.

(b) In no event shall WPI or the author be liable for any damages whatsoever (including without limitation damages for loss of business profits, business interruption, loss of business information, or any other pecuniary loss) arising from the use of or inability to use the Book or the Software, even if WPI has been advised of the possibility of such damages.

(c) Because some jurisdictions do not allow the exclusion or limitation of liability for consequential or incidental damages, the above limitation or exclusion may not apply to you.

7. U.S. Government Restricted Rights. Use, duplication, or disclosure of the Software for or on behalf of the United States of America, its agencies and/or instrumentalities "U.S. Government" is subject to restrictions as stated in paragraph (c)(1)(ii) of the Rights in Technical Data and Computer Software clause of DFARS 252.227-7013, or subparagraphs (c) (1) and (2) of the Commercial Computer Software - Restricted Rights clause at FAR 52.227-19, and in similar clauses in the NASA FAR supplement, as applicable.

8. General. This Agreement constitutes the entire understanding of the parties and revokes and supersedes all prior agreements, oral or written, between them and may not be modified or amended except in a writing signed by both parties hereto that specifically refers to this Agreement. This Agreement shall take precedence over any other documents that may be in conflict herewith. If any one or more provisions contained in this Agreement are held by any court or tribunal to be invalid, illegal, or otherwise unenforceable, each and every other provision shall remain in full force and effect.

BUSINESS, CAREERS & PERSONAL FINANCE

0-7645-9847-3

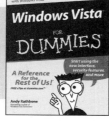

0-7645-2431-3

Also available:
- Business Plans Kit For Dummies
0-7645-9794-9
- Economics For Dummies
0-7645-5726-2
- Grant Writing For Dummies
0-7645-8416-2
- Home Buying For Dummies
0-7645-5331-3
- Managing For Dummies
0-7645-1771-6
- Marketing For Dummies
0-7645-5600-2

- Personal Finance For Dummies
0-7645-2590-5*
- Resumes For Dummies
0-7645-5471-9
- Selling For Dummies
0-7645-5363-1
- Six Sigma For Dummies
0-7645-6798-5
- Small Business Kit For Dummies
0-7645-5984-2
- Starting an eBay Business For Dummies
0-7645-6924-4
- Your Dream Career For Dummies
0-7645-9795-7

HOME & BUSINESS COMPUTER BASICS

0-470-05432-8

0-471-75421-8

Also available:
- Cleaning Windows Vista For Dummies
0-471-78293-9
- Excel 2007 For Dummies
0-470-03737-7
- Mac OS X Tiger For Dummies
0-7645-7675-5
- MacBook For Dummies
0-470-04859-X
- Macs For Dummies
0-470-04849-2
- Office 2007 For Dummies
0-470-00923-3

- Outlook 2007 For Dummies
0-470-03830-6
- PCs For Dummies
0-7645-8958-X
- Salesforce.com For Dummies
0-470-04893-X
- Upgrading & Fixing Laptops For Dummies
0-7645-8959-8
- Word 2007 For Dummies
0-470-03658-3
- Quicken 2007 For Dummies
0-470-04600-7

FOOD, HOME, GARDEN, HOBBIES, MUSIC & PETS

0-7645-8404-9

0-7645-9904-6

Also available:
- Candy Making For Dummies
0-7645-9734-5
- Card Games For Dummies
0-7645-9910-0
- Crocheting For Dummies
0-7645-4151-X
- Dog Training For Dummies
0-7645-8418-9
- Healthy Carb Cookbook For Dummies
0-7645-8476-6
- Home Maintenance For Dummies
0-7645-5215-5

- Horses For Dummies
0-7645-9797-3
- Jewelry Making & Beading For Dummies
0-7645-2571-9
- Orchids For Dummies
0-7645-6759-4
- Puppies For Dummies
0-7645-5255-4
- Rock Guitar For Dummies
0-7645-5356-9
- Sewing For Dummies
0-7645-6847-7
- Singing For Dummies
0-7645-2475-5

INTERNET & DIGITAL MEDIA

0-470-04529-9

0-470-04894-8

Also available:
- Blogging For Dummies
0-471-77084-1
- Digital Photography For Dummies
0-7645-9802-3
- Digital Photography All-in-One Desk Reference For Dummies
0-470-03743-1
- Digital SLR Cameras and Photography For Dummies
0-7645-9803-1
- eBay Business All-in-One Desk Reference For Dummies
0-7645-8438-3
- HDTV For Dummies
0-470-09673-X

- Home Entertainment PCs For Dummies
0-470-05523-5
- MySpace For Dummies
0-470-09529-6
- Search Engine Optimization For Dummies
0-471-97998-8
- Skype For Dummies
0-470-04891-3
- The Internet For Dummies
0-7645-8996-2
- Wiring Your Digital Home For Dummies
0-471-91830-X

* Separate Canadian edition also available
† Separate U.K. edition also available

 WILEY

SPORTS, FITNESS, PARENTING, RELIGION & SPIRITUALITY

0-471-76871-5

0-7645-7841-3

Also available:

- Catholicism For Dummies
  0-7645-5391-7
- Exercise Balls For Dummies
  0-7645-5623-1
- Fitness For Dummies
  0-7645-7851-0
- Football For Dummies
  0-7645-3936-1
- Judaism For Dummies
  0-7645-5299-6
- Potty Training For Dummies
  0-7645-5417-4
- Buddhism For Dummies
  0-7645-5359-3

- Pregnancy For Dummies
  0-7645-4483-7 †
- Ten Minute Tone-Ups For Dummies
  0-7645-7207-5
- NASCAR For Dummies
  0-7645-7681-X
- Religion For Dummies
  0-7645-5264-3
- Soccer For Dummies
  0-7645-5229-5
- Women in the Bible For Dummies
  0-7645-8475-8

TRAVEL

0-7645-7749-2

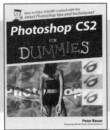

0-7645-6945-7

Also available:

- Alaska For Dummies
  0-7645-7746-8
- Cruise Vacations For Dummies
  0-7645-6941-4
- England For Dummies
  0-7645-4276-1
- Europe For Dummies
  0-7645-7529-5
- Germany For Dummies
  0-7645-7823-5
- Hawaii For Dummies
  0-7645-7402-7

- Italy For Dummies
  0-7645-7386-1
- Las Vegas For Dummies
  0-7645-7382-9
- London For Dummies
  0-7645-4277-X
- Paris For Dummies
  0-7645-7630-5
- RV Vacations For Dummies
  0-7645-4442-X
- Walt Disney World & Orlando
  For Dummies
  0-7645-9660-8

GRAPHICS, DESIGN & WEB DEVELOPMENT

0-7645-8815-X

0-7645-9571-7

Also available:

- 3D Game Animation For Dummies
  0-7645-8789-7
- AutoCAD 2006 For Dummies
  0-7645-8925-3
- Building a Web Site For Dummies
  0-7645-7144-3
- Creating Web Pages For Dummies
  0-470-08030-2
- Creating Web Pages All-in-One Desk
  Reference For Dummies
  0-7645-4345-8
- Dreamweaver 8 For Dummies
  0-7645-9649-7

- InDesign CS2 For Dummies
  0-7645-9572-5
- Macromedia Flash 8 For Dummies
  0-7645-9691-8
- Photoshop CS2 and Digital
  Photography For Dummies
  0-7645-9580-6
- Photoshop Elements 4 For Dummies
  0-471-77483-9
- Syndicating Web Sites with RSS Feeds
  For Dummies
  0-7645-8848-6
- Yahoo! SiteBuilder For Dummies
  0-7645-9800-7

NETWORKING, SECURITY, PROGRAMMING & DATABASES

0-7645-7728-X

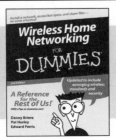

0-471-74940-0

Also available:

- Access 2007 For Dummies
  0-470-04612-0
- ASP.NET 2 For Dummies
  0-7645-7907-X
- C# 2005 For Dummies
  0-7645-9704-3
- Hacking For Dummies
  0-470-05235-X
- Hacking Wireless Networks
  For Dummies
  0-7645-9730-2
- Java For Dummies
  0-470-08716-1

- Microsoft SQL Server 2005 For Dummies
  0-7645-7755-7
- Networking All-in-One Desk Reference
  For Dummies
  0-7645-9939-9
- Preventing Identity Theft For Dummies
  0-7645-7336-5
- Telecom For Dummies
  0-471-77085-X
- Visual Studio 2005 All-in-One Desk
  Reference For Dummies
  0-7645-9775-2
- XML For Dummies
  0-7645-8845-1